About Island Press

Island Press is the only nonprofit organization in the United States whose principal purpose is the publication of books on environmental issues and natural resource management. We provide solutions-oriented information to professionals, public officials, business and community leaders, and concerned citizens who are shaping responses to environmental problems.

In 1994, Island Press celebrated its tenth anniversary as the leading provider of timely and practical books that take a multidisciplinary approach to critical environmental concerns. Our growing list of titles reflects our commitment to bringing the best of an expanding body of literature to the environmental community throughout North America and the world.

Support for Island Press is provided by The Geraldine R. Dodge Foundation, The Energy Foundation, The Ford Foundation, The George Gund Foundation, William and Flora Hewlett Foundation, The James Irvine Foundation, The John D. and Catherine T. MacArthur Foundation, The Andrew W. Mellon Foundation, The Pew Charitable Trusts, The Rockefeller Brothers Fund, The Tides Foundation, Turner Foundation, Inc., The Rockefeller Philanthropic Collaborative, Inc., and individual donors.

About the Pollution Prevention Education and Research Center

The Pollution Prevention Education and Research Center (PPERC) addresses a broad range of issues associated with industrial production processes and the use of hazardous materials. The Center's mission is to conserve resources and reduce or eliminate the use of toxic substances through an interdisciplinary program of education, research, and outreach grounded in a philosophy of prevention rather than control. Through the collaborative efforts of its members, PPERC is shifting the focus from "end-of-pipe" pollution control techniques to a front-end, systems approach which analyzes technologies, cycles of production and consumption, industrial structures, and policy instruments to reduce toxics use and protect human and environmental health.

Reducing Toxics

Reducing Toxics

A NEW APPROACH
TO POLICY AND
INDUSTRIAL
DECISIONMAKING

Edited by
Robert Gottlieb

Pollution Prevention Education and Research Center
University of California, Los Angeles

ISLAND PRESS

Washington, D.C. • Covelo, California

Library of Congress Cataloging-in-Publication Data

Reducing toxics: a new approach to policy and industrial
  decisionmaking / edited by Robert Gottlieb.
    p. cm.
  Includes bibliographical references and index.
  ISBN 1-55963-336-0 (pbk.)
    1. Pollution—Government policy. 2. Industrial management—
Environmental aspects. I. Gottlieb, Robert, 1944–
HC79.P55R43   1995
658.4'08—dc20   94-46257
                                                                                                              CIP

Printed on recycled, acid-free paper   ✪

Manufactured in the United States of America
10   9   8   7   6   5   4   3   2   1

Contents

PART II

Industry Settings: Opportunities and Limits for Pollution
Prevention

Contributors

DAVID ALLEN is a codirector of the UCLA Pollution Prevention Education and Research Center. He is professor and chair of the UCLA Department of Chemical Engineering. He has written extensively on pollution prevention education and industrial ecology and served on a number of national advisory committees on pollution prevention, including EPA's American Institute for Pollution Prevention and the Pollution Prevention Group of EPA's National Advisory Council for Environmental Policy and Technology (NACEPT).

TAMIRA COHEN is a Ph.D. candidate in the UCLA Department of Environmental Health Sciences in the School of Public Health, focusing on issues of industrial hygiene and occupational safety and health.

JOHN FROINES is a codirector of the UCLA Pollution Prevention Education and Research Center and professor of toxicology and chair of the Department of Environmental Health Sciences at UCLA. He is also director of the UCLA Center for Occupational and Environmental Health, is a member of the National Academy of Science's Committee on Environmental Epidemiology, and was deputy director of the National Institute for Occupational Safety and Health (NIOSH).

ROBERT GOTTLIEB is a codirector of the UCLA Pollution Prevention Education and Research Center and coordinator of the Environmental Analysis and Policy area of the UCLA Department of Urban Planning. He has written extensively on environmental, resource, and industrial policy, including *Forcing the Spring*, *War on Waste*, *Thirst for Growth*, and *Empires in the Sun*.

JANICE MAZUREK is a research associate with Resources for the Future. She holds a master's degree in urban planning and is a Ph.D. candidate in the UCLA Department of Urban Planning. She was formerly a senior research associate with the UCLA Pollution Prevention Education and Research Center.

JULIE ROQUE is a codirector of the UCLA Pollution Prevention Education and Research Center and is an assistant professor in the UCLA Department of Urban Planning. In 1994 she was on leave from UCLA as a senior policy analyst in the Office of Science and Technology Policy. At OSTP she was engaged in a wide range of projects, including evaluating management and legislative strategies for toxics, and reviewing the White House's proposal for a national environmental strategy.

RANIA SABTY has a master's degree in public health and is currently a Ph.D. candidate in the UCLA Department of Environmental Health Sciences, focusing on industrial hygiene and occupational health and safety.

PETER SINSHEIMER is a senior research associate with the UCLA Pollution Prevention Education and Research Center. He is a Ph.D. candidate in the UCLA Department of Urban Planning and received a master's degree in public health at the University of California, Berkeley.

MAUREEN SMITH is a senior research associate with the UCLA Pollution Prevention Education and Research Center. She is the author of *The Paper Industry and Sustainable Production: An Environmental Argument for Industrial Restructuring,* to be published later this year.

PAMELA YATES is an environmental audit manager for a Fortune 500 company. She is also a Ph.D. candidate in the UCLA School of Public Health and was a senior research associate with the UCLA Pollution Prevention Education and Research Center.

Acknowledgments

This book is a collaborative effort of faculty and researchers associated with the UCLA Pollution Prevention Education and Research Center. The Center was established in 1991 to address a broad range of issues associated with industrial production processes and the use of hazardous materials. The Center's mission is to conserve resources and reduce or eliminate the use of hazardous materials through an interdisciplinary program of education, research, and outreach embedded in a philosophy of prevention. This book emerged in part out of the need to identify and analyze such an approach.

As editor of this volume, I have appreciated the enormous value of collaboration. As part of that process, each of the codirectors of PPERC, including myself, Julie Roque, John Froines, and David Allen, made specific contributions as authors and/or coauthors of several of the chapters. A major role in research and writing for the book was undertaken by PPERC's current or former research associates, Maureen Smith, Janice Mazurek, Pamela Yates, Tamira Cohen, and Peter Sinsheimer, each of whom authored or coauthored one or more chapters. Janice Mazurek also played a crucial role in restructuring and ultimately cohering the overall manuscript. Research assistance for several of the chapters was provided by PPERC research associates Deborah Fryman, Andrea Gardner, Peter Hein, Joseph Powers, Helene Wagner, and Nola Kennedy. Linda Ashman Hicks, PPERC's associate director, reviewed the overall manuscript and made important changes that both strengthened and refined the final product. Funding for the project was provided by the University of California Toxic Substances Research and Teaching Program and the UCLA Center for Occupational and Environmental Health.

Ultimately, each of these individual efforts was part of the collaborative, interdisciplinary model of research and analysis that the Pollution Prevention Education and Research Center has sought to foster. It is an approach we see as essential to the task of establishing this new paradigm for policy and decisionmaking.

Introduction

Robert Gottlieb
Janice Mazurek

As we approach the new millennium, citizens in the U.S. and throughout the world have begun to forcefully insist that the range of environmental hazards present in everyday life needs to be *reduced* in all its manifest forms. This argument has become particularly linked to the generation, use, and disposal of toxic and hazardous materials. Successful reduction strategies depend in part on expanding present interpretations of what we understand to mean "environmental hazard" or "toxics." The term *toxics* as it is referred to in this book, would in fact include all materials and processes which may cause harm to human health and the environment.

For more than two and a half decades, various government policies and industry responses have been developed to manage hazards present at each stage of the production cycle. These policies and activities, however, have failed to significantly address the problem of toxics generation and use beyond the question of management and disposal. At best, more narrowly conceived and at times contradictory efforts toward reducing these hazards have been introduced both in policy arenas and through industry activities. Yet, the greater the public focus on toxics, the greater the pressure on government and industry to more fully develop new strategies or new paradigms for policy and industrial decisionmaking. One starting point for analyzing such a shift in strategies is by distinguishing between two key contrasting approaches in the policy area, most often characterized as *prevention* and *control,* and by identifying two contrasting reference points along a continuum for industry decisionmaking, from *public input and intervention* to *voluntarism.*

With respect to policy, pollution control has remained the dominant framework for most forms of legislative and regulatory interventions and industry responses during much of this two-and-a-half-decade period. In the process, a vast number of businesses and support services have been established, including waste disposal, engineering and construction companies, and consulting and specialized control technology firms. These businesses collectively constitute an "environmental" or pollution control industry, a direct product of the legislative and regulatory focus on the management and treatment of environmental hazards.

Despite its dominance as a set of policy instruments and limited success in addressing immediate and visible forms of emissions, the pollution control system nevertheless became problematic in terms of its stated objectives. For one, media-specific, end-of-pipe regulations often failed to sufficiently address toxics, a pernicious and often hard to pinpoint subset of pollution whose genesis, use, and exposure routes often departed radically from nonhazardous pollutants related to household solid waste, thermal water emissions, or partially treated sewage. Subsequent prevention-based statutes, such as the Toxic Substances Control Act of 1976, seen as alternatives to the single-media, end-of-pipe focus, nonetheless failed in part because of the statute's limited depiction of toxic uses. As discussed in this study, toxics reduction requires distinguishing among the nature, use, and location of hazardous substances—a framework absent from the end-of-pipe statutes.

In addition to analytic distinctions, the regulations also posed practical problems. For one, the economic costs of pollution control became increasingly prohibitive. During the 1970s and 1980s, both disposal and liability costs rose dramatically, creating pressures on policymakers and industry to move beyond their preferred focus on management and treatment. Cost created added implementation pressures as EPA increasingly bore the burden of proving its programs cost effective. New political pressures arising in opposition to the construction or continued operation of treatment and/or disposal facilities also forced policymakers to seek ways to shift some of the focus away from pollution control toward new kinds of policy instruments aimed at minimizing or reducing wastes. This shift has been most pronounced in the area of hazardous wastes, where control strategies turned out to be most costly. Pollution control outcomes, as a public health or environmental objective, also were seen as limited or contrary to the stated goals of this policy system. Hazards throughout the production cycle were shifted or transferred by medium and/or escaped regulatory purview, while the emphasis on technology add-ons (such as scrubbers) or engineering controls (such as respirators) failed to address the problem of toxics generation and use. Similar to the debates over costs, the continuing presence and at times concentration of hazards in new forms via pollution control established both an environmental and public health interest in a policy shift. As pollution control fell out of favor, waste minimization, then pollution prevention, gained increasing support; indeed by 1990, with the passage of the Pollution Prevention Act, this concept had become the buzzword of environmental policymaking.

While policymakers engaged in efforts to shift toward a prevention-based framework, industry leaders responded by emphasizing their preference for voluntary action as distinct from regulatory interventions. Even as the most prominent polluting industries learned to adjust to end-of-pipe control requirements during the 1970s and simultaneously supported market incentives as a better way of achieving environmental objectives (while maintaining decisionmaking control), the new interest in prevention (and related heightened public concerns about waste issues) also caused a shift in focus during the 1980s for industry groups. Led by such companies as 3M and trade groups such as the Chemical Manufacturers Association (through its "Responsible Care" program), industry sought to construct through its voluntarist perspective a "corporate environmentalism." Yet the arguments that emerged about this approach, similar to the policy debates within and among government agencies and legislators, revealed unresolved and contentious issues, primarily focused on decisionmaking questions.

In this book, we have developed a more comprehensive definition of reduction or prevention that seeks to eliminate hazards in all environmental media. The definition is expanded along the production chain to encompass not only environmental releases but occupational exposures and product use. This definition requires new ways of exploring public input and intervention, including the use of conventional policy instruments such as environmental taxes, product or substance bans, or regulatory instruments, including facility-wide permitting. Preferably, this new type of approach will also be able to help renovate the process of industry decisionmaking during the design phase—well before the product is manufactured, marketed, and consumed. Criteria questions for pollution prevention call for a critical examination of what is being produced, why it is produced, as well as how it is produced. Such criteria must be central considerations for industry decisionmaking, and must parallel such core industrial design and structure criteria as costs, markets, product innovation, production efficiency, and material and process flexibility. These criteria must be applied to the continuum of the industrial cycle; both upstream from the production process, in materials extraction, as well as downstream, in consumer use, recycling, and disposal. These criteria and debates surrounding implementation and strategies are developed in Chapter 5.

Despite the growing interest in developing a new framework for toxics policy, the transition from control to prevention continues to remain an elusive objective for policymakers, generators, and citizen groups. At the same time, there has been no systematic examination of the nature of that transition and the issues involved. The situation is comparable to earlier discussions of waste minimization: in the early 1980s when the concept was first introduced, there were no comprehensive laws at the state level and only a few which even partially incorporated waste minimization objec-

R. Gottlieb and J. Mazurek

tives. By the mid 1990s, however, nearly every state in the country had established waste minimization legislation and related mechanisms for implementation.[1] Over the same period, the published literature on the subject had increased significantly. Today, at an early stage of pollution prevention discourse, a review of the academic, trade, and technical literature indicates a relative dearth of material on the concept and practice of prevention or reduction, despite the rapid increase in related policy initiatives currently underway.

This book illustrates how pollution prevention emerged from the extant control framework and analyzes the initiatives and policy debates which have shaped their development and influenced the effectiveness of that framework. Proceeding from the general to the specific, Part I examines the regulatory and institutional setting of these initiatives and prescribes possible definitions and strategies for developing a prevention framework, the subject of the part's concluding chapter. These principles are then applied through case study analysis at the industry and facility level, the subject of Part II. These snapshots, which target different "decision points" in the production process, clarify definitions developed in Part I and develop evaluative techniques for various approaches to pollution prevention. Such a framework is crucial in understanding the intent and limits of particular legislative and industry initiatives, as well as in evaluating the ability of such initiatives to reach their stated environmental goals. Through analysis of these case studies, the authors explore the potential conflicts between industry-supported voluntarist approaches and more publicly framed, prevention-based policies. Based on the structural and organizational analyses of pollution prevention presented in Parts I and II, we conclude that pollution prevention still lacks coherence in terms of its definition, institutional implementation, and day-to-day application.

Reducing Toxics is a collaboration among faculty and research associates affiliated with the Pollution Prevention Education and Research Center (PPERC), an interdisciplinary program at the University of California at Los Angeles. PPERC includes participants from the Department of Chemical Engineering, the Center for Occupational and Environmental Health within the School of Public Health, and the Environmental Analysis and Policy area of the Department of Urban Planning.[2] By integrating engineering, toxicological, and public policy approaches within this new framework of pollution prevention, the authors have sought to directly confront the complex of unresolved issues now facing policymakers and industry. This book represents the contextual starting point for a longer term investigation into how certain environmental hazards, which arguably represent some of the most protracted and unmanageable problems confronting policymakers today, can be addressed in the years to come.

We began this book seeking to answer a basic set of questions: what is the nature and extent of pollution prevention research and activity currently underway, and how can these efforts eventually be designed in a more comprehensive and holistic manner? This book addresses the first question and establishes a framework of inquiry and analysis for the second. Ultimately, answering the question of feasibility—can pollution prevention become the option of choice for policymakers and industry?—requires full public discussion of the issues at stake. This book, we hope, will contribute to that process.

Notes

1. U.S. General Accounting Office, *Pollution Prevention: EPA Should Reexamine the Objectives and Sustainability of State Programs,* (GAO/PEMD-94–8), 1994; see also *An Ounce of Toxic Pollution Prevention: Rating States' Toxics Use Reduction Laws,* (Boston and Washington D.C.: National Environmental Law Center and the Center for Policy Alternatives, 1991); *State Legislation Relating to Pollution Prevention,* (Minneapolis: Waste Reduction Institute for Training and Applications Research, Inc., 1991).

2. See University of California Pollution Prevention Education and Research Center, *Program Description and Summary of Activities, 1991–1994,* (Los Angeles: UCLA Pollution Prevention Education and Research Center, 1994).

Part I

The Difficulty of Getting There: The Evolution of Policy

Robert Gottlieb

If the 1970s was, in the environmental policy arena, the decade of pollution control, and the 1980s was the decade when pollution policies began to shift toward such approaches as waste minimization and marketing incentives, then the 1990s has clearly come to be defined as the decade of pollution prevention. But legislation and policy directives notwithstanding, policymakers are still asking just what pollution prevention means.

Pollution prevention is a concept in search of a policy framework. Its definitions remain contested, its terrain remains unclear. Is pollution prevention a form of exhortation by way of technical assistance, an encouragement of the market to achieve presumably more efficient outcomes, or a new type of planning? Is it a matter exclusively for environmental agencies and regulators, or does it necessarily address other arenas such as workplace and product regulation? More than an abstraction but still less than a coherent policy, the pollution prevention initiatives and debates of the 1990s in fact point to some of the problematic features of environmental policymaking itself in a period when the role of government has become the subject of a highly charged debate. And while pollution prevention has become widely accepted in its broadest, least-focused terms, examining the evolution of toxics policy from the 1970s to the 1990s serves the function of better understanding how we got to where we are today, as well as sorting out pollution prevention's multiple reference points and diverse implications for policy.

Part I of *Reducing Toxics* examines how we shifted from the dominant pollution control discourse to the more open-ended and often ill-defined pollution prevention approaches that have emerged during the past decade. The origins and development of pollution control during the 1970s, the authors of Chapters 1 and 2 argue, involved a complex process with sometimes unintended outcomes, influenced significantly by certain dominant assumptions and biases in environmental policymaking. Constructed in an era of rising environmental advocacy, great urgency in mitigating visible problems of pollution, increased reliance on a federal role in regulating such pollutants, and a continuing belief that solutions were primarily technical in nature and that technologies could be located to address the pollutant of the moment, pollution control policies were developed as part of an ambitious but largely unimplementable agenda. At the same time (as Chapter 3 authors have described) there were other potential paths for environmental policymaking, including the 1976 Toxic Substances Control Act, that were never sufficiently explored. Those initiatives were constrained in part by the prevailing structures of policymaking, resistance from the regulated, and an unwillingness of policymakers to follow the logic of such new policies into the hitherto proprietary domain of industry decisionmaking.

The pollution issues, notably the question of toxics generation and use, were not exclusive to the environmental domain, where policies were most concerned with the endpoint in the flow of toxics or pollutants, specifically the management of wastes at their point of release into the environment. The focus on toxics generation and use shifted the focus to include questions of both production (how things were produced) as well as consumption (what things were produced and what they were used for) rather than environmental management as external to those processes (e.g., post-production or postconsumption wastes). But policymaking in the areas of workplace and product safety regulation, as discussed by the authors of Chapter 4, remained even more distant than environmental policy from the sources of the pollution or the hazards embedded in production and consumption processes. By the 1990s, however, pollution prevention appeared to be fully on the rise, as the authors of Chapter 5 discuss. But the nature of that paradigm shift in policy, whether in terms of the definition of such policy, the role of information, the search for new policy instruments, evaluations of risk, or the reemergence of state and local governments as major players, has been filled with uncertainties and ambiguities, making it, at the very least, an open-ended process.

Thus, we come face to face with a core dilemma in contemporary environmental policymaking. It is better, as is now commonly accepted, to prevent or reduce at the source various forms of environmental hazards or (more generically) pollution itself, rather than to simply manage such pollution, once it has become a problem requiring attention. But there is neither consensus nor a significant number of examples of successful policymaking in how to prevent pollution. To resolve such a dilemma—the need to make pollution prevention a successful and implementable guide to policy in light of the uncertainties of how or even whether to undertake such policies—becomes then the task of environmental policymaking in the years to come.

1

The Pollution Control System: Themes and Frameworks

Robert Gottlieb
Maureen Smith

Managing Pollution: Policy Conundrums

At the heart of contemporary toxics policy reside a series of conundrums. For at least a century, policies related to human health and the environment reflected what was considered to be a basic truth of contemporary industrial society: that many products and materials produced and used by industry, including those that were hazardous, have made "life worth living," as a notable chemical industry promotional campaign once declared.[1] Increasingly, policymakers are confronting the fact that these same products and processes potentially pose widespread risks to human health and the environment. To resolve this dilemma of production, an elaborate set of legislative and regulatory initiatives at both the federal and state levels were developed to address the concerns about toxics. More generally, policies focused on the larger issue of pollution as a whole. Yet most such initiatives remained aloof from core production decisions regarding what to produce, how to produce, and why specific materials and processes were used. Although these early policies, which imposed high costs of regulation, focus on the endpoint of the production process, they also served to highlight opportunities for intervention in the early stages of production, when decisions regarding what to produce are made. Debates over these policies ushered in new forms of environmental conflict over the degree and nature of public intervention in production activities and decisions.

Opportunities for intervention first occurred in a significant way during the 1960s, when growing public concerns about environmental hazards increased pressure on Congress to authorize federal funds aimed at reversing the most visible forms of environmental pollution. Prior to this period, federal efforts for the most part had been limited to grant programs to ease the burden on state and local communities which were ill-equipped and often reluctant to tackle such issues. As a result, the policy debates began to shift toward establishing a more expansive federal role—a shift related in part to the increasing political prominence of environmental issues. Within a remarkably short period of time, a new national environmental policy or pollution control system was constructed, based on a series of new laws enacted after 1970 and new regulatory agencies established in part to carry out the mandates specified in those acts.

These new legislative mandates and regulatory activities focused on various forms of pollution resulting from a wide range of industrial processes and products. Regulatory targets included the creation of hazardous wastes, nonhazardous solid wastes, and various other byproducts of manufacturing and energy generation; the deliberate or inadvertent introduction of hazardous constituents of manufacturing processes into the air and often into surface water or groundwater; the occupational risks stemming from production activities; and the incorporation of hazardous constituents into products.

Until the 1970s, solid and liquid wastes from manufacturing processes had been disposed of by simply dumping them into pits, landfills, or waste ponds, or by discharging them into surface waters, deep wells, or the oceans. Disposal of volatile chemicals generally had been accomplished by evaporation or percolation into the ground. Occupational exposures received limited attention, with only a handful of workplace hazards subject to regulatory intervention. Product review was even more narrowly conceived, with such known hazards as tetraethyl lead in gasoline or asbestos in building materials escaping regulatory review.

By the 1970s, however, a sense of crisis had come to dominate the environmental policy discourse. Lakes and rivers were polluted to the degree that they were no longer fit for recreational use. Fish, shellfish, birds, and other wildlife were seen as threatened to the point of extinction due to chemical contamination originating from industrial processes and agricultural practices. Air quality in many parts of the United States had reached unhealthy levels for large populations—as many as 150 million people, according to Clean Air Act attainment standards. Industrial chemicals, primarily organic solvents and metals, were found in measurable quantities in drinking water wells and groundwater aquifers, creating a new and unanticipated environmental threat. Dump sites, including many that previously had been abandoned, posed substantial risks to nearby communities, even forcing evacuations of houses and neighborhoods. Serious occupational hazards, with allowable risks at significantly lower thresholds than environmental standards, were identified in a number of industries. The environmental crisis, defined increasingly as a priority policy area, came to be conceived in part as a toxics crisis.

In response, the pollution control system took shape. Yet instead of addressing the sources of pollution and contamination or their multiple exposure routes, policymakers focused on managing specific kinds of wastes and emissions. This focus, in turn, resulted in separate policies designed to (i) capture and control some types of air emissions; (ii) place certain limits on discharges to water; (iii) regulate treatment, storage, and land disposal of hazardous solid wastes; and (iv) designate best available treatment technologies to establish limits on these adverse effects of industrial processes. Legislation also was introduced to address other nonenvironmental routes of exposure (occupational or product-based) and to respond to the continuing introduction of new hazardous substances into the environment.

The structure of legislation and regulatory review conceived in the early and mid 1970s and broadly implemented by the end of the decade created an environmental management system centered on the treatment of wastes after they had been generated. Emphasis was placed on industries meeting regulatory limits by their identifying demonstrated, available, and proven control technologies. The policy shift that began taking place in 1970 with the passage of the Clean Air Act and other legislation and the creation of the Environmental Protection Agency specifically augmented the federal role in terms of regulating discharges and disposal techniques while expanding various support mechanisms to enhance such management strategies. With the passage of the Resource Conservation and Recovery Act (RCRA) six years later, the federal role evolved further. EPA, in particular, took center stage in terms of its broad oversight of wide-ranging regulatory initiatives, from the phasing out of land disposal methods to the creation of a hazardous waste tracking system. This new federal role, moreover, led to an increasing centralization and concentration of functions and activities in relation to both regulatory agendas and a new and rapidly expanding waste management or "environmental" industry that arose in response to such regulatory requirements.

Establishing federal policies on pollution, wastes, and hazards, however, had only limited success in stemming the flow of toxics through production systems and into the environment. The scale of the problem involved in both managing existing waste streams as well as in monitoring and reviewing the hundreds of chemicals introduced each year overwhelmed the available resources of the regulators. The sheer number of chemicals to review, as mandated by the Toxic Substances Control Act alone, presented a formidable obstacle for effective oversight.

The emphasis on pollution control increased the difficulty in addressing and quantifying the widespread presence of environmental hazards throughout the production cycle. Pollution control strategies were designed to treat or remove toxic contaminants from waste streams. But, as it was increasingly pointed out, the technologies used often simply shifted the location of the pollutants. Further, since pollution control technology could not be designed to destroy one hundred percent of the toxics released from industrial processes, it followed that at least traces would be discharged to the environment. Such releases often were completely unregulated or were permitted if maintained within established limits. As a consequence, hundreds of thousands of separate, distinct sources were allowed to release toxic chemicals in quantities that now are recognized as staggering when considered in total. [2]

The limits of pollution control also became visible in the deficiencies of the waste management, treatment, and disposal programs put in place subsequent to RCRA and CERCLA (legislation establishing the clean-up of hazardous waste sites). The regulation of hazardous waste facilities has been implemented slowly, with EPA continually seeking to meet Congressionally designated deadlines. These included "hammer" provisions provided under the 1984 amendments to RCRA for land disposal bans for certain solvents and other wastes, standards related to underground storage tanks, or regulations affecting small quantity hazardous waste generators. [3] The enforcement of many of these regulations posed yet another set of problems for the regulators. As a result, from these and other policy puzzles, pollution control, though established as the dominant policy system, increasingly was seen as an ineffective approach to managing pollution flows.

Seeking Change: The Emergence of Pollution Prevention

By the mid to late 1980s, the extensive pollution control system had come under attack from a variety of sources both inside and outside of government. Numerous reports were issued which challenged the assumptions, capabilities, costs, and results of pollution control as a comprehensive environmental protection system capable of addressing hazards at each stage of the production cycle. In this period, a new approach was sought, which some defined as source reduction, others as waste reduction, or, as EPA called it, waste minimization. In the process, a debate emerged over both the terms and related programmatic content of what might constitute a new approach, or new policy "paradigm." The focus on managing pollution through treatment and disposal methods shifted to a more generic argument over how best to handle the toxics issue.

In January 1989, the EPA issued a statement in the Federal Register on Pollution Prevention that sought to demonstrate the Agency's new commitment toward a different approach to toxics.[4] Yet pollution prevention, even as its definition evolved and as efforts were established to create new, cross-media or multimedia forms of regulatory review, essentially remained an ambiguous concept and framework for policy. Despite its apparent purpose in stopping pollution at its source, pollution prevention as first introduced by EPA had no center of gravity for policymaking and instead appeared to mask certain fundamental differences in approach regarding the role of policy in addressing questions of production design and decisionmaking.

As a widely heralded new policy framework, pollution prevention increasingly became defined in contrast to pollution control, and the language of fundamental change—even of paradigm shift—in turn became pervasive. Pollution prevention seemed to signal a major break from the particular regulatory formats and the conceptual frameworks of pollution control that had become rigid over nearly two decades, as local authorities, then states, and then the federal government attempted to address the unwanted environmental byproducts of an advancing industrial society. Pollution prevention also was viewed as a response to the failures and limitations of the pollution control regime, among them, the continuing chemical pollution of the environment and the high costs to both industry and the public imposed by the bureaucratic inefficiencies of pollution control regulations.

In differentiating pollution prevention from pollution control, two core themes, or axes of change, have tended to be emphasized. The first referred to the necessary progression from a "single medium" to a "multimedia" basis for regulations. By the 1980s, this important regulatory format had in fact become fully constituted as its own specialty under the label of "integrated pollution control,"[5] seeking to differentiate itself from the narrow, single-medium focus of the dominant control strategies primarily embedded in EPA's program offices (Air, Water, Solid Waste, etc.). The single-medium system of pollution control had, from the outset, focused on the individual entry points of various pollutants into the environment (the "end of the pipe"), and had given rise to separate and uncoordinated bodies of regulation organized primarily around air, water, land, workplace, and consumer products, with fragments of each administered by multiple federal agencies. Indeed, by the late 1970s, the system already appeared dysfunctional: for example, the federal regulation of vinyl chloride, as David

Doniger pointed out, was addressed through fifteen different statutes and five federal agencies, creating an extraordinarily complex process with no clear outcomes.[6]

Integrated pollution control, building jointly from the efficiency arguments of organizational specialists and the ecosystems perspective of biologists, emphasized the common bases and interconnectedness of medium-specific problems, and began to seek and support approaches to address them more comprehensively at common points of origin. This orientation of integrated pollution control to common sources of multimedia pollution problems came to embody the "upstream," or preventative interests ascribed to pollution prevention policy.

The other core theme that came to be emphasized in defining pollution prevention policy was more nebulously cast in terms of a "new relationship" (typically a "partnership") between regulators and the regulated (primarily industry). Broadly speaking, pollution prevention was considered by some to be headed away from the historical dependence on what was by then known as the "command-and-control" format for pollution control regulation. That term loosely connoted the particular mixture of available regulatory instruments and other tools of intervention employed to carry out pollution control policies, which included (as with air regulations) highly detailed and specific standards directly enforced at the unit-process level through operating permits.

What pollution prevention headed *toward* along this axis remained far less clear, but various ways of thinking about it began to emerge. One concept, often touted by industry, reemphasized the economist's analysis of the pollution problem as a defect in the free market; namely, that "spillover" or external costs of production (pollution, noise, etc.), are not borne by producers, and not reflected in the prices of products and services. These products and services do not, therefore, reflect their true "social cost." Because the remedies available through common law to those who do suffer the external costs are generally inadequate, some form of additional government intervention was seen as justified. Since neoclassical economists (several of whom figured prominently in constructing the economic discourse for environmental policy) nevertheless tended to have great respect for what they considered the otherwise efficient and flexible characteristics of free market forces, their criticism of pollution control and view of pollution prevention tended to emphasize the need for regulatory options that mimicked or recreated competitive markets.[7]

Thus, one view of pollution prevention (indeed, of regulatory reform in general) became substantially characterized by the application of market-based incentive mechanisms for the "harnessing" of market forces in the service of a cleaner environment. Most prominent among the mechanisms advanced has been the creation of highly regulated regional markets in which quantified rights to pollute can be traded. In Southern California, for example, a recorded exchange involved the Anchor Glass Container Corporation of Huntington Park and Union Carbide Corporation's Torrance facility. Under the exchange, Anchor Glass purchased 3,446,478 pounds of nitrogen oxide emissions from Union Carbide for a price of $1,275,197.[8]

Emissions taxes also continued to receive some attention. This perspective similarly tended to suggest that intrusive federal micromanagement—particularly the uniform point-source standards that have inhibited flexibility, and thus innovation and efficiency—needed to be, at a minimum, deemphasized and reworked for compatibility with alternative market-based tools. This market-focused conceptual approach has also become a frame of reference for the advocacy of pollution prevention voluntarism, or what the Business Roundtable (the organization of CEOs of the largest industrial corporations) described as creating successful facilities "when they are not told how to approach pollution prevention."[9]

Another view, by no means totally incompatible with either a market-failure analysis or an interest in market-based tools, has tended to focus more on the structural and institutional nature of both pollution and pollution control problems. It has sought to explore more interventionist mechanisms and reforms (whether traditional or new) through which pollution prevention mandates and incentives could be inserted into areas which were previously partly or wholly off-limits, such as transportation and land-use policy, trade and, perhaps most notably, forms of "industrial policy" or economic development strategies. In certain respects, this approach has remained somewhat less interested in the particular tools than in the integration of pollution policy with other policy areas.[10] Between these areas (market-based and voluntarist strategies versus more direct roles for public policy initiatives) have resided a range of other strategies and policy instruments. These include such approaches as technical assistance, planning requirements, and right-to-know initiatives, that collectively have come to constitute the axis of pollution prevention.

The analysis of each of these axis points—the single-medium/multimedia dimension, and the particular mix of policy instruments and targets favored at various points in time and described along this continuum from voluntarist to interventionist—is indeed critical to advancing the definition and interpretation of pollution prevention. If pollution prevention is to become a truly pathbreaking departure from the failures of pollution control, however, a larger set of themes that characterize the evolution of pollution control policy also must be considered. Only some of these themes have been addressed in recent federal and state pronouncements on pollution prevention, and often only superficially. These central themes thus need to be considered through an overview of the core statutes of pollution control and their histories of interpretation and implementation.

Conceptual Themes in Pollution Control

As the environmental policy system emerged during the 1970s, a set of core factors and approaches evolved with it. These included: the tendency toward maintenance of (or incremental change in) the status quo; the importance of crises in the formulation of policy; the development of tools to allocate risks and address the burdens of uncertainty in defining and managing those risks; the central role of information in establishing policies and conflicts over access to such information; the evolution of the problem domain from a focus on "conventional pollution" to a focus on "toxic chemical pollution"; the technology fixation of policy in the search for solutions; and the development of entry points for regulation that emphasize "adding on" to, rather than redesigning, production facilities and systems. Each of these themes also tended to reinforce the others, creating in turn a policy domain for the management of hazards as byproducts rather than focusing on sources and the structures that mediate generation and use.

The incremental nature of pollution policy, for example, appears most strikingly when technology-based standards are established to address specific pollutants, which, in turn, create a new market for add-ons (such as scrubbers) and a new range of regulatory activities based on the cross-media transfer for which such technology add-ons are responsible. The problems become circular while the solutions increasingly are more expensive; the management of pollutants remains exogenous to considerations of how industrial facilities are designed or products and processes are selected, let alone how pollutants might derive from the way in which systems are organized and structured (e.g., transportation systems). The regulatory patterns in this instance become a classic representation of Lindbloom's concept of "disjointed incrementalism," where policymakers and regulators operate through a remedial process of action, "a planning without overarching goals."[11]

Similarly, the crisis management focus of pollution control policy continually has separated the crisis point for regulatory activity from the institutional and industrial settings in which such crises are embedded, with management strategies careening from one crisis to the next. "Some see the history of air pollution control," one analyst wrote as early as 1959, "as bearing out a 'catastrophe theory of planning'."[12] That this has continued to characterize pollution control is nowhere more evident than in the emergency preparedness and related legislation of the mid-1980s that developed in response to the catastrophic methyl isocyanate release at the Union Carbide plant in Bhopal, India. For further discussion of these, see Chapter 2.

While the importance of crises has continued to be a dominant theme in the formulation of pollution policy, the nature of the crises, and the ways in which they are constructed and perceived, have become far more complex, reflecting in part the absence of such incontrovertible eyewitness evidence as the disaster of Bhopal, or the "killer fog" and burning river episodes prominent in earlier years. In the 1990s, as pollution prevention searches for a definition, the crises of ozone depletion, global warming, rising cancer rates, and massive species extinction have become, in pace with the growing magnitude of their implications, ever more abstract and debatable, and their effect on policy more difficult to describe.

The need to address problems as crisis points is compounded when the problems are elaborated upon in terms of scientific uncertainty, another major feature of pollution control regulatory activity. This conundrum—the need to act immediately when uncertainty is present—was explored in a voluminous literature and huge body of case law in the late 1970s and 1980s. These explorations are most directly concerned with the ways in which scientific uncertainty can be managed and, in particular, how the burden of uncertainty is to be allocated. Specifically, the burden has been conventionally allocated to those who claim harm and seek change. This became in fact the major focus of the pollution policy debates in the 1980s both in terms of the forced distinction between "risk assessment" (seen as scientific), and "risk management" (seen as political); and in terms of the degree to which "good science"—in the face of overwhelming scientific uncertainty—became a strategic platform for de facto deregulation.[13] In both cases the debate was sharpened by interpretations of highly varied feasibility and risk/benefit balancing requirements for pollution control regulations. By intervening earlier, pollution prevention could be seen as avoiding the need to precisely define the magnitude of risk prior to establishing the need to act, at least where the ability to act becomes evident.[14] However, it has yet to reverse the allocation of the burden of uncertainty.

Strongly intertwined with uncertainty issues and the crisis driven nature of policymaking is the central role of information in policy elaboration, or what some call "the production of knowledge" associated with the design and implementation of pollution control policy.[15] This theme is itself many-faceted, having to do with questions of basic research such as timing, focus, and sponsor, and with evolving requirements for monitoring, record-keeping, reporting, and planning by both agencies and those regulated as sources of pollution. An equally important aspect has been the question of public access to the systematic knowledge thus produced and collected. This first clearly emerged in the late 1970s; the nature of data sources and the evolving role of public access had become a central concern by the 1980s; and the improved but still sharply limited access gained in those years has in turn become a driving force in the development in particular of current pollution prevention policy.

Underlying the issues of knowledge and uncertainty has been the shifting focus of policy from "conventional pollutants" to "toxic chemical pollutants." Conventional pollutants generally refers to a class of substances that share the characteristics of being released in large volumes, and of being both highly visible and comparatively easy to link to particular health and environmental effects. As a shorthand, one can distinguish this class of pollutants by the fact that they create more "obvious" (in the sense of acute or short-term) problems, although they might also be associated with more complex, subtle, and long-term effects. The conventional pollutants, and in many cases their primary source categories, are comparatively few in number. The second class consists of the thousands of known "toxic" pollutants, typified by carcinogens, that are invisible and otherwise more difficult to detect, and which may affect health and cause environmental damage at trace concentrations or very low exposure levels, although the degree of uncertainty tends to be very high. While they may be associated with short-term hazards, they are at least of equal concern due to their persistence in the environment, and/or their ability to cause serious disease after long latency periods. The successes of pollution control have largely been organized around conventional pollutants, while the failures are most prominently associated with toxic chemical pollutants, thus posing a particular challenge for pollution prevention.

Perhaps the most pervasive theme in pollution control that has profoundly infused and shaped its evolution is the question of "technological fixation." The deeply entrenched single-medium regulatory focus has often been viewed as the most difficult characteristic to change within the bureaucracies responsible for implementing pollution policies and their complex statutory mandates. However, the *technocentrism* of pollution control infuses not only the bureaucracy and its charters but also dominant institutions and constituencies in the society it serves. The continuing technocentrism of existing statutes, bureaucracies, policymakers and, apparently, the society at large has largely short-circuited attempts to move the policy focus more than just slightly upstream of the machinery and unit production processes with which it remains preoccupied. Pollution prevention requires expanding conventional approaches to industrial production and consumption, and assumes that production involves more than a bundle of discrete technologies. Indeed, from this perspective, consumption involves more than a bundle of products. These prominent themes are illustrated in Part II.

Policy Tools in Pollution Control

The themes discussed in the previous section can also shed light in turn on the nature of the policy tools selected as part of the pollution control framework. There are, of course, many competing schemes for classifying the set of tools from which the government may draw in attempting to effect policy objectives—since they ultimately are as broad as the full set of powers held by the government—and no classification scheme is entirely satisfactory. For our purposes, and to lend order to the following discussions, the following definitions and system of classification will be used.

Policy, particularly pollution policy, will be defined as the overarching body of problem analysis and general objectives that provides the conceptual framework and motivation for government action in a given area. It is obvious, but worth emphasizing, that the most significant defining characteristic of any body of policy (or piece of legislation), is how the underlying problem has been bounded and the subject matter labeled. It will be argued later that the rigid divisions made between "pollution policy" and, for example, "health policy," "natural resource policy," "environmental policy," or "economic policy," pose significant barriers to pollution prevention.

Regulation will be viewed as one body of options for effecting policy objectives, and most specifically for remedying problems that arise out of the failures of the unregulated marketplace. Other classes of options, however, are less obviously "regulatory" (or economic) in nature. They may be less mechanistic and/or focused than classical regulatory tools, or more grounded in the generic doctrines and remedies of common law, or in the broader powers (e.g., taxing and spending) of government. They are thus more difficult to classify. To deal with some of these complexities, the approach here will begin by observing the distinction made by Stephen Breyer between "classical" and "alternative" modes of regulation.[16] Generally, the classical forms of regulation tell firms or other subjects of regulation what to do, and create what Breyer calls a "detailed web of affirmative legal obligations." The alternative forms of regulation are more oriented toward altering the preconditions of competition, rather than toward specific remedies for the defects in the competitive marketplace.

Among the six *classical modes of regulation* Breyer describes, two are most applicable and have been extensively used in the control of pollution: (1) standard setting and (2) individualized screening (the others primarily involve price or rate setting and resource allocation). Although they play out very differently in implementation, the two can be seen as mirror images: when relatively precise standards for what is required or desired cannot be effectively formulated, more general standards that provide mechanisms for a detailed case-by-case screening-out of unwanted products, substances, or activities can be utilized.

Of the *alternative modes of regulation,* only a few have been substantively employed in the control of pollution, although several have received significant attention in the development of pollution prevention policy. They are: the application of antitrust laws; disclosure requirements; regulatory "taxes" or surcharges (distinguished from fines, and generalized income, sales, or corporate taxes); the creation of marketable property rights; changes in liability rules; bargaining; product bans; and nationalization or other government ownership. For our purposes, and in light of developments that became particularly significant during the 1980s, it will be useful to further divide disclosure into reporting and labeling requirements, on the one hand, and planning and modeling requirements on the other. Both may, to some extent, apply not just to the regulated sector, but to the regulators themselves (i.e., agencies and independent regulatory commissions). The latter case—agency disclosure requirements—corresponds more closely to the regulatory reform options described below.

In addition to the regulatory body of policy tools, there are two other general classes of tools. The first, also described by Breyer, identifies a set of *generic regulatory reform options.* They include: procedural changes to improve fairness, efficiency, and legitimacy; structural changes in the relationships between the agencies and independent regulatory commissions, and the three branches of government (e.g., provisions for congressional and/or executive veto power over agency rules); the creation of new institutions (such as a "science court," or a consumer protection agency, or cross-agency bodies); and the use of "sunset" provisions, and other mechanisms to mandate periodic substantive review of regulations.

To the reform options, we add a final class of instruments we call, simply, *generic policy tools.* They consist of: the ability to set policy and legislative boundaries referred to above; the provision of subsidies and development funds; and, most generally, what has been called "moral suasion": the ability to influence policy goals through leadership, publicity, and the manipulation of popular opinion.[17]

There is yet another distinction that can be made in the discussion of policy tools; namely, the degree to which their targets are direct or indirect. This is similar to the difference between classical and alternative modes of regulation (i.e., the difference between altering the market conditions that influence outcomes, and altering the outcomes themselves). However, it applies even within the classical modes of regulation, as discussed below, in terms of both "technology-forcing" and "nontechnological" standards. Although both may take the form of focused rules that describe a specific desired outcome, it is often the network of indirect or systemic effects they may set up that is of most interest.

Alternatives to classical, direct regulation often may hold the greatest potential for substantive change; however, they will often be greeted with justifiable mistrust by those who suffer most from the problem to be corrected, or those who may suffer most from the implied solution, or those who generally fear the breadth of change that may occur. The processes and outcomes, although potentially providing greater scope for flexibility and innovation, will be difficult or impossible to track, and will thus create greater uncertainty. The more indirect mechanisms may impose the strongest requirements for accompanying procedural and institutional reform if they are to be accepted.

This brief discussion of themes and policy tools identifies a series of interrelated paths along which the federal system of pollution control has evolved. Pollution prevention policy ultimately must be derived from our experiences, evaluation, and critique of control systems. Understanding how this new paradigm has emerged from the core statutes of pollution control provides the starting point for understanding both the barriers to and possible opportunities for forging the path toward prevention.

Notes

1. Instead of questioning the equation of "progress" and "pollution," policymakers had also long assumed that the means by which the conundrum could be resolved was through "pollution management" (that is, through a system of controls), rather than by challenging the bias associated with the equation itself. The 1965 Report of the Environmental Pollution Panel of the President's Science Advisory Committee, for example, put it this way: "The production of pollutants and an increasing need

for pollution management are an inevitable concomitant of a technological society with a high standard of living. Pollution problems will increase in importance as our technology and standard of living continue to grow." See *Restoring the Quality of Our Environment,* (Washington D.C.:The White House, November 1965).

2.Various estimates have placed the amount of waste tonnage at as much as 10.5 to 12 billion pounds. See David T. Allen and R. Jain, eds., *Hazardous Waste and Hazardous Materials,* Volume 9 (1) (1992): The estimate of the chemical industry's implied total waste and byproduct generation (dry basis) based on its average process yield is of the order of 50 million tons per year. See the discussion in Chapter 8.

3. U.S. Congress, Hazardous and Solid Waste Amendments of 1984, P.L. 98–616 (98 Stat. 3221), November 8, 1984.

4. EPA Pollution Prevention Statement, Federal Register, January 26, 1989, 54 CFR 3845–3847.

5. On "integrated pollution control," see Nigel Haigh and Frances Irwin, eds., *Integrated Pollution Control in Europe and North America* (Baltimore, Maryland: The Conservation Foundation, 1990). For a survey of the field, see also, "Integrated Pollution Control: A Symposium," *Environmental Law* 22 (Winter 1992).

6. David Doniger, *The Law and Policy of Toxic Substances Control: A Case Study of Vinyl Chloride* (Baltimore and London, Johns Hopkins Press, 1978).

7. *Environmental Improvement through Economic Incentives,* Frederick Anderson, Allen Kneese, Philip Reed, Serge Taylor, and Russell Stevenson, (Baltimore: Johns Hopkins Press for Resources for the Future, 1977); *Economics and the Environment: A Materials Balance Approach,* Allen V. Kneese, Robert U. Ayres, and Ralph C. D'Arge, (Baltimore: Johns Hopkins Press for Resources for the Future, 1970); "Environmental Markets in the Year 2000," Robert Hahn and Roger Noll, *Journal of Risk and Uncertainty,* Vol. 3, pp. 351–367, 1990.

8:The exchange is the second such swap since the program was instituted in January 1994. Under this negotiation, Union Carbide converted existing emissions reduction credits, achieved through process changes, into trading credits with Anchor Glass. By purchasing credits achieved through Union Carbide reductions, Anchor Glass can delay pollution control efforts or choose to emit more than its objectives stated under the exchange. Officials expect future exchanges to be more straightforward. (Personal communication with Sam Atwood, South Coast Air Quality Management District, 1994.)

9. "Government regulation should not prescribe given measurements," the Business Roundtable argued, "but rather individual facilities should

develop their own measurements which would vary according to process and products." See *The Business Roundtable Position Paper: Pollution Prevention*, n.d.

10. See, for example, the approaches described by Nicholas Ashford ("A Unified Technology-Based Strategy for Incorporating Concerns About Risks, Costs, and Equity in Setting National Environmental Priorities"), Barry Commoner ("Pollution Prevention: Putting Comparative Risk Assessment in Its Place"), and Mary O'Brien ("A Proposal to Address, Rather than Rank, Environmental Problems"), papers presented at an EPA/Resources for the Future conference, "Setting National Environmental Priorities: The EPA Risk-Based Paradigm and Its Alternatives," (Washington DC: Resources for the Future, 1993).

11. "Planning without overaching goals" is from John Friedmann's critique of the Lindbloom approach, *Planning in the Public Domain: From Knowledge to Action*, John Friedmann, (Princeton: Princeton University Press, 1987), p. 131. Charles Lindbloom's famous essay is "The Science of Muddling Through," *Public Administration Review*, Spring 1959, Vol. 19, No. 2, pp. 79–99.

12. See C. Haar, *Land-Use Planning*, (Boston: Little, Brown, 1959), pp. 130–1, cited in James E. Krier and Edmund Ursin, *Pollution and Policy: A Case Essay on California and Federal Experience with Motor Vehicle Pollution, 1950–1975* (Berkeley and Los Angeles: University of California Press, 1977).

13. The debates over what constituted "good science" in regulatory judgments, most notably during the Reagan administration's first term, are discussed in "Good Science, Bad Regulation, and Toxic Risk Assessment," Howard Latin, *Yale Journal of Regulation*, 5(1), pp. 89–148. See also "Deregulation: The Failure at EPA," Richard N. L. Andrews, in *Environmental Policy in the 1980s: Reagan's New Agenda*, Norman J. Vig and Michael E. Kraft, (Washington, DC: Congressional Quarterly, 1984), pp. 161–180.

14. See "When to Act and What is Known: Health Impacts and Risk Assessment in the Context of Toxics Reduction," John Froines, Pollution Prevention Education and Research Center, working paper, UCLA, 1994.

15. Krier and Ursin, *Pollution and Policy*, p. 263.

16. Stephen Breyer, *Regulation and Its Reform* (Cambridge, Massachusetts, Harvard University Press, 1982).

17. William Baumol and Wallace Oates, *Economics, Environmental Policy, and the Quality of Life* (Englewood Cliffs, New Jersey: Prentice Hall, 1979), p. 218.

2

By Air, Water, and Land: The Media–Specific Approach to Toxics Policies

Robert Gottlieb
Maureen Smith
Julie Roque

Introduction

The development of far-reaching environmental laws and regulations since the 1970s has also generated a host of unresolved questions. Although Congress has often provided detailed instructions and implementation schedules, the laws have been both broad in scope and vague as to how mandates were supposed to be fulfilled. Congressional passage of media-specific legislation, aimed specifically, yet separately, at the "three pollutions, or three routes of pollutant exposure: air, water, and land," further influenced the mode of implementation, creating a sharp division of labor both within and among regulatory agencies.[1] The following discussion examines the advent of these media–based laws, including the Clean Air Act, the Clean Water Act, and the various strategies aimed at land-based hazardous and nonhazardous solid waste. What emerges is that this environmental regulatory or pollution control framework has sought to direct industry to alter its behavior, but without specifically addressing structural factors in industry decisionmaking.

With respect to industry, the pollution control system has largely been structured in relation to technology-based standards. Through implementation of regulations and promulgation of rules, regulatory agencies, particularly the U.S. Environmental Protection Agency (EPA), have become large and unwieldy bureaucracies, organized largely on the basis of a medium-by-medium and substance-by-substance approach. These agencies have also had to answer to an increasingly impatient and frustrated Congress, itself responding to growing community concerns over toxics.

The media-based legislation established targets, incentives, and disincentives based on varying regulatory philosophies, as described in the previous chapter. From the least direct forms of government action (voluntarism) to the more elaborate (detailed standards and mandated controls),
diverse regulatory approaches (including such varied reference points as
zero discharge goals, voluntary reductions, regulatory flexibility, right-to-
know, market incentives, technology-forcing standards and cost-benefit
criteria) often lacked strategic coherence and direction. Yet collectively,
these disparate sets of approaches came to define today's pollution control
system over the past two decades.

Air

The origin of the pollution control system is often traced to the environmentally turbulent months of 1970 that coincided with events surrounding the first Earth Day. In addition to the passage of the Clean Air
Amendments of 1970, commonly known as the Clean Air Act of 1970,
which provided for an aggressive and profound amplification of federal
authority in the regulation of air quality, the year marks the signing of the
National Environmental Policy Act (NEPA) with its broad vision of environmental protection. And, following the emergence of a powerful grassroots movement of miners, 1970 also witnessed the passage of the
Occupational Safety and Health Act (OSHA).

Despite the elevation of environmental issues to the forefront of the
national agenda, and the comparatively holistic, ecological approach
reflected in NEPA and Earth Day rhetoric, the Clean Air Act (similar to
OSHA) simultaneously embodied key aspects of the reductionism and
fragmentation that ultimately describe the central features of pollution
control. While the Act regulated stationary industrial sources of air pollution, it simultaneously sought to control a very different type of air pollution associated with personal use of automobiles. It was in fact in the area
of transportation that the Act sought to pose potentially far-reaching prevention mechanisms. But, prevention opportunities were for the most part
passed over in favor of standard attainment through largely end-of-pipe
technological fixes.

One explanation for this was the single-medium focus of policy that
became crucially elaborated in this new legislation. Indeed, the Clean Air
Act of 1970 (CAA), addressing the first of the three pollutions that constituted the primary domain of pollution control efforts, also set the style and
framework for the subsequent expansion of federal efforts to control water

pollution, solid waste, and toxic pollutants. Indeed, the CAA has been called the "flagship of the environmental protection fleet" in recognition of its crucial role in the construction of modern federal pollution control policy.[2]

Prior to the 1960s, the federal government had played almost no role in the protection of air quality, which was left to be hammered out at the municipal, county, and state levels. The Air Pollution Control Act of 1955 marked the first federal foray into the area, but was limited to the provision of technical and financial assistance to the states.[3] With the rapid industrial growth and rise in fossil-fuels-based energy production and consumption in the post-war decades, the extent of the problem had come to be underlined by catastrophic air pollution episodes in heavily industrialized regions such as Donora, Pennsylvania, or the London "killer fog" of December 1952, which was implicated in as many as 4,000 deaths. The 1952 events were succeeded ten years later by another London episode that caused some 700 deaths. These events, occurring shortly before the second National Conference on Air Pollution in the U.S., became a force behind the passage of the federal Clean Air Act of 1963. The effects of yet another air crisis, a 1966 episode in New York City which fell a month before the third National Conference on Air Pollution, were also reflected in the federal Air Quality Act of 1967. A series of less catastrophic smog episodes, particularly in California, drove state efforts to control vehicular emissions, and were eventually reflected in the federal Motor Vehicle Pollution Control Act of 1965.[4]

These laws gave the federal government authority to intervene directly around specific areas (for example, in the setting and enforcement of vehicle emission standards and in issues of interstate pollution), but remained substantially focused on the support and supervision of state-led efforts. However by decade's end, the failures of both state and federal efforts to effectively contain either industrial or vehicular pollution were undeniable. Polls found that air pollution was perceived as the most widespread and intractable of the three pollutions. One survey found that 69 percent of the people interviewed considered air pollution a "very serious" or "somewhat serious" problem, up from 28 percent just four years earlier.[5] Unlike previous local ordinances and state and federal law which developed substantially in response to specific episodes of pollution, the Clean Air Act of 1970 responded to a more generalized sense of systemic environmental crisis.

The new, more profound environmental crisis apparent through air pollution has been described as a "crisis in thought," in which "it suddenly occurred to many people that perhaps government did not know what it was, or should be, doing."[6] These concerns led directly to a modified Clean Air Act of 1970 that not only authorized greater federal involvement in air pollution control, but in fact constituted a giant step in the federalization of pollution control.

The overriding policy goal of the Clean Air Act of 1970 (CAA) was "to protect and enhance the quality of the nation's air resources in order to promote the public health and welfare and the productive capacity of its population."[7] Its major provisions were organized around the attainment of ambient air quality standards, and various procedural mechanisms for implementation, enforcement, and judicial review. Although the CAA contained provisions to regulate toxic air pollutants ("hazardous air pollutants" in the language of the Act), their regulation languished in a gridlock of scientific uncertainty, expanding tests for economic impact, and court battles throughout the 1970s and 1980s.

The National Ambient Air Quality Standards (NAAQS) program provided specific air quality objectives to be met in every region of the country. Under this program, the EPA (its implementing authority) was required to develop two sets of maximum ambient air concentration standards for particular pollutants. *Primary* ambient air quality standards were to be sufficient to "protect the public health," and *secondary* standards (more conservative) to "protect the public welfare." Pollutants for which such standards were to be set were limited to those posing public health and welfare risks, emitted by "numerous sources," generally falling within the class of conventional pollutants (such as carbon monoxide or nitrous oxides) resulting in a variety of acute health effects. In the case of air pollution they came to be known as *criteria pollutants* (because for each pollutant to be addressed by an ambient standard, the agency was required to compile documentation describing the criteria by which it was targeted). By 1971, standards had been established for six criteria pollutants (to which none has since been added). All were strongly associated with fossil fuel combustion generally, or gasoline specifically. These criteria pollutants are: oxides of nitrogen (NO_x); ozone (O_3), which is formed from a combination of NO_x and hydrocarbons (HC); particulate matter (PM10); carbon monoxide (CO); lead (Pb); and oxides of sulfur (SO_x).

The states were required to develop plans, known as SIPs (State Implementation Plans), for meeting the NAAQS concentration ceilings. The most direct mechanism—and the one emphasized in the Act—for meeting ambient concentration standards in regions where they were being exceeded, was the imposition of emissions limitations on the major sources of criteria pollutants. The general categories of sources to be thus addressed were *stationary sources* (e.g., utilities and manufacturing plants) and *mobil sources* (motor vehicles). The term *non-point source* later came into use to distinguish the obvious tailpipe or smokestack *point sources* from, for example, leaks, evaporation, and numerous other sources that were more difficult to pinpoint and target. The term *indirect source* (sometimes called "complex source") was also introduced by the EPA (although the category was never effectively regulated) to describe sources such as roads and parking lots that attract and concentrate mobil sources of pollution.

Performance standards were intended to work within models of aggregate emissions that would allow ambient air standards to be met. Yet in practice they usually worked forward from the status of available technology. Thus regulators surveyed the emissions rates of like point sources, and expressed their conclusions in terms such as: LAER (lowest achievable emissions rate), BAT (best available technology economically achievable), BADCT (best available demonstrated control technology), RACT (reasonably available control technology), and so forth. As the terms indicate, they factored in qualifications such as reasonableness and practicability, and various other economic tests that were present in the statutes, interpreted by the agency or the courts, or, eventually, added by executive order.

From these standards was born the phenomenon of "technology stalling," in which uniform performance standards would bring existing point sources up to a demonstrated standard of performance—and no further. Standards for new sources, however, which imposed less-costly design rather than retrofitting requirements, provided an opportunity to impose more stringent uniform requirements, which eventually tended to be expressed in such terms as MACT (maximum available control technology). They also potentially provided for what became known as "technology forcing." In one of the more controversial sections of the Act, Congress required that by 1975 new car emissions must be reduced by 90 percent on the general assumption that the technology could be developed with sufficient motivation.

The states were given primary authority (which was largely delegated to state regulators operating in regional "airbasin" jurisdictions) to define regional emissions limitations for *existing sources* (with some significant exemptions, such as federal facilities). The federal government reserved primary authority for itself in the construction of uniform national emissions standards for *new or modified sources*. It also reserved the authority to write its own SIPs if the states failed to produce adequate plans. Thus a complex system was established whereby state regulators would juggle among establishing their own regional emissions standards; implementing and customizing federal emissions standards; developing air monitoring systems and complex models for predicting air quality as a function of total emissions, weather patterns, pollutant interaction, etc.; and imposing (at least theoretically) whatever other controls would be necessary to bring regional airbasins into compliance with the overarching NAAQS standards.

As has often been pointed out, the decision to emphasize a classical regulatory approach was among the key choices made.[8] Notwithstanding the significance of this top-level choice, the more specific and complex issues of what *kind* of controls were imposed was perhaps even more important. Standard-setting, once decided upon as a general course of action for pollution control, offers a wide range of alternatives, including ambient and emissions standards. Each may fall in a different place not only in the continuum from direct to indirect mechanisms, but in terms of a distinction that is commonly made between *technological and nontechnological standards*. The difference essentially turns on the degree to which a particular technology is the first or primary subject of a rule, distinct from whatever larger objective it is intended to work toward. Emissions limitations applied to particular sources of pollution are usually constructed in the form of technological (or "technology-based") standards. However, they can, for example, also take the form of nontechnological operating or workplace standards, in which a particular technology is less at issue than the frequency or competence with which it is deployed. Fuel composition standards— particularly the highly effective restrictions on lead additives discussed in Chapter 6—represent another type of nontechnological standard, as do other forms of product composition or product design standards.

One of the most portentous yet overlooked prevention-oriented clauses of the Act requires that SIPs address all measures necessary for meeting ambient standards, including "land-use and transportation controls." These significantly include not just proscriptive rules, but the possibility of highly focused surcharges that are essentially a form of regulatory tax intended to influence both private behavior and urban form.

A wide variety of transportation controls seeking to address the enormous contribution of motor vehicle sources to air pollution have been potentially available, including: parking controls and surcharges, auto-free zoning, mandatory bus and carpool lanes, bridge and highway tolls, vehicle retrofitting, and inspection and maintenance requirements, selective driving bans, mandatory four-day work weeks, and gas surcharges and rationing schemes.[9] In turn, they represent important tools (as do new source emissions standards) for any serious effort to influence land-use patterns, along with the more traditional land-use control mechanisms such as rent controls, real estate and other taxes (or tax exemptions), and zoning regulation.

Except for the vehicle inspection and maintenance requirements (which were really subsidiary components of tailpipe emissions standards, and became the only real survivors among transportation controls by the end of the decade), the rest of the options were mostly nontechnological controls that sought to provoke a larger network of effects. Indeed, as R. Shep Melnick observed: "The result of such restrictions (and, for some supporters, their purpose as well) would have been a fundamental shift in urban and suburban residential patterns."[10]

The early demise (by 1977) of serious federal efforts to enforce transportation management programs as a component of air quality regulation could probably have been predicted, given the powerful biases toward controls and add-ons that had emerged from the origins of the federal pollution control system, even as the transportation option was being formulated. Instead, transportation management became at most a stepchild of the engineering bias inherent in transportation planning agencies, with the federal environmental effort becoming applicable only in isolated circumstances (for example, with California's 2% electric vehicle mandate, which is discussed in Chapter 9).

Among the many barriers that emerged to the imposition of transportation and land-use management controls, the most important included the enormous technical and scientific uncertainties associated with accurately quantifying the effect of such controls on ambient air quality (and thus in meeting legal tests for requiring them). Several decades of experience had disclosed the unmistakable correlation between vehicular emissions and smog episodes. Far less was known about the chemistry by which, for example, photochemical oxidants such as ozone are produced as a function of reactions between NO_x and hydrocarbons under different conditions of sunlight, temperature, and humidity. That motor vehicles are a major source of air pollution was a central premise of the Clean Air Act. How many vehicles, operating under what environmental and traffic conditions, cause how much pollution represented a far more complex question, and the unachievable burden of quantifying the chain of causation lay with the EPA. At the same time there is a longstanding tradition of state and local jurisdiction in most areas of transportation and land-use planning, and an enormous array of associated political forces opposed to federal intervention in these areas. Finally, the policy framework—air quality—under which these controls were advanced was far too narrow.

At the state and local levels, transportation systems and land-use patterns emerge out of the complex interactions of a wide variety of different governmental jurisdictions; there is, for example, no single obvious and competent authority to be charged with what is effectively a form of regional

planning. The multiple social and environmental benefits of mass transportation systems and increasing urban density potentially achieved by limiting private vehicle use were simply too broad to be meaningfully contained or advanced—more-or-less through the back door—within the
comparatively limited framework of a medium-specific environmental
statute. While many analysts of the failure of the Clean Air Act's transportation control provisions have concentrated on the technical, administrative, and enforcement complexities, and in particular on the tensions of
a federal system, it is worth considering what might have been the benefits of even a limited attempt at the hard work of policy integration at the
federal level. If, for example, the transportation control efforts advanced
under the Clean Air Act had been accompanied by a significant redirection
of federal highway funds to public transit development; or transportation
controls of the sort outlined above had been made a direct condition of
receiving any federal transportation funds—the other barriers might have
seemed far less insurmountable.[11] The much-cited American love affair
with the automobile and the implied resistance to alternatives evolved over
decades in which (for many Americans) there were no "practicable," "reasonable," or "feasible" alternatives available. Transportation policy was competing as an equally valid framework, not simply because the air quality
problem was a spillover from production, but equally because it was a
spillover from a system of product use and the spatial organization built up
around it.

Indeed, in the vast body of literature on the subsequent history of pollution control, the terms *direct control* and *direct regulation* have become
effectively (and inaccurately) synonymous with technological control. This
is attributed to the comparatively limited attention, and great resistance,
paid to nontechnological alternatives such as transportation controls. Of
the "fixations of pollution policy" observed by James Krier and Edmund
Ursin in their discussion of the Clean Air Act, the "technological fixation"
and the "fixation with regulation" go hand-in-glove. As they write: "Not
only are technological fixes quicker, easier, and more predictable than
'social engineering,' they are also less disruptive of the status quo" than
nontechnological alternatives.[12] As early as 1955, however, public health
officials in California, faced with mounting health effects from air pollution problems, had observed that "too much emphasis [is] placed upon
cure, once smog has occurred, and not enough upon prevention and determination of cause," even though "preventative measures taken before air
pollution becomes a problem would undoubtedly be more effective and
less expensive for all concerned."[13] Although the Clean Air Act primarily
advanced the curative methods of the technological fix, the five words

"transportation and land use controls" could be read as an early opening for a nontechnological preventative approach, although the door quickly slammed shut.

By the end of its first decade, regulation under the Clean Air Act resulted in net reductions of estimated total annual emissions of each of the criteria pollutants.[14] The single most significant reduction was in lead emissions, which declined by more than 65 percent due largely to a combination of vehicular exhaust system control technology and restrictions on the use of lead additives in gasoline. However, total emissions of sulfur oxides, nitrogen oxides, and particulates from transportation sources had increased as growth in motor vehicle use outpaced the effects of the technological controls imposed. With the notable exception of lead additive restrictions, however, nontechnological controls had been largely ignored or abandoned, and the alternative modes of regulation remained largely untried. Many regions of the country remained (and still remain) out of compliance with the NAAQS standards, while comparatively pristine areas had seen air quality worsen due both to growth, and interregional air pollution transport. In fact some pristine areas had begun to see water quality worsen as a transboundary air pollution problem transmuted into acid rain.

The Clean Air Act Amendments of 1977 attempted to address the issues of increased air pollution in formerly clean airbasins by developing provisions for the "prevention of significant deterioration."[15] Acid rain would not be addressed until the end of the following decade. The 1977 amendments also sharply restricted the EPA's authority to impose transportation control requirements. In most other respects the Amendments were focused on the development of improved mechanisms and sanctions to be used in what had become less of an NAAQS attainment requirement than a negotiated approach to demonstrable progress on that front. The Clean Air Act would not be significantly amended again until 1990, when the influence of the new pollution prevention approach would begin to be felt. However, the basic approach established in the 1970 Act would be almost immediately reproduced in the efforts addressed to cleaning up the water and making it safe to drink, providing further elaboration of a system driven by its technology-focus and its attention to the medium rather than the source.

Water

The events influencing the design of the Federal Water Pollution Control Act Amendments of 1972 (commonly known as the Clean Water Act) and the Safe Drinking Water Act of 1974, as well as the basic structure of their approaches, had a good deal in common with the Clean Air Act in the construction of the federal pollution control system of the 1970s.[16]

Historically, the issue of "water quality" divided between the focus on "clean" water, signifying the degradation of pristine water bodies and the need to clean up such waters, and "safe" drinking water, referring to an earlier era of waterborne diseases. Water "pollution" was the common reference point, although the primary focus of policy was environmental— rather than health-based. The prevailing assumption was that drinking water treatment impacting potable water supplies had been more effectively addressed than treatment or management of discharges, spills, or accidents that affected source waters.

Historically, the series of health crises that set the framework for this policy, began with typhoid, cholera, yellow fever, and other disease outbreaks in the 19th century, which eventually became linked to pathogen-contaminated drinking water supplies. These crises had led, by the early 20th century, to the introduction of water and sewage filtration and chemical treatment systems by cities, which appeared to eliminate the problem of waterborne diseases but only partially addressed the problem of water pollution as an environmental issue. The support and oversight of such treatment facilities eventually became a central focus of federal efforts to control water pollution, beginning with the Federal Water Pollution Control Act (FWPCA) of 1948, which formally established the federal policy of subsidizing publicly owned sewers and treatment works. The 1962 publication of Rachel Carson's book *Silent Spring* dramatically highlighted the effects of pesticide (and other petrochemical) pollution of ground and surface waters, and was a force behind the more generalized sense of environmental crisis—which prominently included water quality as an environmental concern—that had emerged by the end of the decade.

As with air pollution control, however, the federal government, accepted only incremental expansion of its jurisdiction in the FWPCA amendments of the 1950s and 1960s, and was reluctant to become involved beyond the level of supervision and assistance. Primary responsibility for water pollution problems thus remained with the cities and states.[17]

In addition to agricultural runoff and municipal sources of pollution, the direct pollution of water bodies by effluent from heavy chemical process industries had also accelerated sharply with postwar industrial growth. Industrial water pollution was never effectively regulated at state and local levels (which were acutely subject to the influence of local industrial interests). The need for federal intervention, however, was dramatically indicated by the time Cleveland's heavily contaminated Cuyahoga River

caught fire in 1969.[18] By the mid-1960s the approach taken in air pollution control of establishing ambient standards and working backward to
control point sources, also had become central to the developing federal
water pollution control strategy.

The Clean Water Act of 1972 provided the muscle to this approach.
From the outset, however, both the medium of water and the sources and
types of its major contaminants were more divisible, and the approach to
water pollution control became even more fragmented than that used for
air quality control. With water quality policy, differentiated frameworks
(often with different goals) built up around discrete types of water bodies,
and the various different "uses" for which they are employed. The purview
of "water quality" management included large lakes and rivers, shallow
streams and ponds, groundwater aquifers, wetlands, coastal estuaries and
bays, and the open ocean.[19] The 1972 CWA was primarily limited in its
direct focus on navigable waters, leaving wetlands and groundwater (at
best) narrowly or indirectly addressed. Wetlands protection, considered to
have significant land use/development as well as environmental implications, became the direct domain of the Army Corps of Engineers (COE).[20]
Groundwater, on the other hand, was assumed to be a relatively protected
source of water on the basis of natural filtration. This position rapidly
eroded, however, after trace contaminants of various chemical pollutants
began to be discovered on a massive scale from 1979 on. Increasingly,
groundwater protection came to be perceived as a function of safe drinking water regulation (with its focus on treatment, as described below), and
generally fell outside the domain of watershed protection or prevention
strategies. At the same time, opportunities for federal action were seen as
constrained by longstanding definitions of groundwater as a local resource.
Finally, open ocean pollution, another critical environmental concern of
the early 1970s, would continue to be approached through an entirely separate body of federal standards and, eventually, international agreements.

The more direct Clean Water Act provisions charged the states with the
task of defining the particular uses to be preserved in various navigable
water bodies, and then with developing water quality standards sufficient
to sustain them. Uses could include, for example, the support of plant and
wildlife populations, recreation, industrial and agricultural water supply,
and, in an effort to relink human health and the environment, at least as an
option of choice, public drinking water supply. Both the states and the federal government would define point source effluent limitations (generally,
technology-based point source performance standards) and state implementation plans would be subject to federal approval. If the state effluent
limitations or water quality standards were insufficient, independently

developed federal standards would be required. States also could develop more stringent point-source standards than the federal effluent limitations. The implementation and enforcement of these standards was housed within a framework known as the National Pollutant Discharge Elimination System (NPDES).[21] The sources to be regulated included direct dischargers, primarily firms and publicly owned treatment works (POTWs). Firms were subject to technology-based standards (BCT, BADCT, and BAT, depending on whether the source was new or existing, and on the class of pollutant). POTWs were required to meet secondary treatment standards, as defined by the EPA, or more rigorous standards if the receiving water quality warranted it. So-called "indirect dischargers," or firms discharging into public sewers, were required to meet specific pre-treatment standards, generally sufficient to allow the downstream POTW to meet secondary standards.[22]

The Clean Water Act called for cleaning up the nation's waters through two key provisions. First, it mandated that all pollutant discharges to navigable waters be eliminated by 1985, including specific toxic discharges, and stipulated that these waters be fishable and swimmable by 1983.[23] In Title I of the law, under the "Declaration of Goals and Policy," the Act states that "the discharge of toxic pollutants in toxic amounts be prohibited"[24] and that it would be "the policy of the Congress to recognize, preserve, and protect the primary responsibilities and rights of States to prevent, reduce, and eliminate pollution...."[25] However, this "prevention" language was subsumed by the strong emphasis on "treatment" (e.g., funding and requirements for publicly owned waste treatment works) and "technological controls."[26] Furthermore, the Act's focus (and particularly EPA's implementation approach) on point sources and more limited emphasis on such nonpoint sources as urban land uses or agricultural runoff (primarily embodied in CWA's Section 208 provisions designed to identify nonpoint sources and to develop plans emphasizing the need to develop regulations and land use measures to control them) represented a missed opportunity to associate "planning" measures (similar to those that might have been made available through the transportation controls of the Clean Air Act) with pollutant reduction objectives.[27]

With respect to its language regarding point sources, the Act set up pollution discharge standards based on the specific existing control technology available for various industrial processes and a permitting system also based on available control technologies (the NPDES) for companies discharging into waterways. EPA was instructed to write guidelines to indicate a "best practicable technology" (BPT) for each industry by 1977 and a "best available technology" (BAT) by 1983.[28] The Clean Water Act also provided for a pretreatment program for municipal sewers and treatment plants (POTWs), which had been underfinanced at the state and regional level in the years prior to it's passage.[29]

Although the Act directed EPA to "… develop comprehensive programs for preventing, reducing, or eliminating the pollution of the navigable waters and groundwaters," the timetables were ambiguous "national goals" rather than specific policies.[30] The Act's definition of pollutant reduction, moreover, involved the development of specific control technologies (BPTs and BATs) rather than actual process changes by industries. At the same time, the Act's costly and often poorly implemented grants program designed to deal with the sewage outflow problem was specifically earmarked for the construction of treatment facilities, rather than reduction-oriented pretreatment programs. Thus, the discharge and permit requirements of the Act institutionalized both "acceptable" pollutant discharge levels and the emphasis on treatment rather than reduction. By the late 1970s, it was already becoming obvious that the zero discharge targets would not be met.[31] Recognizing that the goals of the Act would not be met also contributed to the deemphasis of the reduction intent of the legislation.

Instead of reducing and eventually eliminating discharges, the Clean Water Act helped to create an elaborate control system which further expanded the media-shifting nature of the regulatory system, an argument that had already been raised in 1973 by the National Water Commission in its critique of the use of technology-based standards to achieve "clean water" goals.[32] Through the 1970s and 1980s, EPA rulemaking for CWA regulations continued to focus primarily on point sources of industrial and municipal discharges to navigable waters and public sewers. Its two main regulatory vehicles were the NPDES permitting process and pretreatment standards for effluent released to sewers. Standards for both types of discharge, which can vary by state and POTW, are coupled to specific industrial waste stream categories and thus fall between both technology based standards (e.g., BPT) and ambient water quality criteria. Spills of approximately 300 hazardous substances, including oil, above specific thresholds must be reported to the National Response Center.[33] Pollutants regulated through permits include conventional pollutants such as suspended solids, grease, organic materials that deplete oxygen, and substances which alter pH levels, as well as toxic substances. Ultimately, the frustrations associated with the failure of regulators to link CWA permitting and discharge standard provisions and technology controls with the emerging pollution prevention objectives of the late 1980s served to make the efforts in the 1990s to rewrite the Clean Water Act (described in Chapter 3) similar to the debates over the 1990 Clean Air Act Amendments—a major battleground for the evolution of pollution policy.

While the debates over the CWA demonstrated the limits of a single-media approach in the clean water area, the problem of drinking water contamination pointed to the difficulties of regulating downstream users of toxics who remained reluctant to address the upstream sources involved. During the early 1970s, public interest groups brought attention to the problem of contamination of drinking water supplies that stemmed from both widespread chemical contamination of surface water, such as from petrochemical plants along the Mississippi River, as well as from potentially carcinogenic chlorine-based byproducts resulting from long-standing water disinfection methods. These concerns brought new attention to water quality as a health-based concern and established a new legislative and regulatory reference point for water pollution legislation. In response to the atmosphere of crisis surrounding these discoveries of new health problems, Congress passed the Safe Drinking Water Act in 1974.[34]

Unlike the Clean Water Act, the language of the SDWA centers primarily on concepts of "protection" as opposed to "control" or "reduction," although methods of compliance are similarly defined as treatment-based and therefore technology-focused. The Act provides for water agencies to test for a range of organic chemical contaminants in the drinking water supply. It also establishes a process to develop standards for contaminants and mechanisms to select appropriate treatment technologies. There is no language in the law that addresses how to control or reduce such contaminants other than the focus on treatment technologies.

As with air toxics regulation, EPA was slow to develop the Safe Drinking Water Act provisions regarding settings for standard drinking water contaminants, despite the impact of more extensive testing and monitoring. Much of the resistance to regulation could be traced to the increasingly aggressive role of the Office of Management and Budget, particularly during the Reagan administration, which established narrow cost-benefit criteria in what should have been an obvious arena for health-based evaluations. Even the technology bias of the system came under challenge in the SDWA process. The obvious (although expensive) choice for BAT, a granular-activated carbon system, was resisted by the water utility industry and received the coup de grace from Reagan's OMB. OMB disassociated the concept of BAT as technology that could achieve the stated goal of pollutant reduction to BAT as most *cost-effective*, read "least costly."[35] Thus, the SDWA proceeded along two parallel tracks: standard setting (which became only partially associated with health risk analysis) and the search for the best technology (which largely became a cost-dominated exercise).

As a consequence, in the first dozen years after passage of the SDWA, only two standards were established: one for trihalomethanes (THMs) (which EPA later identified as inadequate, given increasing evidence of THM and other chlorine disinfection byproduct health risk) and another for radionuclides.[36]

In 1986, Congress overwhelmingly passed new Amendments to the Safe Drinking Water Act, specifying a timeframe for EPA to develop standards for 83 different organics (a provision similar to the air toxics provisions of the 1990 CAA Amendments).[37] The support for the amendments stemmed from dissatisfaction with the implementation of the 1974 law and, in particular, OMB's role in placing obstacles in the path of standard setting. The 1986 Amendments also raised the question of preferred-treatment technology but failed to include any language about pollution prevention or even watershed or source protection, after some initial attempts to include such language was opposed by the water utility and chemical industry interests.[38]

While the legislation was designed to speed up the standard-setting process and press for more advanced treatment, it had no framework in which to evaluate and address the source of the problem. By the early 1990s, legislative pressure on EPA to establish new standards also had resulted in yet another water utility industry counterattack on the costs, impracticality, and scientific uncertainties in the standard-setting process. These criticisms, some of which were endorsed by EPA, sought to challenge the basis of regulation rather than reevaluate the regulatory focus in order to better identify ways to reduce contaminants prior to treatment.

Most significantly, the language in the SDWA Amendments regarding the issue of disinfection byproducts (suggesting the need for more stringent treatment) served to explicitly shift the regulatory burden to a downstream player (namely the water utilities) rather than to chlorine producers, given the central, historical role of chlorine (or its derivatives chlorine dioxide and chloramines, or chlorine plus ammonia) as the most widely used disinfectants. Trihalomethanes are the best known and only regulated chemicals among the numerous byproducts of the disinfection process. In particular, the health risks of chloroform have generated a growing body of literature. Due in part to the exclusive emphasis on treatment, combined with the water utility industry's long-standing reluctance as a downstream player to fully assess alternatives to chlorine use, the focus of disinfection byproduct regulatory activity stimulated by the SDWA (with its far-reaching implications in terms of numbers of people and water utilities affected) has remained a classic trade-off between the costs of technology controls and what standards to set, with far less attention paid to possible reduction strategies. Yet the chlorination debate offers a potential glimpse of how regulatory policy can potentially be reframed along a reduction path. This could occur if the regulatory approach would lead regulators and the regulated downstream players (the water utilities) more directly to the question of alternatives to the regulated practice itself. As with the Clean Water Act, however, the focus on treatment and controls within a limited single-medium domain—even when the subject of public health has been the prominent concern—has served as a continuing barrier in the design of new reduction-based approaches.[39]

Land

During the 1960s, land contamination, the "third pollution," grew in parallel with the increasing concern about air and water pollution. In this period, both municipalities and industrial interests had shifted to land disposal following the significant decline of incineration as a waste disposal technology that resulted in part from air emission restrictions imposed by the 1963 and 1967 Air Quality Acts.

As late as the 1960s, most land disposal methods involved the use of untended open pits, often located at the edge of a municipality where land was still cheap and transportation costs insignificant. Increasingly, these open pits or dumps were perceived as a public health hazard, a problem compounded by the fact that urban growth now situated many of the dumpsites next to residential communities.[40] Up to this point, waste disposal was seen as a local concern, similar to sewage disposal. And like the sewage issue, municipalities (and industries) were unwilling to fully underwrite the development of more advanced (and expensive) disposal methods. As the problems of open dumps became a major target of environmental protest, Congress finally agreed to new mechanisms for federal intervention with the passage of the Resource Recovery Act in 1970.[41]

The RRA was largely an amalgam of earlier legislation providing for federal funding for research and demonstration projects. It enlarged this role by increasing the amount of funds available and by relating their use to the concept of "resource recovery." The Act relied heavily on the language of "conservation," linking the recovery of energy and materials to more effective "waste management" systems. Though the law did not establish an overall approach in such areas as recycling and waste-to-energy incineration, it did provide funds to help support the construction of several new incineration projects. It also emphasized the need for the private sector to develop new treatment technologies, which resulted in a (partially intended) consequence of stimulating a more comprehensive waste management industry.[42] As with the Clean Air and Clean Water Acts, the emphasis on new technologies in the RRA laid the groundwork for the rapid emergence of pollution control as a set of industries introducing technologies designed to meet the system's regulatory requirements.

Concerns about land pollution sharpened with the growing regulatory interest in wastes defined as *hazards* as well as the problem of volume or disposal capacity. During the 1975/1976 legislative session, Congress debated two distinct though related proposals: the Toxic Substances Control Act (TSCA), which was designed to address the hazards related to the introduction of new chemicals into the market, and the Resource Conservation and Recovery Act (RCRA), which was designed to deal with the management of waste.[43] The problem of land disposal of chemical (and other hazardous) wastes as well as municipal solid wastes had been the primary focus of the Resource Recovery Act. The development of the provisions in RCRA, which distinguished between hazardous and non-hazardous solid wastes and established the elaborate "cradle-to-grave" tracking system for hazardous substances, was far less controversial than either the debate over TSCA or even some of the more bitterly contested issues highlighted in RCRA's solid waste sections, including its provisions in (Subtitle D) for closure of open dumps.[44] With the passage of RCRA and its less controversial (Section C) provisions governing the management of hazardous wastes, Congress laid the groundwork for a major new focus on end-of-pipe regulation, waste treatment, and clean-up oriented programs whose costs would ultimately reach into the billions of dollars.

RCRA allowed the federal government to recast its ability to restrict land disposal, and define and manage hazardous wastes. Unlike earlier legislation, RCRA distinguished between nonhazardous solid waste and hazardous waste that presents "special dangers to health and requires a greater degree of regulation than does non-hazardous solid waste."[45] Defining wastes as hazardous if they are either ignitable, corrosive, reactive, or toxic,[46] and allowing EPA to intervene if such wastes presented "an imminent and substantial endangerment to health and the environment,"[47] the legislation incorporated a long list of substances into this definition. The law excluded wastes produced by small quantity generators (anyone producing less than 220 pounds a month), wastes covered by other federal laws (e.g., radioactive materials), and certain controversial wastes such as incinerator ash, whose exemption under RCRA continued to be a major policy dispute over the next two decades.[48]

RCRA required all generators of hazardous wastes to maintain records that would identify the quantities of hazardous waste generated. The manifest system was designed to insure that wastes were designated for proper treatment, storage, and disposal. Any treatment, storage, or disposal of wastes *off-site* also fell under the purview of RCRA, which provided EPA with the authority to prohibit any open dumping of hazardous waste as well as to require a permit for anyone undertaking its treatment, storage, or disposal. Ultimately, the RCRA system was assumed to be straightforward in its construction and simple in its execution: EPA decides what constitutes a hazardous waste; standards are established for the wastes to be properly handled through treatment, storage, and disposal facilities; permits are then issued for such facilities that comply with the standards; and the generators and transporters of such wastes have to conform to specified handling procedures as well as to fill out the manifests that track those wastes. Further, it was also hoped that such a system would relieve the problem of what to do with new wastes needing disposal that had been created by treatment of air emissions and water discharges.

Even more than the air and water legislation enacted earlier in the decade, RCRA situated the disposal and treatment orientation of legislation designed to deal with the three pollutions. In its definition of a hazardous waste, the legislation explicitly linked the nature of the hazard to its being "*improperly* treated, stored, transported, or disposed of or otherwise managed" (our italics).[49] Thus, the legislation implied that a hazardous waste, if properly treated, would no longer represent a threat to the environment or human health. By distinguishing between proper and improper treatment as well as by establishing "RCRA wastes" as a new category in environmental management, RCRA crucially elaborated the pollution control system from the generation, release, and transport of toxic substances to include their ultimate fate.

Despite its role as a legislative anchor among the pollution control laws, RCRA, like its single-medium antecedents, also suffered from a range of implementation difficulties, including delays in establishing rules for TSD facilities and problems in developing adequate distinctions among types of waste and thus in designing rules for their disposal. These problems were compounded in the early 1980s by the active hostility of the new Reagan administration regarding regulations governing landfills, incinerators, pits, ponds, and lagoons. Further, that situation was greatly exacerbated by the administration's unsuccessful efforts to suspend the ban on the dumping of bulk liquids into landfills.[50]

It had become clear by the 1980s that the environmental management system was heavily dependent on the media-specific treatment of wastes, emissions, or discharges. Yet precisely due to their elaborate and costly mechanisms for media-specific disposal, treatment, and standard setting, these laws also generated new industry concerns about the costs and liabilities associated with clean-up and waste management problems. In this way, RCRA, the most significant, elaborate, and waste specific of the pollution control laws of the 1970s, had also inadvertently served to question the reliance on pollution control as the best way to address the presence of toxics in the environment. That unanticipated outcome became even more sharply delineated with the problem of the management of hazardous waste sites, itself the regulatory end point in this treatment and disposal-based system.

Shortly after the passage of RCRA, the issue of proper treatment and effective management of land disposal became significantly complicated by the discovery that *existing* waste sites in places like Love Canal in upper New York State, Times Beach, Missouri, and Glen Avon, California represented a new and extraordinarily costly environmental and regulatory problem. The belated discovery of various health risks for communities adjacent to hazardous waste sites potentially extended the regulatory purview to include the most notorious of those long-standing or abandoned waste sites. The dramatic events at places like Love Canal (where an EPA official was "kidnapped" at one point to dramatize the community's concerns about the slowness and inadequacy of the regulatory response to the "discovery" of hazardous waste sites)[51] created a sense of urgency regarding the need to clean up such sites. The passage of the Comprehensive Environmental Response, Compensation, and Liability Act (CERCLA) in December 1980,[52] occurring in the midst of an anti-regulatory backlash (a process already gathering momentum during the last two years of the Carter administration that would intensify during the first term of the Reagan administration), testified to the potency of the community groups directly affected by these hazardous waste sites and the power of the "crisis" mode in establishing waste-related environmental policy.

CERCLA, with its "shovels first, lawyers later" conceptual approach, was explicitly designed as an emergency-oriented clean-up and remediation program. Though it failed to address reduction issues directly, the statute did indirectly elevate reduction strategies as a potential alternative by providing industry with strong disincentives to continuing to pursue land disposal. These were primarily associated with CERCLA's elaborate program of identification of sites and establishment of liability of potential responsible parties (PRPs) through the legislation's strict, joint and several liability provisions.[53] Beyond the recovery of costs through the PRP process, the cleanup of sites was to be financed through a $1.6 billion Hazardous Waste Trust Fund (Superfund) to pay for the cleanups in situations where responsible parties could not be identified or held fully liable for the entire costs or where emergency situations involving hazardous substances warranted immediate intervention.

From the outset, implementation of CERCLA involved substantial conflict and controversy. EPA officials in the Reagan administration, responding to the antiregulatory signals from the Office of Management and Budget, sought to limit Superfund activity in terms of the number of sites selected, the kinds of cleanup strategies employed, and the amount of funding made available. However, instead of these efforts serving to downplay or minimize the issue, public concern about inadequate implementation intensified, further pressuring Congress to intervene more forcefully in developing new legislative mandates. At the same time, the growing Superfund-related EPA focus on developing and supporting new hazardous waste treatment technologies such as incineration (which also came to be included in EPA's definition of "waste minimization") also came under attack, led by community groups who opposed the siting of such treatment facilities in their neighborhoods. These political conflicts produced a regulatory standoff, essentially immobilizing cleanup plans. The failure to adequately implement CERCLA not only pushed Congress toward new legislation, it also contributed to escalating costs and liability concerns associated with hazardous waste disposal activities. As a consequence, despite (or perhaps influenced by) its tendency toward immobilization, Superfund (like RCRA) contributed to an interest in reduction as an alternative to an increasingly costly pollution control and cleanup approach.

Media-Specific Administration

While Congress helped shape the legislative framework for toxics policy based on a pollution control paradigm, the executive branch, through its rulemaking and implementation powers, was also directly responsible for helping craft this system. The cornerstone of that executive branch policymaking was the Environmental Protection Agency, defined from its birth as the central player in federal environmental management.

As the most prominent of the regulatory agencies in the toxics area, EPA had initially been conceived as a broad-based agency that would centralize the tasks of combatting pollution and protecting the environment. Prior to its formation, much of the pollution-oriented regulatory activity had been divided among a myriad of agencies with few significant cleanup or regulatory powers. These included the National Air Pollution Control

Administration (founded in 1955 and housed in the Department of Health Education and Welfare) and the Federal Water Quality Administration (originally established as a program in the Public Health Service but transferred to the Department of the Interior in 1966). Other agencies, such as the Bureau of Solid Waste Management, also housed in Health, Education, and Welfare, were underfunded, and experienced personnel turnover and shifting locations.[54]

Though some of these agencies were provided with additional regulatory powers during the 1960s, they were largely hamstrung by inadequate enforcement mechanisms, a dilution of responsibilities, and uncertain mandates. As a result, the federal presence in environmental management was weak, uncoordinated, and incapable of responding to growing public concerns.

Federal legislation was thus developed to provide a broad policy mandate on the environment. This legislation, the National Environmental Policy Act (NEPA), was passed by Congress in late 1969 and signed into law by the President on January 1, 1970, in effect ushering in a new decade of environmental policy. In its few pages of text, NEPA offered a broad vision of environmental "protection." Its purposes included the promotion of "efforts which will prevent or eliminate damage to the environment and biosphere and stimulate the health and welfare of man." NEPA also established (in Title II) a Council on Environmental Quality (CEQ) to provide the administration with expert advice on environmental matters while also providing for NEPA-mandated environmental impact analysis to force federal officials to consider how federal actions might significantly affect "the quality of the human environment."[55]

A few weeks after NEPA was signed into law, President Nixon used the occasion of his State of the Union message to declare that environmental issues would be a priority item for his administration.[56] Soon after, concerned with criticisms and his possible political vulnerabilities, he laid out a 37-point environmental program focused primarily on water and air pollution policy.[57] A White House committee, the Ash Commission (named after its chair, Roy Ash), followed up this effort with a proposal to establish a single, independent agency to coordinate the environmental initiatives of the Administration and Congress. The Ash Commission argued that the primary mission of the existing departments would bias any of their decisions concerning the environment, especially those that involved other agencies and departments. Commission members, including Ash himself, had at first explored the concept of a new Department of Environment and Natural Resources, but Commission staff had argued against such an approach as too cumbersome and potentially incapable of reconciling the conflicting goals of resource development and environmental quality. Instead, a new agency, the commission staff successfully argued, needed to more directly focus on the "comprehensive" management of the wastes or "unwanted byproducts" of an affluent society.

On July 9, 1970, the President endorsed the Commission's recommendations and sent a reorganization plan to Congress to establish an Environmental Protection Agency.[58] This "strong independent agency," as Nixon characterized his proposed EPA, would presumably consolidate the functions of all existing entities dealing with environmental issues, although Nixon, also fearful of a potential antiindustry bias emerging within this new agency, still reserved certain key environmental research and regulatory functions for other agencies [e.g., National Oceanic and Atmospheric Administration (NOAA) to the Commerce Department][59]

The new EPA was charged with establishing and enforcing environmental standards, undertaking research, assisting CEQ in developing new policies for environmental protection, and developing cleanup strategies. Through this process of consolidation and expansion of duties, EPA became an instant bureaucracy, incorporating existing programs, entire agency units, and nearly 6,000 employees, based on an initial budget of $1.4 billion (80% of which initially was construction grant money). Programs related to air quality, water quality, solid waste, pesticides, and radiation issues, formerly based at such agencies as HEW, the Interior Department, the Food and Drug Administration, the Atomic Energy Commission, the Department of Agriculture, and the Federal Radiation Council, were now under the EPA umbrella. The President used the language of systems analysis in his charge to the new agency, urging it to "give unique direction to our war on pollution" and to treat "air pollution, water pollution and solid wastes as different forms of a single problem."[60]

EPA began operations on December 2, 1970. The Agency was immediately faced with the problem of rulemaking and legislative mandates provided by the Clean Air and Resource Recovery Acts. EPA's first Administrator, William Ruckelshaus, initially devised a strategy that skirted the line between keeping intact the media-specific program offices (reinforced by the mandates) and pursuing the charge to identify a holistic systems approach. As part of that effort, Ruckelshaus initially combined the media-specific programs into two program offices to be headed by an Assistant Administrator for Media Programs (air and water pollution) and a second Assistant Administrator for Categorical Programs (pesticides, radiation, and solid waste).[61]

EPA also initially sought to demonstrate its regulatory independence by highlighting its enforcement efforts and its promotion of innovative pollution control technologies. This approach was reinforced with the growing legislative road map for pollution control based on treatment and technology-driven standards. The Agency began to define itself in part in relation to its technology transfer functions through the underwriting and development of new technologies and new pollution control businesses, an approach deemed successful due to sharp reductions in certain of the more visible and previously uncontrolled emissions and discharges such as sulfur dioxide and BOD that were negatively affecting the environment.

But by the mid 1970s, it was becoming clear that EPA's original organizational plan could no longer effectively respond to the increasing array of media-specific Congressional mandates. The Agency's early balancing act had begun to erode between its executive-derived "systems" function aimed at establishing a pollution control framework for cleaning up the environment across media boundaries and its "program"-oriented mandates framed by Congressional legislative action that had largely weighed in on the side of program-based regulation and technology-driven rulemaking. One immediate result was the decision to reestablish separate rather than consolidated administrative units in the areas of air, water, solid waste, pesticides, and radiation. Research and enforcement functions were also divided into these separate units. Thus, there never effectively developed any "environment-wide" focus to Agency activities, and even the broader programs in education and technology transfer tended to be designed for industries seeking compliance with individual standards rather than as product or process changes in production or front-end design considerations. The research work sponsored by the Agency also tended to reflect distinctions between its technology-derived functions (nearly all of which were media-specific and control-oriented) and its health-based and ecology- or ecosystem-related research, both of which also tended to reflect certain media-specific research questions. Finally, EPA's reliance on its ten regional offices to address compliance and statewide program implementation was directly influenced by the way funding was channelled through the program offices. With the passage of TSCA, which sought to address toxics problems through a substance-by-substance regulatory approach, EPA (which by then had a six-year track record of media-specific rulemaking, implementation, and organizational division) was organizationally ill-equipped to deal with TSCA's premanufacturing, front-end focus. The Office of Toxic Substances, the unit established to implement TSCA, was immediately hamstrung by the Agency's limited capacity to implement TSCA (as will be discussed in Chapter 3). Implementation of TSCA, which proceeded slowly and unevenly, remained a stepchild of the larger Agency emphasis on pollutant regulation and disposal and treatment management and review, reinforced notably by the passage of RCRA in the same time period. Yet, the increasing prominence of hazardous waste and toxics issues by the late 1970s was causing the Agency to define itself in terms of public health as much as environmental terms but without the capacity to structurally attack the issues generating public health concern.

These problems were soon compounded by the general counteroffensive launched during the mid and late 1970s by several industries who complained of increasing compliance costs and the failure to more fully incorporate economic criteria in the development of pollutant standards and regulations. A powerful antiregulatory mood swept Washington during the late 1970s and early 1980s, culminating in a number of regulatory reforms aimed at EPA and other toxics and pollution-oriented agencies such as OSHA and the Consumer Product Safety Commission (CPSC). During the Carter administration, a Regulatory Analysis and Review Group (RARG) was established by executive order, in part to conduct economic impact analyses on specific regulations.[62] These included OSHA's widely criticized (by industry) cotton dust standard and EPA's proposed ozone standard. Subsequently, the Reagan administration, through Executive Order 12291, authorized the Office of Management and Budget to review and potentially revise or veto on economic grounds any regulation, standard, or enforcement action to be undertaken by the Agency. The order also mandated agencies like EPA to undertake cost-benefit analyses on any proposed rules to ensure that benefits exceeded costs and that a least-cost option ultimately would be selected. OMB also was given the authority to delay any proposed regulation until changes were made to its satisfaction.[63]

From its outset, the Reagan administration sought to diminish EPA's regulatory powers, cut its budgets, and essentially eliminate its policy role. Entire media-specific programs, such as the resource-recovery programs (e.g., solid waste recycling and treatment by incineration) that had been encouraged under both RCRA and the Resource Recovery Act, were now underfunded and/or effectively eliminated through budget cuts. Executive branch reorganization, (e.g., the creation of the Cabinet Council on Natural Resources, initially chaired by Interior Secretary James Watt, which excluded EPA despite the Council's environmental focus), assumed major new policy responsibilities. This included, for example, the Council's discussions of Clean Air Act revisions. Ultimately, these administrative initiatives, combined with the leadership overhaul at EPA during the early 1980s, greatly extended the trend toward inclusion of economic criteria in agency decisionmaking, provided strong industry access to the decision-making process, and sharply scaled down or delayed a number of agency activities that had been mandated by legislation, such as Superfund cleanup or enforcement of TSCA's prenotification provisions. The failure to set a standard for formaldehyde, a widely used industrial chemical, illustrated, as one crucial example, how the administration sought to influence the agency's regulatory review process.[64]

This antiregulatory backlash proved to be short-lived, however. Public outcry, particularly in the toxics area, as well as new Congressional initiatives, redirected EPA back toward new rulemaking, clean-up activities, and technological controls. These renewed Congressional directives still segmented EPA actions and authority. The Agency found itself with a largely restored staff and budget; a series of new directors (William Ruckelshaus, career official Lee Thomas, former Conservation Foundation director William Reilly, former Congressional staffer and state environmental official Carol Browner) who in turn sought to rebuild the Agency's tarnished reputation; and increased responsibilities, such as oversight of emergency response planning and new industry reporting requirements for toxic emissions and discharges. Yet EPA, its media-specific programs insulated and largely powerless to significantly affect the flow of toxics (most specifically as waste entering the environment), seemed incapable of achieving even the most modest of its mandated goals. By the late 1980s, with Congress increasingly preoccupied with the problem of the costs, liabilities, health risks, and public anger concerning the hazardous wastes problem, EPA tentatively began to search for ways to extend its organizational mission beyond pollution control toward waste minimization and, ultimately (by the 1990s) to pollution prevention. That search, however, remained confined to managing byproducts while avoiding the path clearly suggested by the failures of pollution control and the promise of pollution prevention: namely, to the substance of industrial decisionmaking and the public's role in shaping that process.

Conclusion

With the level of reported toxics releases in the billions of pounds and the costs and liabilities of cleanup continuing to increase at a rapid rate, all the parties—citizen groups, government regulators, and industry generators—have agreed that current toxics policy requires fundamental restructuring. Yet there is little or no consensus as to how this restructuring should take place.

If the great problems associated with pollution control are to be attributed largely to classical regulation, then we must acknowledge that within the standard-setting mode, only technological standards have been thoroughly exercised, while nontechnological standards have been mostly ignored.

These laws have essentially sought to remediate contamination through containment strategies. As a result, pollution was often transferred but not eliminated, controlled but not reduced. When successful, the regulations merely ameliorated the more conventional forms of pollution, such as smoke from industrial point sources or direct discharge to water bodies. The problem of toxics, often involving more subtle exposure routes which can be difficult to pinpoint, isolate, and track, remain an intractable reality of industrial pollution. From these early regulatory gaps, it has become increasingly apparent that establishing a framework to attack pernicious problems associated with hazardous substances requires a proactive management approach which is systemic, as opposed to focused on single sources and technical solutions.

Pollution prevention had become the new byword for controlling toxics in the 1990s, but a new framework for reducing toxics had yet to be established. Though different in scope, philosophy, and targeted pollutants, the legislation of the 1970s and the regulatory framework established for implementation instead became the cornerstone of a media-specific, technology-driven, pollution control policy. Despite well-earned criticism, pollution control continued to be the dominant regulatory strategy through the late 1980s and into the 1990s. As a result, the embrace of pollution prevention has failed to dislodge the media-specific framework for toxics policy, while the development of new strategies has continued to be largely dependent on regulation of the three pollutions at their respective routes of entry: air, water, or land. The development of the various legislative and regulatory tracks, and the contentious issues that arose in relation to their role in the formation of policy, revealed both the problems and opportunities arising from government efforts to confront environmental hazards. It had become a truism of toxics policy that the old paradigm was no longer viable, but, despite the system's failures, a new paradigm of environmental governance in this area had yet to emerge.

Notes

1. The term "three pollutions" was first introduced in the late 1960s by William Small, a staff aide to Senator Edmund Muskie's Committee on Air and Water Pollution. See, *Third Pollution: The National Problem of Solid Waste Disposal*, William Small, (New York: Praeger, 1971).

2. R. Shep Melnick, *Regulation and the Courts: The Case of the Clean Air Act* (Washington, D.C.: The Brookings Institution, 1983), p. 24.

3. On the history of air pollution control prior to 1970 see, Krier and Ursin, *Pollution and Policy* (cited in note 12 of Chapter 1); Richard Stewart and James Krier, *Environmental Law and Policy* (Indianapolis: Bobbs-Merrill, 1978); and J. Clarence Davies and Barbara Davies, *The Politics of Pollution*, 2nd ed., (Indianapolis: Bobbs–Merrill, 1975).

4. On the London episodes: See Krier and Ursin, *Pollution and Policy*, pp. 20, 171; Davies and Davies, *The Politics of Pollution*, p. 46. On Donora: H.H. Schrenk *et al.*, *Air Pollution in Donora, Pa.: Epidemiology of the Unusual Smog Episode of October 1948*, Public Health Bulletin No. 306, (Washington D.C.: Public Health Service, 1949); James G. Townsend, "Investigation of the Smog Incident in Donora, Pa. and Vicinity," *American Journal of Public Health*, Vol. 40, No. 2, February 1950, pp. 183–189: On New York: Krier and Ursin, pp. 106, 263, 264. On California episodes (and the history of vehicular pollution control in general), see Krier and Ursin.

5. Figures are from Opinion Research Corporation surveys from 1965 to 1970 which are cited in Hazel Erskine, "The Polls: Pollution and Its Costs," *The Public Opinion Quarterly*, Vol. 36, No. 1 (1972), pp. 121–122. The consequent potential for mobilization of the public around air quality issues was reflected in the fact that the group established to organize the April 22, 1970 Earth Day events immediately sought to focus on the proposed Clean Air Act legislation as the centerpiece of their activities for the event, and for post-Earth Day efforts (personal interview with Denis Hayes in 1992).

6. Krier and Ursin, p. 299. On the complex links between the emergence of a national environmental movement in the late 1960s and early 1970s and the social turmoil and activism of those years, see Robert Gottlieb, *Forcing the Spring: The Transformation of the American Environmental Movement* (Washington D.C.: Island Press, 1993), Chapters 3 and 4.

7. Generally, 42 U.S.C. §§ 7401 *et seq.* Both Sidney Wolf (although writing prior to the 1990 Clean Air Act Amendments), and Roger Findley and Daniel Farber (in the West Publishing Company "Nutshell Series") have provided useful guides to the technical provisions of the Clean Air Act and other core statutes of pollution control. See Sidney Wolf, *Pollution Law Handbook: A Guide to Federal Environmental Laws* (New York: Quorum Books, 1988), and Roger Findley and Daniel Farber, *Environmental Law in a Nutshell*, 3rd ed. (St. Paul: West Publishing Co., 1992).

8. "Rather than offer subsidies for pollution control, impose taxes on pollution, or establish a system of marketable emission rights, Congress and the executive branch opted—almost without thought—for what has

become known as 'command-and-control' regulation," Melnick, *Regulation and the Courts,* p. 43.

9. Although these measures have not been adopted as part of a coherent federal program establishing such transportation controls, many of them have been applied on an *ad hoc* basis in emergency provisions such as the 1994 Los Angeles earthquake, and subsequently lifted once the "emergency" has passed.

10. Melnick, *Regulation and the Courts,* p. 300.

11. As Melnick documents, in the mid-1970s Senator Edmund Muskie (a major force in pollution control policy and a chief Congressional supporter of transportation control strategies), attempted to force the transportation and appropriations committees to spend more money on mass transit (Melnick, pp. 310–311). However, this largely unsuccessful political maneuvering was quite different from the overt policy integration and coalition-building that was, and still is, needed. The 1990 amendments to the Clean Air Act did, however, provide new sanctions against nonattainment regions that could include the cutoff of federal highway funds (Findley and Farber, p. 119), establishing at least one concrete link between the two contending policy and legislative frameworks.

12. Krier and Ursin, *Pollution and Policy,* p. 277.

13. California Department of Public Health, *Clean Air for California* (Initial Report, 1955), p. 47, cited in Krier and Ursin, *Pollution and Policy,* p. 253.

14. U.S. Environmental Protection Agency, Office of Air Quality Planning and Standards, *National Air Pollutant Emission Estimates 1940–1989* (Research Triangle Park, North Carolina, U.S. EPA Publication No. EPA-450/4–91–004, March 1991).

15. For an overview of how PSD (prevention of significant deterioration) requirements arose see R. Shep Melnick, "Significant Deterioration: A Tiger by the Tail," Chapter 4 in *Regulation and the Courts.*

16. Federal Water Pollution Control Amendments Title 33 § 1344 (*et seq.*).

17. On the history of water pollution control prior to 1970 see, in general, Davies, *The Politics of Pollution.* For a historical perspective on the complex relationship between water quality issues and water supply and development issues see Robert Gottlieb, *A Life of Its Own: The Politics and Power of Water* (San Diego: Harcourt Brace Jovanovich, 1988).

18. On the failure of state efforts to control industrial discharges in the 1960s, see *Public Regulation of Water Quality in the United States,* N. William Hines, prepared for the National Water Commission, Report # NWC-L-72–036, (Washington D.C.: National Water Commission, 1971).

19. 33 § 1252.

20. See "Permits for Dredged and Fill Material," Section 404, Public Law 92–500, and the court case that subsequently obliged the Corps to assume a broad permitting authority with respect to wetland areas [*Natural Resources Defense Council v. Calloway, 392 F. Supp. 685 (1975)*]; On the Corps' reluctance to use its permitting authority to block development, see *Can Organizations Change?: Environmental Protection, Citizen Participation, and the Corps of Engineers,* Daniel A. Mazmanian and Jeanne Nienaber, (Washington DC: The Brookings Institution, 1979).

21. 33 § 1342.

22. 33 § 1342 9 (n) 14.

23. 33 § 1251(a)(1)(2).

24. 33 § 1251(a)(3).

25. 33 § 1251(b).

26. 33 § 1251(a)(5)(6).

27. For a discussion of EPA's failure to implement Section 208 planning, see *Environmental Quality 1980,* Council on Environmental Quality, (Washington DC: Government Printing Office, 1981), p. 133. On background to CWA and its early implementation, see "Preserving the Clean Water Act: The Appearance of Environmental Victory," Helen M. Ingram and Dean E. Mann, in *Environmental Policy in the 1980s: Reagan's New Agenda,* Norman J. Vig and Michael E. Kraft, eds. (Washington DC: Congressional Quarterly Press, 1984), pp. 251–271.

28. 33 § 1311(b)(1)(a).

29. 33 § 1311(b)(1)(b).

30. 33 § 1251.

31. "Preserving the Clean Water Act," Ingram and Mann, pp. 251–272.

32. The National Water Commission presciently argued that CWA's focus on technology and construction grants would in fact be both prohibitive and media-shifting. *A Water Policy for the American People,* National Water Commission (Washington DC: Government Printing Office, 1973), p. 70.

33. 40 CFR Sections 116.4, 117.3.

34. Safe Drinking Water Act, Title 42 § 300f (*et seq.*).

35. See "A History of the Attempted Federal Regulation Requiring GAC Adsorption for Water Treatment," James M. Symons, *Journal of the American Water Works Association,* August 1984.

36. The 1979 THM standard can be found in the Federal Register 44, No. 231, 68624–68707 (November 29, 1979); on EPA's statement of the inadequacy of the THM standard see, "Regulating Organics: An Interview

with Michael Cook, EPA," *Journal of the American Water Works Association,* January 1987.

37. Safe Drinking Water Act Amendments of 1986, Public Law 99–339, Title 42 § 300f (*et seq.*).

38. Interviews with Jerry Dotson (aide to Congressman Henry Waxman) and Duane Georgensen (Los Angeles Department of Water and Power, 1987). For background discussion of the position of the water utility industry, see *Thirst for Growth: Water Agencies As Hidden Government in California,* Robert Gottlieb and Margaret FitzSimmons, (Tucson: University of Arizona Press, 1991), pp. 152–161.

39. Ultimately, in terms of the THM regulation issue, a negotiated rule-making process (reg-neg) was concluded in 1994, a process which involved both EPA, water utility interests, and environmental groups. The reg-neg proposed phasing in a tightening of THM standards (from 100 ppb to 80 ppb and eventually to 40 ppb), influenced in part by new technologies available that were capable of meeting such standards.

40. For a review of the hazards of open site landfills, see for example, *Closing Open Dumps,* Office of Solid Waste Management, U.S. Environmental Protection Agency, (Washington DC: Government Printing Office, 1971); *An Environmental Assessment of Gas and Leachate Problems at Land Disposal Sites,* Office of Solid Waste, U.S. Environmental Protection Agency, 530/SW-110-OF (Washington DC: Government Printing Office, 1973).

41. Resource Recovery Act of 1970, Public Law 91–512, Title 42 § 6901 (*et seq.*).

42. See *Resource Recovery and Waste Reduction, Report to Congress,* U.S. Environmental Protection Agency, 530/SW–118, (Washington DC: Government Printing Office, 1974). See also "Solid Waste Management: Planning Issues and Opportunities," Robert Gottlieb, American Planning Association, Planning Advisory Service Report No. 024/425.

43. Resource Conservation and Recovery Act of 1976 (Public Law 94–580).

44. RCRA 42 U.S.C. 6943–6944 Sections 4002–4003.

45. This language in the bill, one of the findings of fact in the legislation, is the only finding concerned with hazardous waste among sixteen overall dealing with solid waste and land disposal issues. Resource Conservation and Recovery Act 42 U.S.C. 6292.

46. RCRA 42 U.S.C. 6921, Section 3001.

47. RCRA 42 U.S.C. 6973 Section 7003.

48. RCRA 42 U.S.C. 6921 Section 3001 (Subtitle C).

49. RCRA 42 U.S.C. 6903, Section 1004, Paragraph 5A.

50. Criticisms of the effort to undo the ban on dumping bulk liquids into landfills included charges of conflict of interest, since a key EPA official involved in the decision, James Sanderson, had previously been an attorney for Chemical Waste Management, a leading hazardous waste landfill operator that would directly benefit from the lifting of the ban. See *A Season of Spoils: The Story of the Reagan Administration's Attack on the Environment*, Jonathan Lash, Katherine Gilman, and David Sheridan, (New York: Pantheon, 1984), pp. 63–66.

51. The "kidnapping" episode is described in *Love Canal: My Story*, Lois Gibbs, as told to Murray Levine, (Albany: State University of New York Press, 1982); see also, *Love Canal: Science, Politics, and People*, Adeline Gordon Levine, (Lexington, Massachusetts: Lexington Books, 1982).

52. Comprehensive Environmental Response, Compensation, and Liability Act, Title 42 U.S.C. 9601 (*et seq.*).

53. Strict liability eliminated the need to prove negligence, while joint and several liability meant that all defendants could be held liable regardless of the amount disposed of or the care exercised in the disposal. Both provisions, along with feedstock fees established a primary focus on large generators of hazardous wastes (e.g., major chemical processing industries, oil refiners), who also led the opposition to the passage of CERCLA and subsequently became some of the most vociferous advocates for revision of Superfund liability as well as other treatment-based, single-media legislation that impacted industry costs. On this issue of liability, see "Liability Under Federal Law for Hazardous Waste Injuries," R.D. Hinds, *Harvard Environmental Law Review* 6 (1982), pp. 1–33.

54. See *Federal Pollution Control Programs: Water, Air, and Solid Wastes*, Stanley Degler, (Washington D.C.: BNA Books, 1971); *The Environmental Protection Agency: Asking the Wrong Questions*, Marc K. Landy, Marc J. Roberts, and Stephen R. Thomas, (New York: Oxford University Press, 1990), pp. 114–122.

55. Public Law 91–190, 42 U.S.C. 4321–4347, January 1, 1970.

56. "Excerpts from the President's State of the Union Address, January 22, 1970," reprinted in *Environmental Quality: The First Annual Report of the Council of Environmental Quality* (Washington, D.C.: Government Printing Office, 1970), Appendix B, p. 243.

57. "The President's Message on the Environment," February 10, 1970 reprinted in *Environmental Quality: The First Annual Report of the Council on Environmental Quality* (Washington D.C.: Government Printing Office, 1970), Appendix C, p. 254.

58. Sources from the following three documents: "Message from the President of the United States Relative to Reorganization Plan Nos. 3 and

4 of 1970, July 9, 1970,"; "Reorganization Plan No. 3 of 1970, Message from the President of the United States Transmitting Reorganization Plan No. 3 of July 9, 1970,"; and "Reorganization Plan No. 4 of 1970, Message from the President of the United States Transmitting Reorganization Plan No. 4 of July 9, 1970," are reprinted in *Environmental Quality, op. cit.* Appendices H,I,J, pp. 294–318.

59. For background on the Ash Commission activities, see John C. Whitaker, *Striking a Balance: Environment and Natural Resources in the Nixon-Ford Years,* (Washington D.C.: American Enterprise Institute for Public Policy Research, 1976), pp. 27–31; see also Alfred A. Marcus, *Promise and Performance,* pp. 32–40; Landy *et al.*; *The Environmental Protection Agency: Asking the Wrong Questions,* pp. 30–33.

60. See "Message of the President Relative to Reorganization Plan Nos. 3 and 4 of 1970 in *Environmental Quality: The First Annual Report of the Council on Environmental Quality,* (Washington DC: Government Printing Office, 1970); see also "The Birth of EPA," Jack Lewis, EPA Journal, November 1985, p. 9.

61. Lewis, "The Birth of EPA," p. 9; Marcus, *Promise and Performance,* p. 105; John Quarles, *Cleaning Up America* (Boston: Houghton Mifflin, 1976), Chapter 9.

62. The growing use of economic criteria in environmental rulemaking caused one environmental advocate to complain that there had emerged during the Carter period "a wholesale effort by certain White House officials to rewrite the nation's environmental laws by administrative decree. Thinly disguised in the economic jargon of cost/benefit analysis and cost-effectiveness, these efforts are threatening to severely undermine the nation's already faltering efforts to improve the quality of the human and natural environment" (statement of Robert J. Rauch, Environmental Defense Fund, in hearings on "Executive Branch Review of Environmental Regulations," before the Subcommittee on Environmental Pollution of the Senate Committee on Environment and Public Works, 96th Congress, First Session, February 26, 1979, p. 175; see also "Presidential Power and the Politics of RARG," Susan J. Tolchin, *Regulation,* July-August 1979, pp. 44–49.

63. On background to Executive Order 12291 (signed February 17, 1981), see *Environmental Forum,* September 1983, pp. 31–34; Antonin Scala (later named to the Supreme Court by Reagan) called Executive Order 12291 "the support beam of his [Reagan's] administration's framework for regulatory reform"; in *Regulation,* January–February 1982, p. 19, cited in "Deregulation: The Failure at EPA," Richard N.L. Andrews in *Environmental Policy in the 1980s: Reagan's New Agenda,* Norman J. Vig and

Michael E. Kraft, eds. (Washington DC: Congressional Quarterly Press, 1984).

64. See "A Hard Look at Federal Regulation of Formaldehyde: A Departure from Reasoned Decisionmaking," Nicholas Ashford, C.W. Ryan, and C.C. Caldart, *Harvard Environmental Law Review*, Vol. 7, No. 2 (1983) pp. 297–370.

3

Shifting to Prevention:
The Limits of Current Policy

Janice Mazurek
Robert Gottlieb
Julie Roque

Introduction

If pollution prevention was not an explicit outcome of federal environmental policies, it nonetheless was an implicit intent of at least some of the legislation. Indeed, at the very moment that the pollution control system was under construction, alternative concepts were being introduced that suggested a different route for toxics policy. Embedded in both NEPA and the Clean Air Act, for example, was a broader, more sweeping language of prevention, not just management. As stated in NEPA, such legislation included the mission "to prevent and eliminate damage to the environment and the biosphere."

This chapter discusses the efforts made in legislating and implementing prevention-oriented policies. Several major statutes, most indirectly dealing with pollution prevention, but one specifically constructed around these goals, comprise the analysis. These include: the Toxic Substances Control Act (TSCA); the Hazardous and Solid Waste Amendments to the Resource Conservation and Recovery Act (RCRA and HSWA); the Clean Air Act Amendments (CAAA) (as well as the continuing debates concerning Clean Water Act reauthorization) and the Pollution Prevention Act (PPA). Unlike TSCA, which presented and elaborated screening, testing, and phase-out provisions for hazardous substances, both RCRA/HSWA and the CAAA represented efforts to reengineer media-specific statutes in part around prevention themes. Both TSCA and RCRA carried sweeping provisions to track hazardous chemicals throughout their production cycle, from development, production, transport, and use. The product phase-out and technology forcing provisions of CAAA, on the other hand, presented an opportunity within its media-specific boundaries to directly influence production decisions. The Pollution Prevention Act attempted to encapsulate and articulate the new policy paradigm.

That preventative approaches did not significantly materialize, or have been ineffective in practice, is explored here in relation to a variety of factors, including EPA's reluctance to intervene directly in industry decision-making processes and, similarly, its preference for voluntary as opposed to mandated policies. Efforts to move forward were also thwarted by the lack of consensus among industry, activists, and environmental managers concerning pollution prevention definitions and, thus, how such policies would be bounded. Furthermore, implementation has been vague, marked by an absence of explicit implementation guidelines and standard performance measurements. Ambiguities in legislative intent and language were often reinforced by EPA's program-dominated internal structure. Finally, as with all new departures such as the prevention paradigm, political maneuvering in rulemaking associated with any highly debated legislation provided stumbling blocks that have caused these statutes to fail to live up to their prevention-oriented promise.

TSCA's Lost Opportunity

In 1971, the Council on Environmental Quality, in its second "State of the Environment" report, highlighted the dangers caused by the unrestricted flow of chemicals into the market and the need to expand federal authority in the arena of toxic hazards. In turn, the CEQ report anticipated the extended debates over how best to legislate such intervention.[1] While these debates remained separate from the medium-by-medium drafting of legislation that established the basic framework for pollution policy, they nonetheless shared some of the same assumptions. Containing the flow of toxic chemicals was not unlike reducing pollution by air, water, or land, policymakers declared; the difference resided in the focus on the *production* of the chemicals as opposed to their *release* as pollutants. This was a task of prevention, an assumed objective that had not yet successfully achieved a regulatory entry point. Ultimately, this objective was incorporated into the much debated Toxic Substances Control Act (TSCA).

Passed in 1976, TSCA could be seen as an extraordinary piece of legislation, both in terms of its expansive view of where and how to intervene in issues of toxics production, as well as in its enormous difficulties in constructing and implementing such an approach. TSCA was to be the starting point, the "jewel in the crown of environmental protection," as an Environmental Defense Fund staff member testified, although, as it turned out, its implementation became "antithetical to the purposes of prevention and information gathering, and a burden upon both the public and the regulated community."[2] The story of TSCA thus becomes the story of the road not taken, illuminating the limits to implementing prevention policies.

During the period of the early to mid 1970s, it had already become clear in policy debates that the magnitude of toxics accumulation in the environment required new forms of public intervention. At least 60,000 different chemicals were on the market in the U.S., with little or no tracking, testing, or premarket clearing mechanism. Prior to TSCA's passage, legislation and regulatory activities had exclusively focused on the end point of this chemical production cycle. Among other consequences, the single-medium approach was seen as deficient in specifically managing or regulating the flow of certain hazardous chemicals (in particular industrial and commercial applications) such as polychlorinated biphenyls (PCBs).

TSCA, highly controversial and much debated during several legislative sessions, was passed in response to the idea that the introduction of chemicals into the market could no longer proceed unimpeded. Because such an approach shifted the focus of policy to the front end of production decisionmaking, TSCA was bitterly contested. Chemical manufacturers, particularly Dow Chemical, objected to the proposed legislation's potential reach concerning the decision about when and how new chemicals would be introduced to the market.[3] Furthermore, chemical industry groups complained that TSCA established a set of mechanisms to review chemical toxicity, and conceivably could allow EPA to regulate chemicals that had already entered the marketplace.

Although not designed explicitly as a pollution prevention measure, TSCA reflected growing Congressional sentiment that direct regulation might offer the most effective way to deal with hazardous chemicals. Chemical pollution had previously been addressed as a set of problems to be managed and regulated (e.g., as air toxics) through a single-medium approach. TSCA remained distinct from such end-point approaches in that it proposed to regulate, at the front end, chemicals as a distinctive class of compounds, separate from the medium in which they appeared as wastes or pollutants. By the 1975/76 legislative session, a series of catastrophic events (most notably the discharge of the highly toxic pesticide Kepone into the James River, and the revelations concerning the tragic occupational exposures to the toxic chemical BCME in a Rohm and Haas chemical manufacturing plant) brought dramatically to the fore the need to regulate chemicals before they became identifiable hazards. These events not only helped ensure passage of the legislation as a "crisis" measure but also to establish TSCA, with its focus on identifying and regulating toxic chemicals prior to their release, as potentially representing a new premise in environmental management.[4]

TSCA appeared to offer the Environmental Protection Agency, as its implementing agency, broad authority to restrict the use of toxic chemicals, although the law explicitly established a timetable to prohibit the use of only one such chemical, PCBs.[5] The primary thrust of the legislation centered on a series of notification procedures, including a 90-day pre-manufacture notification of the public health and environmental effects of any new chemical prior to its introduction, and a separate notification process for any significant new use of an existing chemical. If the Agency determined that such notification information was insufficient to evaluate potential risks, it had the power to prohibit the manufacture of that chemical until sufficient data was provided.[6] The law also included a set of provisions that allowed EPA to control the production, importation, marketing, or use of any chemical found to present an "unreasonable risk of injury to health or the environment."[7] These controls ranged from the labeling of products as hazardous, to limiting or banning the production of a particular toxic chemical. The law further sought to encourage technological innovation within the chemical industry as one way to bring about changes consistent with the purposes of the Act.[8]

Though the authority provided EPA to restrict the production and use of toxics was quite broad, TSCA has nevertheless proven to be a legislative shell, a "sleeping giant," as one EPA official described it.[9] Although the warning provision has been implemented more extensively, few restrictions on the production and use of toxics have actually been imposed. In its first fifteen years after passage, EPA, under TSCA, instituted regulatory restrictions against only five chemical substances (PCBs under Section 6(e) of the Act, CFCs in aerosols (see Chapter 11), nitrites in metal-working fluids, dioxin in relation to disposal requirements, and asbestos in relation to inspection and removal), while reviewing only an additional 16 test results.[10] Even the TSCA restrictions on PCB use exempted specific applications, although the stringency of the regulation helped bring about various product innovations from PCB manufacturers who quickly introduced a number of PCB substitutes.

In the nearly two decades since its passage, the continuing high growth rate of new chemicals introduced to market and the absence of information on even high production volume chemicals indicates that TSCA has played a minor role in controlling and regulating that flow of chemicals. TSCA's "failure," much debated by analysts and policy makers, reflects the difficulties inherent in the enormity of its tasks, the controversial nature of its mission, and the lack of specificity in its provisions for implementation. The EPA's focus on "environmental" problems to the exclusion of other routes of exposure (such as occupational) further weakened TSCA. The regulatory division in turn reinforced the narrow focus of agencies on specific substances or sources of contamination, rather than industry activities or decisionmaking structures. That, combined with the growing desire by regulators through the 1980s to favor voluntary action, also undercut the regulatory mission of TSCA.

Given its failures, can TSCA still be salvaged as a foundation stone for pollution prevention as a regulatory strategy? The answer to that question can provide crucial insight into the nature, limits, and future opportunities of pollution prevention in the legislative arena.

The heart of TSCA in fact has been its provisions which require that industry have the burden of proof for demonstrating that its products do not pose "unreasonable risk" to human health and the environment. Section 4 of the Act provides authority for the EPA Administrator to require industry to test new and old chemical substances and mixtures if the Agency lacks sufficient data to determine "unreasonable risk" (itself a concept which is never elaborated in the legislation), and if the chemical substance or mixture is or will be produced in substantial quantities and may enter the environment in substantial quantities.[11]

Perhaps more than any other part of the Act, the Section 4 testing provisions (along with Section 5 and Section 8 data gathering provisions) had shown EPA to be ineffective in using TSCA to influence industry decisionmaking. As of 1990, for example, Section 4 programs had considered for testing just 386 chemicals, or less than 1 percent of the more than 70,000 chemicals in commercial production or imported to the U.S. Further, EPA had obtained complete test data for only six chemicals, even though the program had been in existence for more than twelve years. "What is even more disturbing," a General Accounting Office report concluded, "is that EPA has not finished assessing any of those six chemicals [up to 11 by 1992] to determine, from a toxicity standpoint, whether they should be regulated."[12]

In response to the critical GAO report and continuing Congressional criticism of the pace of TSCA implementation, EPA tentatively initiated some efforts to reorient TSCA along prevention lines. Since 1990, for example, the agency has, with some success, revised and streamlined its testing procedures. A new testing program inaugurated on behalf of the European Organization for Economic Cooperation and Development (OECD) members which targeted 1,500 of the highest volume chemicals (about which there was little available test information) enabled EPA to

increase testing volumes. Between 1980 and 1989, EPA had proposed testing action for 201 chemicals, but during 1990 and 1991 alone, testing
actions were proposed for 262 additional chemicals, of which 163 were
related to the OECD.[13]

In addition to expediting testing of existing chemicals, the EPA also
began to reform its existing chemicals analysis process by dividing it into
several stages, or "decision points." The first phase of review is called Risk
Management 1 (RM1) where scientists and analysts make "qualitative
judgements" (i.e., no testing to determine risk at this stage) as to whether
a chemical poses a significant risk. After RM1, the chemical is either
cleared or referred for testing or information-gathering under TSCA
Sections 4 and 8. These chemicals are then examined individually or in
chemically similar "clusters." The RM1 program itself is also seen as an
extension of a pollution prevention approach since both potentially hazardous substitutes as well as viable, nonhazardous chemical substitutes can
be identified.[14]

The second phase of the program involves either dropping certain
chemicals from further action, placing others on a master testing list where
testing is inaugurated, or sending still others through another process
which is called Risk Management 2 (RM2). RM2 includes a pollution
prevention assessment and additional risk reduction analysis of the chemicals identified from the RM1 phase. The RM2 phase also involves "stakeholder dialogues," among producers, consumers, policymakers, and activists
to explore cost–effective production alternatives. At the conclusion of the
RM2 process, EPA can then decide whether to drop further review, initiate collaborative prevention strategies, or initiate rulemaking. As part of the
agency's growing embrace of nonregulatory routes for pollution prevention, it has established a "voluntarist" rather than regulatory end point for
the RM1/RM2 process. If risks are identified, EPA (instead of initiating
rule-making) will instead send "letters of concern" to companies that manufacture, process, or use the targeted substance. Such letters advise companies about the risks involved and encourage them to initiate pollution prevention steps to reduce exposure and releases. In the first two years of the
program, 85 "concern" letters (in lieu of regulatory action) were sent, with
some (though not all) of the companies responding with claims of voluntary chemical substitutions or emission reductions.[15]

The EPA's response to testing deficiencies under Section 4 reveals its
continuing uneasiness with TSCA's essential mandate for front-end regulatory intervention. On the one hand, the streamlined and accelerated test
cases since 1990 indicate that TSCA provisions can be successfully implemented, in this case simply by clarifying testing protocol. On the other

hand, EPA's use of its "letters of concern" program reflects the Agency's desire to avoid industry regulation at the front end by seeking pollution reduction through voluntary industry action. Section 4 reforms, while defining the statute's "objectives and scope," nevertheless underline the Agency's unwillingness to adhere to the spirit of TSCA's regulatory mandate.

Such front-end regulatory reluctance is even more evident in EPA's interpretation of the "confidential business information" (CBI) provisions in Section 14 of TSCA. The legislation (especially Section 8) was in fact designed to make information about chemicals—including their health and environmental effects—publicly available. As such, it is consistent with prevention efforts in that TSCA is an enforceable mechanism with which to procure data about the myriad chemical substances in production, and could conceivably represent a rich data source for health professionals and prevention advocates.

TSCA's data-gathering authorities, spelled out in Section 8, require manufacturers, distributors, and importers of chemicals to report information about production and use as well as health and environmental effects and exposures. Both Sections 8(a) and 8(b) (involving production and use data) as well as 8(d) (involving health and environmental effects and exposures and methods of disposal) are quite detailed in their reporting requirements. The framers of TSCA therefore assumed they could conceivably reveal trade secrets. As a result, Sections 14(a) and 14(b) provided trade secret protection by allowing information submitted or obtained under TSCA to be claimed as confidential. However, 14(a) explicitly limits confidentiality to the protection of "trade secrets or financial information," while also allowing disclosure if necessary to prevent "unreasonable risk." Section 14(b), which deals with data submitted under health and safety studies, even more narrowly confines confidentiality claims to data that reveal "processes used in the manufacturing or processing of a chemical substance or mixture or, in the case of a mixture ... any data which discloses the portion of the mixture comprised by any of the chemical substances in the mixture." Essentially Section 14 has afforded confidentiality protection only for proprietary information that reveals processes and mixture composition and proportions.[16]

Unlike the continuing complaints about EPA's single-medium regulatory permitting, standard setting, and enforcement activities, EPA's implementation of Section 14 CBI confidentiality claims has failed to register any industry objections. To the contrary, despite nearly two decades of collecting toxics data, EPA has thoroughly adhered to the confidentiality process, maintaining CBI protection as if national security secrets were at stake.[17] At the same time, however, CBI claims by industry during this period have become so excessive that they, more than any single aspect of the Act's implementation, have fundamentally frustrated the intent of TSCA and transformed a treasure trove of information potentially available for pollution prevention into a guarded fortress of inaccessible data. The extraordinary use of CBI claims extends throughout TSCA's data-gathering and notification provisions, including premanufacturing notices (where CBI claims have covered over 90 percent of all premanufacture notices on new chemicals), substantial risk notifications (where CBI claims have covered more than 25 percent of such notification, with 80 percent of such CBI submissions involving claims for chemical identity), and health and safety studies (where CBI claims have covered more than 20 percent of all such reported studies).

With respect to TSCA's new chemicals program (where manufacturers must submit a notice of intent to manufacture 90 days before production commences), of the more than 2,000 premanufacture notices (PMNs) that EPA receives each year, 90 percent or more will contain CBI claims. Some of these forms are submitted entirely blank. Others fail to report mandatory information on the PMN section that requests health and safety data. Yet such premanufacture notices comprise the bulk of new chemical manufacture data in the U.S. By purging such data from the public record via CBI claims, these data have been rendered virtually useless.[18]

More pressing than confidentiality claims on new chemical data are the CBI claims on health and safety studies as required under Section 8 of TSCA. Section 8(e) requires manufacturers, processors, and distributors to notify the EPA immediately if they obtain information indicating that a chemical presents a "substantial risk of injury to health or the environment." Failure to report substantial risks is punishable by a $25,000 per day fine. Most CBI claims in this area have been based on chemical identity, but also have included claims based on submitter identity (i.e., the company name), use toxicity, and use and environmental data. These claims have significantly undercut EPA activity in this area; one 1992 study (the Hampshire Report) on CBI and TSCA prepared for EPA in fact found blatant abuses of CBI claims in these categories. For example, a recent program initiated by the Office of Pollution Prevention and Toxics (OPPT) (formerly the Office of Toxic Substances) (EPA's office assigned to implement TSCA provisions) sought to review and potentially challenge some of the industry CBI claims under Section 8(d) health and safety studies and 8(e) notices of substantial risk. Between September 1990 and May 1991, 106 Section 8(e) notices and 351 Section 8(d) notices were submitted. Of those, OPPT decided to challenge 52 (49 percent) of the 8(e) notices and

77 (22 percent) of the 8(d) notices. In each case where challenged, the company involved decided to amend its CBI claims.[19]

The combination of inadequate testing, failure to initiate rulemaking, and excessive CBI claims has enormously frustrated any significant attempt at TSCA implementation. Of these shortcomings, the spotlight currently surrounds the question of proprietary information. In early 1994, Congress initiated reauthorization hearings. In June 1994, EPA released a plan to reform CBI reporting.[20] The EPA action plan articulates a set of proposals aimed primarily at teaching industry how to reduce egregious proprietary claims. The plan calls for CBI reporting workshops and dissemination of sample CBI claims prepared by EPA which show what information may and may not be claimed as confidential. Other proposals suggest that older information flagged as CBI be sunsetted, as product ingredients and process methods are disseminated among producers and thus disclosure no longer threatens to endanger sensitive trade secrets. Finally, in recognition of TSCA's stated objectives to improve public awareness of potential risks posed by some chemicals, EPA, in cooperation with industry, will attempt to make more data about hazards reported under TSCA available to the public. As part of this reform process, EPA plans only to modify one existing regulation. It plans to stiffen up-front reporting methods, requiring senior managers to sign off and thus verify company information submitted under TSCA.

At the same time, EPA has long stated its opposition to TSCA reauthorization, preferring less confrontational methods such as those outlined in the action plan. While improved education programs to industry may indeed reduce some egregious claims, reform efforts fail to correct TSCA's fundamental statutory flaws. For example, one reason that egregious claims persist is that the statute only imposes penalties for wrongful disclosure on government employees, yet, unlike other statutes such as SARA, fails to impose fines on industry for egregious CBI claims. However, the heart of TSCA's shortfall involves not Section 14 disclosure penalties, but the statute's central premise that environmental risk can be removed by flagging and removing "a few bad chemicals" as former CEQ official Warren Muir put it.[21] But chemical toxicity alone, he adds, is not the problem. Human and environmental exposure hazards are a result of chemical use:

> The heart of the problem of toxic chemicals is not their ability
> to produce harmful effects, but instead the particular uses of toxic
> chemicals in specific settings that allow harmful effects to
> occur.[22]

TSCA framers viewed toxic risks arising from industrial production as singular: concentrated under one factory roof, and relatively unchanging over time. Emerging approaches to industrial policy, however, take the opposite approach, acknowledging that how production takes place, where it takes place, and the processes and inputs involved, vary as a function of economic adaptation. Put another way, these systems (to borrow from evolutionary biology) are dynamic.[23] Muir argues that a single agency such as EPA is unable to track and monitor the millions of risks posed every day in local settings by the 70,000 chemicals in use throughout the U.S. economy.[24] Instead, he argues that public policy should seek to formulate principles regarding chemical production and use. Once such policy is articulated, it should, in turn, guide industrial decisionmakers to assess the risks of different uses while assuring that those uses (and risks) that are chosen are not "unreasonable" as TSCA stipulates.

TSCA's lack of specificity regarding the nature, use, and location of hazardous substances illustrates the difficulties and lost opportunities embedded in its implementation. This failure also highlights the continuing decision by the Agency to approach pollution prevention by other means and through other regulatory tools. EPA's reluctance to make TSCA reauthorization a major legislative priority underlines its reluctance to place TSCA at the center of its regulatory approach.[25] At the same time, the development of other toxics-related legislation (such as the 1990 Pollution Prevention Act and the 1990 Clean Air Act Amendments) and other EPA initiatives (such as its Industrial Toxics (33/50) project and its Common Sense Initiative), has shifted the focus of pollution prevention away from regulatory intervention regarding front-end production decisions toward both voluntary actions and an expansion of the single-medium approach, albeit with limited reduction objectives. "While we want to utilize the traditional regulatory tools which TSCA provides," EPA official Linda Fisher has argued, "we also see opportunities to use our statutory authorities in fresh ways, consistent with new trends in environmental management."[26] TSCA, one-time stalking horse for a new regulatory paradigm, has ended up as an uncomfortable reminder for both legislators and regulators that establishing new regulatory approaches beyond the entrenched pollution control framework has remained as difficult as ever.

Reconfiguring Single-Medium Regulation

With TSCA a legislative sideshow to the debates about new approaches in regulatory strategy, much Congressional attention has turned to recasting single-medium legislation as part of an effort to escape the "black box" bias toward technological add ons that characterized the pollution control system. During the early 1980s, Congressional concern about land disposal hazards created interest in ways to minimize waste, including new treatment technologies, notably hazardous waste incineration. In 1984, the Hazardous and Solid Waste Amendments to RCRA more explicitly elevated the reduction of hazardous waste as a matter of national policy. HSWA stipulated, in its first section, that "wherever possible, the generation of hazardous waste is to be reduced or eliminated as expeditiously as possible."[27] To achieve this objective, the act required that the 1976 RCRA manifest (the cradle-to-grave tracking mechanism) certify that the hazardous waste generator had a program in place to reduce the volume and toxicity of that waste to a degree that was economically feasible. It further required that each hazardous waste generator submit a biennial report on (1) the quantity and nature of hazardous waste generated, (2) efforts taken to reduce the volume and toxicity of waste generated, and (3) changes in volume and toxicity achieved during the year.

In terms of the certification and reporting program, HSWA specified a public release of the biennial reports. The first of these reports was compiled at the state level and was initially made public in 1987.[28] This and subsequent reports were immediately criticized for their lack of information and guidance to generators concerning what constituted waste reduction or waste minimization activities and the consequent broad and ultimately meaningless interpretation by numerous industries regarding how such forms should be filled out, if at all. Difficulties in data compilation were also traced to general industry ignorance and unfamiliarity with hazardous waste data and collection procedures; the inability of government agencies to effectively track down all generators of hazardous waste to ensure compliance; and resistance by a number of generators who simply wouldn't comply with the reporting provisions. Some generators cited (as part of their waste "reduction" effort) waste treatment technologies that even EPA had not incorporated into its waste minimization definition, or simply quoted the certification language in the report (e.g., that they had a waste reduction in place, without identifying it), while others acknowledged the absence of any program or left that section of the report blank.[29]

For more deep-seated reasons rooted in the structure of RCRA/HSWA classifications, however, even quantitative descriptions of RCRA waste reductions (which have been volunteered from various quarters) have been of equally limited utility, since they provide no evidence of the reduction of specific toxic constituents (dramatic waste reductions can be accomplished, for example, by using less water in the generating process, producing a more concentrated toxic waste), and because they will not reveal any accompanying shifts of toxics to forms and media that fall outside of

RCRA's hazardous waste definitions. Despite these critical flaws, descriptions of "waste reduction" efforts by both industrial trade groups and individual companies still commonly use the language of RCRA wastes, similar to the biennial report procedures.

The focus on wastes as hazards that emerged through RCRA and its subsequent amendments paralleled the evolution of single-medium policy approaches seeking to address toxic releases to the air and water. For example, the language in the Clean Air Act regarding toxic or "hazardous air pollutants" (metals like cadmium and chromium, organics such as benzene, polyaromatic hydrocarbons (PAHs), polychlorinated dibenzo-p-dioxin (dioxins), and acid gases such as hydrogen chloride and sulfuric acid), did provide EPA with the authority to establish regulations on a pollutant-by-pollutant basis, but did not provide a clear direction for connecting this rulemaking with prevention objectives. Section 112 of the Act, the National Emission Standards for Hazardous Air Pollutants (NESHAP) provision, did mandate an up-to-date list of toxic air pollutants hazardous to human health, with emission standards to be set within one year of the decision to add a pollutant to the list. But while health-based only standards were to be set for CAA criteria pollutants, the NESHAPs were to be technology-based and at the discretion of the administrator who could take economic criteria (the costs to industry) into account in setting final standards.[30] To meet the standards for air toxics, both EPA and the states responded by writing industry-specific requirements for point sources of pollutants. These technology-based standards were developed by determining how much emission control was actually achievable with particular control technologies, and then by setting emission standards within achievable ranges. Further reinforcing its control emphasis, the Clean Air Act had also included a provision for EPA to provide information on various pollution control techniques to help achieve compliance.[31]

During the 1980s, the Clean Air Act's standard-setting process and imposition of controls was further eroded by the inaction of the Reagan and Bush administrations, especially with respect to air toxics and the growing concerns regarding acid rain. Among the literally thousands of air toxics that had been identified during this period, only a handful of hazardous air pollutant (HAP) standards had been promulgated by the end of the decade.[32] As a consequence, sufficient pressure had emerged both inside and outside Congress to rewrite the Clean Air Act and address some of its limitations, including the lack of any pollution prevention focus. That debate coincided with efforts to reauthorize the CAA, which included the active intervention by the Bush administration to tie together regulatory flexibility with both "free market" and "prevention" objectives.

Coming after several years of protracted debate, the 1990 Clean Air Act

Amendments established, according to the EPA, new ways to control air pollution above and beyond traditional control strategies. These included both the mechanisms to "harness market forces" and an additional emphasis on "pollution prevention."[33] The key strategic thrust of the legislation, however, was its effort to provide sufficient flexibility to industry both in controlling and in reducing emissions to break the twenty-year stalemate for the Agency in managing most air toxics.

The 1990 Amendments consisted of fourteen different titles with a wide range of policy objectives.[34] Three provisions of the legislation most directly sought to promote pollution prevention: Title III (Hazardous Air Pollutants)[35]; Title IV (Acid Deposition)[36]; and Title IX (Clean Air Research).[37]

Title III of the Amendments ("Hazardous Air Pollutants") directly reflected Congress's frustration with EPA's inability to list and regulate the vast majority of the hazardous air pollutants that had been provided under the 1970 Act but which continued to be emitted routinely nationwide. The Title lists 189 compounds to be regulated, and defines a two-tiered approach.[38] The first tier requires EPA to prioritize industrial source categories to be regulated and then develop technology-based standards for each category and pollutant.[39] Standards for various source categories are to be phased in over several years. The second tier of Title III requires EPA to evaluate the residual health risks associated with the remaining emissions from each source, eight years from the time that a source category is required to be in compliance with the technology-based standards. If the residual risks are determined to be "unreasonable," EPA is directed to promulgate additional standards based solely on health considerations.[40] Sources would be required to install additional controls (or modify or shut down processes) to meet the health-based standards. The purpose of the two-tiered approach is to require the installation of best control technologies prior to any determination (and likely debate and possible delay) over what a health-based target ought to be. Title III does seek to provide incentives for reduction through its provisions that allow EPA to issue permits to generators without technology controls if they demonstrate that they have reduced their emissions by 90% (95% for particulates) before any technology standards for their sector are proposed. EPA's criteria for defining "reduction," however, remains open-ended; for example, whether transferring emissions to other media will qualify as "reduction" or whether the 90% target applies only to a specific pollutant or can be defined by a combination of pollutants is not clearly specified in the legislation.[41]

The CAA Amendments are more specific in their reduction objectives in Title IV which addresses emissions of precursors to acid deposition. Title IV established annual reduction targets of 10 million tons for sulfur dioxide (SO_2) and 2 million tons for nitrogen oxides (NO_x) from the base year of 1980 in the lower 48 states and the District of Columbia.

Title IV is of particular note in how it attempts to link market factors to reduction objectives.[42] The debate over how to control acid rain was a primary factor in delaying earlier bills to amend the Clean Air Act prior to passage of the 1990 Amendments. Those debates between mainstream environmental organizations and large Midwestern electric utilities ultimately were resolved through a compromise measure whose centerpiece was a market-based system of emissions trading for utilities. In the end, Title IV distinguished between emission reduction requirements defined as "economically feasible" to be accomplished through technology-based controls and a system that allowed for the transfer or trading of "emission credits" to facilities where the effort to reduce emissions by controls is more expensive and not economically feasible.[43] At the same time, the total emissions of SO_2 and NO_x are capped, with new emission sources or facilities not permitted to come on line without purchasing emissions allowances from existing facilities. Overall emissions reductions are to be achieved by establishing decreasing emissions limits in two phases over a ten-year period.

Finally, Title IX of the Amendments (the "Clean Air Research" section) specifies that EPA undertake research in a number of areas, including the development of new control technologies and new policy mechanisms.[44] Some of the language in Title IX suggests the need for "prevention" by stipulating that EPA "conduct a basic engineering research and technology program to develop, evaluate and demonstrate nonregulatory strategies and technologies for air pollution prevention."[45] Like nearly all the other titles in the Act, however, a schedule and format for this research are not specified, and it is conceivable that the problem of cross-media transfers and the need for reduction strategies in place of end-of-pipe controls may be overlooked.

Thus, in sum, the Clean Air Act Amendments, despite the claims that they were written for new regulatory "flexibility," establish a reduction or prevention framework that remains only incidental to its continuing end-of-pipe emphasis on how to limit emissions. Air toxics regulation was assumed to be, but never directly became, the occasion for pollution prevention, remaining the stepchild of a far more pronounced system of technology controls and end point management.

Similar to the air toxics debates, the concern over poorly controlled toxic discharges and frustration with the inability of regulators to link the

permitting and discharge standard provisions of the Clean Water Act with
pollution prevention objectives also emerged as a main area of contention
in the Congressional debates over accomplishing pollution prevention
strategies within a single-medium frame of reference. Reauthorization legislation for the Clean Water Act (the occasion of this debate over water and
toxics) was introduced during both the 1991–1992 and 1993–1994
Congressional sessions. These bills included provisions for linking both
Clean Water Act permitting (the NPDES system described in Chapter 2)
and state grant funds to the development of pollution prevention programs
and statewide management plans with prevention objectives. For example,
in one of the draft bills introduced, EPA was to "rely upon and require, to
the maximum extent practicable, source reduction measures and practices"
in developing future technology-based standards. Similarly, companies were
required to prepare a "pollution prevention plan" as a condition for obtaining a permit under Section 402 of the Clean Water Act. These approaches
nevertheless remained subsumed under the single-medium permitting and
standard setting still prevailing in the Act rewrite.[46] The single medium
focus for CWA reauthorization was further reinforced by Congressional
jurisdiction disputes based on the committee system which mirrored the
medium-by-medium approach of the regulators. These intricacies of legislative tracking and jurisdiction also served to narrow the likelihood of
passage of a bill with a more inclusive/cross-media prevention framework
which had no specific committee to help advocate such an approach.
Given the essential focus of the Clean Water Act to "comprehensively [pro-
tect] the ecological integrity of water bodies," water quality rather than
pollution prevention remained the centerpiece of reauthorization
debates.[47]

The most controversial recommendation for a front-end prevention
approach during the Clean Water Act reauthorization debates was the
Clinton administration's proposal to "comprehensively assess the use, environmental and health impacts of chlorine and chlorinated compounds and
relative efficacy and safety of substitutes for these substances."[48] The direct
motivation for such a study were the impacts, particularly non-point
source contamination, on water bodies by chlorinated compounds used by
the pulp and paper industry, agriculture (pesticides and herbicides), solvents, plastics, and in publicly owned treatment works and drinking water
systems. The chlorine ban concept had in fact emerged as a major campaign objective of Greenpeace, one of the larger, more direct-action–oriented environmental groups. The chlorine ban concept had also received
support from a number of established policymaking and professional
sources, including the American Public Health Association and the

International Joint Commission on the Great Lakes, and had strong European Community interest.[49] Greenpeace was especially quick to applaud Browner's CWA announcement, even though the EPA director had simply advocated researching *the feasibility* of instituting such a ban or phase out rather than advocating the process itself.[50] Nevertheless, Browner's remarks unleashed a highly visible counterattack on the part of the chlorine industry that argued that thousands of lives would be lost and potential economic disruption would ensue if such a ban were to be (even partly) instituted. Though Browner refused to directly abandon her position on the chlorine study, a besieged EPA, under parallel attacks for its advocacy of "unfunded mandates," its presumed willingness to seize private property ("takings"), and its failure to use the science of risk assessment in allocating resources (see Chapter 5), seemed unprepared to defend the possibility of using single-medium legislation for pollution prevention purposes. The mix of pollution prevention and the Agency's single medium approach, reinforced by its limited and often uncertain legislative mandates, left open the question of which direction toxics policies might pursue.

The Ambiguities of Pollution Prevention Legislation and Regulation

During the late 1980s, the concern about constructing a new approach shifted gears in both legislative and regulatory arenas, as new debates emerged over what in fact constituted "pollution prevention." These debates took on a legislative dimension in the form of a free-standing bill first introduced as the Waste Reduction Act and, subsequently, during the 1989–1990 Congressional session (to accommodate EPA concerns), as the Pollution Prevention Act.[51] EPA, along with most industry lobbyists, had initially opposed the legislation, objecting to its language defining pollution prevention as "source reduction," and placing this concept at the top of a waste reduction hierarchy.[52] The legislation in fact defined source reduction as "any practice which reduces the amount of any hazardous substance, pollutant, or contaminant entering any waste stream or otherwise released into the environment (including fugitive emissions) prior to recycling, treatment, or disposal...."[53] Recycling and treatment were specifically excluded from the definition of pollution prevention.

At the same time, the authors of the legislation had wanted the Pollution Prevention Act, as a free-standing bill, to avoid the traps of legislative committee infighting over jurisdiction.[54] As part of that effort, the bill had been successfully attached to the budget recommendation package. After months of intense negotiations with industry groups, environmentalists, administration officials, and key members of Congress, a compromise was reached: the language about pollution prevention as "source reduction" would remain intact in exchange for a more voluntarist definition of the intent of the legislation. A parallel compromise also was achieved about the legislation's reporting or "right-to-know" provisions. On the one hand, efforts to more directly address CBI/trade secret abuses were abandoned in exchange for provisions to strengthen the reporting requirements under the Toxics Release Inventory established by EPCRA (see Chapter 5). On the basis of these compromises, the Chemical Manufacturers Association, through the efforts of the lobbyist from Dow Chemical who saw the Act as an important example of "regulatory flexibility," signed off on the legislation.[55] At the same time, many of the environmental groups, represented primarily by a Sierra Club lobbyist, also agreed to the changes. However, the Bush administration still remained lukewarm about it,[56] and it also was actively opposed by a number of Republican Senators who saw the legislation as unduly interventionist, despite its voluntarist intent. With maneuvering that lasted until just one hour before the close of the 100th Congress, the Pollution Prevention Act passed with a bare minimum of votes, a reluctant EPA, and an uncertain future in relation to both policy and industry interpretation of its intent. Nevertheless, the legislation set a new standard for toxics policy, expanding on the HSWA definition by asserting that pollution needed to be "prevented or reduced at the source whenever feasible."[57]

The Pollution Prevention Act offered a bit of something for each of the parties signing off on the legislation. For environmentalists and toxics use reduction advocates, the legislation provided a tighter definition of pollution prevention, albeit a definition still limited specifically to waste streams and environmental releases rather than more comprehensively incorporating occupational and product-based hazards or addressing use issues. Nevertheless, the Act's new definition remained paramount to environmentalists. By focusing specifically on source reduction, it also underlined the importance of the new reporting requirements for TRI established by the new legislation. This included both reporting the amount of wastes treated or recycled prior to release or disposal as well as provisions for estimating future toxic releases and detailing pollution prevention or source reduction plans in relation to those future wastes.[58] These new provisions, along with the much anticipated executive order broadening TRI to include all federal facilities (signed by President Clinton in August 1993),[59] had clearly established TRI as a primary source of information and pressure point for the environmental groups.

Both EPA and industry, meanwhile, supported the Act's voluntarist approach. As opposed to TSCA's front-end regulatory potential and RCRA and HSWA's burdensome reporting requirements and land disposal restrictions, the Pollution Prevention Act established no new direct regulatory powers for EPA (other than the new reporting requirements), and specifically defined pollution prevention as essentially an industry-only activity. The only recommendations in the Act specifically directing EPA were instructions that the Agency consider the effects of existing programs on future "source reduction" efforts, review all current Agency regulations in relation to those efforts, and develop standards for measuring reduction and identifying potential reduction goals. To accomplish those tasks, the Act had little to say about the Agency's internal single-medium oriented organization, other than to suggest that expanded pollution prevention education programs be developed and that a new Office of Pollution Prevention be established to potentially implement such goals.[60] Thus, the Act tended to obscure the question of how pollution prevention would become the basis for future policy other than to leave to Agency discretion the interpretation of its new mandate and to allow "regulatory flexibility" so that industry would be given the opportunity to demonstrate its commitment to this new approach. While the Pollution Prevention Act presented an invitation to change, it did not state how such changes were to be accomplished nor guarantee their acceptance as the basis for either industry decisionmaking or future policy.

For EPA, pollution prevention implementation, compounded by the open-ended/let-industry-do-it mandate of the Pollution Prevention Act, continued to have a difficult and often tortuous path, residing at the margins rather than at the center of Agency activity. Prior to the 1990 legislation, the passage of the Hazardous and Solid Waste Amendments to RCRA of 1984 had provided the Agency with its first explicit instructions to report to Congress on how it intended to compel or persuade industry to reduce or eliminate hazardous waste. EPA interpreted this mandate along two lines: the promotion of voluntary programs as opposed to specific mandatory standards for waste reduction; and a conceptual framework which included treatment as well as recycling (both on-site and off-site) as part of its overall definition of waste minimization, the initial concept of preference for EPA in responding to HSWA's directives.

By the late 1980s, EPA's waste minimization strategy was under attack from a number of different quarters. Community and public interest groups remained strongly opposed to the Agency's continuing preference for advanced treatment techniques, including incineration. Agency officials saw incineration as the most feasible alternative to land disposal of wastes, which was increasingly restricted through regulatory measures such as HSWA's land ban provisions. For example, EPA's interpretation of the requirement in the 1986 Superfund Amendments for states to develop hazardous waste capacity assurance plans[61] provided a visible and controversial example of Agency bias in favor of treatment rather than reduction as the most direct method of handling hazardous wastes both within and between states.

Despite criticism from the Office of Technology Assessment, members of Congress, and environmental and public interest groups who objected to EPA's conceptual reliance on waste "minimization" and its continuing focus on treatment and technology-based standards, the Agency continued to resist adopting a more stringent, reduction-oriented approach. In 1988, when the Waste Reduction Act was first introduced in Congress, EPA remained strongly opposed to any restructuring of its activities. An EPA Assistant Administrator testified against the legislation, arguing that a separate Waste Reduction Office within EPA, as advocated in the legislation, would "serve to diffuse the [agency's] effort, not intensify it."[62]

Increasingly wary of the criticism in an election year and pushed by its critics to shift directions, EPA decided, in the summer of 1988, to establish a small Pollution Prevention Office within its Office of Policy Planning and Evaluation and a Waste Minimization Branch for its research lab in Cincinnati. These moves anticipated EPA's decision to initiate its own major new policy initiative, which first appeared in the form of an Agency Statement that was published in the Federal Register on January 26, 1989. This Pollution Prevention Policy Statement was designed to answer the Agency's critics and define EPA's commitment "to a preventive program to reduce or eliminate the generation of potentially harmful pollutants."[63]

The publication of EPA's Pollution Prevention Policy Statement was immediately touted by administration officials as a new course for the Agency, moving it away from the media-shifting, "environmental merry-go-round effect" of pollution control toward a policy emphasizing "source reduction and environmentally sound recycling practices," as one Agency figure put it.[64] Yet the Statement remained ambiguous about both its interpretation of pollution prevention and its proposed methods of implementation.

For one, while the Statement appeared to elevate source reduction (which included closed-loop, in-plant recycling) over other management practices, it still included off-site recycling as part of its prevention framework. This inclusion was significant, given the strong preference by industry for off-site recycling as a means of complying with various waste reduction mandates and targets. For example, the initial release of TRI data (the 1987 TRI results were made public just a few months after the Pollution Prevention Statement was published) indicated that recycling (including the transfer of waste to off-site recycling centers) was identified by two-thirds of the industries submitting reports as their waste reduction method of choice.[65] When EPA subsequently conducted its own review of industry "prevention" activities through a survey conducted by its Source Reduction Clearinghouse, as many as 90% of the examples identified involved recycling activities. Even where "recycling" involved an "on-site" activity, the question of what appropriately constituted "prevention" became "nuanced in terms of what you measure," as EPA official Eric Schaffer put it. "It depended on what you meant by recycling," Schaeffer declared. "Was it processing? Was it distillation? And weren't these activities that would otherwise occur?"[66]

Second, despite the Pollution Prevention Statement's distinction between source reduction and recycling and those forms of treatment previously included in its waste minimization approach (e.g., incineration), it continued to insist that "safe treatment, storage and disposal, for pollution that couldn't reasonably be reduced at the source or recycled, will continue to be important components of an environmental protection strategy."[67] EPA programs, in fact, continued to reflect the Agency's historical emphasis on treatment and control. For example, shortly after the Statement's publication, EPA awarded about $5 million in grants to establish Hazardous Substance Research Centers at five different university consortia. This grantmaking had been authorized under provisions in SARA which provided for as much as $25 million over five years to establish and maintain such centers. Of these grants, however, the majority of the funds were directed toward various waste treatment studies, with little money directly earmarked for prevention or source reduction research.[68]

The mechanisms for implementation of the new pollution prevention program as outlined by the Statement and subsequent passage of the Pollution Prevention Act also appeared to rely heavily on exhortation and education rather than on any expanded jurisdiction or redefinition of the media-specific—oriented offices within the Agency. The Pollution Prevention Office established prior to the Statement's publication failed to emerge as a significant factor in reshaping the Agency's organizational structure and focus of activities (and consequent policy bias). Without any clear and specific mandate on how to proceed and with only a minuscule operational budget (more than two years after its founding the PPO still had a staff of only 15), the Pollution Prevention Office represented in this period at best only a weak symbol of Agency intent.[69]

At the same time, Agency-wide implementation of pollution prevention appeared to reside elsewhere. The 1989 Pollution Prevention Statement emphasized, for example, that each of the media-specific and regional offices would be instructed to incorporate the pollution prevention philosophy "into every feasible aspect of internal decisionmaking and planning," institutionalizing the concept by creating a "pollution prevention culture" within the Agency. The Statement also called for an Advisory Committee of senior Agency managers to help direct the pollution prevention program and "assure the participation of the entire Agency in this important mission." Part of this effort included a review of the existing programs and offices to identify where pollution prevention opportunities might exist and whether the existing programs encouraged, were neutral to, or impeded pollution prevention. As with a number of other programs, the Statement also called for support for state and local programs and an educational or outreach program aimed at state and local governments, industry, and consumers "designed to effect a cultural change emphasizing the opportunities and benefits of pollution prevention."[70]

Despite the directive to reexamine at an institutional level the control biases within the Agency, even the minimal efforts designed to accomplish such a change were met with resistance and institutional inertia. For example, within the Office of Solid Waste, a Source Reduction and Recycling Plan was put in place in October 1990 to establish a pollution prevention review of OSW's rules and permits under RCRA as well as the permitting and enforcement activities taking place at the state level. Through the initiation of the program's key advocate, Manik Roy (who had been hired by EPA partly on the basis of his pollution prevention experience in the state of Massachusetts), focus groups were established for permitting officials as well as for those who wrote the rules and regulations within the Agency. Although the response within the Agency of those interested in participating appeared strong, there were numerous and lengthy delays in obtaining EPA approval for the program management plan. Given the delays, the unwillingness of the Agency to make a collective decision for implementation at the program office level, and the clear disinterest in the regulatory possibilities associated with a pollution prevention approach, Roy left the Agency by 1992 to take a position at the Environmental Defense Fund. He represented a casualty of the continuing single medium/control biases within the Agency.[71]

The decision to maintain EPA's existing structures, perhaps the single most important barrier untouched by the new program, also meant that the role of the Pollution Prevention Office became limited to such tasks as training its own and other federal agency staff to "identify pollution prevention opportunities," collecting and disseminating information primarily for educational and promotional purposes, and providing small amounts of funding especially for small businesses, defined as a primary pollution prevention constituency. A comprehensive review of EPA-defined pollution prevention activities in the Agency's various program and regional offices between 1989 and 1991 also underscored the divorce between control and treatment-based single-medium permitting and enforcement activities (the heart of program office mandates) and "prevention" activities that were largely promotional and informational in nature. These ranged from award programs for innovative pollution prevention projects, publication of materials for better housekeeping measures (e.g., Office of Solid Waste brochures aimed at the metal plating industry, which were often repetitious of similar state and even other OSW brochures on the same subject), or even programs designed to identify wastes as "below regulatory concern" to escape further hazardous waste classification. Most significantly, funding for pollution prevention at the regional level largely arrived through federal program offices (Air, Water, Solid Waste, etc.), which in turn biased the design of resulting programs.[72]

In response to continuing criticism of EPA's limited approach to prevention, several new initiatives were launched during the early 1990s that sought to demonstrate an expanded Agency commitment to pollution prevention. These involved, most notably, (1) EPA Administrator William Reilly's announcement of a 2% budgetary set aside program for funding pollution prevention activities; (2) a much-heralded 33/50 program to reduce the release of seventeen toxic chemicals; (3) the issuance of a new Pollution Prevention Strategy Statement (in response to passage of the Pollution Prevention Act), which sought to clarify the Agency's approach to prevention and define its work more strategically in this area; and (4) implementation of the "institutionalization" concept through the creation of an industry cluster or sector approach.

The 2% program was created to help support pollution prevention projects throughout the Agency. The program was funded by setting aside two percent of the Agency's budget (originally designed for fiscal years 91 and 92) and then establishing a competitive grants system whereby EPA offices could submit proposals to obtain funding. The first set of funding proposals received reinforced the Agency's approach to prevention. It included, among other projects, an award program of $25,000 for small businesses demonstrating innovative pollution prevention programs, a consumer product life cycle analysis project, and an industry-linked pilot project to reduce VOC emissions through alternative coating materials and processes. Most significantly, the 2 percent set aside, as an *external* grants program, failed to confront EPA's own *internal* organizational biases, including its own substantial internal budgetary resources favoring the control orientation of program offices. By way of example, no 2% set-aside money was earmarked for developing a cross-media approach to the regulations that were to be established through the Clean Air Act Amendments, nor were any funds designated for the Agency's most ambitious pollution prevention initiative at the time, the Source Reduction Review Project.[73]

The 33/50 program became even more indicative of EPA's failure to establish within its own operations an explicit Agency culture favoring prevention. The program, as originally defined by the Bush administration's William Reilly and described in the Agency's 1991 Pollution Prevention Strategy, was aimed at highlighting the possibilities of a voluntary approach by industry to accomplishing prevention goals. The concept was simple: EPA would identify 17 high use toxic chemicals. Industries that committed to the program would then pledge to reduce their releases of those seventeen chemicals by an amount of 33 percent by 1992 and 50 percent by 1995. Reductions would be measured by TRI numbers. [The seventeen chemicals that were in fact selected in 1992 accounted for 22 percent of the total releases reported to TRI in 1988 (1.4 out of 6.4 billion pounds) and were handled by many of the industries represented—as defined by SIC codes 20–39—in the TRI database). There were no specific pledges that the reduction would be accomplished through pollution prevention, while the actual targets of 33 and 50 percent reductions were to be aggregate reductions by company rather than chemical specific. In other words, a company could reduce far less of one chemical but not reduce another chemical and still achieve a 33/50 target. The program would complement existing voluntary industry programs such as the Chemical Manufacturers Association's Responsible Care program as well as efforts by individual companies such as Dow's "Waste Reduction Always Pays" (WRAP) program or Chevron's "Save Money and Reduce Toxics" (SMART) initiative, and would ultimately become a significant measure of corporate citizenship or "corporate environmentalism" (see Chapter 6). Finally, 33/50 would demonstrate the cooperative spirit of voluntarism as opposed to the then current regulatory-driven system that was often seen as establishing an adversarial relationship between regulator and regulatee.[74]

The design of 33/50, moreover, was not linked to any specific ongoing pollution prevention Agency regulatory activity and further underlined the *ad hoc* nature of how the Agency interpreted its pursuit of "prevention." The selection of the seventeen chemicals, for example, had no regulatory reference point (such as being based on TSCA information). Instead, chemical selection relied on informal feedback from program and regional offices which sought to identify those chemicals that seemed to offer the best (and often the easiest) opportunities for reduction, as well as chemicals already targeted (or about to be targeted) for reduction or waste minimization activities by various companies. The reductions were to be measured by comparing TRI numbers in 1988 with later target dates, although there were no criteria established to distinguish among "reduction" approaches. Rather, the language encouraged participants to voluntarily report how the reductions in their releases were achieved (e.g., by a condensation or distillation of the chemical, by a new technology, by a new process, by a substitution such as water-based solvents, and so forth), thus leaving entirely open whether the reduction actually represented a form of pollution prevention.[75]

Despite its strong emphasis on "voluntarism," when the 33/50 approach was first introduced by the Bush administration, it encountered significant opposition from the Office of Management and Budget, as well as from CEQ and the Council on Competitiveness chaired by Vice President Dan Quayle. OMB and the others argued that because EPA would select the 17 chemicals, such action was itself "coercive" and not a true voluntary approach. OMB officials insisted in fact that if pollution prevention measures were indeed economical for a company, they would have already been instituted, given the logic of the market. The reliance on TRI numbers, OMB further argued, was proximate to "extortion," subjecting companies to unnecessary and unwanted public pressures. EPA strongly disagreed with the OMB position, calling it "an antiempirical" approach, as one EPA official put it, since even significant simple process changes had failed to materialize among numerous companies. Despite the criticisms, a number of industry groups, with only a few exceptions, supported the 33/50 concept, largely in recognition that TRI and other "right-to-know" initiatives were becoming a significant factor driving toxics policy, thereby creating pressures on industry to respond through some kind of visible demonstration of reduction efforts.[76]

In 1991, 33/50 was formally launched with much fanfare by the Agency. Letters were sent out to the "Top 600" companies with TRI emissions, with a larger round of letters and meetings with industry officials subsequently taking place. By December 1992, when the 1992 target figures were announced, the number of firms participating had increased to 812. Of those participating, 684 companies (84 percent of the total) had submitted quantifiable reduction goals that would ultimately allow EPA to determine the total reductions in releases and transfers by 1995.[77]

Despite the strong interest in the program, 33/50 proved to be, by the time of its first interim target date, an uncertain example of the link between "voluntarism" and pollution prevention. In terms of the numbers, as of December 1992, the total aggregate reductions from the 1988 figure of 1,456 million pounds amounted to 342 million pounds, or a reduction of 25% rather than the proposed target of 33%. Those numbers, further-more, were neither adjusted for reductions resulting from production declines (a significant factor in a period of economic recession) nor with respect to treatment or recycling on-site (a new reporting requirement for TRI created by the 1990 Pollution Prevention Act legislation).[78] EPA in fact was defining 33/50 as a "release reduction program," never having pursued for reporting purposes the more stringent "source reduction" characterization contained within the Pollution Prevention Act and EPA's own Pollution Prevention Strategy when the original 33/50 program was first announced. Finally, the 33/50 numbers were not analyzed with respect to "paper" or "phantom" reductions based on how the reporting was undertaken, a major criticism of the TRI process itself.[79] At the same time, many of the reductions were related to chemicals specified for regu-latory action under the Clean Air Act Amendments, and thus simply antic-ipated reduction goals (in terms of reducing emissions for possible waivers from CAA mandated controls) that were about to be established.[80]

For EPA, however, 33/50 has continued to be seen as a way to make companies aware of (and less hostile to) pollution prevention opportuni-ties. Despite the smaller than hoped for numbers, EPA has touted the pro-ject as a means by which reductions are achieved faster than otherwise may be obtained by waiting for statutes to be implemented. The program, according to EPA officials, also represented an effective voluntary method for targeting specific chemicals for specific reductions, perhaps the most notable aspect of the project, according to both state officials and EPA reg-ulators.[81]

But does 33/50 constitute pollution prevention? Not if pollution pre-vention is considered "source reduction," the basis of the new EPA defin-ition developed as early as 1991, following the lead of the Pollution Prevention Act. In that definition, pollution prevention was stipulated as the equivalent of "source reduction" and seen as "the first step in a hier-archy of options for reducing the risks to human health and the environ-ment from pollution."[82] In this definition, "responsible" recycling and "safe" treatment methods, although acceptable if the wastes could not be "reduced at the source," would nevertheless not be considered "true" pol-lution prevention.[83] Through definitions provided by 33/50, however, participating companies specifically included recycling and treatment in their discussions of how 33/50 targets were to be accomplished.[84]

While EPA's new definition—parallel to the language used in the Pollution Prevention Act—created inconsistencies in its interpretation of 33/50 as pollution prevention, it did underline (through its elevation of source reduction to the top of a management hierarchy) the need for a new framework for pollution prevention. Such a need came to be most directly associated with the Agency's Source Reduction Review Project, initiated in 1992. The SRRP grew out of two initiatives: an attempt to review regulatory actions for the pulp and paper industry as a "cluster" or "sector" (an action precipitated in part by growing public criticism of the environmental impacts of chemical use by that industry); and the attempt to institutionalize a "pollution prevention culture" among senior Agency managers and within program offices, a process further defined by Section 4(b) of the Pollution Prevention Act which required EPA to "review regulations of the Agency prior and subsequent to their proposal to determine their effect on source reduction."[85]

The SRRP was first established by action of the appropriations committee within the EPA Administrator's Office as a means to get the managers of the powerful single-medium units to begin talking to each other. A SRRP workgroup was to consist of both Assistant and Deputy Administrators from those units plus a small staff for the Council itself. Meetings were to be arranged on a quarterly basis with perhaps two to three recommendations for pollution prevention initiatives at each meeting to be forwarded to the Administrator. The Council also sought to assure that the definition of pollution prevention as source reduction would guide such recommendations; that pollution prevention criteria would be employed in the rule development process (e.g., the use of chemical substitution as a form of compliance); and that industries that faced more than one rule would be selected for SRRP activity (in other words, instead of developing guidelines and rules that might, for example, govern chlorine use on a medium-by-medium basis, the concept of eliminating chlorine within an industry altogether would now guide the rule development process).[86]

The key to the SRRP was its focus on cluster industries. Sixteen additional industries, aside from pulp and paper, were selected for potential cross-medium/pollution prevention action. The Council would then facilitate industry-wide surveys, help evaluate different pollution prevention technologies, and conceivably synchronize regulatory timetables. The cluster approach could also allow for greater communication regarding multimedia or cross-media impacts (for example, examining whether the air regulations influencing the shift to water-based solvents might in fact be creating a new water quality problem). Most importantly, it could alter future rulemaking by incorporating cross-media and pollution prevention considerations into early stages, while seeking to integrate pollution prevention approaches into existing rules. Enforcement and permitting actions would also be critical since pollution prevention could be established as a settlement outcome and permitting and inspections could be structured to explore whether pollution prevention activity was being pursued. The logic of such an enforcement/permitting/inspection approach was to define regulatory action not by medium but by the "whole facility," an approach initiated on an experimental basis in Massachusetts but which had never been integrated into EPA's own permitting and enforcement activities nor into any of its state-mandated instructions.[87]

For SRRP to succeed, however, it required, as SRRP staff coordinator Eric Schaeffer put it, that the "media programs talk to each other," a process that faced numerous barriers and structural constraints. The program offices, with their rulemaking, standard-setting, permitting, and enforcement authorities, continued to define the locus of power and activity at the Agency. At best, the SRRP remained grafted on to that structure, an untested experiment in an Agency whose ways had solidified from twenty plus years of single-medium control and treatment-oriented legislation and rule making. At the same time, the Agency had clearly indicated a preference for voluntarism rather than regulatory action, an approach codified in the 1991 Pollution Prevention Strategy which stipulated that it would neither "expand EPA's existing authority" nor propose "new regulatory requirements." Rather, the Agency would "encourage voluntary actions by industry that reduce the need for EPA to take action under statutes like the Toxic Substances Control Act."[88]

At the same time, Agency officials in the new Clinton administration decided that the cluster approach and other pollution prevention initiatives lacked focus and were vulnerable to criticism about the lack of "stakeholder" input. In 1994, EPA Administrator Browner announced a new Common Sense Initiative (CSI) as a further attempt to refocus the Agency away from media-specific management to sectoral analysis. Six industries or sectors—auto manufacturing, computers and electronics, iron and steel, metal finishing and plating, petroleum refining, and printing—were selected for an approach that combined pollution prevention, regulatory review, more simplified record keeping and permit streamlining, and the promotion of innovative environmental technologies. The CSI program also sought to include industry, worker, and environmental stakeholders in its development, though each of the groups either remained skeptical of its intent (e.g., environmental criticism of the lack of resources provided to ensure participation). CSI continued the quest for new environmental management strategies, but faced obstacles associated with sharply divergent views of how to get there.[89]

Conclusion

The preference for voluntary action rather than regulatory intervention as illustrated in both legislation and rulemaking also paralleled the EPA's limited focus on environmental releases to the exclusion of other hazards or routes of exposure (i.e., those that were occupational or product-based). As TSCA's own history suggested, regulatory (or voluntary) action that ignored occupational and product-based concerns avoided confronting some of the most critical aspects of toxics use and greatly compounded the difficulties in framing any pollution prevention policy. While the search for pollution prevention policies remained problematic in environmental arenas, the barriers to prevention seemed even more insurmountable in other policymaking venues. Even within those environmental agency arenas, most notably at EPA, a pollution control "status quo" had become entrenched in the program offices and in the other structures of the Agency, with both budgets and mandates themselves dependent on the pollution control structure of environmental regulation. Ultimately, as the voluntarist-oriented Bush administration gave way to a Clinton administration which sought to maintain this voluntarist approach while pursuing limited new initiatives such as the chlorine ban feasibility study, pollution prevention remained little more than a popular concept embraced by policymakers, but without any effective basis for actually carrying out a prevention policy itself.

Notes

1. *Environmental Quality*, The Second Annual Report of the Council on Environmental Quality, pp. 17–18, (Washington, D.C.: Government Printing Office, 1971).

2. See the statement of Karen Florini, Environmental Defense Fund, in "Whatever Happened to the Toxic Substances Control Act," hearing before the Subcommittee on Environment, Energy, and Natural Resources of the House of Representative's Committee on Governmental Operations, 100th Congress, 2nd Session 134 (October 3, 1988).

3. A former member of the Council on Environmental Quality who coordinated Administration policy on TSCA through three Congressional sessions argued in 1994 testimony for TSCA reauthorization that it was the new chemical review provisions of Section 5 in TSCA which "aroused great controversy," in contrast to the broad reporting provisions of Section 8 or the testing authorities of Section 4 or even the broad controls available in Section 6. See testimony of Warren R. Muir before the United States Senate Committee on Environment and Public Works Subcommittee on Toxic Substances, Research and Development, May 17, 1994; See also, on Dow's opposition and the debates concerning TSCA, Luther Carter, "Toxic Substances: Five Year Struggle for Landmark Bill May Soon be Over," Science, vol. 194, no. 4260, October 1, 1976, pp. 40–42; Samuel Epstein, Lester O. Brown, and Carl Pope: *Hazardous Waste in America,* (San Francisco: Sierra Club Books, 1982).

4. On the Kepone episode see, "Kepone," Devra Lee Davis *et al.,* in *Basic Science Forcing Laws and Regulatory Case Studies: Kepone, DBCP, Halothane, Hexane and Carbaryl,* (Washington, D.C.: Environmental Law Institute, 1980); on BCME, see *Rohm and Haas: History of a Chemical Company,* Sheldon Hochheiser, (Philadelphia: University of Pennsylvania Press, 1986), pp. 168–177; Willard S. Randall & Stephen D. Solomon, *Building Six: The Tragedy at Bridesburg,* (Boston: Little Brown, 1976).

5. See Toxic Substances Control Act 15 USC 2605 § 6(e).

6. 15 § 2604(e).

7. 15 § 2601 [Section 2(b)(2)].

8. 15 § 2601 [Section 2(b)(3)].

9. Statement by George Bonina, deputy director of the Information Management Division, OPPT, U.S. EPA in "TSCA and CBI Review," October 14, 1992, p. 2.

10. See H. Reid testimony in "Implementation of the Toxic Substances Control Act," Hearing before a Subcommittee on Toxic Substances, Environmental Oversight, Research and Development, U.S. Senate, March 25, 1992, p. 30.

11. 15 § 2603.

12. See the testimony of R. Hembra in "The Failure of the Toxic Substances Testing Program," Hearing before the Environment, Energy, and Natural Resources Subcommittee of the Committee on Government Operations, House of Representatives, June 20, 1990, p. 13.

13. Testimony of Linda Fisher, Assistant Administrator of the Office of Prevention, Pesticides and Toxic Substances (OPPT) in Hearings (note 10).

14. See Linda Fisher testimony, *op cit.*

15. See Linda Fisher testimony, note 7, p. 43.

16. "Influence of CBI Requirements on TSCA Implementation," March 1992, Hampshire Research Associates, Inc., Alexandria, VA, EPA Contract Number: 68-DO-0165/68-DO-0200.

17. See "Influence of CBI Requirements on TSCA Implementation," Hampshire Research Associates, Inc. March 1992, p. 25 (hereafter referred to as "Hampshire Report").

18. See the testimony of EPA official Scott Sherlock, in "Environmental Protection Agency Public Hearing: TSCA and CBI Review," October 14, 1992, p. 9.

19. Hampshire Report, p. 18.

20. "Final Action Plan: TSCA Confidential Business Information Reform," June 24, 1994. U.S. Environmental Protection Agency Office of Prevention, Pesticides, and Toxic Substances, in the Office of Pollution Prevention and Toxics.

21. Testimony of Warren R. Muir, Ph.D., president, Hampshire Research before the United States Senate Committee on Environment and Public Works Subcommittee on Toxic Substances, Research and Development on Reauthorization of the Toxic Substances Control Act, May 17, 1994.

22. Muir, Testimony in TSCA Reauthorization, May 17, 1994.

23. Nelson, R. and S. Winter, *An Evolutionary Theory of Economic Change*, (Cambridge, MA: Harvard University Press, 1982); Amendola, M. and J.L Gaffard, *The Innovative Choice: An Economic Analysis of the Dynamics of Technology*, (New York: Basil Blackwell, 1988).

24. Even where EPA has sought to invoke TSCA powers directly to force production changes [as with its Section 6(d) immediate rulemaking], should the Agency find a chemical substance "likely to result in an unreasonable risk of serious or widespread injury to health and the environment," it has had to retreat in the face of legal challenges, as with its Asbestos Ban and Phaseout Rule. Asbestos was in fact the first substance to be considered for regulatory action under this section since PCBs, but the Fifth Circuit Court of Appeals, in *Corrosion Proof Fittings v. EPA*, challenged the Agency's interpretation of the necessary steps to be taken in its rulemaking, specifically EPA's risk analysis techniques of accessing exposure, the risks of substitutes, and the regulatory costs involved. EPA interpreted the court ruling to assume that the Agency now had burden of proof responsibilities; in effect, this undercut the intent of TSCA and paralyzed EPA's use of Section 6(d) powers. 947 F. 2d 1201 (5th Circuit, Oct 18, 1991, p. 1229).

25. EPA's approach to TSCA, including its approach to CBI claims, ultimately came under increasing criticism from environmental and public

interest groups, with OPPT recommending changes (during TSCA reauthorization proceedings in 1994) that did meet some of those criticisms. In
the area of CBI, EPA's proposed changes included requiring companies to
substantiate CBI claims, requiring a senior company official to sign CBI
claims, and more broadly defining "health and safety studies" to reduce
potential secrecy claims. EPA's proposed changes, however, did not provide
for eliminating provisions that allowed the company name and address to
remain secret, establishing a sunset provision for current CBI claims, making data more accessible, or establishing provisions to address false CBI
claims. Beyond CBI, another significant battleground between community
and industry groups had become the question of state access to TSCA data.
Despite EPA's efforts to promote TSCA reauthorization, it still remained a
far more limited legislative priority even within its commitment to pollution prevention than its parallel efforts around reauthorization of the Clean
Water Act and Superfund. On the CBI issues, see "Confidential Data
Reform Ahead," in *Working Notes on Community Right-to-Know*,
March–April 1994, p. 2. The reauthorization hearings for TSCA began in
May 1994 before the Senate Committee on Environment and Public
Works Subcommittee on Toxic Substances, Research and Development.

26. Linda Fisher testimony, p. 45.

27. HSWA, PL 98–616 Sec. 1002(b), Title 42 § 6901 (*et seq.*).

28. RCRA, 42 U.S.C. Section 6922(a)(6)(C) (as amended November 8,
1984), see 40 CFR Section 262(a)(6) (1987).

29. Despite being touted as the most aggressive federal mandate for pollution prevention documentation to date, the information gathered from
the biennial reports contributed predictably little to clarifying either problem or solution. As a National Wildlife Federation staff member testified in
hearings on the subject:

> Responsible in part for the failure to collect relevant information
> is the biennial reporting form itself. The 1985 biennial report was
> the first to request generator waste reduction information. Part
> XVI of that report requested information on "Waste
> Minimization—[narrative description]." The agency gave so lit-
> tle guidance to generators concerning what constitutes "waste
> minimization," that respondents often cited waste treatment
> technologies outside the scope of even EPA's broad definition of
> the term, merely quoted the certification language [stating they
> had a program to reduce waste in place], admitted having taken
> no waste reduction efforts or else simply allowed Part XVI to
> remain blank.

See "Oversight of Right-to-Know Pollution Data: Hearing Before the Subcommittee on Superfund, Ocean, and Water Protection of the Senate Committee on Environment and Public Works," 101st Congress, 1st Session, 38 (May 10, 1989), statement of Gerald Poje.

30. Clean Air Act of 1970, 42 § 7400.

31. 42 § 7408(b) as amended in 1977.

32. Prior to passage of the 1990 Clean Air Act Amendments, only a handful of hazardous air pollutants had been regulated (including asbestos, benzene, beryllium, mercury, radionuclides, radon-222, and vinyl chloride) for a limited number of sources specific to each pollutant. Mercury emissions, for example, had been regulated for mercury ore processing, mercury chlor-alkali cell production, and sewage treatment sludge incineration, but not for coal-fired power plant emissions.

33. "Project 88—Harnessing Market Forces to Protect Our Environment: Initiatives for the New President," A Public Policy Study sponsored by Senator Timothy E. Wirth, Colorado, and Senator John Heinz, Pennsylvania, (Washington, D.C., Dec. 1988).

34. See P.L. 101-549, November 15, 1990, 104 Stat. 2399, Title 42 § 7400 (*et seq.*).

35. 42 § 7412.

36. 42 § 7651.

37. 42 § 7403. Title VI (Stratospheric Ozone Protection), developed as a formal response to the 1987 Montreal Protocols, also included provisions establishing a schedule for phasing out the use of specific ozone depleting compounds such as chlorofluorocarbons (CFCs), carbon tetrachloride, methyl chloroform, and hydrochlorofluorocarbons (HCFCs). Unlike Title IV, however, no specific incentives or regulatory instruments were mandated or proposed to accomplish reduction objectives.

38. 42 § 7412(b).

39. 42 § 7412(b)(2).

40. 42 § 7412(f)(2)(A).

41. 42 § 7412(i)(5).

42. 42 § 7671.

43. 42 § 7671(f).

44. 42 § 7403(a).

45. 42 § 7403(g).

46. See testimony of Carolyn Hartmann, U.S. Public Interest Research Group, before the Senate Environment and Public Works Committee Subcommittee on Clean Water, Fisheries and Wildlife on "Toxic Pollution Prevention in the Clean Water Act, July 1, 1993; see also testimony of

Jessica Landman, senior attorney, Natural Resources Defense Council at the same hearing, July 1, 1993.

47. Clean Water Act, Title 33 § 1251(a); also personal communication with Kate English, 1993.

48. See "Study of Chlorine and Chlorinated Compounds" in President Clinton's Proposal for the Clean Water Act, January 28, 1994, pp. 22–24.

49. See *The Product is the Poison: The Case for a Chlorine Phase-out,* Joe Thornton, (Washington D.C.: Greenpeace Great Lakes Project, 1991); "Recognizing and Addressing the Hazards of Chlorinated Organic Chemicals," resolution passed 10/28/93, Annual Meeting of the American Public Health Association, San Francisco; *A Strategy for Virtual Elimination of Persistent Toxic Substances,* (Windsor, Canada: International Joint Commission on the Great Lakes, 1993).

50. The legislative director for Greenpeace's Toxics Campaign called the chlorine study announcement "the most meaningful position taken by the Administration in keeping with their campaign rhetoric on pollution prevention, since they have taken office." Cited in "Clinton and Senators Detail Ambitious Measures for Cleaner Water," John H. Cushman Jr., *New York Times,* February 2, 1994.

51. Waste Reduction Act, Title 42 § 6901 (*et seq.*); Pollution Prevention Act, 42 § 13101 (*et seq.*).

52. Testimony of William K. Reilly, Administrator, Environmental Protection Agency before the Subcommittee on Transportation and Hazardous Materials Committee on Energy and Commerce, U.S. House of Representatives, May 25, 1989, "Consideration of H.R. 1457, The Waste Reduction Act."

53. Pollution Prevention Act of 1990, 42 § 13103.

54. Jurisdictional issues were frequently defined in terms of a single-medium bias; that is, committees which had oversight over one set of environmental issues defined by the medium involved (e.g., air, water, or land pollution). These committees and their chairs would at times seek to contest or bottleneck legislation if their committees were excluded from the review process, or, most frequently, would claim jurisdiction despite efforts to identify legislation as having a cross-media purpose, such as the Pollution Prevention Act. Interview with Kate English, 1993.

55. The one notable exception to the final industry approach of support or neutrality of the Pollution Prevention Act was the 3M company, which remained adamantly opposed to the provisions excluding recycling and treatment in the definition of pollution prevention (see Chapter 12).

56. Prior to passage of the Pollution Prevention Act, the Bush administration had unsuccessfully introduced its own pollution prevention bill that

had been centered on solid waste issues and reflected EPA's primary focus on RCRA in driving waste policy.

57. Pollution Prevention Act, 42 § 13101(b); see also, Stephen M. Johnson, "From Reaction to Proaction: The 1990 Pollution Prevention Act," *Columbia Journal of Environmental Law,* Vol. 17, No. 1, pp. 153–204 and interviews with Eric Schaeffer and Kate English (all 1993).

58. Pollution Prevention Act of 1990, 42 § 13107(a).

59. Executive Order 12856 of August 3, 1993, "Federal Compliance with Right-to-Know Laws and Pollution Prevention Requirements."

60. Pollution Prevention Act of 1990, 42 § 13105–13106.

61. Capacity Assurance Plans, Section 104(c)(9) of the Comprehensive Environmental Response, Compensation and Liability Act, Title 42 § 9601 (*et seq.*).

62. See EPA Assistant Administrator James Barnes testifying before the U.S. House of Representatives' Energy and Commerce Committee's Transportation, Tourism, and Hazardous Materials Subcommittee....A separate waste [reduction] office within EPA would "serve to diffuse the [agency's] effort, not intensify it," as cited in Gary Cohen and John O'Connor, eds., *Fighting Toxics: A Manual for Protecting Your Family, Community and Workplace,* (Washington, D.C.: Island Press, 1990) p. 304.

63. EPA Pollution Prevention Statement, January 26, 1989, Federal Register 54 CFR 3845-3847.

64. Gerald Kotas, U.S. Environmental Protection Agency in "The Environmental Professional," Vol. 11, pp. 185–189, (Washington, D.C.: Government Printing Office, 1989) EPA/0191-5398/89.

65. By 1991, the first year the additional data mandated by the Pollution Prevention Act for TRI reporting became available, the enormous preferences for off-site recycling was still striking. Of the production-related quantities in waste, 3.3 billion pounds alone were from off-site recycling compared with 3.8 billion pounds of total quantities released to air, land, and water. Even more striking was that the quantities released were only 10 percent of the total production-related quantities (which included both on- and off-site recycling, on- and off-site energy recovery, and off-site treatment). 1991 Toxics Release Inventory: Public Data Release, Office of Pollution Prevention and Toxics, May 1993, EPA-745-R-93-003, May 1993. See also EPA's 33/50 Program Second Progress Report: Reducing Risks through Voluntary Action. U.S. Environmental Protection Agency, Office of Pollution Prevention and Toxics, EPA/TS-792A, February, 1992.

66. Interview with Eric Schaeffer, 1993.

67. Pollution Prevention Statement, January 26, 1989.

68. Freeman, Harry, U.S. Environmental Protection Agnecy Pollution

Prevention Research Branch, Current Projects, Risk Reduction Engineering Library, Cinncinnati, OH, 1990.

69. Interview with Jocelyn Woodman, 1991.

70. January 26, 1989 Statement 54 FR 3845.

71. Roy also felt that his efforts in identifying and pursuing pollution prevention opportunities would be more effective outside the Agency. Interview with Manik Roy, 1993. However, in 1994 Roy was offered a new position at EPA (as Director of the Pollution Prevention Policy Staff in the Office of the Administrator), which he accepted.

72. Interviews with the following EPA staff: Jocelyn Woodman, 1990; Elizabeth Cameron, 1990; and Eric Schaeffer, 1993. Data derived from Pollution Prevention Strategy Summary, 1989–1991 EIES database for the following EPA offices: Pesticides and Toxic Substances; Air and Radiation; Policy Planning and Evaluation; Water; Solid Waste; and Regions 1, 2, 4, 9, and 10.

73. G. Kotas, *op cit.*

74. EPA 1991 Pollution Prevention Strategy, Federal Register, Vol. 56, p. 7850; EPA's 33/50 Program Second Progress Report, *op cit.*

75. EPA's 33/50 Program Second Progress Report, *op cit.*; interview with Eric Schaeffer, EPA, 1993.

76. "Right-to-know legislation has been a major contributor to what the public knows about environmental performance and how it views industry," asserted one *Chemical and Engineering News* article, commenting on TRI and programs like 33/50. See Ann M. Thayer, "Growing Exchange of Information Spurs Pollution Prevention Efforts," *Chemical and Engineering News,* July 26, 1993, p. 8.

77. EPA's 33/50 Program Second Progress Report: Reducing Risks through Voluntary Action. U.S. EPA Office of Pollution Prevention and Toxics, TS-792A, February, 1992.

78. 1991 TRI figures revealed that on-site treatment, energy recovery, and recycling accounted for 77 percent of total production-related quantities in waste compared with only 10 percent for pollutant releases—the yardstick of 33/50; 1991 Toxics Release Inventory: Public Data Release, *op cit.*

79. For example, a survey undertaken by the public interest group, Citizen Action, discovered that 47 of 50 companies reported reductions of TRI chemicals based on "changes by EPA in the chemical releases that had to be reported, changes in waste estimation techniques, lower levels of production, or other factors beyond the control of the facility, such as decreased runoff due to less rainfall." See Manufacturing Pollution, (Washington, D.C.: Citizen Action, 1992) cited in "Waste Solution Must Involve Water, Air, Land" Manik Roy and Eric V. Schaeffer, *Forum for*

Applied Research and Public Policy, Spring 1993, Vol. 8, No. 1, pp. 116–124; see also "Phantom Reductions," (Washington, D.C.: National Wildlife Federation, 1990).

80. EPA's 33/50 Program Second Progress Report, *op cit.*; see also, "A Voluntary Approach to Environmental Regulation," Seema Arora and Timothy N. Cason, *Resources,* No. 116, Summer 1994, pp. 6–10.

81. When EPA sought to establish in 1994 a 33/50 Project award ceremony for specific companies meeting their 33/50 targets at a "Promoting Pollution Prevention by Voluntary Initiatives" conference in Williamsburg, Virginia, environmental and public interest groups called on EPA to cancel the awards on the grounds that the program ignored off-site shipments to recycling and that reductions specified on-site might have included control methods or even hidden off-site shipments not recorded. See Working Notes on Community Right-to-Know, March–April 1994, p. 2.

82. It should be noted that occupational and product-based exposures were not included in this definition.

83. Environmental Protection Agency Pollution Prevention Strategy, Federal Register, February 26, 1991, Vol. 56 No. 38, p. 7855.

84. For example, Chevron chairman K.T. Derr, in a letter to EPA Administrator William Reilly, argued that while the company would "stress source reduction, meeting the goal [of 33/50 reductions] will require the use of recycling and treatment." Letter from K. T. Derr to William Reilly, May 10, 1991; Dow Chemical's chair Frank Popoff argued along the same lines, stating "*to the maximum extent possible,* we will rely on source reduction and *recycling* in preference to other methods for achieving emission reduction" (emphasis added). Letter from Frank Popoff to William Reilly, April 29, 1991.

85. Pollution Prevention Act, 42 § 13103(b)(2).

86. U.S. Environmental Protection Agency, "Source Reduction and Review Project," Office of Pollution Prevention and Toxics, EPA/100/R-92/002, (Washington, D.C.: Government Printing Office, August, 1992); U.S. Environmental Protection Agency, "Source Reduction and Review Project: Guidelines for EPA Work Groups," Office of the Administrator and Office of Pollution Prevention and Toxics, EPA/100/R-92/003, (Washington, D.C.: Government Printing Office, August, 1992); interview with Eric Schaeffer, 1993.

87. "Waste Solution Must Involve Water, Air, Land," Manik Roy and Eric V. Schaeffer, *Forum for Applied Research and Public Policy,* Vol. 7, No. 1, Spring 1992, pp. 116–124

88. EPA Pollution Prevention Strategy, Federal Register, Vol. 56, p. 7850, February 26, 1991.

89. See "Browner Names Six Industries in Plan to Improve

Environmental Protection," U.S. Environmental Protection Agency, Communications, Education and Public Affairs, R-177, July 20, 1994; "Crossing Agency Boundaries," W.C. Cleland-Hamnet and J. Retzer, *The Environmental Forum,* March–April 1993.

4

Disassociating Toxics Policies: Occupational Risk and Product Hazards

John Froines
Robert Gottlieb
Maureen Smith
Pamela Yates

The Problem of the Workplace

The limits to constructing a new approach in environmental policy beyond media-specific regulations and related emphasis on treatment and control extended to other policy arenas where the toxics issue had emerged. These limits were further magnified by the divorce of environmental policy from other policy settings. Such a divorce was most acutely felt in relation to workplace hazards. In 1976, Nicholas Ashford, an MIT professor and director of its Center for Policy Alternatives, argued along these lines in his classic text *Crisis in the Workplace:* "Efforts to clean up the factory may result in polluting the general environment, and, conversely, efforts to 'contain the pollution' may mean increased pollution within the plant," Ashford wrote. "The problems of the general and workplace environments are thus intimately connected and must be attacked together."[1] Following the creation of EPA in 1971 and the Occupational Safety and Health Administration in 1970 and continuing thereafter during the nearly two decades since Ashford's words were written, regulatory and policy frameworks with respect to workplace and environment have remained distinct—a separation that has significantly reinforced the end-of-pipe emphasis of the government's approach to the toxics issue.

During the first half of the twentieth century, exposure to toxics in the workplace received far less attention than occupational injuries, job-related accidents, and the development of worker compensation laws. Only well-known toxicants such as lead, silica, and beryllium received any kind of focus from occupational health scientists. While there was recognition that certain materials, such as asbestos, could create occupational hazards (i.e., a chronic lung disease called asbestosis), there was little appreciation of their carcinogenic potential. Aside from the notable efforts of occupational health pioneers like Alice Hamilton and the well-publicized disasters such as Gauley Bridge where hundreds of workers died from silicosis, occupational exposures to toxics and hazardous materials were largely ignored as workplace hazards. Little attention was given to prevention of occupational disease, even though the effects of lead, silica, and other chemical agents were recognized.[2] Congressional hearings held as a result of the Gauley Bridge disaster focused not on prevention of silicosis through social legislation, but more on the adequacy of worker's compensation. At the 1936 hearings, then Congressman Jennings Randolph stated that only 11 states in the U.S. had laws in which silicosis was compensable.[3] By the end of 1937, 46 states had enacted compensation laws covering workers with silicosis, but there was little legislation establishing preventive strategies for occupational disease.[4]

After World War II, with the dramatic expansion of the chemical industry and the introduction of tens of thousands of new toxic and hazardous substances, occupational hazard issues changed substantively and quantitatively, both in relation to the manufacture and the downstream use of these agents. There also emerged compelling evidence that older, widely recognized toxicants such as lead and silica remained uncontrolled at the workplace and in the general environment. Indeed, recent data in the United States continues to indicate that exposure to high levels of lead and silica can be found across a broad range of industries, and that measurements of lead levels in the blood of workers reveal a large danger of lead-related illness. Exposure in the workplace to other recognized toxicants such as beryllium, mercury, asbestos, arsenic, chromium, and organic solvents also continues to be well-documented, further suggesting that attempts to eliminate health hazards from exposure to specific toxic chemicals whose effects are well characterized, have been largely unsuccessful.

Diseases associated with exposure to modern chemicals have been identified in recent years. The numerous cancers derived from exposure to the toxic chemicals bischloromethyl ether (BCME) and vinyl chloride became signposts in the 1970s, indicating that exposure to chemical carcinogens in the workplace conceivably represented an occupational health problem of major proportions. Exposure of workers to the pesticide dibromochloropropane (DBCP) in Lathrop, California during this same period also demonstrated that certain organic chemicals can have adverse effects on reproductive capacity. In this instance, male workers in the Lathrop plant became sterile as a result of workplace exposure to this pesticide.[5]

During the 1970s, there were other key examples of occupational exposures to toxics resulting in serious illnesses. For instance, outbreaks of neurological disease related to occupational exposure to methyl butyl ketone, dimethylaminopropionitrile (DMAPN),[6] kepone, and Lucel-7 were all substantially documented.[7] Each of these four agents produces extremely debilitating neurological diseases which have potential long-term consequences on the exposed worker's central and peripheral nervous systems. Interestingly, while the outbreaks associated with these four chemicals were severe, they also came to represent examples of pollution prevention insofar as three of the four chemicals were removed from production in the United States and no longer represented a workplace threat in this country. A similar reduction success story came to be associated with the banning of DBCP, although trace amounts of DBCP continued to be found in groundwater wells throughout California more than fifteen years after the pesticide was barred from production and use in the United States.[8] It is also worth noting that exposure to acrylonitrile, vinyl chloride, and DBCP occurred primarily during the manufacture and subsequent preparation and/or formulation of plastics, whereas the most notable exposures to the neurotoxicants cited above occurred during the use of those products in manufacturing other goods.

The methods available for evaluating chemical carcinogens, reproductive toxicants, or neurotoxins have markedly advanced since these outbreaks of occupational exposures that occurred during the mid and late 1970s. Today, it has become more possible to identify the toxicity of these agents prior to their introduction to the market and to either substitute alternatives or establish different designs of production processes to eliminate thier use. However, while detection capabilities have advanced, the regulatory framework established to deal with workplace exposures has not addressed these issues.

The first occupational safety and health legislation enacted in the United States occurred at the state level. Massachusetts passed legislation in 1852 and 1877, and by 1890, 22 states had promulgated regulations of safety in mining and 14 had enacted legislation providing for industrial workplace inspections.[8] Still, as the Office of Technology Assessment pointed out, there was, on average, only one occupational health staff member at the state level for every 108,000 workers. State safety and health programs were underfunded, lacked authority, or in many states were even nonexistent—a situation that still prevailed into the 1960s.[9]

The first federal legislation providing protection of workers was the Walsh–Healy Act of 1936, later supplemented by the McNamara–O'Hara Act of 1966, and the Construction Safety Act of 1969. These laws covered employees working for employers who had contracts with the federal government and required those employers to comply with Walsh–Healy safety and health standards. Inspections were conducted by the Bureau of Labor Standards, and penalties included "blacklisting"—the prohibition of bidding on federal contracts for up to 3 years. These Acts clearly affected workplace conditions, but, overall, the performance of these agencies indicated a need for more comprehensive federal legislation. A Department of Labor study described as "inadequate" and "fragmented" the nation's health and safety laws.[10] By 1968, President Lyndon Johnson proposed federal legislation to establish safety and health regulatory programs that would provide for occupational standards, but the legislation never reached the floor of Congress. However, the stage was set for legislation that was to follow, and for a new era in occupational health policy.

The Occupational Safety and Health Act

As the 1960s came to a close, it was apparent that new policies were needed to address health and safety in the 5 million workplaces that employed approximately 90 million workers in jobs ranging from service/clerical work to high technology professional employment to heavy industry with its myriad of recognized health and safety hazards. It was estimated at the time that 14,000 employees were dying annually in accidental deaths; that there were injuries resulting in 2 million lost workdays each year; and that an estimated 390,000 new cases and 100,000 deaths were occurring annually from occupational disease.[11] Ultimately, new legislation, both broad in scope and representing a major step forward in providing protection for the tens of millions of American workers, was introduced. Though significant as breakthrough legislation, the new Occupational Safety and Health Act, like its environmental counterparts discussed in earlier chapters, nevertheless failed to address the issue of pollution prevention.

The purpose of the OSH Act was "to assure so far as possible every working man and woman in the Nation safe and healthful working conditions." The legislation established two agencies to implement the Act: the Occupational Safety and Health Administration (OSHA) for enforcement purposes, and the National Institute for Occupational Safety and Health (NIOSH) to undertake research related to the Act's goals and programs. The OSH Act was structured to deal with worker health and safety by "authorizing enforcement of standards...."[12] The Act provided for NIOSH to conduct research on occupational disease-derived exposure to toxic chemical and physical agents. This research was to lead to the development of mandatory occupational safety and health standards to be enforced through unannounced inspections. Establishing appropriate health and safety standards represented the central theme of the Act. Those standards were to be the foundation of the enforcement program as well as the basis for education and training and voluntary compliance.

The central role of the Occupational Safety and Health Administration (OSHA) (located in the Department of Labor) was the promulgation and enforcement of standards in businesses and industries within the jurisdiction of the Act. Standards were considered crucial because they defined the minimum level of health and safety practice for industry to meet. They formed the basis around which a business would plan its health and safety program, and they provided information for workers on appropriate conditions for their work environment. The adequacy and enforcement of standards was therefore to be a crucial test of the effectiveness of the administering agencies.

In contrast to its more developed research and enforcement provisions, the OSH Act failed to address toxics reduction in the workplace. Reduction strategies such as substance bans or product substitutions and process changes were not included in the legislation. It provided no guidelines for OSHA (or EPA) with respect to the intersection of environmental and occupational hazards and exposures. The regulatory philosophy embodied in the Act establishes enforcement of occupational health standards as the primary approach to controlling workplace exposures, with the emphasis on meeting specific limits; presumably through the use of traditional control technology such as ventilation and enclosure rather than substitution. The basis of this approach derives from earlier assumptions that there are safe levels of exposure to chemical agents and that threshold levels exist below which there are no adverse effects. It is now recognized, however, that certain chemical agents, including a large number of chemical carinogens, some reproductive toxicants, and one of the most widely recognized toxicants, lead, do not have an apparent threshold. To maximize worker protection, product substitution or process change or reformulation would be significantly more protective.

The Role of Standards

Following passage of the OSH Act, OSHA immediately faced the issue of how to establish standards to begin an enforcement effort. The Act provided a two-year time frame during which OSHA could adopt existing standards developed by consensus standards bodies or already promulgated applicable federal standards. These standards would be exempt from the rulemaking procedures required by the Administrative Procedure Act, and they would be immediately effective.

In the health area, OSHA adopted recommendations developed by two "consensus" standards organizations, the American National Standards Institute (ANSI), and the American Conference of Governmental Industrial Hygienists (ACGIH), founded in 1938 by industrial hygienists employed in government agencies.

ACGIH is noteworthy because of its development of "threshold limit values" (TLVs). TLVs refer to the airborne concentrations of chemical substances and physical agents to which nearly all workers may be repeatedly exposed day after day without adverse health effects. Using its authority under Section 6(a) of the Act, OSHA adopted the 1968 TLVs which had previously been incorporated in 1969 by the Bureau of Labor Standards using the authority in the Walsh–Healy Act. Approximately 400 chemicals were included in this list. Since 1971, OSHA has adopted 24 permanent standards, but the 1968 TLVs remain the operative standards for most of the chemicals regulated by OSHA. There is today, however, a growing consensus that many of the TLVs are inadequate and do not provide necessary protection to workers.[13]

The ACGIH TLVs and ANSI standards that were adopted by OSHA define the maximum level of exposure to which a worker may be exposed over a workshift. The intent of such standards has been to limit exposure through traditional control technology rather than through substitution or elimination by process redesign, as would be embodied in a pollution prevention strategy.

Establishing permanent occupational safety and health standards was envisioned by Congress as being central to achieving the goals of the OSH Act. In order for the agency to establish permanent standards, it was necessary for Congress to define the criteria that OSHA would use in promulgating standards. If those criteria were vague, they would lead to standards being continually challenged in the courts and therefore defeat the Act's objectives. If they were too strictly defined, it was felt, they might place the agency in a regulatory straitjacket.

Section 6(b)(5) of the Act states the criteria that the Secretary of Labor must meet in promulgating permanent standards for toxic materials or harmful physical agents. "The Secretary...shall set the standard which most adequately assures, to the extent feasible, on the basis of the best available evidence, that no employee will suffer material impairment of health or

functional capacity even if such employee has regular exposure to the hazard dealt with by such standard for the period of his working life." Key
areas of debate that emerged included what Congress meant by the terms
feasibility and *material impairment*. The former has particular relevance once
the Agency begins to address the issue of the type of controls appropriate
to limit exposure to safe levels.

The term "to the extent feasible" represents the core language in
Section 6(b) that addresses the criteria for standard setting under the OSH
Act within the context of pollution prevention. The U.S. Supreme Court
addressed the issue of feasibility in its decision upholding OSHA's standard
for controlling exposure to cotton dust, the term used to define worker
exposure to airborne particulates in the textile industry.[14] Since Congress
had not provided a specific definition of "feasible," the court sought to
determine the meaning of the term by going to *Webster's Third New
International Dictionary*, the *English Oxford Dictionary*, and *Funk and Wagnall's
New Standard Dictionary*. In this manner, *feasible* can be defined, literally, as
"capable of being done," and thus the court ruled that Section 6(b)(5)
directs the Secretary to issue the standard that "most adequately
assures...that no employee will suffer material impairment of health," limited only by the extent to which this is "capable of being done."

Several other major decisions on feasibility arose in court cases involving coke oven emissions[15] and lead.[16] Coke oven emissions have been
causally associated in epidemiologic studies with increased risks of lung
cancer, and OSHA had moved to regulate these exposures in the late
1970s. In its decision, the District Court of Appeals ruled that OSHA can
impose a standard which requires an employer to implement technology
"looming on today's horizon" and is not limited to issuing a standard solely
based upon technology that is fully developed today.

The court also clarified the meaning of economic feasibility in this standard. It determined that a standard is not economically infeasible because
it is financially burdensome or even because it threatens the survival of
some companies within an industry.

> Nor does the concept of economic feasibility necessarily guaran-
> tee the continued existence of individual employers. It would
> appear consistent with the Act to envisage economic demise of
> an employer who has lagged behind the rest of the industry in
> protecting the health and safety of employees and is consequently
> financially unable to comply with new standards as quickly as
> other employers.[17]

However, the court ruled that a standard could be considered economically infeasible if an entire industry were dislocated, that is, if it affected the competitive stability of an industry or led to undue concentration.

In the lead decision, the U.S. Supreme Court also acknowledged that providing a reasonable time for an industry to comply with a standard would result in an enhancement of economic feasibility and prevent injury to competition. The time provided for compliance with a new standard could therefore be considered an important variable in defining the economic feasibility of the standard.

Each of these decisions has specific relevance in determining whether OSHA has authority under the OSH Act for the use of pollution prevention strategies for controlling occupational exposures to toxic chemicals. There is nothing in the Act, nor in the legal decisions that have followed, that precludes OSHA from banning substances or requiring the use of substitutes or process change, as long as the standard meets the court's requirement of "feasibility"; that is, "can it be done." For example, substitution of one chemical for another is certainly acceptable if a less toxic chemical is available and its introduction will not result in severe economic dislocation of an entire industry. OSHA could accept the use of ventilation and respirators over an extended period of time but require implementation of a pollution prevention strategy that was "looming on the horizon" at the time of the promulgation of the standard, if it provided a suitable period of time for introduction of the new technology or substance.

While nothing in the original Act precludes the use of pollution prevention, there is no specific language that provides a positive framework for the use of this approach to controlling workplace hazards (in contrast to the provisions found in the Toxic Substances Control Act, see Chapter 3). As with TSCA, neither Congress nor the executive branch has sought to amend the OSH Act to incorporate a pollution prevention framework. OSHA itself has, in fact, rarely considered pollution prevention strategies throughout its 25-year history. Instead, the agency has focused more narrowly on the use of respiratory protection rather than requiring implementation of engineering controls. This focus contrasts sharply with approaches in environmental policymaking where respiratory protection for the public has never been considered as an alternative to control technology, let alone pollution prevention strategies for process or product changes. Such a debate over approaches has only occurred with respect to workplace settings.[18]

In fact, none of the permanent standards promulgated by OSHA since the passage of the Act has addressed substitution or banning of a substance with the exception of a generic cancer policy (established during the Carter administration but never implemented). Ultimately, the failure to pursue pollution prevention as a means of controlling exposures emerged more as a matter of Agency policy and as a result of a lack of research on chemical and process substitutes than ambiguities in the Act itself. For OSHA, confronting the range and breadth of workplace hazards came to be defined as a question of which set of controls to adopt. Standard setting and regulation of workplace exposures then became not so much a scientific activity designed to identify a safe level of exposure, but rather a public policy question about the level of risk that would be deemed acceptable.

Acceptable Risk—Benzene

The question of acceptable risk was particularly highlighted in the late 1970s during the debates over benzene exposures in the workplace. In 1978, OSHA promulgated a permanent standard for benzene which reduced the permissible exposure limit (PEL) from 10 parts per million (ppm) averaged over an 8-hour workday to 1 ppm in order to reduce the risk of leukemia from exposure to benzene in the work environment. The evidence in the record for benzene firmly established a causal relationship between benzene exposure and leukemia. The permanent OSHA standard was first litigated before the Fifth Circuit Court of Appeals which invalidated the standard, and, later, before the U.S. Supreme Court which upheld the Appeals Court ruling.[19] In the benzene decision, the U.S. Supreme Court ruled that OSHA had a duty to demonstrate whether a specific toxic substance poses a significant health risk in the workplace and that any new, stricter standard had to be shown to be "reasonably necessary." In other words, the agency now had an affirmative duty to demonstrate in its rulemaking for a toxic substance that a stricter standard be considered reasonably necessary, by showing an incremental benefit in terms of lives saved, disease avoided, or some other criterion in reducing the standard from one level to another.

A problem in OSHA's developing standards for toxic substances is that the evidence for health effects is often collected at levels of workplace exposure to the chemical in question. These exposures, in turn, are substantially greater than the exposure which is being considered for regulation. Animal studies are often conducted at very high administered doses of the chemical in question, known as the "maximum tolerated dose." Even in the case of human epidemiology, the exposures are often greater than the projected regulation precisely because of the need for protection at levels that would not produce overt disease. OSHA must mathematically extrapolate from the higher dose or exposure levels where studies have been conducted to lower hypothetical doses or exposure levels which have been defined as being "safe" as a matter of regulatory policy.[17]

At the time of the benzene rulemaking, OSHA defended its policy of setting the PEL for a carcinogen at the lowest "feasible" level because there was no threshold for chemical carcinogens, and therefore, no absolutely "safe" level. The risk of developing cancer from exposure to benzene increased linearly from zero dose and there was a risk of disease at any measurable exposure. In its decision invalidating the benzene standard, the Supreme Court declared that "the Agency [OSHA] applied its standard policy with respect to carcinogens, concluding that, in the absence of definitive proof of a safe level, it must be assumed that *any* level above zero presents *some* increased risk of cancer." The court rejected this argument and stated that OSHA has an affirmative duty to demonstrate that a place of employment is unsafe insofar as significant risks are present and can be reduced or eliminated by a change in the standard. OSHA also has a duty to meet the feasibility requirements of the OSH Act, but it must first demonstrate that a significant risk is present.

The Supreme Court did agree that experimental (animal) evidence is appropriate for use in defining significant risk. In fact, it ruled that OSHA has substantial leeway in defining significant risk: "As several courts of appeals have held, this provision requires a reviewing court to give OSHA some leeway where its findings must be made on the frontiers of scientific knowledge. Thus, so long as they are supported by a body of reputable scientific thought, the Agency is free to use conservative assumptions in interpreting data with respect to carcinogens, risking error on the side of overprotection rather than under-protection."

What then constitutes "significant risk" in chemical carcinogenesis? Since there is often no threshold for carcinogenesis, there is risk at any level of exposure. In environmental settings, the risk of one excess cancer in a million persons has generally been considered the standard for significant risk. The Environmental Protection Agency (EPA) has adopted a general policy that a lifetime cancer risk of one in 10,000 for the most exposed person might constitute acceptable risk and that the margin of safety should reduce the risk for the greatest possible number of persons to an individual lifetime risk of no higher than one in 1 million. The Supreme Court was not explicit in its findings. It stated that a risk of one excess cancer in a million persons is not significant, but that a risk of one in a thousand would be considered significant. But that left six orders of magnitude between those two values. Subsequent to the benzene decision, OSHA has used the one in a thousand risk as the defining criteria for significant risk. There is clearly no "gold standard" for risk, and the selection of a one in a thousand risk is controversial since it results in a less protective posture for occupational exposures than is used for environmental risks. This issue of what constitutes significant risk, or, conversely, an acceptable risk, will continue to be debated, but the benzene decision has been one of the important decisions that has led to an emphasis on quantitative risk assessment. This emphasis on quantitative risk assessment has itself been a central feature of environmental and occupational health regulation for more than a decade. OSHA has used the exposure that produces a risk of 1 excess cancer per 1000 exposed as the defining level of significant risk since the benzene decision. Thus the agency has focused its attention on two defining features in standard setting: feasibility and significant risk. While the former does not preclude an approach to standards promulgation that incorporates pollution prevention approaches, the latter has resulted in the agency's focusing attention on the control strategies that could achieve this level of risk resulting in what might be considered an undue focus on traditional control strategies to the exclusion of pollution prevention.

Setting Priorities at OSHA—Problem Identification

Identifying the chemical compounds that constitute the most serious workplace problems is critical to establishing inspection, standard setting, education, and pollution prevention priorities. To date, OSHA has given little attention to pollution prevention issues, but this could change in the future. One means of identifying such problems—and opportunities for action—is through hazard surveillance, the quantitative characterization of exposure to toxic chemicals in the work environment. There are limited sources of information on exposure of workers to chemical toxicants in the workplace, but they are potentially important for priority setting. Priority setting could also derive from epidemiologic data and case studies; that is, health surveillance information. Information of that nature can be derived from NIOSH research studies and can be used to identify etiologic agents and dose–response relationships that could establish causality with subsequent attention to pollution prevention as a means to eliminate exposures.

Both federal OSHA and authorized state OSHA departments conduct facility inspections for approximately 450 different chemical and physical hazards for which permissible exposure limits have been set. Of these, approximately 340 are "chemical" hazards, although they include agents such as wood dust and limestone. A review of such inspections, however, revealed that more than seventy percent focused on only 21 of the known chemical and physical hazards.[20]

The results of OSHA inspections are compiled into a national database known as the Integrated Management Information System (IMIS).[21] Quantitative results of samples taken for particular chemical substances are expressed both in terms of airborne concentration, and as a severity level (airborne concentration divided by the PEL). The OSHA IMIS database represents the most comprehensive quantitative data available on exposure to toxic substances in the workplace, although it is plagued by extremely uneven and incomplete coverage of both exposure agents and industries.[22]

Two one-time surveys conducted by the National Institute of Occupational Safety and Health constitute the only nationally focused supplement to the IMIS database. The National Occupational Hazard Survey (NOHS), conducted in 1974, and the National Occupational Exposure Survey (NOES), completed in 1984, both conducted on-site inspections of more than 4,000 facilities in various regions of the country. NOES inspectors recorded the presence of more than 10,000 different potential chemical, physical, and biological hazards in nonagricultural, nonmining, and nongovernmental establishments, although no samples were taken.[23] Results of the NOES survey have been compiled into a summary format known as the Job Exposure Matrix (JEM), which does not break down data by region. The data found in the NOES database is limited to identification of which chemicals are found in specific industries. There is no quantitative information on worker exposure. NIOSH Health Hazard Evaluations (HHEs) do contain quantitative information on workplace exposure, but the number of HHEs is limited and the data are not computerized in a readily accessible form.

Given the limitations of the nature and applicability of OSHA data, workplace right-to-know efforts, primarily associated with OSHA reform, have broadly paralleled community right-to-know efforts. Both have focused on the need for more detailed provisions for pollution prevention planning, although the proposed OSHA reforms have tended to be more limited in scope than community right-to-know proposals. For example, although improved toxic exposure data collection has been proposed as part of the OSHA reform effort, the reporting of toxic chemicals use data has not, nor have pollution prevention goals been proposed from the workplace context.

Beyond the issue of OSHA reform, workplace hazard information could be significantly strengthened by better integrating EPA's Toxics Release Inventory (TRI) and other environmental exposure information with workplace exposure information. The other databases available for this purpose have recently been reviewed by UCLA Pollution Prevention Center researchers.[24] In particular, the reporting of process-specific sources for each reported TRI chemical would be a major source of information for workplace exposure assessment, especially if it were coupled with the number of workers potentially exposed to each source. Although workplace and environmental exposures can involve potentially different sources, the failure to integrate facility-level data ultimately only serves to reinforce the historic regulatory and policy division that has long existed between the environment and the workplace.

In addition to intractible data collection and analysis problems, OSHA has developed only 24 permanent standards and does not have any means of identifying the scope of worker exposure to substances not currently regulated by the agency. Accordingly, W. Kip Viscusi wrote in 1983:

> OSHA's emphasis on perhaps the most critical type of hazards, those posing the risk of occupationally related cancer, has been disturbingly modest. The carcinogens for which OSHA initiated rulemaking in the 1970s include asbestos, vinyl chloride, coke oven emissions, arsenic, benzene, acrylonitrile, beryllium and a group of cancerous substances that OSHA has dubbed the 'fourteen carcinogens.' Indeed, the total number of all types of toxic and hazardous substances covered has increased very little since the initial list of OSHA standards. As a result, OSHA standards address but a small portion of the roughly 2,000 substances in the workplace for which there is some evidence of carcinogenicity.[25]

OSHA has developed a generic hazard communication standard which provides information to workers on the hazards of the chemicals they encounter in the work environment. However, OSHA does not collect the information on industry use for priority setting purposes nor is the industry required to provide information to workers on non-OSHA regulated chemicals. OSHA has made no attempt to access information found at the state or local levels under "right to know" for use in setting priorities for pollution prevention or for any other relevant purposes. For OSHA, data sources remain an opportunity not seized in developing pollution prevention targets and strategies.

Enforcement—Are Pollution Prevention Strategies Available?

Besides the problem of the pace and substance of standard setting, the limits of enforcement mechanisms has exacerbated the failure to reduce environmental hazard exposure in the workplace. Even on those occasions where OSHA developed comprehensive rules for a specific substance, the results have been unsatisfactory in terms of workplace protections. For example, OSHA established a landmark standard for lead in 1978. A subsequent study on lead and air toxics documented that airborne lead concentrations continued to be excessive and that there were more industries with high lead levels than originally envisioned in the 1978 standard.[26] This information was compounded by the growing health-related evidence identifying lead as far more toxic than was thought when the 1978 lead standard was adopted. Even the presence of a comprehensive standard such as that for lead is no guarantee that the substance is adequately controlled and not a candidate for pollution prevention strategies.

The limits of enforcement is a key factor that obviates an alternative paradigm, such as pollution prevention. Since its inception, OSHA has measured success on the basis of input variables such as the number of inspections, fines levied, and the number of violations in each inspection rather than by output variables, such as the implementation of controls to reduce exposures. Similarly, OSHA has not adequately evaluated abatement of any particular toxicant overexposure, and companies have not received adequate follow-up inspections to determine if necessary controls have been implemented.

There is in fact strong resistance on the part of industry to implement such controls. They are costly (e.g., the estimated $500 million in projected costs calculated for compliance with OSHA's 1980 cotton dust standard) and rules such as this tend to be responsive to industry influences. In this kind of setting where costs influence the rulemaking and the rulemaking (focused on control outcomes) can influence costs, a cycle of regulatory failure may occur. With companies hesitant to make large capital investments in aging plants, OSHA is unwilling or unable to pursue compliance around abatement. Many workplace exposures thus remain unattended. Workers are often merely required to use devices such as respirators for protection, which represent inadequate measures of control. Workers often resist these forms of personal protection, resulting in continuing full exposure to the environmental hazards present in the work setting.

This cycle of regulatory failure has become characteristic of efforts to deal with workplace exposures. OSHA has never established the means to evaluate these issues as a matter of agency policy and therefore has not developed the mechanisms to judge the efficacy of its efforts beyond the setting of standards and recording inspection numbers. The simultaneous efforts by other regulators to reduce or manage hazardous or toxic substances that exit the workplace environment as hazardous wastes can at times compound the problem of workplace exposures. A number of industries which have reduced significantly their discharges into the environment may in fact still generate significant occupational exposures. For example, environmental impacts from the automobile battery industry have been largely controlled. Approximately 97 percent of the automobile batteries manufactured in this country are now recycled. In modern battery recycling plants, moreover, lead emissions from furnaces and lead in the wastewater are extracted and returned to the production cycle, and sulfuric acid is neutralized before its discharge. Still, even with extensive ventilation systems, worker exposure in some sections of these plants exceeds OSHA's own limited permissible exposure limits.[27]

The focus on control strategies for the workplace and divorce between environmental and workplace frameworks for policy has not simply been limited to OSHA. For example, a 1985 Office of Technology Assessment (OTA) report entitled "Preventing Illness and Injury in the Workplace" discussed in just one paragraph the idea of substitution of less toxic materials. On the other hand, an entire chapter was devoted to the hierarchy of controls limited to the two types of control discussed earlier: engineering controls and respiratory protection. The report failed to address workplace process changes, design changes, and other approaches associated with pollution prevention or waste reduction strategies, a significant omission given the elaborate argument put forth by OTA just one year later about the importance and value of waste reduction strategies for the general environment. OTA's omission was also representative of how policymakers distinguished between workplace hazards (which often received more limited attention and weaker controls) and the problems of pollution in the general environment.[28]

In reviewing OSHA's and EPA's regulatory histories and the legislative acts which established their mandates, it becomes clear that a pollution prevention strategy needs to address both occupational and general environment exposures *simultaneously,* as part of a consistent and integrated approach. Such a policy also needs to provide an alternative to the current costly, difficult, and inadequate process of establishing appropriate workplace controls (parallel to the end-of-pipe requirements in EPA regulations). This system has ultimately established neither the capability nor the desire to effectively address the kinds of environmental hazards found in the workplace nor their complex relationship with the wastes and hazards present in the environment. Reform of this workplace policy system has become as essential to a pollution prevention approach as the restructuring of EPA and overall environmental policy.

Consumer Product Hazards

Ideally, from both a commercial chemical life cycle and toxics release perspective, the incorporation of toxic substances as constituents in both formulated products and durable goods should be viewed as another route of release or transfer to those usually of concern (i.e., land, water, air, various treatment works, and underground injection). Examination of the advent and performance record of consumer protection regulations (e.g., the Consumer Product Safety Commission or CPSC), illustrates how the regulatory conception of consumption continues to be a missing link in attempts to account for the use and release of toxic chemicals in manufacturing. It is also excluded in the development of a comprehensive picture of consumer product hazards, as well as in the analysis of hazardous municipal waste constituents.

Issues related to consumer product hazards have long been associated with an extended yet episodic history of legislation and regulation. At the turn of the century, muckraking journalist Upton Sinclair's bestselling exposé of the meatpacking industry, *The Jungle,* helped lead to the passage of the 1906 Food and Drug Act, the first of a series of consumer product hazard legislative initiatives.[29] Similarly, the passage of the 1938 Food, Drug, and Cosmetics Act, and the 1960 Hazardous Substances Labeling Act were influenced by public concerns about false consumer product advertising, mislabeling, and the rush to market of products with particular toxic ingredients later discovered to be harmful to human health.[30] Workplace exposures and regulation have also had direct bearing on the question of subsequent exposure through product use and the adequacy of product regulation.

There has been a concurrent extensive history in this country of advocacy regarding issues of worker health and safety and consumer product hazards. During the 1910s and 1920s, advocacy researchers such as Alice Hamilton and John Andrews demonstrated that workplace hazards were related to such toxic substances as white phosphorous used in match production, and consumer advocates also began to challenge a wide range of product hazards, such as lead additives in gasoline or radium in watch dials.

Both consumer safety and occupational health advocates joined forces in highly visible efforts to ban such products.[31]

Government intervention regarding product hazards emerged more significantly in the 1930s with the passage of the Food, Drug, and Cosmetic Act, again in the wake of a series of consumer campaigns and bestselling exposés concerning hazardous food additives, patent medicines, cosmetic and pharmaceutical ingredients, and widely used insecticides such as lead arsenate.[32] Growing concerns about petrochemical-based products, especially pesticides and food additives, emerged during the 1950s, generating new efforts at regulatory intervention such as the Food and Drug Administration's adoption in 1954 of "tolerance limits" for chemical residues on food, and passage of the "Delaney Clause" in 1958 legislation that banned any toxic ingredient in food.[33]

These approaches, however, failed to fully alleviate public concern about toxic ingredients in products. During the 1950s and 1960s, another round of consumer-related scares exacerbated those concerns, including the discovery during the1959 Thanksgiving holiday period that cranberries had been contaminated by amitrole, a pesticide known to cause cancer in rats, and the growing number of incidents of lead poisoning stemming from children ingesting lead from the paint peeling off the walls of predominantly inner city homes.[34] Cases such as these resulted in new legislation or regulatory bans that focused on a particular product of concern. But even these efforts, such as the restrictions on lead ingredients in paints, failed to fully eliminate associated product-based hazards. The passage of the 1971 Lead Paint Poisoning Prevention Act, for example, reduced the exposure to lead-based paints in new housing stock. Although it contained provisions to underwrite efforts to strip lead paint from existing federally subsidized housing, it still left intact (twenty years after its enactment) potentially toxic lead-based paint in as many as 900,000 units of public housing and 40 million units of private housing. Lead-based paint and dust thus represented, as one analyst put it, "a health menace" for an estimated 3.8 million U.S. homes of children seven years of age or younger.[35]

A new upsurge in consumer politics by the 1960s placed many of these same issues back on policy agendas. Consumer concerns with product hazards came to be linked with environmental concerns over toxicity, flammability, and safety. These issues in turn helped stimulate the rise of an environmentally oriented consumer movement which first took shape during the late 1960s and early 1970s under the leadership of consumer advocate Ralph Nader. Nader, who had expanded his own interest in automobile safety issues to broader questions of corporate accountability, helped initiate the coalition that generated political support underlining the push for new consumer hazard related legislation. Thus, President Lyndon Johnson sent a "consumer protection"-related message to Congress in February 1967, wherein he argued that the "march of technology" which had brought "unparalleled abundance and opportunity to the consumer," had also exposed the consumer to "new complexities and hazards." In response to the President's message, Congress established the National Commission on Product Safety to analyze consumer problems, including those associated with household hazardous products.[36] Soon after the Commission published its findings, new coalitions, focusing on the concepts of "quality of life" which broadly intersected with the new environmentalism, eventually led to the 1972 passage of the Consumer Product Safety Act.[37] This was accomplished despite the opposition of then President Richard Nixon who preferred that product safety issues be addressed directly by the executive branch. The Act, instead, established a Consumer Product Safety Commission (CPSC) based on significant independence from executive branch direction.[38] The Commission would have the power to develop safety standards for consumer products, undertake research regarding potential risks associated with particular products, and open its proceedings to the public to ensure public participation.

The Consumer Product Safety Act (CPSA) defined its mission as preventing "unreasonable risks" posed by "unacceptable" products, language that would later broadly parallel TSCA's "unreasonable risk" standard.[39] The CPSC in addition to setting safety standards, was also to serve as a consumer clearinghouse and research agency. Under the Act, however, the Commission's powers were neither comprehensive nor clearly demarcated. Yet like the OSH Act (which provided OSHA with the authority to undertake product bans), the CPSA did provide its Commission with the potential power to ban products "when necessary" to "adequately protect the public." That reduction-related opportunity, however, was limited by language and jurisdictional constraints. For one, product hazard areas regulated under other statutues were specifically excluded from CPSC`s mandate. These included pesticides, tobacco and tobacco products, motor vehicles and motor vehicle equipment, and food, drugs, and cosmetics. In addition, a number of other federal agencies maintained jurisdiction over consumer product regulation, including the Food and Drug Administration (mandated by the Food Drug and Cosmetic Act), EPA (mandated by the Federal Insecticide, Fungicide, and Rodenticide Act to regulate pesticide use), the Federal Trade Commission (mandated by the Fair Packaging and Labeling Act), and the Department of Transportation (mandated by the Hazardous Materials Transportation Act).

The Consumer Product Safety Act further limited the regulatory purview of the new agency by applying only to consumer products manufactured and used in this country. At the same time, while it sought to identify and regulate consumer product hazards, there was nothing in the language of the Act that addressed the question of how to *reduce* the toxicity of products. In this vein, the most serious risks were considered to be amputation, electrocution, burns, and asphyxiation. While cancer was also included as a serious risk, it was largely ignored as an issue requiring regulatory intervention. Instead, the Commission's regulatory focus led it to address the more visible, safety-oriented rather than health-based product hazards. Thus, from the outset, the Commission largely abdicated its ability to intervene to eliminate or prevent consumer product hazards at an earlier stage of production (i.e., prior to a product's entry to market).

With a limited budget and a diffuse jurisdiction, the CPSC's lack of intervention contrasted with the widespread presence in consumer products of varying kinds of hazards and toxic ingredients. Although the Act provided CPSC with the power to set standards and ultimately ban products through its "unreasonable risks" benchmark, CPSC generally avoided utilizing these powers (similar to EPA's unwillingness to pursue TSCA authority under a parallel "unreasonable risk" standard), and it even failed to identify the types and amounts of toxic ingredients found in particular products. Like the Occupational Safety and Health Act which established a broad mandate but included inadequate mechanisms to address the presence of workplace hazards, the Consumer Product Safety Act appeared to broaden the regulatory focus regarding consumer product hazards but failed to provide for the mechanisms necessary to directly reduce those hazards.

While, as implemented, the CPSA contributed little to the regulation of toxic hazards in consumer products, it played an even more limited role in developing an understanding of the nature and extent of those hazards. The current state of information about the presence of toxic constituents in consumer products is extraordinarily limited. This persists even though toxic exposures associated with the use of a few products (such as art supplies and carpet installation materials) have been relatively well documented in recent years. Indirect evidence (such as alarming signals from wells downstream including toxic leachate from municipal landfills) has also been largely ignored. A 1987 EPA study underlined this issue by revealing that of 1000 brand name household products reviewed by EPA, 126 contained at least one of six well-documented toxic chlorinated solvents. More than half of those products themselves contained concentrations by weight of more than 1 percent of the solvent. Even more disturbing, as an Inform analysis pointed out, was EPA's discovery that, despite CPSC rules on product labeling,[40] some 55 of the 126 products (or 44 percent) had failed to disclose the solvents on product labels.[41]

Through the late 1980s, the CPSC initiated direct regulatory action or analysis around only a handful of highly toxic chemicals.Vinyl chloride and methylene chloride were controlled with respect to their use as propellants; labels were required on consumer products containing asbestos; a proposed rule to ban products containing 0.1 percent or more benzene was withdrawn; and a ban on urea formaldehyde foam insulation was overturned by the Fifth Circuit Court of Appeals, and the CPSC declined to directly regulate formaldehyde exposures from pressed wood products.[42] The Commission's basic approach has been one of waiting until a serious problem is identified through public concern rather than proactively seeking to identify highly toxic constituents and potential exposure problems. A combination of factors accounts for the CPSC's dismal record around toxics and makes it unlikely that in the foreseeable future the Commission will prove to be a useful source of information on toxic chemicals in products.

A review of the history of the Commission's regulatory performance further underlines this point. During the 1970s, the CPSC became involved in various consumer product safety and hazardous substance issues. These ranged from regulations limiting the asbestos and formaldehyde content of products to labeling requirements for hazardous ingredients in such items as turpentine, antifreeze, and the contents of fire extinguishers. Through additional legislative authority (partly due to pressure from consumer groups), CPSC also became involved in such issues as child-resistant containers and flammability standards for clothing fabrics, children's sleepwear, mattresses, carpets, and vinyl plastic film.[43]

Despite its mandate for regulating hazardous substances in consumer products (based in part on the broad, and somewhat ambiguous language in the CPSA), CPSC's capacity to act was framed from the outset as limited in scope and narrow in design. Early opposition by President Nixon delayed Commission appointments and established an ongoing battle between the Administration and the CPSC which lasted until Nixon resigned from office. During the Ford years, CPSC faced continuing criticism from both Congress and consumer groups concerning its inactivity and chairman S. John Byington's hostility to consumer-oriented legislation and regulation. It was only during the Carter years that the Commission began to more clearly identify specific administrative powers, and extend certain of its regulatory powers, including those addressing questions of product hazards and "toxicity." This involved recasting some existing voluntary standards into mandatory ones, and requiring manufacturers to notify the commission if they planned to export products that had been banned or regulated in this country. The CPSC also strengthened its regulatory role through more direct liaison with other environmental agencies through such forums as the Interagency Regulatory Liaison Group and by participating in a linked review process with respect to specific hazards, most notably the use of CFCs in aerosols.[44] However, as with the regulatory/deregulatory squabbles confronting EPA, the Carter CPSC was also continually required to address charges that its regulatory activity imposed burdens on industry, pressures that often ended up making "dollar costs, not the health effects" the driving force of the regulatory process, as Carter's CPSC chair Susan King put it.[45]

By 1981, with the election of Ronald Reagan, those arguments had crystallized into a frontal attack on the more active interpretation of the CPSC mission itself. Soon after Reagan's election, David Stockman, the new head of the Office of Management and Budget and a leader in the antiregulatory drive against environmental agencies, accused the CPSC of having "adventured too far in some areas of regulation," especially with product bans and mandatory standards. This position was sustained by the Heritage Foundation, a conservative think tank that had played a key advisory role during the transition to the new administration. The Foundation recommended abolishing the CPSC, or, at the least, to "continue the agency, but with drastic cutbacks in funds, permitting CPSC to operate only as an educational and informational agency." This fallback position was codified in part by the passage of Amendments to the Consumer Product Safety Act in 1981, which shifted the Commission toward a voluntary compliance approach away from imposing any form of mandatory standards. This included the elimination of product design standards and restricting the public disclosure of hazards, a position that ran counter to the "right-to-know" approach that would become central for subsequent legislation such as the reauthorization of Superfund (SARA) in 1986. At the same time, the Reagan and Bush administrations effectively carried out much of the Heritage Foundation's agenda. This included the dismantling of interagency links such as the IRLG, a substantial cutback of both funds and staff for the agency, and ultimately assigning a low priority status to the Commission in the area of environmental policy. The status issue was further underlined by the lengthy periods of time that elapsed before submission of names of new commissioners to Congress, which in turn produced lengthy stretches of time when a lack of quorum prevented the Commission from conducting any official business.[46]

A major interagency focus for the Commission regarded CFC use in aerosol propellants during the 1970s. This came to represent during the Reagan and Bush years of the 1980s a direct example of Commission reluctance to intervene regarding specific product hazards identified in other forums. After EPA action under TSCA in the late 1970s had established a ban on the use of CFCs in aerosols, aerosol producers began substituting methylene chloride (Meth) for CFCs. Meth, a toxic substance that enjoyed widespread use in a number of other household products, was also the subject of a substantial body of toxicity research.[47] In this context, the Consumer Federation of America petitioned the CPSC to ban all uses of methylene chloride from household products. The Commission formally denied the petition, and instead proposed the voluntary development of appropriate warning labels. In September 1987, the Commission, under increasing pressure from both Congress and consumer groups, reworked its labeling approach to include standards for mandatory warning labels, but still failed to interpret its "unreasonable risk" mandate as applying to a Meth ban. As a consequence, the Consumer Federation of America petitioned the agency to review this refusal to initiate a product ban. Court action was subsequently initiated around the new petition, with the Chlorinated Solvents Industry Alliance deciding to intervene on behalf of the CPSC. In an attempt to respond to the petition, CPSC in 1990 ordered manufacturers to submit to the Commission data on formulations for consumer products containing >1.0% methylene chloride. Since the order applied to packagers and labelers as well as product importers, it basically covered the range of aerosol producers, a primary target for the CFA action. The purpose of the order, which included information on the actual label as well as the product formulation and product sales information, was framed so as to establish the effectiveness of the labeling guidelines issued in 1987 but to not pursue directly the possibility of a product ban.[48] One of the Commission members involved in these decisions (who subsequently resigned to become a public relations consultant representing, among other clients, the aerosols industry), echoed the Commission sentiment when she declared in a February 1991 aerosol trade publication that the aerosols industry was "environmentally sound."[49]

CPSC's limited regulatory terrain was also compounded by the fact that over its lifetime (with the brief exception of the IRLG experiment), its regulatory focus was isolated from the environmental and occupational mandates of EPA and OSHA. At the same time, CPSC's ability to address product hazards was further circumscribed by the mandates established for other product-oriented regulatory agencies such as the Food and Drug Administration. These regulatory divisions effectively separated the issue of product hazards from the broader question of determining environmental hazards at each stage of any given production system. As a consequence, product hazard issues emerged as a subset for environmental policy.

At times, the actions of other regulatory agencies directly underlined the weaknesses in product regulation. For example, one consequence of EPA's strong interest in solid waste recycling strategies, heightened with the passage of RCRA in 1976, was its unwillingness to discourage construction companies from using waste oil (a potential hazardous product-related regulatory target) as a dust suppressant on asphalt roads, especially in rural areas. Given waste oil's high concentrations of heavy metals such as lead, cadmium, and chromium, and other toxic pollutants such as benzene, PCBs, and polycyclic aromatic hydrocarbons, its use as a dust suppressant frequently resulted in product-use–based contamination issues, including the widely publicized Times Beach, Missouri episode where EPA was forced to place (and then later withdraw) an entire town on its National Priorities List of contaminated sites. (Interestingly, later debates within EPA about Times Beach concerned the risk assessment approaches used rather than the problem of inconsistent policy objectives and regulatory activities).[50]

Underlining this limited focus on product regulation within the environmental policy system, was the growing number of products with toxic ingredients or representing chronic hazards (from household cleaners to cosmetics to lawn care products) that expanded their respective market shares, despite being potential targets for regulatory intervention. These products were generally without the kinds of immediate "safety" hazards that primarily preoccupied the CPSC, although they nevertheless represented a range of environmental hazards, from solid waste disposal to air toxic emissions to indoor air pollution concerns. EPA's own evaluation of relative types of environmental risks identified indoor air pollution (a concern significantly related to product use) as one of the "high risk" areas among environmental hazards evaluated.[51] Yet the policy focus for agencies like EPA or the CPSC regarding hazardous products continued to focus on back-end strategies, such as expensive household hazardous waste collection centers and disposal programs, rather than on specific product-related pollution prevention strategies.

Besides the potential environmental risks associated with certain consumer products, industrial product use has often represented a far more significant problem of exposure. Exposure routes for such hazardous industrial products as chlorinated solvents occur both in the original production of the solvents and in their later use in subsequent industrial processes such as for painting and coating purposes or for cleaning in electronics or aerospace production. A wide variety of hazards based in the production process, some known and many others unknown, can in fact stem from the end uses of industrial products rather than from their original production. For example, man-made mineral fibers are widely available industrial products that are themselves substitutes for asbestos in a variety of industrial processes. Workplace exposure to these fibers appears to be low in the manufacturing process but higher in their end use.[52]

With the CPSC basically removed from the process of reviewing consumer and industrial product hazards, government action has gradually begun to shift to states and local communities. By the late 1980s, several states began to pass a range of product liability laws or to institute actions regarding specific products (such as art products for schools) which contained toxic substances. In Los Angeles, for example, the South Coast Air Quality Management District initiated actions that sought to present a "consumer product profile" as part of its regulatory attack on toxic air emissions. In that context, SCAQMD proposed a phased-in ban or stringent regulations regarding two high profile consumer items—barbecue lighter fluids and aerosol spray paints—in order to reduce or eliminate their release of toxic air contaminants. In a similar vein, dozens of communities and states passed measures banning or regulating the use of polystyrene foam containers, addressing both their toxicity and ozone depleting capacities as well as their contribution to solid waste problems.[53]

The widespread introduction of these kinds of measures, some of which came to be duplicated by other states or localities, put increasing pressure on industry to respond, either by creating different products for different markets or by shifting toward alternative products to be introduced nationally.[54] The most effective of these measures—those that were duplicated by the largest number of states or communities—had evolved into a kind of de facto national regulation. In response, industry groups such as the Chemical Specialties Manufacturer's Association sought to refocus regulatory action on the national level, with the CSMA specifically calling for a national labeling standard regarding toxic materials in consumer products as an alternative measure.[55] In this context, the limited role of the CPSC, combined with the control-oriented, narrow purview of OSHA and the unfulfilled paradigm shift of EPA, has had the unintended consequence of highlighting what was emerging as the most significant recent trend in government toxics policy: namely a more expansive role of states and local communities.

Today, the question of product hazards with both consumer and industrial products remains largely unfocused and often unaddressed within the broader arena of toxics policy. In order to confront such issues, reduction strategies necessarily need to focus on earlier stages of the production process where products and processes are identified, rather than the current regulatory focus on the post-production cycles of use and disposal. In this way, pollution prevention can also be seen as an issue of production (and product) design, an issue that goes to the heart of the problem of toxics generation and use and situates pollution prevention as the conceptual underpinnings of a strategy of front-end policymaking. Such front-end policymaking specifically needs to integrate decisions about the workplace and about product use with the issues of environmental regulation in general. Failure to do so only compartmentalizes the issues of toxics generation and use and perpetuates the end-of-pipe approach that refuses to be dislodged from the modus operandi of policymakers.

Notes

1. Ashford, N.A., *Crisis in the Workplace* (Cambridge: MIT Press, 1976).

2. Corn, J.K., "Historical Aspects of Industrial Hygiene: II. Silicosis," *Am. Ind. Hyg. Assoc. J.* 41:125, 1980.

3. U.S. Congress House Committee on Labor, *An Investigation Relating to Health Conditions of Workers Employed in the Construction and Maintenance of Public Utilities*, Hearings on H.R. 4973, 96th Congress, 1st Session, 1936.

4. Cherniak, M, *The Hawks Nest Incident* (New Haven: Yale University Press 1986).

5. Whorton, M.D., "Male Reproductive Hazards," *Occupational Medicine: State of the Art Reviews* 1, pp. 375–379, 1986.

6. Keogh, J.P., Pestronk, A., Wertheimer, D., and Moreland, R., "An Epidemic of Urinary Retention Caused by Dimethylaminopropionitrile," *JAMA* 243, pp. 746–749, 1980.

7. Landrigan, P.J., Kreiss, K., Xintaras, C., Feldman, R.G., and Heath, Jr., C.W., "Clinic Epidemiology of Occupational Neurotoxic Disease," *Neurobehavioral Toxicology* 2, pp. 43–48, 1980.

8. Office of Technology Assessment, *Preventing Illness and Injury in the Workplace*, Washington D.C., U.S. Congress, OTA-H256, 1985.

9. Page, J.A., and O'Brien, M.W., *Bitter Wages* (New York: Grossman, 1973).

10. MacLaury, J., "The Job Safety Law of 1970: Its Passage Was Perilous," *Monthly Labor Review* 104(3), pp. 18–24, 1981.

11. Castleman, B.I., and Ziem, G.E., "Corporate Influence on Threshold Limit Values," *Am J. Ind. Med.* 13, pp. 531–559, 1988.

12. 29 USC 651.

13. Roach, S.A., and Rappaport, S.M., "But They Are Not Thresholds:

A Critical Analysis of the Documentation of Threshold Limit Values," *Am. J. Ind. Med.* 17, pp. 727–753, 1990.

14. U.S. Supreme Court, 452 U.S. 490 (1981).

15. U.S. District Court of Appeals, 577 F.2d 825 (3d Cir. 1978)

16. U.S. District Court of Appeals, 647 F.2d 1189 (D.C. Cir. 1980).

17. U.S. District Court of Appeals, 577 F. 2d 825 (3d Cir. 1978).

18. During the promulgation of the cotton dust standard an important issue that emerged within the Carter administration concerned the use of engineering controls versus respiratory protection to reduce worker's exposure to cotton dust. Available engineering controls included exhaust ventilation, dilution ventilation to reduce the concentration of the contaminant, isolation, or enclosure. Historically, OSHA had provided for a hierarchy of controls, with respirators to be used only during the period that engineering controls were being implemented. Respirators could not be considered a permanent method of protecting workers but needed always to be viewed as an interim method of control.

At the time the debate over the cotton dust standard was occurring, economists such as Stuart Eizenstadt and Charles Schultz inside the Carter administration objected to what they considered an inflexible policy on control strategies, and they rejected the OSHA policy on the hierarchy of controls. They argued that respiratory protection was an entirely appropriate method of control, as such a method would be decidedly less expensive than engineering controls. The issue was resolved at a 1978 White House meeting attended by President Carter and Vice President Mondale (which also included one of the authors of this chapter). At the meeting, the Administration economists argued for the use of respirators over engineering controls as a cost-saving measure which would continue to make the U.S. textile industry competitive in a world market. They were opposed by then Secretary of Labor, Ray Marshall, and the Assistant Secretary for OSHA, Dr. Eula Bingham, who argued that OSHA's regulatory policy that emphasized engineering controls was a preferred strategy. President Carter agreed that the traditional hierarchy of controls was most appropriate, and that policy has continued to remain in effect. Despite this victory in more "stringent" protection, the "respirators versus traditional engineering controls" debate illustrates OSHA's failure to pursue more innovative technological change and pollution prevention as necessary strategies for progress in occupational health.

19. U.S. Supreme Court, 488 U.S. 607 (1980).

20. Froines, J.R., Dellenbaugh, C.A., and Wegman, D.H., "Occupational Health Surveillance: A Means to Identify Work Related Risks," *Am. J. Pub. Health* 76, pp. 1089–1096, 1986.

21. Froines, J.R., Wegman, D.H., and Eisen, E.A., "Hazard Surveillance in Occupational Disease," *Am. J. Pub. Health* 79 (supplement), pp. 26–31, 1989.

22. See Cisternas, M., Smith, M., and Froines, J.R., "Industries with Increased Risk of Occupational Disease in California," Report to the State of California Compensation Insurance Fund, 1992.

23. Cisternas *et al. Ibid.*

24. Cisternas *et al. Ibid.*

25. Viscusi, W. Kip, *Risk by Choice: Regulating Health and Safety in the Workplace* (Cambridge: Harvard University Press, 1983).

26. Froines, J.R., Baron, S.L., Wegman, D.H., and O'Rourke, S., "Characterization of the Airborne Concentration of Lead in U.S. Industry," *Am. J. Ind. Med.* 18, pp. 1–17, 1990.

27. See Bak-Boychuk, Laura *et al.*, *Impacts of the Reclamation of Lead-Acid and Nickel-Cadmium Batteries for Electric Vehicles*, report prepared for the Pollution Prevention Education and Research Center, Preventing Pollution class, Winter 1994, UCLA.

28. Office of Technology Assessment, *Preventing Illness and Injury in the Workplace*, 1985.

29. Sinclair, Upton, *The Jungle* (New York: Doubleday 1906).

30. Federal Food, Drug and Cosmetics Act, 1938 Title 21 § 300 (*et seq.*); Federal Hazardous Substances Labeling Act, Title 15 § 1262 (*et seq.*).

31. The occupational hazards from match production are discussed in Lee, R. Alton, "The Eradication of Phossy Jaw: A Unique Development of Federal Police Power," *The Historian*, Vol. 29, No. 1, November 1966, pp. 1–21; The radium dial painting episode is discussed in Goldmark, Josephine, *Impatient Crusader: Florence Kelley's Life Story*, (Urbana: University of Illinois Press, 1953); The lead additives issue is discussed in Chapter 6. See also Gottlieb, Robert, *Forcing the Spring: The Transformation of the American Environmental Movement* (Washington D.C.: Island Press, 1993), Chapter 2.

32. See, for example, Kallet, Arthur, and Schlink, F.J., *100,000,000 Guinea Pigs: Dangers in Everyday Foods, Drugs, and Cosmetics* (New York: Vanguard Press, 1932).

33. Title 21 § 321 *et seq.*; Regs at 21 CFR 1-1300.

34. Quinn, Michael, *Lead Paint Poisoning in Urban Children: An Annotated Bibliography* (Monticello, IL: Council of Planning Librarians, 1976).

35. The "health menace" quote is from a *New England Journal of Medicine* editorial, "Exposure to Lead in Childhood—The Importance of Prevention," Kathryn R. Mahaffey, Vol. 327, No. 18, October 29, 1992, pp. 1308–1309; Department of Housing and Urban Development, 1990.

36. The Johnson speech is reproduced in *National Commission on Product Safety*, a Hearing before the Consumer Subcommittee of the Committee on Commerce, United States Senate, Ninetieth Congress, 1st Session, March 1, 1967, p. 6.

37. Title 15 § 2051 (*et seq.*).

38. Title 15 § 2053.

39. Title 15 § 2051(a)(1).

40. The product labeling rules were published by CPSC in the Federal Register. 1 *Federal Register* 57 (197): 46627, October 9, 1992. These rules significantly extended the requirements for labeling for chronic hazards (that in 1990 had first been stipulated for art products) to all products under CPSC jurisdiction.

41. See *Household Solvent Products: A "Shelf" Survey with Laboratory Analysis*, Office of Toxic Substances, U.S. Environmental Protection Agency, (Washington D.C.: U.S. Environmental Protection Agency, 1987). The Inform study is Lilienthal, Nancy, Ascione, Michele. and Flint, Adam, *Tackling Toxics in Everyday Products*, (Washington D.C.: Inform, 1991).

42. See "Consumer Product Safety Commission Reauthorization: Hearing Before the Subcommittee on Commerce, Consumer Protection, and Competitiveness of the House Committee on Energy and Commerce," 100th Congress, 1st Session, 79–84 (1987).

43. "Consumer Product Safety Commission Reauthorization: Hearing Before the Subcommittee on Commerce, Consumer Protection, and Competitiveness of the Committee on Energy and Commerce," United States House of Representatives, 100th Congress, 1st Session, June 4, 1987.

44. The Interagency Regulatory Liaison Group was created in 1977 and included EPA, OSHA, and the Food and Drug Administration (FDA), as well as CPSC. Part of its success for CPSC was measured by increased coordination and collaboration on hazard assessments that might not have been accomplished or even undertaken by any of the agencies independently (particularly CPSC). "At a time when regulators were being attacked from every quarter, we took preventive regulatory policy further than it had ever gone before," CPSC's Susan King said of the IRLG. King's statement is cited in Landy, Marc K., Roberts, Marc J., and Thomas, Stephen R., *The Environmental Protection Agency: Asking the Wrong Questions*, (New York: Oxford University Press, 1990), p. 199.

45. See Susan King's remarks in Conference on Environmental Law—Toxic Substances, *Proceedings*, Marshall-Wythe School of Law, College of William and Mary, Williamsburg, Virginia, 1979.

46. See Klayman, Elliot, "Standard Setting Under the Consumer Product Safety Amendments of 1981—A Shift in Regulatory Philosophy,"

The George Washington Law Review, November 1982, Vol. 51, No. 1, pp. 96–112.

47. See, for example, California Air Resources Board Report, Part B: "Health Effects of Methylene Chloride," 1989.

48. "Self Pressurized Products Containing CFC's," 16, Code of Federal Regulations, p. 1401.

49. "Aerosol Age," February 1991.

50. See Gorman, Christine, "The Double Take on Dioxin (Scientists Are No Longer Sure Dioxin Is As Dangerous a Carcinogen As Originally Thought)," *Time,* Vol. 138, No. 8 (August 26, 1992), p. 52.

51. See *Unfinished Business: A Comparative Assessment of Environmental Problems,* Office of Policy Analysis, U.S. Environmental Protection Agency (Washington, D.C.: Government Printing Office, 1987).

52. *On the Evaluation of Carcinogenic Risks to Humans: Man-Made Mineral Fibers and Radon,* IARC Monograph, Vol. 43, (Lyon, France: World Health Organization—International Agency for Research on Cancer, 1988).

53. See Blumberg, Louis, and Gottlieb, Robert, *War on Waste: Can America Win Its Battle with Garbage?* (Washington, D.C.: Island Press, 1989).

54. An interesting case involving the development of a national product to meet certain environmental regulations (specifically emissions of polynuclear aromatics or PNAs) based on a regional product line was the Amoco Oil Company's decision to market nationally a colorless premium gasoline (which significantly eliminated PNAs) that had been developed as early as 1915 but had been only sold in limited Eastern markets under the brand name White Crown. See Feder, Barnaby J., "Behind the 'Clear' Trend," *New York Times,* June 6, 1993.

55. See *The Consumer Products Handbook: A Comprehensive Guide to Today's Household Chemical Products* (Washington D.C.: Chemical Specialties Manufacturer's Association, 1992).

5

New Approaches to Toxics: Production Design, Right-to-Know, and Definition Debates

Robert Gottlieb
Maureen Smith
Julie Roque
Pamela Yates

The Debate Over Terms and Strategy

At the center of the debate about how to construct new toxics policies has been the question of definition. The declarative judgment of the Hazardous and Solid Waste Amendments to RCRA (HSWA) in 1984—that it would now be a matter of national policy for the generation of hazardous waste to be "reduced or eliminated as expeditiously as possible"—suggested that a new policy era was indeed about to emerge.[1] On what basis such policies would be constructed, however, remained a matter of interpretation, often contested among various stakeholders. The first part of this chapter examines the genesis and conflicting interpretations among several key federal agencies and offices regarding nascent prevention terminology. The second part focuses on the debate over the actual language in stipulating what constituted "reducing" or "eliminating" hazardous waste. Finally, we offer an expanded interpretation of pollution prevention policy, which derives from the legislative analyses developed earlier in Part I, and is applied to the industrial decisionmaking approaches which unfold in Part II. The chapter sets the stage for Part II by assessing how a clearer understanding of the debates, strategy, and terms can serve to identify barriers to pollution prevention. We encourage debate over terms and strategies as a means of enriched understanding and to further prevention aims.

The Debates

The first major study to initiate discussion on this subject—the National Research Council's (NRC) "Reducing Hazardous Waste Generation—An Evaluation and Call for Action"—was published in 1985. The NRC report argued that while industrial waste reduction programs were bound to increase in sophistication over time, nontechnical factors that influenced such decisions were also likely to vary in importance, depending on the industry and types of wastes involved. Thus, the NRC report called for government programs to primarily gather data and document successful waste reduction programs, assure regulatory flexibility in order to accommodate diverse waste reduction efforts, develop research on waste reduction techniques, and ultimately establish effective risk management mechanisms to assess the "tradeoffs between protection of public health and the environment and costs."[2]

In contrast to the NRC's more limited conception of the framework for waste reduction policies, a more directed and comprehensive analysis of the issue was undertaken in 1986 by the Office of Technology Assessment (OTA) following a request by Congress to document alternatives to pollution control approaches. The OTA study concluded that reduction would be a more economical alternative to pollution control[3] and thus reinforced the calls for changing the conceptual basis for toxics policymaking.

While the OTA study (similar to NRC) argued for the importance of regulatory flexibility, it also pointed out that waste reduction, despite its enormous potential, remained minimal. OTA argued that a federal policy on waste reduction could be developed along one of three lines: (1) by maintaining current voluntary waste reduction programs, with no new action to direct or support industry actions; (2) by initiating federal efforts to expand those few programs that did exist; or (3) by putting in place a new, highly visible waste reduction program to be mandated through new legislation. OTA called for a broad policy debate over both the desirability and the specifics of a waste reduction approach in order to choose a direction.

Just one month after the OTA report was released, EPA published its own analysis of preferred pollution reduction alternatives, which the Agency defined as "waste minimization."[4] For EPA, waste minimization signified any action taken to reduce the volume or toxicity of RCRA-regulated hazardous wastes, including treatment technologies such as incineration, and chemical and biological processes ordinarily identified as end-

of-pipe pollution control technologies. EPA also argued that various on-
site and off-site recycling measures were equally integral to a waste minimization strategy. The Agency concluded that the three basic components
of a waste minimization approach included treatment, recycling, and
source reduction.[5]

The EPA waste minimization conceptual approach was immediately
critiqued by OTA, at the behest of Congress, in a June 1987 study. OTA
pointed out that EPA had created two contradictory definitions for "waste
minimization." One incorporated waste treatment as an acceptable option.
The second, by linking minimization to "source reduction," appeared to
exclude treatment. The significance of including "treatment" in a definition was enormous; treatment strategies, as proven, available technologies
exogenous to existing production processes, were clearly preferred by
industries concerned that waste reduction potentially represented
unwanted intrusions into exclusive industry domains of what to produce
and how to produce it.[6]

The EPA, OTA, and NRC reports, as well as other studies published by
nongovernment groups (INFORM, Environmental Defense Fund, the
Public Interest Research Groups, and the National Toxics Campaign, most
prominently)[7] exacerbated rather than resolved the reduction/minimiza-
tion debate. Each of the studies incorporated significantly different definitions, with such terms as "waste reduction," "waste minimization," "source
reduction," and "toxics use reduction" (the concept introduced by community and public interest groups), differing with respect to both methods
and goals. The proliferation of terms in turn created conceptual ambiguities at the policy level.

This conceptual confusion also extended to the "building block" concepts of toxics policy, often reflecting their introduction through earlier
end-of-pipe legislation and regulations. These differences also related to the
regulatory framework regarding routes of exposure. Different definitions of
terms like "hazard" or "hazardous substance" came to be used even when
referring to the same chemical or manufacturing facility.

Further, the definition debates reflected differences over the nature of
specific reduction or minimization activities themselves. The OTA study,
for example, defined waste reduction as: "in-plant practices that reduce,
avoid, or eliminate the generation of hazardous waste so as to reduce risks
to health and the environment."[8] Actions taken away from the waste generating activity, including waste recycling or treatment of wastes after they
had been generated, were excluded from this approach. Also, an action that
merely concentrated the hazardous content of a waste to reduce waste vol-

ume or diluted it to reduce the degree of hazard was not considered waste reduction.

EPA's definition of waste minimization, on the other hand, included a wide variety of recycling approaches which were excluded in OTA's definition. EPA's language also tended to be less specific. It interpreted waste minimization as reduction of hazardous substances generated, treated, stored, or discarded, which appeared to limit the approach to RCRA-defined wastes. EPA's interpretation included: "...any source reduction or recycling activity undertaken by a generator that results in either: (1) the reduction of total volume or quantity of hazardous waste; or (2) the reduction of toxicity of hazardous waste, or both, provided that reduction is consistent with the goal of minimizing present and future threats to human health and the environment."[9]

The distinction that emerged during the mid 1980s between "waste reduction" and "waste minimization" was primarily concerned with whether or not to include waste treatment and recycling. EPA considered both on-site and off-site recycling and most forms of waste treatment, such as incineration, as acceptable waste minimization practices. Its definition of recycling in the 1986 study incorporated both on-site and off-site recycling as well as certain types of treatment linked to a recycling process. Thus, EPA referred to recycling as "the use or reuse of a waste as an effective substitute for a commercial product, or as an ingredient or feedstock in an industrial process... [which could] also involve various types of treatment to facilitate the recycling process."[10]

EPA's interest in treatment was linked directly to the Agency's interpretation of its various waste-related mandates; most notably, reducing RCRA hazardous wastes intended for landfill disposal. In that context, incorporating waste treatment and the full range of recycling options within a waste minimization framework helped the Agency achieve its mandated goals. Most industry groups supported EPA's approach for identifying how they in turn could reduce their RCRA wastes.

Compounding these conceptual differences was the use of the term "source reduction." In its 1986 report to Congress, EPA described source reduction as:

> any activity that reduces or eliminates the generation of a hazardous waste within a process...that most closely corresponds to the concept of waste avoidance. Source reduction measures can include some types of treatment processes, but they also include process modifications, feedstock substitutions or improvements

in feedstock purity, various housekeeping and management practices, increases in the efficiency of machinery, and even recycling
within a process.[11]

The Agency's concept of source reduction, which was adopted by several environmental groups as well as by EPA, focused on in-plant changes
that reduced exiting wastes but also included off-site recycling. At the same
time, as elaborated in the EPA definition, it also included such treatment
processes as incineration or condensation.

Toxics Use Reduction and Pollution Prevention

These conceptual distinctions also became a focus of concern for public
interest and community activist groups which criticized the more exclusive emphasis on RCRA-regulated hazardous *wastes* (i.e., what exited a
system, rather than inputs, processes, or products) shared by EPA, OTA,
EDF, and Inform. The question of occupational exposures provided one
significant area of dispute. For example, although OTA's definition
appeared to be sufficiently broad to include workplace hazards as part of
its concept of "all environmental media," the OTA report specifically
excluded occupational exposures. This approach, as well as EPA's more limited focus on RCRA-defined wastes and inclusion of off-site recycling and
treatment, contrasted with the approach taken by the National Toxics
Campaign and the Public Interest Research Groups (PIRGs). These groups
sought to restructure toxics policy on the basis of a more comprehensive
view of the exposures involved and the parties affected by such exposures.
Linked to the "right-to-know" campaigns of the mid 1980s, activist groups
began to employ the term "toxics use reduction" in reflecting their own
constituent-based advocacy concerns. The Public Interest Research
Groups described this concept as:

> Changes in production processes, products or raw materials that
> reduce, avoid, or eliminate the use of toxic or hazardous sub-
> stances or the generation of hazardous byproducts per unit of
> production, so as to reduce overall risks to the health of workers,
> consumers, or the environment without shifting risks between
> workers, consumers or parts of the environment.[12]

By introducing the term "toxics use reduction," these groups sought to
incorporate into the definition of environmental hazards those hazards also
experienced by workers and consumers. The groups further sought to refo-

cus regulatory policy on the input end of the production cycle as an arena for intervention, which in turn provided the highest potential for preventing hazardous waste generation. If the use of a toxic material was eliminated, these groups argued, then all subsequent waste reduction, minimization, management, or pollution control became secondary to the main thrust of policy and industry activity.

The increasing prominence of the grassroots antitoxics movements that shifted the toxics discourse away from treatment and management to consideration of sources set the stage for a new round of conflicts and policy debates during the late 1980s and early 1990s regarding what kinds of product or process changes would be encouraged for industry to pursue. Both EPA (which had distanced itself from those regulatory tools available through TSCA) and industry (increasingly concerned about its vulnerabilities from "right-to-know" evidence of the extent of industry-generated toxic hazards)[13] began to seek a more inclusive (as well as voluntarist) concept to counter the criticisms about industry and regulatory failures in the toxics area. This search ultimately led to the introduction of the concept of *pollution prevention*, a concept seen as separate from rather than informed by toxics use reduction. In its January 1989 Pollution Prevention Statement published in the Federal Register, EPA first sought to demonstrate "a preventive program to reduce or eliminate the generation of potentially harmful pollutants" that would be broad in its definition. For EPA, pollution prevention represented:

> The reduction or elimination of pollutant discharges to the air, water or land. Pollution prevention approaches include: 1) Reducing the quantity and/or toxicity of pollutants generated by production processes through source reduction, waste minimization, and process modifications; 2) Eliminating pollutants by substituting non-polluting chemicals or products (e.g., material substitution, changes in product specifications); and 3) Recycling of waste materials (e.g., reuse, reclamation).[14]

The EPA definition explicitly focused on issues associated with solid and hazardous RCRA wastes. This definition incorporated distinctive approaches: waste reduction, waste minimization, process modifications, material substitution, and off-site and on-site recycling. This *was not* a policy-specific definition; that is, it allowed divergent strategies such as front-end process or material substitution changes, traditional process-specific activities (e.g., condensation or distillation), or certain forms of treatment which in turn created new forms of waste (e.g., on site incineration). Indeed, many of the techniques associated with early pollution prevention definitions were nothing more than extensions of media-specific regulatory approaches. Thus, pollution prevention, like waste minimization before it, was introduced as a catch-all phrase, revealing more the ambiguities, contradictions, and ultimately the single-medium focus of EPA's toxics policy rather than its restructuring.[15]

The Pollution Prevention Act of 1990, largely created through compromises between public interest groups and industry with a lesser role for EPA, began to shift the pollution prevention definition more sharply in the direction of reduction as substitution or process changes (e.g., "source reduction") as part of an overall conceptual hierarchy of approaches. The Act defined as national policy the objective that "pollution should be prevented or reduced at the source whenever feasible" which linked the concept of prevention to "source reduction," the concept at the top of the Act's conceptual hierarchy. In this context, the Act situated prevention as a practice which excluded waste recycling and treatment (unlike EPA's earlier definition of "waste minimization"). Thus, pollution prevention was represented here as:

> any practice which reduces the amount of any hazardous substance, pollutant, or contaminant entering any waste stream or otherwise released into the environment (including fugitive emissions) prior to recycling, treatment, or disposal....[16]

Acknowledging the dominance of the pollution control programs within EPA and the barriers they represented in the development of a primary focus on source reduction, the Act sought to circumvent such constraints by charging EPA to consider the effects of its existing programs on future "source reduction" efforts as well as to review all current Agency regulations in relation to those efforts. Though the Act did not attempt to set out a measurable goal for source reduction nor spell out specific programs to accomplish such objectives, it suggested that the groundwork for the future establishment of such goals could be accomplished by EPA's developing standards for measuring reduction and identifying potential reduction targets. In recognition of the increasing importance for environmental groups of right-to-know as the most effective route to pollution prevention, the Act also modified reporting requirements that had been established through the Toxics Release Inventory (discussed below) which became effective with the 1991 reporting year.[17]

Aside from these changes in reporting and definition, the Pollution Prevention Act still failed to address issues outside a "waste" or "emissions" framework. Most significantly, it ignored the occupational and product-related issues addressed directly by a "toxics use reduction" conceptual approach, which had been a primary concern of reduction advocates. Its most significant accomplishment as a policy tool was its attempt to provide a source-based definition, and its linkage of pollution prevention to information and reporting requirements. Although substantial provisions for data collection had been found throughout the sphere of single-medium pollution control legislation and regulation, its significance as a pollution prevention policy tool emerged more directly as the availability of data sources came to be associated with the concept of "right-to-know." This concept itself evolved into an approach that suggested a powerful, albeit inconsistent and sometimes flawed, arena for change.

Right-to-Know: The Role of Information

With the emergence of the "toxics use reduction" concept and the expanding influence of the community-based antitoxics groups who promoted it, new pressures came to bear on EPA and Congress to extend and revise the information that could be made available in order to sustain the changes associated with a toxics use reduction approach. The passage of Title III of the Superfund Amendments, the Emergency Planning Community Right-to-Know Act (EPCRA) establishing the Toxics Release Inventory, shifted attention from front-end regulation to identifying the nature and extent of the toxics release issue. The passage of Proposition 65 in California further elaborated this approach, linking "labeling" strategies with right-to-know approaches, by seeking to influence industry activities more as a result of public pressure than regulatory intervention. While "right-to-know" undoubtedly increased pressures on industry to pursue front-end changes, it further shifted attention away from the legislative and regulatory route for front-end policymaking, as indicated by the low priority status of TSCA described in Chapter 3. Nevertheless, right-to-know measures, most notably TRI, became the most visible, and frequently most effective source of such pressures at a time when the interest in pollution prevention still failed to translate into any effective, coordinated set of policy tools for accomplishing its ambitious goals.

The Toxics Release Inventory was established in 1987 as a computerized national database of toxic chemical releases by individual manufacturing facilities. Created under the authority of Section 313 of Title III of EPCRA, it was quickly established as the first publicly accessible computer database ever required by a federal law.[18] TRI came to provide the most comprehensive information on national toxic pollution at both a chemical and facility-specific level, despite significant exclusions of both chemicals and industries.

Section 313 stipulated that an annual report be submitted to the EPA by each industrial manufacturing facility in the U.S. that had ten or more employees, that imported, manufactured, processed or otherwise used more than an identified threshold level for some 329 toxic chemicals and classes of chemicals, and that fell within Standard Industrial Classification (SIC) Codes 20–39. The reporting threshold for facilities importing, manufacturing, or processing TRI chemicals was 75,000 pounds in 1987, declining to 50,000 pounds in 1988, and to 25,000 pounds in 1989 and thereafter. Facilities using 10,000 pounds or more of any one TRI chemical were also required to report.

Reporting facilities were required to estimate the quantity of each listed chemical released through various routes, including air, surface water, and land, and to underground injection wells and publicly owned treatment works, as well as the quantity transferred to off-site locations for treatment, storage, or disposal. TRI reports also required basic facility identification and some on-site waste treatment and recycling information. It further provided for optional reporting of waste reduction efforts, and exempted chemicals transferred to off-site recycling facilities from reporting requirements. Since the passage of the original law and the release of the first TRI report covering 1987 releases, various expansions of both the original reporting requirements and the number of TRI chemicals involved have been designated or proposed through subsequent legislation, and are discussed below.[19]

When results from the first year of TRI reporting (1987) were publicly announced in June of 1989, they indicated that more than 20 billion pounds of TRI chemicals were released or transferred, with more than 80 percent of that amount in the form of direct releases to air, surface water, or land.[20] The news was greeted with reactions that generally ranged from surprise to shock. Yet, as EPA's Director of the Office of Toxic Substances observed, the 20 billion pounds "could have been any [other] number," due to the absence of any prior baseline.[21] A few weeks after the data were released, the OTA suggested that a more accurate picture of the "national toxic loading of the environment" could be obtained by multiplying the figures by a factor of two to account for both intentional and inadvertent underreporting and failure to report by industry, and by a factor of ten to account for other toxic chemicals known to be used and released by industry, producing a rough estimate of 400 billion pounds annually.[22] Yet in the second year of reporting (1988), the total dropped to 6.2 billion pounds (due primarily to the delisting of six TRI chemicals which had accounted for more than fourteen billion pounds of all releases reported in 1987), with the EPA estimating that only two-thirds of all facilities required to report actually did so.[23]

Despite such fluctuations, the TRI data immediately came to be viewed as the most serious and well-articulated indictment to date of the failure of preceding decades of pollution control efforts to safeguard public health and the environment. It was also seen as an unprecedented and powerful source of information that could assist the goals of pollution prevention. Clearly a dramatic improvement on the ambiguous and highly porous data derived from RCRA reporting requirements (as in HSWA's biennial reports described in Chapter 3), the TRI immediately emerged as a central force in the debate on pollution prevention policy.

The driving force for passage of both the TRI and other EPCRA provisions had been the movement advocating worker and community right-to-know laws and regulations, several of which had first been introduced at the state and local levels during the late 1970s and early 1980s. This movement included occupational health advocates led by a handful of unions such as the Oil, Chemical and Atomic Workers (OCAW) and worker support groups such as the Committees on Occupational Safety and Health, as well as the community and public interest groups such as the National Toxics Campaign which had organized an effective, right-to-know linked "Superdrive for Superfund" campaign around the reauthorization debate. The central mission of "right-to-know," as presented by these groups, was to establish a democratic right to information within a toxics-related production system. Such a right was described by Minnesota state representative Darby Nelson during the debates over reauthorization:

> We simply must provide people with information that may, in fact, impact their chances of developing cancer, producing children with birth defects, and other health problems. The issue is fundamental and simple. People want to have maximum direct control over their own lives.[24]

By 1985, 29 states, primarily influenced by these community movements, had passed some form of right-to-know law, of which 25 covered worker right-to-know, and 18 covered the right-to-know of the community at large. These state laws, supplemented in some cases by municipal laws, provided the first vehicles by which workers and community residents could obtain information about the specific chemical hazards to which they were exposed.[25]

The major opponents to the right-to-know provisions in EPCRA were a number of different industry groups, led by the chemical industry, which sought to confine the reporting requirements to the Hazard Communication Standard approach established by OSHA earlier in the decade (described in Chapter 4). During the Superfund reauthorization hearings, these industry groups initially and strongly advanced the position that federal community right-to-know requirements should be based primarily on community access to Material Safety Data Sheets (MSDS). Industry spokesmen were particularly emphatic in recommending that the OSHA Hazard Communication Standard trade secrets provisions be preserved, and that states be precluded from imposing their own chemical hazard communication requirements. In contrast to this industry position, certain state legislators supporting federal community right-to-know legislation argued that they were largely motivated by their own frustrated attempts to pass state community right-to-know laws which had been undermined by industry threats to relocate.[26]

In their final form, the EPCRA provisions were substantially stronger than the OSHA standard, influenced largely by the intervening Bhopal disaster. In particular, EPCRA was explicitly designed to supplement, rather than preempt, state and local community right-to-know laws, and trade secret-based exemptions were made more difficult to establish in all EPCRA provisions. In 1988, for example, only 23 trade secret claims were allowed among the more than 70,000 TRI forms filed.[27] Facing legislation that was certain to go beyond a minor extension of the MSDS approach, the fall-back position of industry was generally organized around what industry groups came to call the public's "right-to-understand"—an approach that has characterized industry responses to the published TRI data. Along these lines the National Association of Manufacturers commented (in 1989 hearings that followed the release of the first year of TRI data) that "such data is clearly not understandable to the lay person."[28]

During the debate over EPCRA (and the TRI provisions), industry groups directly sought to limit how much and what kind of information would need to be reported. They suggested, for example, that inventory information not be required for chemicals that posed long-term exposure risks but did not create health risks in the event of an emergency release, or, conversely, that annual emissions data not be required for chemicals that posed only acute, short-term risks. Industry advocates also proposed limiting the distribution of certain elements of community hazard information to health and safety officials.[29] Industry response to the release of TRI data similarly focused on the maximum interpretation of results before widespread dissemination. The CAER (Community Awareness and Emergency Response) program of the Chemical Manufacturers Association (inaugurated in the year preceding the passage of SARA), typified this approach by emphasizing "the dissemination of information on risk *communication*—how to present information in meaningful ways so that citizens can evaluate actual risks in their community and take appropriate action" (our emphasis).[30]

Ultimately, the debates over what to include within a right-to-know framework were never successfully resolved. On the one hand, the initial list of TRI chemicals was remarkably indifferent to the major existing federal regulatory lists. The language of Section 313 included chemicals known to cause both chronic and acute health effects, and also (uniquely among the three EPCRA lists) provided for the inclusion of chemicals solely on the basis of adverse environmental effects. By the time of the EPCRA debate, Congress had the ability to choose from and/or incorporate elements from some five or six federal lists of regulated toxic chemicals. There were also various advisory lists from both professional and government health organizations which could have been used as a basis for TRI reporting. The state of West Virginia, for example, had in 1985 passed a community right-to-know law requiring annual emissions reports. The law adopted OSHA's definition for physical hazards, and added chemicals for which threshold values had been established by the American Conference of Government Industrial Hygienists as well as those specified in the National Toxicology Program's Annual Report on Carcinogens. Through this method, the law arrived at an initial list of 670 chemicals.[31] Instead, Congress based its list primarily on lists generated under right-to-know acts in New Jersey and Maryland to arrive at its original total of 329 chemicals and chemical classes (such as lead compounds). Fewer than 25 percent of the combined CERCLA and EPCRA hazardous substances were represented, while more than 100 substances were unique to the TRI list. According to data published by the Working Group on Community Right-to-Know, as of 1991 (i.e., accounting for listing and delisting actions since the original list) the TRI chemicals list remained limited to only 173 of 189 CAA hazardous air pollutants; 40 of 126 CWA priority pollutants; 140 of the 316 RCRA-regulated "P" (acute toxics) and "U" (chronic toxics) chemicals; 90 of 101 reproductive toxins and 202 of 351 known or probable human carcinogens listed by California's Safe Drinking Water and Toxic Enforcement Act of 1986 ("Proposition 65"); 41 of 129 chemicals listed as known or probable human carcinogens by the EPA Cancer Assessment Group; and 69 of 117 FIFRA special review pesticides.[32]

If the list of chemicals seemed somewhat arbitrary, the two reporting thresholds (one for use; one for import, manufacture, or processing) were equally so. During the debates preceding passage of SARA, threshold levels discussed ranged from facilities using 500 pounds or more of any listed

chemical, as some state laws required, to those manufacturing or processing 200,000 pounds or more. And while the differentiation between "use"
and "manufacture and processing" appeared to reflect a consensus that use
leads to proportionately greater total releases, it also meant that the distinction in thresholds could conceivably lead to an interpretation that
defined what constituted "manufacture and processing" in overly vague
and broad terms.[33]

Perhaps most important, however, were the large number of facilities
that were excluded from reporting by the SIC code criteria. Particularly
striking omissions included utilities, mining operations, oil and gas production, agribusiness, municipal waste management facilities, and all federal facilities; or, in other words, many of the same sectors exempted under
RCRA, and more recently by the CAA hazardous air pollutant (HAP)
source categories. In the case of RCRA, these exemptions, particularly for
primary extractive industries, were largely supported by a "high volume,
low risk" argument, and by a developing sentiment that the complicated
RCRA system may have reached its natural limits. The TRI approach, on
the other hand, seemed eminently well-adapted to address the high-vol-
ume low-risk considerations, and appeared to provide the basis for an alternative regulatory approach.

A 1990 report by the San Diego Environmental Health Coalition,
"Communities at Risk: Your Right to Know About Toxics in San Diego,"
provided some illustration of the significance that various loopholes in TRI
reporting criteria have had at a local level. The authors combined information derived from the 1988 TRI database with information from the
San Diego County Department of Health Services Hazardous Materials
Management Division to obtain an overview of toxics and hazardous
materials use and release. The Coalition found that the manufacturing SIC
code requirement excluded 90 percent of the facilities under permit from
San Diego County hazardous materials regulators, including utilities,
chemical supply firms, propane and fuel storage facilities, and service firms
such as exterminators and clinical and research facilities. Similarly, the
threshold reporting requirements excluded 68 of 70 facilities known to use
chlorine at California-reportable thresholds (55 gallons, 500 pounds, or
200 cubic feet), and 141 of 151 acetone users.[34]

Perhaps the most notorious early example of an omission was revealed
through a reporting error in which the 1987 TRI figures released by
Kennecott Utah Copper provided a much remarked, one-time glimpse
into the potential significance of TRI's exclusion of the mining sector. In
its 1987 TRI report, the company mistakenly reported releases for both its
Primary Metals (SIC 33) and mining (SIC 10) operations. In 1988, in

reporting only on Primary Metals activities, releases of copper alone decreased from 130 million tons to 4 million tons.[35]

Since then, there have been numerous occasions where omissions, reworked numbers, or other reporting inconsistencies have produced staggering changes in the releases reported. These inconsistencies were made even more dramatic when information about toxics *use* within facilities was able to be contrasted with the toxics *release* information. A reporting bill established by the state of New Jersey, for example, which included use, inventory, and receiving data (under the generic category of toxics use) was particularly revealing when contrasted with TRI release data. According to an Inform report contrasting the New Jersey law with the TRI, a Shell Oil facility had, through the TRI, indicated releases in 1992 of 4,876 pounds of benzene. But data on benzene use within the facility was, through the New Jersey law, reported to be 110 *million* pounds. As a result of these and other powerful contrasting data sources, EPA began in 1994 to explore the development of a Chemical Use Inventory system, modeled in part on the New Jersey and Massachusetts laws.[36]

Despite its enormous gaps and problems in the data, the TRI has nevertheless represented a breakthrough in the content and value of the right-to-know approach. Prior to the TRI, national toxics release information consisted primarily of sketchy, variable, and typically media-specific permit data buried under multiple layers of bureaucracy in permit files and reports around the country. Some of this information was potentially accessible through Freedom of Information Act requests and through local permit authorities, but only to the most diligent and informed of citizens. The development of the TRI, despite its obvious and significant limitations and disadvantages, offered new opportunities for linking the reporting and availability of information with a prevention framework. The advantages posed by a publicly accessible computer database containing site- and chemical-specific emissions data for the entire country, while apparently underestimated at conception, cannot be overstated.

Such advantages, moreover, exist not only for citizens who can be significantly empowered by a right-to-know approach, but also for the EPA (for both its existing regulatory programs, and for its developing pollution prevention interests)[37] and for industry as well (despite its lack of enthusiasm for right-to-know in general and TRI specifically). While industry initially tended to view the TRI as a public relations nightmare and has subsequently opposed efforts to expand its scope, for many facilities the preparation of TRI reports represented the first internal attempt to account for total emissions of specific chemicals and the first integrated view of their own toxic chemicals use and production.

In recognition of its potential role in encouraging reduction efforts, the seven-page Pollution Prevention Act of 1990 modified TRI reporting requirements (effective beginning with the 1991 reporting year) to make mandatory a "source reduction and recycling report," which closed the off-site recycling loophole, and required that a ratio of production in the reporting year to production in the previous year be provided for each chemical.[38] Those changes were further strengthened when the President also expanded the list of facilities required to report, including most notably federal facilities (e.g., military-based facilities) whose absence had constituted an enormous gap in TRI information.[39]

After passage of the Pollution Prevention Act in 1990, public interest groups helped put together a more powerful and far-reaching expansion of both the TRI and the federal commitment to pollution prevention objectives in the form of The Community Right-to-Know More Act, first introduced by then Congressman Gerry Sikorski (D-Minn.) in 1991.[40] Under this law, TRI reporting requirements would be extended to apply to all facilities that employed 10 or more employees and met a different threshold test for listed chemicals. This test would be dramatically revised to apply to chemicals released in amounts greater than or equal to 100 lbs for metals or metal compounds, and 2,000 lbs for other listed substances (replacing the 10,000 lbs use, and 25,000 lbs manufacture, processing, and import thresholds and distinctions). The content of reports would require that maximum hourly rates of release of each chemical be correlated with specific sources, that the amount of each listed chemical present as a product constituent be expressed per unit of product output (essentially defining a comprehensive materials accounting system), and that substitutions that result in a discontinuation of the use of listed chemicals be identified regardless of whether the substitutes were themselves listed. Other provisions called for the preparation of detailed toxics use reduction plans, for strong inspection and enforcement powers, and for a variety of mandates and mechanisms integrating "toxics use reduction" with existing environmental statutes and regulations.[41]

Through the early 1990s, efforts to pass some version of a Community Right-to-Know More Act failed to develop sufficient support in Congress, as industry groups successfully raised their concern about regulatory burdens (including reporting requirements) as a counter to right-to-know. Ultimately still situated at the margins of policy, this more aggressive use of right-to-know as a policy tool pointed to the vast distance that lay between the current state of pollution prevention information and activity, and a pursuit of the broader objectives of a more comprehensive pollution prevention strategy. Right-to-know had opened up new possibilities for comprehension and action on the toxics front, but the availability of data has provided, at best, opportunities for review rather than information tools for restructuring.

Nevertheless, right-to-know, as embodied in the evolution of the TRI, has emerged as one of the most striking pollution prevention successes to date. Chemical industry officials, for one, have noted that the public nature of the information has provided a powerful incentive for industry activity, certainly at the level where specific process changes (as described in Chapter 8) can result in dramatic improvements in the numbers. Where right-to-know remains an incomplete tool for action is in the divorce of information from policy intervention conceived as a strategic goal in addressing sources. Absent that linkage and caught in the throes of continual debate about the value of intervention in the first place, pollution prevention continued to take a back seat to the contentious arguments about how environmental policy should be conducted.

Reducing Government's Role: Comparing Risks, Creating Markets, and Emphasizing Technologies

Although pollution prevention had emerged by the 1990s as every policymaker's favorite strategy, EPA became more directly associated with a number of other policy approaches, each of which had its own potentially contrasting implications for interpreting a pollution prevention mandate. These included the elevation of "comparative risk" as a process to evaluate risks and influence the allocation of Agency resources; the continuing shift toward voluntarist measures, including the use of "market" incentives as a flexible strategy for accomplishing such results; and a renewed emphasis on environmental technologies which failed to distinguish between technologies of control or prevention.

The "comparative risk" concept was given major prominence as a guide to policy with the publications of *Unfinished Business: A Comparative Assessment of Environmental Problems in 1987* and *Reducing Risk: Setting Priorities and Strategies for Environmental Protection* in 1990.[42] The "Unfinished Business" study, undertaken by senior EPA officials, had been initiated by EPA administrator Lee Thomas in order to re-elevate the concept of scientific risk assessment as a means of ranking different environmental problems and then using such ranking for purposes of allocating Agency resources. The "Reducing Risk" study, a product of EPA's Science Advisory Board, urged EPA to target its actions in terms of its risk reduction potential. This study, in turn, was promoted heavily by EPA

Administrator William Reilly, who argued that EPA needed to ground itself in "solid science" as opposed to "middle class enthusiasms." Risk analysis as solid science would provide the basis for distinguishing the "big environmental problems from the small ones."[43] And although the Clinton administration's EPA placed less emphasis on comparative risk as an evaluation tool, the Agency found itself increasingly on the defensive from Congressional and press criticisms of its overresponsiveness to public concerns. Instead, these critics argued, EPA's risk-based evaluations (and resource allocations) needed to occur outside the public discourse; that is, in the neutral, value-free arena of science.[44]

At the time that the "Unfinished Business" and "Risk Reduction" studies were undertaken, the role and conceptual underpinnings of risk assessment had already evolved considerably from its initial introduction as a tool for environmental policy in the late 1970s. Risk assessment was first perceived during the protracted debates over policy and regulation during the late 1970s as providing a mechanism for shifting the focus from the zero emissions/discharge targets embedded in the language of the Clean Water Act and Clean Air Act to a more "flexible" position regarding standard-setting (with respect to the regulated industries), akin to such other policy innovations at the time as the "bubble" concept and cost–benefit analysis. Risk analysis, it was posited, would clarify a "safe threshold" comfort level in relation to regulatory action. This could be accomplished through the use of science in the standard setting process, which in turn underlined the emphasis on how to best manage rather than reduce toxics use (whether in terms of controlling the level of emissions or of discharges to air, water, or land or as an occupational hazard).

Despite its basic argument that it was grounding policy decisions in scientific analysis and thus presumably removing it from political contention, quantitative risk assessment became a controversial tool from the outset. As an evaluative method, it was continually beset with arguments over what constituted "safe" thresholds (or whether, for certain substances, there was *any* safe threshold), the nature of the assumptions used in determining risk levels, and whether the risk assessment process itself was distinct from the policy implications of the assessment (i.e., the nature of the relationship between risk assessment and risk management). These controversies were compounded by specific standards established by both OSHA and EPA which were attacked as either too weak (where the risk assessment process was superseded by cost considerations, as with the 1979 standard for THMs in drinking water sources[45]) or too stringent (as with OSHA's benzene and cotton dust standards, both of which became subject to later regulatory modification or court action which established additional criteria for regulatory action and/or which mandated the use of a more comprehensive risk assessment as a prerequisite for standard setting[46]). Political influences within the regulatory agencies during the early 1980s further compounded the arguments over what constituted "good science," and whether risk assessment itself needed to be subordinated to other considerations (e.g., impact on industry activities).[47]

In 1983, the National Research Council published its major review of the risk assessment question and significantly (given the controversies at the time) sought to distinguish and separate directly the process of assessment from management.[48] This judgment was underlined by the new EPA Administrator William Ruckelshaus, brought back as Agency head in the midst of charges about industry influence and the corruption of the regulatory review process. Ruckelshaus was particularly concerned with demonstrating EPA's renewed commitment to scientific analysis, with its capabilities of generating high quality data to inform the policy process.[49] By the mid to late 1980s, risk assessment (despite its considerably evolving status as an instrument of science) had not only become standard operating procedure in informing policy judgments and used to justify particular regulatory actions, but had itself become the primary link or "logical common denominator" between EPA's different program offices in how they each defined priorities for Agency action. However, this "logical common denominator,"[50] though a widely used tool for regulatory activity, had yet to receive status as the defining instrument in assigning priorities (for cleanup funds, regulatory intervention through standard setting, etc.) for the Agency as a whole. Without such an instrument, Agency officials feared they would continue to be subject to what they considered an emotional, unscientific process of legislative mandates influenced by players removed from scientific judgments (e.g., citizen groups, industry, environmental advocates, etc.).

With the publication of "Reducing Risk" in 1990, the Bush administration sought to extend the role for risk assessment by launching a new program (the Comparative Risk Project) to be undertaken at the state level, while strongly promoting legislation on this subject that had been introduced at the federal level by Senator Patrick Moynihan (D.-NY) on behalf of the Agency.[51] Both of these efforts were designed to more formally elevate traditional risk assessment in assigning Agency priorities. On the one hand, the state projects were to specifically "rank" different risks on the basis of a risk assessment review as a way to structure decisionmaking on Agency resource allocations. At the same time, the Moynihan legislation would establish a Committee on Relative Risks as well as a Committee on Environmental Benefits, both consisting of technical experts capable of "ranking" risks and estimating the quantitative benefits of reducing specific risks.

Both the Moynihan bill and the risk-ranking exercise at the state level were immediately criticized on the basis of the biases inherent in the latter. This included the absence of public participation in the evaluation process and the inability to identify both cumulative risks and concentrated risks for specific populations ("hot spots"), a core argument of those community groups identified with a burgeoning environmental justice movement.[52] More directly, in relation to the question of pollution prevention, was the concern that the risk ranking focused on existing risks (and thus treatment and control options in managing such risks) rather than future risks (and thus pollution prevention opportunities for reducing or eliminating particular risks as a management priority). By promoting risk ranking as both an evaluative tool and a guide for management, EPA and its counterparts at the state level further removed the debate over standard setting and enforcement from the question of how best to influence the way industries operated in the context of their generation and use of hazardous substances and processes.

At the same time, both the Bush and Clinton EPA strongly emphasized the centrality of voluntary waste reduction efforts by industry, established through specified targeted plans such as EPA's 33/50 plan designed to reduce releases of seventeen major chemicals appearing on the TRI list. The focus on "voluntarism," the major objective of industry associations such as the Chemical Manufacturers Association, was further reinforced, particularly during the Bush administration, by industry access to key new environmental policy-oriented administrative structures, such as the Competitiveness Council chaired by Vice President Dan Quayle. The Council reassumed the role the Office of Management and Budget had previously played during the early 1980s through its implementation of Executive Order 12291 in deemphasizing regulatory interventions. Though the Clinton administration abolished the Competitiveness Council and sought to establish equal access to both industry and environmental groups, it maintained the Bush administration's emphasis on market solutions to help extend the focus on voluntary initiatives. It did this significantly by associating toxics release reductions with industry flexibility in determining both the nature and timing of such reductions. Market-derived or voluntary reductions, however, frequently differed from pollution prevention initiatives by their reliance on "media-shifting" of pollutants; use of recycling and treatment strategies to reduce regulated toxic releases; and less frequent reliance on specific changes in the actual use of toxic or hazardous substances or processes. These approaches, along with the elevation of comparative risk, provided EPA a set of contrasting strategies that further removed the policy process from a restructuring emphasis associated with a prevention mandate.

The most significant policy shift associated with the Clinton administration was its emphasis on "environmental technologies" as a strategy designed to create economic benefits associated with environmental goals, while specifically seeking to expand those benefits through an aggressive export strategy for those same technologies. The emphasis on technologies resembled arguments put forth during the 1970s by pollution control advocates seeking to counter claims of job loss from environmental regulation. Pollution control, with its emphasis on technology add-ons, was said to provide net economic benefits by establishing new industries and related stimulator effects for local economies.[53] Such an argument was reinforced by the rapid emergence of a pollution control or "environmental" industry involved in the development of those technologies. These became the classic technologies of pollution control; the incinerators, landfill liners, scrubbers, condensation and distillation equipment, and other technological instruments for regulatory compliance. Pollution prevention technologies, particularly where those technologies assumed significant structural changes in the products or processes used, tended to be more marginal to this environmental technology concept, with the major exception of electric vehicle technology, itself driven by a media-specific regulatory requirement (see Chapter 9 for a discussion of EV issues). The failure to directly associate pollution prevention with the definition of environmental technology simply served to reassert the dominance of the pollution control industry as a core actor on the policy stage, and, increasingly, in the export of pollution control at the global level. Clean technology, as a pollution prevention concept, remained at best a device to make facilities more efficient and less wasteful, rather than addressing the question of the purpose and nature of both the technology and the processes and products associated with it.

Locating Other Entry Points: State and Local Efforts

Unlike their historical role in managing environmental concerns in such areas as air emissions, water discharge, or solid waste disposal, the involvement by states and local communities in the management of toxics has been more recent. Hazardous waste federal legislation such as RCRA and CERCLA and toxic substances control legislation such as TSCA mandated federal agencies to be the primary authority in rulemaking and enforcement, although some of the implementation occurred at the state level. It was not until the mid 1980s, linked in part to the development of EPA's waste minimization approach, that more extensive state and local programs began to be initiated. In 1981, only two states had established specific waste minimization programs; by 1988 the number of programs had increased to twenty-nine, according to a National Governor's survey. But nearly all these programs focused primarily on technical assistance and educational efforts, and were quite small. Overall waste minimization program budgets averaged only about $150,000 per year, with minimal staffing for implementation.[54]

By the early 1990s, however, several states and local communities began to explore a broader and more expansive approach. This shift was significantly influenced by the role of community, environmental, and public interest groups dissatisfied with existing toxics policies. These groups successfully lobbied legislators or undertook local initiatives to establish new kinds of programs. Such programs ranged from more comprehensive pollution prevention or waste reduction-oriented legislation (e.g., those in Massachusetts and New Jersey) to community bans on products like polystyrene foam containers or barbecue lighter fluids, to state right-to-know and toxics labeling initiatives such as New Jersey's right-to-know legislation or California's Proposition 65. Although these programs and initiatives varied in terms of their scope and approach, they collectively demonstrated, despite their often limited role, a more aggressive stance of state and local communities, which began to factor into the debates over appropriate pollution prevention strategies. By the 1990s, states and local communities had become actors in their own right in the toxics policy arena.

The first two states in the country to embrace broad-based reduction-oriented legislation were Massachusetts and Oregon, both of which enacted laws on the same day, July 24, 1989. The more explicitly reduction-focused of the two laws, the Massachusetts Toxics Use Reduction Act (TURA), was enacted after an extensive debate and negotiating process lasting more than three years. This process also influenced the reorganization of the state environmental agencies, primarily through the establishment of a Bureau of Waste Prevention, which consolidated hazardous waste, air quality, industrial wastewater, solid waste, and right-to-know programs. The Bureau was created in part to implement a "whole facility approach," with regulations (and enforcement procedures) designed to treat each facility as an entity rather than regulating on a medium-by-medium basis.[55] The provisions of TURA were in fact structured to provide a legislative mandate for the whole facility approach (including planning and reporting requirements for each facility, such as identifying the costs of using toxic materials throughout the facility and across all media), although the reorganization that ultimately took place still left intact, as separate entities, the air, water, hazardous waste, and solid waste programs, while eliminating the right-to-know program.

The passage of TURA was accomplished after negotiations among the Massachusetts Public Interest Research Group (MASSPIRG), state agency officials and legislators, and industry groups led by chemical, electronics, and aerospace companies (e.g., Polaroid and Monsanto) finally reached a successful conclusion.[56] The law, similar to state initiatives stipulating solid waste diversion reductions, established an ambitious statewide goal of 50% reduction in toxics use by reporting facilities by 1997. The legislation identified "toxics use reduction" as the guiding policy instrument, and defined it as "in-plant changes in production processes or raw materials that reduce, avoid, or eliminate the use of toxic or hazardous substances or generation of hazardous byproducts per unit of product, so as to reduce risks to the health of workers, consumers, or parts of the environment."[57] The legislation further described how such in-plant changes could be achieved: through input substitution, product reformulation, production unit redesign or modification, or improved operation and maintenance. The legislation also identified on site recycling (defined as recycling integral to the production process) as part of the state's reduction approach, while specifically excluding off-site recycling, a key issue for several of those industries who ultimately opposed the final version of the bill.

To implement its provisions, TURA established an Office of Toxics Use Reduction Assistance and Technology to provide technical assistance and guidance for industry, and a Toxics Use Reduction Institute at the University of Massachusetts at Lowell for research, training, and information gathering purposes. The bill also established a "Large Quantity Toxics Users" category, which included both TRI reporting firms as well as certain industries and chemical users exempted from TRI reporting. These large quantity users were required to inventory the chemicals used within facilities and to prepare (by 1994) Toxics Use Reduction plans on a facility-by-facility basis. Such plans were to include (1) a statement of management commitment to toxics use reduction, (2) a process-by-process evaluation of the potential for toxics reduction, and (3) an overall plan for reducing the use and/or disposal of toxic materials. These plans would then be approved by "Toxics Use Reduction Planners," a new group of officials who would be trained and certified through a program run by the Toxics Use Reduction Institute at Lowell.[58]

The Massachusetts program was the most comprehensive effort in the area of toxics use reduction in 1989. Many of its supporters in the environmental and public interest community who had helped draft the original legislation felt that the Massachusetts legislation provided the first significant legislative opportunity at the state level to "have a great impact on reducing toxic waste," as one key advocate put it. Some industry groups decided to support the final amended version in part because, as John Gould of the Associated Industries of Massachusetts put it, the passage of some sort of toxic waste legislation appeared inevitable. Other industry groups, however, argued that the legislation needed to be extended to other states, at least on a regional level, to avoid competitive disadvantage.[59]

As it turned out, the Massachusetts law became more a harbinger of changes at the state level than an isolated case of innovative legislation passed by a state known for its strong environmental and public interest groups. When the state of Oregon, after a similar process of debate and negotiation, enacted its own reduction–oriented legislation on the same day as the Massachusetts legislation was signed into law, it became clear that the focus on new approaches had largely shifted to the states. The Oregon law was similar to Massachusetts's TURA by requiring hazardous waste generators to submit detailed toxics use reduction plans to the state. The state, in turn, was to provide technical assistance, particularly to small quantity generators. Unlike TURA, however, the Oregon law did not set any specific goals for toxics use reduction, in response to the objections of a number of industries who argued that the quantity of toxics produced could also be considered an indicator of economic growth in the state. In contrast to the Massachusetts law, the Oregon law also failed to distinguish between on–site and off–site recycling, a major area of contention between industry and environmentalists. But what most distinguished the Oregon legislation from its Massachusetts counterpart was its emphasis on the development of a voluntary planning process to be developed by industry in seeking to reduce both the use of toxics and the amount of hazardous wastes to be generated. Industry performance goals were to be established and annual waste reduction progress reports were to be issued relative to each of the specific performance goals identified. Although the Oregon legislation failed to identify specific market mechanisms or other economic incentives to achieve such goals, it reinforced the federal EPA focus on voluntary reduction that became increasingly prominent during the Bush and Clinton administrations.[60]

Following the enactment of the Oregon and Massachusetts legislation, a number of states adopted laws or reorganized their environmental agencies as part of their proclaimed goal of instituting pollution prevention or waste reduction-based objectives. Several states, such as New Jersey, Minnesota, and Washington, established target goals from a baseline figure, some as high as 50%, for reduction of toxics use or hazardous waste disposal to be accomplished within various timeframes, from five years in the New Jersey legislation to nearly twenty years in Minnesota's law. Several of the state laws provided for technical assistance programs, user fees to finance implementation of the legislation, and various kinds of reporting and planning provisions, some of which were mandatory (though most remained voluntary). Some legislation established new administrative agencies, typically a Pollution Prevention Office of some kind, partly to administer the law and partly to consolidate various hazardous waste–oriented functions scattered through the state bureaucracies. What most of the legislation failed to address, however, were the forms of direct intervention potentially capable of accomplishing specific reduction goals, whether in relation to product bans, process changes, or larger industrial policy questions regarding the nature of the industrial base within the state.

At the same time, much of the language and intent of the reduction-oriented legislation of the late 1980s and early 1990s, though identifying pollution prevention or reduction as the concepts of choice, failed to extend beyond the problem of waste generation and disposal. It was the disposal question, primarily, which continued to preoccupy state planners concerned about diminishing landfill capacity and strong community-based opposition to maintaining (let alone expanding) existing landfill operations. Unlike the Massachusetts experience and the approach of a few other states such as New Jersey, Maine, Vermont, Oregon, and Washington, this focus on waste also reflected a limited or even nonexistent focus on use, whether in terms of production issues (e.g., occupational hazards) or product use. While state efforts to extend their toxics policies beyond the narrower frame of waste minimization had become widespread, with as many as 105 state programs identified by the General Accounting Office having a presumed pollution prevention focus, these legislative initiatives failed to fully reflect the kind of paradigm shift implicit in the pollution prevention concept. With fully 80% of such programs considered "nonregulatory" (which, according to the GAO, "typically rely on widespread education of business and industry sectors to promote voluntary pollution prevention" while not requiring any kind of formal pollution prevention planning), the thrust of such programs ended up taking "a somewhat passive and reactive approach to their customers rather than one of active outreach."[61]

Still, the new state laws did offer dramatic evidence that a change in policy direction was not only possible but, for some, central to the question of how to address toxics generation and waste disposal in a given location. In the state of Indiana, for example, where toxics generating and toxics using industries, such as pharmaceutical and chemical companies, had long dominated legislative and policy discussions in relation to toxics issues, new toxics legislation was passed less than a year after the Massachusetts and Oregon laws were signed into law. The Indiana legislation, for one, duplicated the Massachusetts rather than the Oregon approach on the recycling issue, despite strong opposition from such key companies as Dow Chemical and the Eli Lilly Company. By specifically excluding such approaches as off-site recycling, waste exchanges, and treatment options such as cement kiln incineration, the Indiana law created a public relations dilemma for companies like Dow and Lilly who had significantly relied on off-site recycling and incineration as the centerpiece of their waste minimization activity. On the other hand, the Indiana legislation was voluntary in intent, without some of the key mandates and regulatory provisions of the Massachusetts legislation. Ultimately, Indiana environmental and public interest groups, led by the Citizen Action League, were able to bring together a bipartisan coalition of legislators and industry groups, particularly small quantity generators, to overcome the resistance of Dow, Lilly, and a number of other large quantity users. The passage of the Indiana law, in a politically conservative state with among the highest per capita generation of toxic substances, strongly identified the potential appeal of a pollution prevention approach at the state level, particularly one with a voluntarist framework.[62]

Parallel to these state efforts, a number of local communities sought to develop programs, establish offices, or associate with larger, regional efforts to explore possible entry points for pollution prevention activity at the local or regional level. Most of these efforts, with the crucial exception of single-medium regulatory agencies which sought to use their mandated compliance and enforcement powers to include a kind of "pretreatment" reduction approach, were also primarily voluntary in nature. They focused on educational or technology transfer activities, such as the city of Los Angeles's use of retired engineers to perform "hazardous waste audits" for small businesses who had little or no access to such resources.[63] What nearly all the local or regional efforts failed to incorporate was a regional planning dimension; that is, defining ways to target industrial activity and infrastructure development (e.g., transportation) as part of a broader perspective on regional issues, whether environmental or economic. The absence of regional planning mechanisms in a context where toxics use and impacts could be considered distinctively regional issues ultimately represented the most powerful barrier to establishing a successful entry point for pollution prevention at the local and regional level.[64]

The Terms: Linking Definitions to Policy

While EPA compounded its uncertain commitment to pollution prevention by embracing such policy approaches as risk ranking, voluntarism, and promoting environmental technologies; and state and local governments sought to expand the arena for possible pollution prevention activity; community, environmental and public interest groups promoted their own agendas. These were, most notably, environmental justice (addressing the burden of multiple and highly concentrated risks), right-to-know and public participation (the public's right to participate in locating opportunities for change and reduction), and most directly, in terms of the discourse around toxics policy, the elevation of the concept of "toxics use reduction" as the most direct way to shift policymaking away from its media-specific, control-oriented emphasis. For community groups and environmentalists, toxics use reduction offered the certainty of substance and process-specific change. The focus on *use* that the toxics use reduction concept provided also served to contrast with the ways in which EPA used the term "pollution prevention" to include approaches that potentially undermined the objectives of a prevention approach.[65]

Still, the emphasis on use raised its own set of questions, particularly by its reference to the actual handling of toxics (from manufacture through use and disposal) but not necessarily including the reasons underlying such use. In that context, the environmentalist interpretation of the toxics use reduction concept focused less on industrial design and structural considerations crucial to industry decisionmaking than on the outcomes of toxics use (e.g., accomplishing specific solvent substitutions, rather than focusing on why and how such solvents were introduced into particular production processes as a means to address their use). While pollution prevention had been introduced as a broad and often ambiguous term of reference, conceptually it still allowed for considerations of design and structural change, as used in this book. Thus, we have identified a design and structure as well as use-oriented pollution prevention concept as one that directly flows from the toxics use reduction approach, while expanding its definition to address questions of what kind of change in production (and consumption) might be required as well as how prevention-oriented changes might be accomplished.

Further, the term "toxics," as OTA had pointed out, potentially limited the conceptual focus for reduction or prevention in that its reference was "poisons," thereby excluding other kinds of environmental hazards (e.g., flammability or explosiveness). In contrast, OTA had sought a more inclusive definition of hazardous waste reduction. OTA's definition referred to "harm to human health or the environment," and to hazardous waste as "outputs from an industrial operation into all environmental media." Although OTA's use of the term "all environmental media" appeared broadly inclusive (potentially incorporating occupational exposures and product hazards), the discussion of "environmental media" in the 1986 OTA report and in the later policy debates between EPA and OTA specifically limited the definition of environmental media to the waste arena.

A more inclusive definition of the terms "toxics," "pollution," or "environmental hazards," as they are referred to (sometimes interchangeably) in this book, would include all materials and processes which may cause harm to human health and the environment. A more comprehensive definition of reduction or prevention should include the reduction or elimination of toxics or environmental hazards in all environmental media, including occupational exposures and product use, at each stage of a production cycle or along a material chain. Such a definition of pollution prevention (one which flows from the toxics use reduction construct) also requires an elaboration of the different forms of intervention (whether through policy instruments or through a reconstituted process of industry decisionmaking) at the design stage of a production cycle. Such a design emphasis would refer not simply to the manufacturing, use, and disposal stages of production but the range of decision points related to how, when, and why products and processes of a specific industry are introduced. In this respect, a pollution prevention–based review or design for the environment[66] seeks to evaluate industry and facility-specific activities in structural terms. That is, *pollution prevention as a category of design or structure* calls for an examination of what is being produced and why it is produced as well as how it is produced. This approach thus affirms "environment" and "pollution prevention" criteria as central considerations for industry decisionmaking, parallel to such core industrial design and structure criteria as costs, markets, performance, product innovation, production efficiency, material and process flexibility or adaptability, both global and regional dimensions of production, and upstream–downstream relationships.

At the same time, the definition of environmental media as used here and following OTA's lead, includes all discharges, whether regulated or within permitted or licensed limits, or those that fail to be detected or reported. This approach also frees the definition—and its policy implications—from the distorting effects of existing regulation. For example, the response of an industry to regulation within a particular environmental medium may be to shift discharges to those media with higher discharge limits or less stringent regulatory restrictions regardless of the environmental consequences of such a media shift. This may move a company from noncompliance to compliance, the core concern of media-specific regulation. However, a comprehensive assessment of environmental impacts (e.g., a design review) must include the new "legal" discharges. When examining or trying to influence the real life behavior of generators of environmental hazards, existing regulatory frameworks must always be considered.

Defining pollution prevention in this way establishes a conceptual hierarchy to promote strategies for reducing the environmental impacts of industrial products and processes. The hierarchy can be structured as follows:

- *Reduction of all Environmental Hazards or Pollution Prevention,* including an environmental design and structural review

- *Waste Reduction,* including all waste stream activities, except for occupational or product-based hazards

- *Waste Minimization,* including off-site recycling, focused primarily on regulated wastes

- *Pollution Control,* including treatment and disposal derived from media-specific regulations

"Pollution prevention," "toxics use reduction," and "source reduction" all belong at the top of this hierarchy. Historically, however, these terms have frequently been used interchangeably with other concepts (waste reduction, waste minimization, and even, in certain instances, with pollution control). Standard "pollution prevention" approaches also frequently omit occupational, product-based, or design issues.

Despite their ambiguities, pollution prevention, toxics use reduction, and source reduction have become conceptual lightening rods—terms of reference associated with policy debates about both the focus of regulation and industry decisionmaking. For example, EPA, in response to the 1990 Pollution Prevention Act as well as criticisms from public interest groups regarding inadequacies in the Agency's definition and interpretation of pollution prevention, has sought on several occasions to redefine the concept, most notably in the wake of the passage of the 1990 Pollution Prevention Act and EPA's subsequent 1991 interpretive statement about its pollution prevention approach. Pollution prevention, on these occasions, referred to "source reduction and only very limited closed-loop recy-

152 R. Gottlieb, M. Smith, J. Roque, and P. Yates

cling"—as one disappointed industry figure characterized the latest EPA approach.[67] This definition also underlined the new reporting requirements for TRI which segregated figures for treatment and recycling, thus suggesting preference for such approaches as product substitution or process changes. The struggle between definitions—namely, industry's preference for "waste minimization" and the promotion of "toxics use reduction" by public interest groups—had ultimately created a policy standoff for evaluating how pollution prevention would or could be accomplished.[68]

The purpose in establishing a prevention hierarchy is presumably to work through such a standoff by demonstrating the greater desirability of approaches in a kind of continuum of strategies designed to deal with the different sources of environmental hazards. In that context, those approaches that fully eliminate or substantially reduce toxic or environmental hazards at each stage of a production cycle and in all environmental media belong at the top of the hierarchy. These can be accomplished by production design changes (through a design review process), structural analysis (locating the barriers for prevention and evolutionary changes in industry structures and location choices), product substitutions (including product bans), or process changes (for example, altering the method for cleaning parts). Certain procedures, such as certain types of process changes (many of which fall within a "good housekeeping" or greater efficiency approach), equipment modifications, and closed loop recycling systems, could constitute acceptable waste minimization and waste reduction practices, but would be considered examples of pollution prevention as well. Unlike a waste minimization approach, however, some forms of pollution prevention may require reexamination of all aspects of a particular production system and may as a result require significant reinvestments in new production facilities and/or a fundamental restructuring of the product or the product's use itself. Thus, pollution prevention also represents a way to inform industrial or economic development policy, insofar as it influences both the processes and outcomes of a given production system.

At the bottom of the hierarchy are those approaches that require controls after the material has become a hazardous waste in some form; that is, traditional pollution control strategies. Implementation of lower steps should take place only after higher-ranking approaches have been adequately reviewed and implemented. Reduction or pollution prevention strategies need to reconstitute the basis for policy, forcing the redesign of existing regulations and policy instruments to reflect the goals of the hierarchy.

Barriers to Prevention

If toxics use reduction, source reduction, or pollution prevention appear to be desirable strategies, why, then, do pollution-control/media-specific policy approaches persist? Why is waste minimization, in the form of improved pollution control and waste management practices, favored by industry and, in many cases, by federal and state environmental agencies over such approaches as design review changes, product substitutions, structural analysis, or, in general, the elimination of environmental hazards from manufacturing processes and manufactured products. Some analysts have noted that pollution control, for one, is "easier to pursue" by regulators ensconced in their media-specific program offices or by industries for whom environmental considerations remain an external cost. Pollution control, furthermore, involves the application of generic technology such as water treatment and filters. Controls do not threaten industrial confidentiality nor do they imply that certain production decisions are subject to social governance. Controls are easy to apply. They can be added to existing processes without altering production methods. Pollution control approaches, as they have been described here, have also been encouraged by the federal government's media-specific regulatory and legislative approach. When an environmental medium is regulated, controls are developed to control discharges to that particular medium and possibly shift those discharges to other less regulated media. This approach in turn has helped establish an industry constituency (the "environment industry") which stands to benefit from the continuation and consolidation of pollution control.

The magnitude of the overall pollution control business has become exceptional, with most of its growth occurring during the past two decades. Pollution control equipment has always been expensive to design and install, and is also expensive to operate. U.S. companies have continued to spend millions of dollars each year to purchase, operate, and maintain such equipment. In 1991, for example, spending in the U.S. for what has been called "pollution abatement control" (treatment, recycling, monitoring, R&D, and so forth) amounted to more than $80 billion, according to U.S. Department of Commerce figures, with industry accounting for more than $50 billion of that amount.[69] These costs have had a major impact at the company and facility level: DuPont, for example, estimated that, by the late 1970s, fully 30% of its new investment was being earmarked for pollution control equipment. By 1992, the company was spending $300 million in capital costs and $900 million for a range of other environmental compliance costs, including remediation costs.[70] And while these figures represented business costs not always directly associated with regulations *per se*, the magnitude of control expenditures had still become breathtaking in its scope. As one consequence, the pollution control business or environment industry, had, by the late 1980s, come to be touted by several Wall Street investment firms as possibly the single fastest growth industry in the country. Even when the pollution control industry experienced slower growth rates during the early 1990s, longer term projections still situated the industry as a premier investment by corporate analysts, a situation underlined by the Clinton administration's emphasis on environmental technology. But by defining pollution control as an environment industry (or by conflating the concept of sustainable technology with pollution control technology), the idea of a nonpolluting or less polluting technology has become intertwined with the recognizable and widely accepted idea of managing the pollution through specific control technologies.[71]

Pollution Prevention: An Environmental and Industrial Strategy

Pollution prevention policy, as distinct from its pollution control variants, remains relatively unexplored (in practice) while continuing to be a potentially challenging approach. Pollution prevention policy requires greater attention to such arenas as occupational exposures and product use—areas that have historically received limited attention as environmental questions. Such intervention, moreover, requires a different framing of the pollution issue, a shift from management (e.g., treatment or disposal) strategies to restructuring a process, a product, or ultimately a production system. The contrasts are obvious. For instance, organic solvents can be effectively managed by removing them from process exhaust air streams by passing the air through a bed of solid adsorbent. The solvent is collected on the adsorbent, and the cleaned air is exhausted. Subsequently, the adsorbent is treated with steam or hot inert gas to remove the solvent from the solid. Finally, the solvent is removed from the steam or gas by condensation and then collected as a liquid. Since none of these steps (nor any control or treatment process) is 100% efficient, some solvent inevitably remains in each medium—in the exhausted air, in the solid adsorbent, and in the steam or gas. This type of media-shifting process has undeniably had significant impacts on human health and the environment, though such impacts have been difficult to quantify since pollutants exhibit different physical and chemical characteristics when present in different media. An approach based on redesign, on the other hand, identifies where and how the use of such solvents can be modified or changed.

A related and widely recognized problem resulting from reliance on pollution control technologies has been the transport of pollutants far from the point at which they are generated. Pollutants discharged to surface waters can be carried to distant rivers, lakes, and oceans, while contaminants not captured or destroyed by air pollution control equipment can travel hundreds of miles where they may also cause environmental damage. The concept of media shifting, in this context, is also a concept of pollution location rather than elimination or reduction.

In contrast, pollution prevention policy, as noted throughout the first part of this book, requires a fundamental rethinking of production methods and innovation techniques, commonly referred to as "know-how." Put in another context (for research, training, and analysis), the end-point oriented analytic reviews of production outcomes have strengthened a similar "end-of-pipe" emphasis in the training and technical requirements for process and design engineers and managers with responsibilities at the front end of the production system. Toxicologists and environmental engineers and planners who prepare quantitative risk assessments and environmental impact statements on behalf of industry function within a well-defined pollution control paradigm based on the concepts of acceptable risk and the management of environmental hazards as a regulatory cost of production. Similarly, the various process, materials, and design engineers, chemists, managers, and others employed by industry at the front end of a production system have their activities situated within certain well-defined parameters such as cost controls, technical and operational requirements, and market considerations. The environmental criteria integrated in recent years into preproduction or early production design stages have primarily involved the cost-related issues associated with RCRA-regulated hazardous wastes or the adoption of greater cost-effective efficiency measures that can also serve to reduce the amount of wastes that might exit from the system. These efforts at waste reduction, or (more properly termed) waste minimization, nevertheless still remain incidental to production planning and design, and are often assumed by operational (rather than design) personnel (including corporate environmental staff) who have the direct task of addressing waste problems.

This form of training (and the production paradigms associated with it), whether for toxicologists, environmental planners, or chemical engineers, can also be found in university course work as well as on-the-job requirements. Chemical engineering or industrial design courses, for example, provide little or no familiarity with toxicological or environmental issues, while environmental planning or toxicology courses have little or no application to industrial design or engineering issues. If such highly toxic substances as mercury, lead, or chromium are used as part of the design of particular industrial or consumer products such as batteries or industrial pigments and primers, the current engineering and design focus continues to identify whether such substances have utility in terms of certain given production criteria (costs, material flexibility, improving the product in market terms, and so forth), while the environmental or toxicological focus continues to be centered on mitigating the impacts and evaluating the risks after the product has been produced. Thus, production design (based on certain production values) and environmental assessment (based on the acceptance of impacts and risks) remain biased toward pollution control and against pollution prevention.

To reorient those biases, environmental and toxicological awareness has to be structured into the design and not just the end uses of production. Such a reorientation would need to begin at the training level, both in terms of university course work and on-the-job training. A new set of production values, most especially the concepts of reduction and prevention, also need to be incorporated into the preproduction and early production design stages. While the environmental impact and risk assessment procedures have helped strengthen pollution control approaches, a new set of procedures—*pollution prevention design review and structural analysis* approaches—need to be developed to underscore a shift to prevention as a primary strategy to deal with the kinds of environmental hazards present at each stage of a production cycle. Recent interest in environmental issues within the industrial design profession suggests that a strong interest in refocusing criteria among designers does exist today, though much of the interest has been limited to solid waste concerns regarding recyclability and volume reduction in products and packaging.[72] The ability to expand that interest to incorporate the overall reduction of environmental hazards (and address other critical environmental factors such as energy use and efficiency, virgin materials usage, and so forth) at the design level remains essential in accomplishing the greatly valued paradigm shift from pollution control to pollution prevention. Similarly, the significant contributions in recent years of evolutionary economics and industrial geography in demonstrating powerful shifts in technology and production helps situate the structural considerations associated with industry activities and technology choices. Yet much of this analysis has failed to identify crucial environmental outcomes of such activities and choices and where pollution prevention would help inform that analysis.[73]

Today, as the language and culture of pollution prevention gradually work their way into policy and industry venues, it has become clear that while some pollution prevention measures are obviously simple, inexpensive, and immediately applicable, others might require the kind of paradigm shift that has become the accepted, albeit theoretical wisdom of pollution control critics. With so much talk of that paradigm shift in the air, this book has sought to analyze the evolution of environmental policy and the limits and barriers to change that still exist. Through such an analysis, we have also sought to identify the ways in which pollution prevention might emerge as the basis of a new environmental policy and as a larger shift in industry activity, as well as the ways it has remained a stepchild in environmental policymaking, mired in the narrow frameworks and constricting outcomes that stubbornly survive today. Policy change beckons, but has yet to find its way.

Notes

1. P.L. 98-616 Sec. 1002(b), Title 42 § 6901 (*et seq.*).
2. *U.S. National Research Council Committee on Institutional Considerations in Reducing the Generation of Hazardous Industrial Waste.* An NRC-staff–prepared digest of the report, "Reducing Hazardous Waste Generation: An Evaluation and a Call for Action," (Washington, D.C.: National Academy Press, 1985).
3. *Serious Reduction of Hazardous Waste for Pollution Prevention and Industrial Efficiency,* Office of Technology Assessment, (Washington D.C.: Government Printing Office, September 1986).
4. U.S. Environmental Protection Agency, "Report to Congress: Minimization of Hazardous Waste," Vols. I and II, EPA/530-SW-86-033 and -034, (Washington, D.C.: EPA, Office of Solid Waste and Emergency Response, October 1986)
5. U.S. Environmental Protection Agency, "Report to Congress: Minimization of Hazardous Waste," *op cit.*, p. 13.
6. *From Pollution to Prevention: A Progress Report on Waste Reduction,* Office of Technology Assessment, (Washington D.C.: Office of Technology Assessment, June 1987), p. 21.
7. Dorfman, M.H., Muir, W.R. and Miller, C.G. "Environmental Dividends: Cutting More Chemical Wastes," INFORM, Inc., New York, 1986, 1992.
8. *Serious Reduction of Hazardous Waste,* p. 10.

9. U.S. Environmental Protection Agency, "Report to Congress: Minimization of Hazardous Waste," *op cit.,* p. ii and p. 6.

10. U.S. Environmental Protection Agency, "Report to Congress: Minimization of Hazardous Waste," *op cit.,* p. ii and p. 7.

11. U.S. Environmental Protection Agency, "Report to Congress: Minimization of Hazardous Waste," *op cit.,* p. 8. See also p. 6 and p. ii.

12. This precise definition of "toxics use reduction" was also adopted as part of the language of the 1989 Massachusetts Toxics Use Reduction Act. [MASS GEN. L. ch. 211 § 2 (1989)]. The Massachusetts chapter of PIRG (MASSPIRG) played an influential role in the drafting of and lobbying for this legislation, which in turn became the model for later policy interpretations of the toxics use reduction strategy.

13. On the impact of "right-to-know" legislation on industry activities in the toxics areas, see "Growing Exchange of Information Spurs Pollution Prevention Efforts," Ann M. Thayer, *Chemical and Engineering News,* July 26, 1993, pp. 8–25.

14. "Pollution Prevention Policy Statement," U.S. Environmental Protection Agency, Federal Register, Vol. 54, No. 16, January 26, 1989.

15. For background to the development of EPA's pollution prevention program in 1988 and 1989, see "EPA's Pollution Prevention Program: Progress and Opportunities," Gerald Kotas, *The Environmental Professional,* Vol. 11, pp. 185–189, 1989; "The EPA's Approach to Pollution Prevention," David G. Stephan and John Atcheson, *Chemical Engineering Progress,* June 1989, pp. 53–58; also, personal communication with Jocelyn Woodman, EPA Office of Pollution Prevention (1990).

16. Pollution Prevention Act, 42 § 13102(5)(a)(i).

17. See, Pollution Prevention Act of 1990, 42 § 13106(b). See also Federal Register 48,475 (proposed rule for "Toxic Chemical Release Reporting: Pollution Prevention Information").

18. U.S. Environmental Protection Agency, 40 Code of Federal Regulations, Part 372 "Toxic Chemical Regulations and Reporting: Community Right-to-Know, Final Rule," Federal Register, Part II, February 16, 1988, for Sections 313 and 318 of Title 311, Superfund Amendments and Reauthorization Act of 1986. For an industry response to the passage of Section 313, see "The Consequences of Section 313," Jeffrey A. Bowman, *Chemical Engineering Progress,* June 1989, pp. 48–52

19. U.S. Environmental Protection Agency, "Toxics in the Community: National and Local Perspectives" 14–16 (1988 National Report on data collected under Section 313 of the Emergency Planning and Community Right-to-Know Act of 1986, EPA 560/4-90-017, Sept. 1990—hereinafter 1988 EPA TRI Report). On the off-site recycling exemption see Working

Group on Community Right-to-Know, "The 'Recycling' Loophole in the Toxics Release Inventory: Out of Sight, Out of Mind" (May 1991).

20. 1988 EPA TRI Report, *op cit.*, p. 24.

21. *Oversight of Right-to-Know Pollution Data: Hearing Before the Subcommittee on Superfund, Ocean, and Water Protection of the Senate Committee on Environment and Public Works,* 101st Congress, 1st Session 38 (May 10, 1989—hereinafter Pollution Data Hearing) (statement of Charles Elkins, Director, Office of Toxic Substances, Environmental Protection Agency).

22. Pollution Data Hearing, *op cit.*, p. 44 (statement of Office of Technology Assessment).

23. An estimated 10,000 facilities did not report. Compliance was highest in the chemical industry, and lowest among manufacturing industries that tend to be chemical users rather than manufacturers, such as the printing and publishing, and apparel industries. U.S. Enviornmental Protection Agency, "Toxics in the Community: National and Local Perspectives," p. 4, EPA/560/4-90-017 (Washington, D.C.: Government Printing Office, September 1990).

24. See *Superfund: Right-to-Know and Hazardous Wastesite Cleanup: Hearing Before the Subcommittee on Commerce, Transportation, and Tourism of the House of Representatives Committee on Energy and Commerce,* 99th Congress, 1st Session 2, 12-13 (Dec. 20, 1985—hereinafter Right-to-Know Hearings) (statement of Darby Nelson, Minnesota State Representative).

25. See, *Reauthorization of Superfund: Hearings Before the Subcommittee on Water Resources of the House of Representatives Committee on Public Works and Transportation,* 99th Congress, 1st Session 1635 (March 26–28, May 1, July 24–25, 1985—hereinafter Reauthorization of Superfund Hearings) (statement of Cathy Hurwitt, Legislative Director, Citizen Action).

26. See for example, testimony by the Chemical Manufacturers Association and Monsanto representatives in "Reauthorization of Superfund Hearings," pp. 1574–1609; see also note at 12-13.

27. See the 1988 EPA TRI Report, *op cit.*, p. 17.

28. See, "Pollution Data Hearings," *op cit.*, pp. 121, 124.

29. See, "Reauthorization of Superfund Hearings," *op cit.*, pp. 11–17.

30. See, "Pollution Data Hearings," *op cit.*, pp. 78–79.

31. See, "Reauthorization of Superfund Hearings," *op cit.*, p. 1619 (statement of Lucas Neas, research analyst, West Virginia Department of Health).

32. *Working Notes on Community Right-to-Know* (April 1991) (Washington D.C.: Working Group on Community Right-to-Know).

33. Pritchard, Jayne, S.A., "A Closer Look at Title III of SARA: Emergency Planning and Community Right-to-Know Act of 1986," 6, *Pace Environment Law Review,* pp. 230–237 (1988).

34. See, *Pollution Prevention and Hazardous Waste Reduction: Hearing Before the Subcommittee on Transportation and Hazardous Materials of the House of Representatives Committee on Energy and Commerce,* 101st Congress, 2nd Session, 10–11 (May 31, 1990—hereinafter "Pollution Prevention Hearing") (statement of Joy Williams, Environmental Health Coalition).

35. 1988 EPA TRI Report, *op cit.*, p. 182.

36. See "Toxics Use Reporting on the Line," Elisabeth Kirschner, *Chemical Week,* February 23, 1994, p. 12. A similar study was undertaken by the Oregon State Public Interest Research Group (OSPIRG) based on evaluation of chemical use data available through Oregon's Toxics Use Reduction Law of 1989. According to the OSPIRG study, the data from the Oregon law revealed that the 16 largest chemical users in the state reported using 310 million pounds of chemicals, or "34 times more pounds of chemicals than reported emitted [under TRI]." *Breaking the Chemical Dependency: The First Data on Oregon's Industrial Toxics Use,* (Portland: OSPIRG, November 1993).

37. See, for example, comments in "Pollution Data Hearing," *op cit.*, pp. 88–107 (statement of Charles Elkins, director of Office of Toxic Substances, EPA).

38. See, "Pollution Prevention Act of 1990," 42 § 13100 *et seq.* See also 56 Federal Register 48,475 (proposed rule for "Toxic Chemical Release Reporting: Pollution Prevention Information").

39. Executive Order 12856 of August 3, 1993, "Federal Compliance with Right-to-Know Laws and Pollution Prevention Requirements."

40. H.R. 3055, 102d Congress, 1st Session (Sikorski).

41. See "Right-to-Know More Bill Introduced," *Working Notes on Community Right-to-Know,* July–August 1991, p.1.

42. *Unfinished Business: A Comparative Assessment of Environmental Problems,* Office of Policy Analysis, U.S. Environmental Protection Agency (Washington D.C.: Government Printing Office, 1987); *Reducing Risk: Setting Priorities and Strategies for Environmental Protection,* The Relative Risk Reduction Strategies Committee of the U.S. Environmental Protection Agency's Science Advisory Board, (Washington D.C.: Government Printing Office, 1990).

43. See William Reilly's testimony in *Reducing Risk: Setting Priorities and Strategies for Environmental Protection,* Hearings on Recent Science Advisory Board Report Before the Senate Committee on Environment and Public Works, 102nd Congress, 1st Session 48 (1991), p. 48.

44. See, for example, the March 21, 1993 article in the *New York Times* that quoted "experts" who argued that "in the last fifteen years environmental policy has too often evolved largely in reaction to popular panics,

Chapter 5. New Approaches to Toxics 161

not in response to sound scientific analyses of which environmental hazards present the greatest risks," "New View Calls Environmental Policy Misguided," Keith Schneider, the first of a five part series in the *New York Times*, March 21–26, 1993

45. On the debate over THM standards, see "A History of the Attempted Federal Regulation Requiring GAC Adsorption for Water Treatment," James M. Symons, *Journal of the American Water Works Association*, August 1984.

46. Title 29 § 655(b)(2),(3),(4).

47. The "good science" debate became most pronounced in the early 1980s regarding the standard-setting process for trichloroethylene (TCE) as a water and toxic air contaminant and its potential impact on the aerospace industry and other industries with high uses of TCE as an industrial solvent. These debates became intertwined with the scandals involving EPA during this period that led to the indictment and conviction of EPA official Rita Lavelle and the subsequent resignation of EPA Administrator Ann Gorsuch Burford. See, "Revisions in Cancer Policy," Eliot Marshall, *Science*, April 1, 1983; *A Life of its Own: The Politics and Power of Water*, Robert Gottlieb, (San Diego: HBJ, 1988), pp. 177–187.

48. *Risk Assessment in the Federal Government: Managing the Process*, National Academy of Science (Washington D.C.: National Academy Press, 1983).

49. Ruckelshaus, the EPA Administrator who sought to elevate risk assessment partly to answer charges of Agency bias, differed considerably in his view of the viability of risk assessment as a scientific tool from Ruckelshaus, the chief executive officer of the country's second largest waste management firm, Browning-Ferris, a position he assumed after leaving EPA for the second time. In 1983, Ruckelshaus, the EPA administrator, stated that he intended to "do everything in my power to make clear the importance of this scientific analysis," while just two years later (and less than a year after he stepped down from his EPA position), he wrote that risk assessment was "a kind of pretense," given the high degree of uncertainty in risk evaluations and the presumption that policymakers "assume that we have greater knowledge than scientists actually possess and make decisions based on those assumptions," in order to "avoid paralysis of protective action that would result from waiting for 'definitive' data." The 1983 speech, given before the National Academy of Sciences, was published as "Science, Risk, and Public Policy" in *Science*, Vol. 221, 1983, pp. 1026–1027. The 1985 article appeared as "Risk, Science, and Democracy" in *Issues in Science and Technology*, Spring 1985, p. 26.

50. The director of EPA's Integrated Environmental Management

Program described quantitative risk assessment as "the logical common denominator for establishing risk reduction priorities among EPA's air, water, and hazardous waste programs," cited in "Reclaiming Environmental Law: A Normative Critique of Comparative Risk Analysis," Donald T. Hornstein, *Columbia Law Review,* Vol. 92:562, p. 566, note 13.

51. The Moynihan legislation, first introduced in the 102nd Congress as § 2132 or the "Environmental Risk Reduction Act" and subsequently in the 103rd Congress as §. 110 or the "Environmental Risk Reduction Act of 1993," proposed that the "ranking of relative risks to human health, welfare, and ecological resources" was a "complex task…best performed by technical experts free from interests that could bias their objective judgment." See, for example, Section 2. Findings and Policy, § 2132.

52. Part of this "environmental justice" critique of risk ranking focused on what was perceived to be an underlying premise of the ranking exercise: namely, assigning a "low" or "lower" priority to such risks as hazardous waste sites, and thus by implication lowering the priority for hazardous waste cleanup. Given the reliance of traditional risk assessment on risks to "population" as opposed to risks to "individuals" (that is, smaller numbers of people in a given geographic area, who might be exposed to higher risks and/or cumulative risks), the weight of evaluation lent itself to assigning higher priority status to broader, potentially more diffuse risks rather than risks that were likely to be experienced in more discriminatory patterns. See "An Environmental Justice Perspective on Comparative Risk," in *Toward the 21st Century: Planning for the Protection of California's Environment,* California Comparative Risk Project, May 1994.

53. See, for example, "Jobs and the Environment," Patrick Heffernan, *Sierra Club Bulletin,* Vol. 60, No. 4, April 1975, pp. 25–26; "Towards an Environmental/Labor Coalition," Alan S. Miller, *Environment,* Vol. 22, No 5, June 1980, pp. 32–39.

54. See *Volume I: The Role of Waste Minimization,* National Governor's Association, Natural Resources Policy Studies Unit (Washington, D.C.: Center for Policy Research, 1989). For a background discussion of the role of state governments in implementation of federal pollution policies, see *The Dimensions of Federalism: State Governments and Pollution Control Policies,* William Lowry, (Durham and London: Duke University Press, 1992).

55. See "Toxics Use Reduction in Massachusetts: The Whole Facility Approach," Manik Roy, *Pollution Prevention News,* U.S. Environmental Protection Agency, February 1990; see also "Waste Solution Must Involve Water, Air, Land," Manik Roy and Eric V. Schaeffer, *Forum for Applied Research and Public Policy,* Vol. 8 No. 1, Spring 1993, pp. 116–124.

56. One of the key negotiators for the agreement argued that the suc-

cessful outcome came about in part when some of the industries involved decided that the legislation was less burdensome than the existing, media-specific regulatory framework. Ultimately, TURA was passed unanimously by the Legislature. Presentation by Ken Geiser, UCLA Pollution Prevention Forum series, May 23, 1994.

57. This definition was in fact lifted directly from the language of public interest advocacy (see footnote 8).

58. By 1994, more than five hundred Toxics Use Reduction Planners had been certified, many of them former engineers, with the group itself highly motivated in establishing its role as a new kind of environmental planner, capable of enabling industry to meet specified targets and ultimately develop a new framework for facility management of toxics use. Presentation of Ken Geiser, UCLA Pollution Prevention Forum, May 23, 1994

59. Ken Geiser, *op cit.*, UCLA Pollution Prevention Forum, May 23, 1994.

60. Toxics Use Reduction and Hazardous Waste Reduction Act of 1989, State of Oregon (ORS 465.003–465.037); see also, "Pollution Prevention Facility Planning: The Oregon Experience," David K. Rozell and Roy Brower, *Pollution Prevention Review,* Summer 1993; *State Legislation Relating to Pollution Prevention: Survey and Summaries,* assembled by the Waste Reduction Institute for Training and Applications Research, Inc., Minneapolis, Minnesota, February 1991; "Toxics Reduction: Policy Tools, Strategies and State Initiatives," Laura Beck *et al.*, March 1992, unpublished manuscript prepared for the Pollution Prevention Education and Research Center.

61. See *Pollution Prevention: EPA Should Reexamine the Objectives and Sustainability of State Programs,* United States General Accounting Office, GAO/PEMD-94-8, (Washington DC: Government Printing Office, 1994).

62. *State Legislation Relating to Pollution Prevention,* WRITAR, pp. 12–14; "Toxics Reduction: Policy Tools, Strategies, and State Initiatives," 1992.

63. "The Los Angeles Small Business Toxics Minimization Project: A Case Study," Elwood M. Hopkins, March 1994, unpublished manuscript prepared for Preventing Pollution Seminar, UCLA; "Regional and Local Pollution Prevention Efforts in Southern California," Julie Roque, Lucile Hise, and Robert Gottlieb, Working Paper, Pollution Prevention Education and Research Center, August 1993.

64. The absence of regional planning mechanisms for pollution prevention is discussed in "Environmenal Planning and Policy in the Los Angeles Region: Opening and Opportunities," Margaret FitzSimmons and Robert

Gottlieb, in *Policy Options for Southern California*, Allen J Scott (ed.) (Los Angeles: Lewis Center for Regional Policy Studies, 1993).

65. See "Toxics Use Reduction and Pollution Prevention," Ken Geiser, *New Solutions*, Spring 1990, pp. 1–8; "Techniques in Toxics Use Reduction: From Concept to Action," Mark Rossi, Michael Ellenbecker, and Kenneth Geiser," *New Solutions*, Fall 1991, pp. 25–32; "Toxics Use Reduction: Pro and Con," Francine Laden and George M. Gray, *Risk—Issues in Health and Safety*, 213 (Summer 1993), pp. 213–234

66. The term "design for the environment" has emerged in recent years as a broad-based concept seeking to illustrate a new approach to introducing products and processes within a production cycle. According to the National Academy of Engineering, for example, "selection and design of manufacturing processes and products should incorporate environmental constraints and objectives at the outset" (cited in "Design for the Entire Life Cycle: A New Paradigm?," Chuck Overby, in *The Environmental Challenge of the 1990s: Proceedings*, International Conference on Pollution Prevention: Clean Technologies and Clean Products, June 10–13, 1990, EPA/600/9-90/039, September 1990, p. 475). Design for the environment has also become an important new EPA buzzword and has served as the basis for a recent EPA program which emphasizes "technology transfer" or information sharing about the "comparative risk and performance of alternatives" for specific industries such as printing and dry cleaning. See, for example, U.S. Environmental Protection Agency, "Design for the Environment: Printing Project—Assessing Alternatives for a Safer Industry," (U.S. Environmental Protection Agency: Washington D.C., 1992).

67. Letter from Dr. Robert P. Bringer, Staff Vice President, 3M Company to Ms. Susan Hazen, Director, Environmental Assistance Division, U.S. Environmental Protection Agency, October 15, 1992.

68. By the early 1990s, industry groups had begun to sharply criticize and challenge the toxics use reduction concept and approach, compounding differences in definition and interpretation. See "Toxics Use Reduction: Prudent or Pernicious?," J.D. Smith, *Environment and Industry Digest*, February 1992; "Toxic Use Reduction Called Threat to Competitiveness," Joe Maty, *American Paint and Coatings Journal*, December 1991.

69. Cited in *Chemical & Engineering News*, July 26, 1993, p. 18.

70. The 30% figure was used by DuPont's top research advisor to the company's executive committee, Richard E. Heckert, at a June 1977 meeting of the executive committee and is cited in *Science and Corporate Strategy: Du Pont R&D, 1902–1980*, David A. Hounshell and John Kenly Smith, Jr.

(Cambridge University Press: Cambridge, 1988), p. 585. The 1992 figures are cited in *Chemical & Engineering News*, July 26, 1993, p. 18.

71. This identification of "sustainability" with pollution control was most recently popularized by the argument put forth by then Senator Al Gore in his book *Earth in the Balance*. It also is suggested in the language of the Clinton administration's "Environmental Technology Initiative" released in 1994. See *Technology for a Sustainable Future: A Framework for Action*, National Science and Technology Council, Washington, D.C., July 1994.

72. Burnette, Charles, "Principals of Ecological Design," *Innovation*, Vol. 9, No. 2, 1990, p. 4; see also other articles in this issue, which is devoted to the subject of industrial design; "Design Alert: The Environment is Our Business," *Innovation*, Vol. 8, No. 3, 1989; *Green Products by Design: Choices for a Cleaner Environment*, Office of Technology Assessment (Washington, D.C.: Government Printing Office, 1993).

73. See the argument elaborated by Janice Mazurek regarding the changing status of wafer fabrication within the semiconductor industry in "How Fabulous Fablessness: The Environmental Policy Implications of Economic Restructuring in the Santa Clara Semiconductor Industry," unpublished M.A. thesis, Graduate School of Architecture and Urban Planning, UCLA, 1994.

Industry Settings: Opportunities and Limits for Pollution Prevention

Robert Gottlieb
Janice Mazurek

If the policy debates concerning pollution prevention remain open-ended and often unresolved, what of the opportunities for prevention within industry settings? The "greening" of American industry, much heralded during the late 1980s and early 1990s by industry officials, policymakers, media commentators, and even, at times, by environmentalists, has continued to generate much dispute and conflicting interpretation, particularly in the area of pollution prevention. How much pollution prevention is actually occurring at the facility or industry-wide level? How should such efforts be characterized and how and why have they occurred? What obstacles are still present, how much toxics use is structural in nature, and how much of it is a matter of organizational practices and biases? How can the nature of decisionmaking at the board or facility level help define appropriate forms of industry restructuring or policy intervention that might be necessary to implement a pollution prevention approach?

Part II of *Reducing Toxics* represents an effort to begin exploring these questions by examining industry issues at a facility, product and/or process-

specific, and sectoral level. This section includes a series of case studies, or
snapshots, each representing different reference points in the production
cycle that help us analyze the overall question of industry decisionmaking
and the intersection of policy directions and industry activities and outcomes. Primarily, the snapshots illustrate how prevention requires managers
to analytically separate the nature, use, and location of hazardous substances.

The studies proceed in focus from general cases (including an analysis
of the structure of the chemical industry and the different ways to characterize the industry that help situate toxics use throughout the society) to
the more specific (including an examination of radiator repair operations:
a downstream industry, where the primary environmental hazards are
occupational and where opportunities for reduction or prevention are
most substantially located upstream). Others, organized along this continuum include:

- *Industrial Process:* An evaluation of the continuum of pollution
  prevention/waste minimization opportunities to establish a
  "cleaner" technology within the chemical industry.

- *Life Cycle Analysis:* An environmental survey of efforts to create a new industry (in this case, electric vehicles) that has been
  significantly influenced and motivated by regulations on
  tailpipe emissions from conventional fuel vehicles. Such an
  emphasis on the question of alternative fuels has largely
  avoided or ignored broader product or industry (automotive)
  or sectoral (transportation) issues. As a consequence, this pol-
  icy-driven effort at industrial innovation has remained narrowly focused in environmental terms.

- *Product Development:* An industry-wide analysis of aerosols
  which examines reduction issues in relation to the creation of
  new markets heavily influenced by the manufacture of new
  consumer "needs." At the same time, such an analysis needs to
  focus on how aerosol producers have also been forced to
  respond to regulatory and policy considerations that heavily
  impact both the nature of the product and the structure of the
  industry itself.

- *Company Voluntarism:* A case study of 3M, which has assumed
  the leadership in this area (focused on the avoidance of regulation). Despite its proven excellence in new product innovation, failure to incorporate prevention into product develop-

ment strategies provides an instructive view of the opportunities and limits of pollution prevention in relation to industry decisionmaking and organizational behavior.

Although these case studies do not fully encompass the range of issues associated with industry decisionmaking, they present snapshots of several of the core themes that guide any evaluation of the "greening" of industry. Promotional campaigns or exhortations about corporate environmental change to the contrary, the cases demonstrate that the need for a prevention strategy is not simply a matter of policy, but a fundamental evaluation of how industry operates. As the several case studies indicate, failure to incorporate the principles which identify reduction opportunities regarding use, medium, and nature of hazard at various points in the production cycle complicates implementation, making actual reduction efforts difficult, if not impossible, to achieve in practice. The greening of industry, as measured by its (varied) applications of pollution prevention, has become in these settings at once a corporate and public concern, the industry counterpart of the search for that "new paradigm of environmental governance."[1]

Note

1. The concept—"new paradigm of environmental governance"—was used by Gus Speth, former head of the Council of Environmental Quality at the "Economic Summit" convened by President-elect Clinton in Little Rock, Arkansas in December 1992, in describing a new approach in the government/industry relationship. *Los Angeles Times,* December 21, 1992.

6

Greening or Greenwashing?: The Evolution of Industry Decisionmaking

Robert Gottlieb
Maureen Smith
Julie Roque

Cautionary Precedents: The Tetraethyl Lead Case

If pollution prevention is to become a new paradigm for production, it is important to understand and evaluate how decisions get made within corporate settings. A key question for any such pollution prevention analysis is what biases or frameworks influence decisionmaking. Put another way, do corporations turn "green" by reconfiguring how they make decisions (and ultimately make products), or does the concept "greening of industry" itself represent an oxymoron, a form of "greenwashing," as some environmental critics have argued?

A useful starting point in the discussion of environmental factors in industrial decisionmaking is its historical evolution. How industry officials have viewed the risks and hazards of the production cycle, whether in terms of occupational exposures or community and environmental impacts, may well offer lessons for today's decisionmakers.

At one level, such lessons appear relatively straightforward. A number of historical examples suggest the absence of environmental criteria in production decisions—a situation characteristic of the evolution of toxics-generating industrial activity for the nearly two centuries since the emergence of a far-reaching chemical industry helped shape the industrial landscape of contemporary societies. Such absences also point to the formidable tasks at hand for pollution prevention. One such example, the introduction of tetraethyl lead in gasoline, which became a product at the center of substantial environmental concerns and disputes for the entire sixty plus years of its market life, provides a valuable case study—a kind of cautionary precedent, helping inform today's greening/greenwashing debate.

This cautionary event is rooted in a sequence of decision points that took place in the early 1920s, when top officials of the General Motors Corporation and E.I. du Pont de Nemours and Company brought to market a new gasoline additive designed to eliminate the "knock" and increase horsepower and fuel efficiency for higher compression engines. Through this new product innovation, the G.M./Du Pont consortia launched a new era in automotive development, establishing a critical link between oil refiners and the chemical industry, and thereby influencing the evolution of both industries and setting a pattern for their subsequent integration and restructuring.[1]

At the same time, the introduction of this additive, tetraethyl lead (TEL), touched off a major debate about the corporate planning that influenced the decision to proceed with the manufacture and environmental release of what was a new and potentially toxic substance. Almost half a century later, new debates concerning TEL and corporate decisionmaking came to be defined by the events surrounding the passage of the 1970 Clean Air Act. Taken together, the two sets of debates mark the rise and fall of tetraethyl lead in the United States, while identifying some core issues associated with industry decisionmaking.

When the antiknocking properties of tetraethyl lead were discovered, both Du Pont and General Motors (already substantially interlocked) became strongly committed to its commercial development as a gasoline additive irrespective of the various toxics issues involved. For General Motors, the development of an antiknock gasoline additive meshed well with its strategy to create demand "not for basic transportation, but for progress in new cars for comfort, convenience, power, and style," as GM President Alfred Sloan later put it.[2] The manufacture of tetraethyl lead also represented a potential windfall for Du Pont, given the product's vast prospective market (already by 1922, it was estimated that 60 million pounds would be required to treat all of the gasoline then consumed annually, a figure that was in fact achieved just sixteen years later).[3] Du Pont, with its prior experience in manufacturing highly toxic products such as explosives and dyes, was also seen as capable of handling the health risks involved in the production of this new additive.[4]

Concern over the toxicity of TEL was not only shared by top GM and Du Pont company officials but by the engineers and scientists associated with Charles Kettering's Dayton laboratory, which had been involved in the research efforts to locate an antiknock compound. Kettering's chief research chemist, Thomas Midgley, who had been directly involved in the discovery of the octane-boosting properties of tetraethyl lead, had within months of his discovery been warned, by a German researcher, of lead poisoning hazards that could arise in its manufacture. Kettering was also aware that the product presented certain problems in its manufacture and use. However, both Kettering and Midgley, and their corporate sponsors GM and Du Pont (as well as Standard Oil, which had also sought to enter the tetraethyl lead market), concluded that while the additive might be dangerous to manufacture, its heavily diluted use in gasoline would not likely present significant environmental problems. In this context, Kettering concluded that the timing was propitious to introduce TEL. Here was a product, Kettering argued, that was "useful to people, or better than what they have otherwise" (thus representing a significant new market), even if, as Kettering also enjoyed proclaiming, "the price of progress is trouble."[5]

The decision to proceed was never in doubt. Even at the manufacturing level where the risks had been more explicitly identified, the pressure to rapidly introduce the new product tended to overshadow the need to adopt measures to minimize occupational exposures. Recognition that TEL potentially represented an explosive new market dominated the decisionmaking about when and how to produce the additive; indeed, as Du Pont company president Irenee Du Pont argued, the rush to produce represented a "war order" priority.[6] In this rush to production, start-up facilities were built without ventilation equipment and occupational safety procedures were largely ignored. This in turn led to several deaths and dozens of cases of lead poisoning at the plant level within the first two years of production.[7]

While the three TEL manufacturing plants constructed between 1922 and 1924 all experienced major lead poisoning episodes, the hazards of tetraethyl lead at first received little public attention. It was only after a disastrous accident occurred in October 1924 at Standard's Bayway facility in Elizabeth, New Jersey, that tetraethyl lead hazards were dramatically brought to public view. Over the course of five days following the Bayway accident, five of the forty-nine workers in the facility would die and thirty-five others would experience severe neurological disorders. Press stories began to label tetraethyl lead "loony gas," creating immediate demands from the press, advocacy groups like the Workers' Health Bureau, and local public officials to halt TEL production. In several cities and states, including New York, New Jersey, and Pennsylvania, various boards of health initiated actions to ban the sale of leaded gasoline while inquiries were initiated regarding tetraethyl lead toxicity. One study, undertaken by the Bureau of Mines and released shortly after the Bayway episode, downplayed both the environmental and occupational risks of TEL. Immediately criticized by other researchers, the report's legitimacy was further under-cut by the fact that it had not only been funded by the Ethyl Gasoline Corporation (the newly organized company established by Du Pont, Standard, and GM to produce TEL), but Ethyl also had final approval of the study's results.[8]

At the height of the controversy, the Surgeon General of the U.S. Public Health Service suggested that the sale of leaded gasoline be temporarily discontinued, which occurred in May 1925. Two weeks after the tempo-rary ban was instituted, the Surgeon General hosted a conference which focused on evaluating the hazards associated with the manufacture of tetraethyl lead. Industry groups at the conference argued that any initial occupational problems were primarily the result of the "carelessness of the men handling it" and the need for "careful discipline" of the workers involved, as Midgley testified.[9] Scientists and public health officials who supported the continued use of TEL also argued that *definitive* proof of a product's hazardous nature had to be required prior to any regulation or banning of such a product.[10] Ultimately, the bottom line for the industry officials was that, despite the limited liability and health risks involved in establishing new products like TEL, they were far outweighed by the cer-tainty of the economic worth and social value of the industrial break-throughs associated with such innovative products. "Our continued devel-opment of motor fuels is essential in our civilization," an Ethyl Corporation spokesman proclaimed in testimony at the conference.[11]

In contrast, public health scientists and advocates like Alice Hamilton (at the time, the foremost investigator of occupational hazards in lead indus-tries), argued that public health considerations, such as those associated with the hazards of lead production and use of lead products, needed to be directly incorporated into industrial research and development considera-tions and that the government had the right to intervene once "poisonous substances" entered interstate commerce. Hamilton bitterly complained that the Kettering group should not have sought to use a lead compound as an additive in the first place, given the already substantial documentation of the hazards of lead in workplace settings. Her argument was not limited to occupational exposures, but included broader environmental impacts as well: "You may control conditions within a factory, but how are you going to control the whole country?" she testified at the Surgeon General's con-ference. "If [as does seem to have been shown] this is a probable danger," she insisted, "shall we not say that it is going to be an extremely widespread one, an extraordinarily widespread one?"[12]

The conference's focus, however, remained fixed on the occupational exposure issues within a framework of balancing public health considerations with industrial needs. As a result, the Surgeon General established a committee of scientists to evaluate the hazards of TEL at the manufacturing level. Their primary task was to identify what controls might be established to reduce occupational risks—not, as Hamilton and other public health advocates had strenuously argued, to determine whether the nature of the risk itself warranted a substitution for the TEL. Given its mandate, the committee indeed concluded in its final report that a ban on leaded gasoline was not warranted, provided "its distribution and use are controlled by proper regulations."[13] However, it did urge further studies, given the likelihood of expanded use and its potential to present environmental as well as occupational hazards in circumstances of "prolonged use or other conditions not now foreseen."[14] Thus, the issue of the context for industrial decisionmaking—in what manner should potential risks or hazards be addressed, given the absence of significant legal or financial constraints—was never directly confronted.

Despite its warnings about the need for further study, the blue ribbon committee's report was quickly embraced by the companies involved in TEL production as justification for continued and expanded production. The central and powerful roles of the automotive, chemical, and oil industries associated with the production and use of TEL strongly influenced the absence of any further government review or regulation of leaded gasoline during the next half century, while also influencing the decline of environmental and toxicological research in this area once the "loony gas" crisis had passed. The blue ribbon committee's recommendation of further study was never pursued, even as production levels of TEL increased dramatically, a factor that had been of direct concern to the committee and which had been the focus of the arguments presented by Hamilton and other advocates such as Dr. Yandell Henderson and Grace Burnham of the Workers' Health Bureau.[15]

Among industry officials, the primary focus remained on continuing high production levels and earnings capacity. Between 1924 and 1947 when various tetraethyl lead patents expired, Du Pont alone was estimated to have earned more than $86 million from TEL, establishing it as one of the two major profit centers for the company. At the same time, the prevailing judgment among company officials and their industry research allies was that a chemical was innocent until proven guilty.[16]

The tetraethyl lead issue, of course, did not disappear once the loony gas fears had dissipated. During the 1960s, new studies on lead pointed to widespread and significant health effects at far lower levels of exposure than previously suspected. Lead use, meanwhile, had increased dramatically, influenced in large part by the huge jump in production of TEL (from

1,000 tons in 1926 to 233,000 tons in 1977). Lead levels in the ambient environment had also increased substantially in the same period as a direct consequence of increased leaded gasoline combustion. The private concerns expressed in 1922 by (then Delaware Senator) Coleman Du Pont over the risk of "lead poisoning in thickly populated centres from the exhaust of autos using gasoline doped with tetraethyl lead" had finally become, five decades later, an unavoidable issue for both public policymakers and industrialists.[17]

The event that most directly influenced the ultimate fate of leaded gasoline in the United States was the decision by General Motors (no longer interlocked with Du Pont nor involved in TEL production by the 1970s) to comply with new Clean Air Act mandates affecting vehicular emissions of carbon monoxide and sulfur dioxide by installing catalytic converters in cars. The use of leaded gasoline, however, turned out to be incompatible with the combination of metals used in the converters, and GM officials therefore argued that leaded gasoline would need to be phased down and eventually eliminated.[18] The General Motors decision, reinforced by EPA rulemaking addressing the lead content of gasoline (rulemaking that was substantially influenced by the successful court actions brought by environmental groups), ultimately forced companies like Du Pont and Ethyl to abandon the highly profitable leaded gasoline market by the late 1970s and early 1980s.

At its peak, in the early and mid 1970s, annual sales of TEL by Du Pont had reached $200 million, with annual operating profits as high as $50 million.[19] The decision to abandon TEL, which some analysts later described as the first major contemporary "pollution prevention" regulatory decision,[20] was in fact a decision primarily forced by a pollution control mandate and the development of a new technology to meet that mandate. Further, this changeover occurred without substantial disruption to either the automotive industry or gasoline producers. The shift in concern from occupational to environmental hazards had clearly played a role in precipitating a more rapid phase-out, but the primary factor underlying the industry decision to abandon leaded gasoline, as Ethyl Corporation officials indicated at the time, had its origins in GM's catalytic converter decision.[21]

What are the lessons of this product's introduction and evolution? For one, it is clear that the debates that marked tetraethyl lead's rise and fall highlighted the tangential nature of toxics issues in production decision-making so prevalent in that era. This remained the case although TEL was widely recognized for its hazardous properties even as it became integral to the structure of gasoline production. The ultimate abandonment of TEL was primarily driven by external forces (e.g., government regulation, public opinion, court action), and did not reflect a restructuring of internal decisionmaking processes and priorities to fundamentally incorporate consideration of environmental and health impacts.

Today, with public policy shifting away from pollution control and toward a prevention-oriented mandate, the subject of industry decisionmaking has reemerged in ways that suggest even more strongly that this area is likely to be disputed terrain. In exploring this terrain, pollution prevention can be viewed as an outcome dependent on organizational cultures and biases as well as structural factors that inform production decisions. Those cultures in turn are illuminated in part by management responses to external constraints on business activities (such as those that arose in connection with the issue of lead emissions from gasoline). Industry decisions do not occur in a political or regulatory vacuum, even as efforts are made to define such decisions as explicitly private rather than having public import and therefore needing public input.

The issues of how and when and in what context decisions are made today thus represent crucial factors in determining the potential for the new prevention-centered paradigm of production design. In situating this potential, the TEL episode suggests some of the barriers that continue to compound the search for new decisionmaking routes within industry settings.

What Gets Decided: Organization and Management Issues

The current public policy debates over the future of toxics regulation have been mirrored by the efforts of industry groups (led primarily by large chemical manufacturers) and industry trade associations to establish programs that address the concerns associated with hazardous materials use. These programs, many originating in response to crisis situations, have also reflected industry concerns over liability as well as the direct and indirect costs of regulatory compliance. Among these efforts have been the development of industrial toxicology and risk assessment programs; the use of environmental audits and life-cycle analyses as "early warning" and compliance tools; "green" marketing and labeling strategies; and various other programs and techniques directed, in varying ways, toward minimizing health risk and environmental damage, minimizing liability, and influencing the public perception of industry activities.

The escalation of industry efforts in these areas has proceeded apace with rising public concern, and, in particular, with the increased public and legislative attention to the "upstream" organizational and decisionmaking arenas that have been highlighted in the pollution prevention debate. While clearly responsive to external factors, the theme of industry voluntarism and self-determination runs strong, and has been used to support claims of a new and improved business/environment relationship (especially in the toxics area) as constituting a form of "corporate environmentalism." Reviewing these organizational and management responses can thus help to clarify the barriers to and opportunities for pollution prevention at the facility, company, and industry levels.

Toxicology and Risk Assessment

Prior to the first outbreaks of TEL poisoning and the public outcry associated with those events, U.S. manufacturing industries had demonstrated little interest in establishing formal programs in industrial toxicology.[22] Most of the initial research in this area had been undertaken by occupational health researchers, such as Alice Hamilton, on behalf of special state or federal government commissions organized to examine occupational hazards in specific industries, including the lead trades and munitions manufacturing. In private correspondence and in her autobiography, Hamilton spoke of strong resistance on the part of employers who "could, if they wished, shut their eyes to the dangers their workmen faced, for nobody held them responsible, while workers accepted the risks with fatalistic submissiveness as part of the price that one must pay for being poor." Despite the mixed impact of the Surgeon General's blue ribbon committee on TEL, Hamilton nevertheless saw the formation of the committee as a positive step by virtue of its exemplifying the need for independent evaluation of toxic hazards in the workplace.[23]

In the wake of the first TEL episodes, concerns about occupational hazards, particularly in the chemical industry, continued to intensify. They were fueled by incidents in the early 1930s at Dow Chemical and at Du Pont facilities where workers exposed to toxic substances (phenol in the case of Dow, benzidine and *beta*-napthylamine at Du Pont) experienced severe illness or death, including the occurrence of more than a dozen cases of bladder cancer at a Du Pont dye plant where *beta*-napthylamine was used. In 1933, responding to a new round of public criticisms of the use of toxic chemicals in industrial facilities, both Dow and Du Pont established their own research laboratories to investigate the causes of the deaths that had already occurred. Such labs were designed "to study the toxicology of all proposed new products in order to give advice as to the proper type of building and equipment before manufacture of the product is started," as the initial appropriation request for the Du Pont facility was phrased.[24] The labs were thus organized to focus primarily on hazard control techniques such as proper ventilation, and more generally on how to determine "the degree of exposure and the ability of each individual to handle that exposure." This approach, in turn, reflected the larger purpose of industry-based toxicology: namely, how "to keep the company out of trouble by producing valid information on toxicity of chemicals," as one Du Pont lab manager put it.[25]

From the outset, the early industry toxicology programs were beset by problems of organizational standing (toxicity assessments were not necessarily accepted or acted upon by other divisions), the slowness of implementation when assessments were finally accepted (it took Du Pont and other chemical manufacturers more than twenty years to cease manufacture of *beta*-napthylamine after research at Du Pont and elsewhere first identified a relationship between bladder tumors and occupational exposure to *beta*-napthylamine), and limits on the publication of research findings (some companies prohibited outside publication; others allowed internal departments with an interest in a particular chemical to have veto power over publication).

By the early and mid 1970s, the inadequacies and limitations associated with industry-based toxics research were further highlighted by a series of well-publicized outbreaks of occupational illness in which the absence or the ignoring of research findings on such substances as vinyl chloride, kepone, DBCP, and bischloromethyl ether (BCME) became the subject of contention and policy review. In the case of BCME, more than fifty deaths had resulted from its use in a single facility. The chemical company involved, Rohm and Haas, had at first resisted contracting with a leading outside toxicological research consultant to analyze BCME toxicity (in order to prevent publication of research findings), and had subsequently rejected a set of research findings regarding BCME toxicity, claiming that BCME use had not yet been conclusively linked to the deaths that had already occurred. Rohm and Haas, which did not have a toxicologist on its staff at the time, was eventually forced to shut down its facility after a major public scandal over the use of BCME erupted. This episode, in turn, contributed to the pressure building for passage of the Toxic Substances Control Act.[26]

The passage of TSCA in 1976 was a pivotal event in the evolution of industry-related toxics research. Like Rohm and Haas, few of the major chemical companies had functioning toxicology programs prior to 1976, but they quickly began to hire staff and organize new research units in order to comply with the research and notification requirements mandated by TSCA. At the same time, some companies with existing programs began to expand these efforts beyond an occupational focus to incorporate considerations of environmental risk. Collective industry research programs, including the Chemical Industry Institute of Toxicology at Research Triangle Park in North Carolina, were also established to help companies comply with new testing regulations, expand the "early warning" function, and, increasingly, to contest the approach of government regulators.

These challenges were aimed at risk assessments for specific chemicals and, more broadly, toward influencing the overall process of risk analysis then being explored in such agencies as EPA, OSHA, the Consumer Product Safety Commission, and the Food and Drug Administration. On the one hand, industry became a staunch champion of the growing use of quantitative risk assessment methods as a "scientific" undertaking that could (at least nominally) be separated from the social and political calculations of risk *management*, and also provide a "rational" basis for intervention. On the other hand, industry groups and researchers became adept at exploiting the vast uncertainties regarding the causal mechanisms of diseases such as cancer, the relationship of animal studies to human health risk prediction, the paths of environmental distribution and concentration of chemicals (a specialty known as "environmental fate" modeling), the effects of multiple exposures and synergistic disease-promoting relationships, and the myriad subtle assumptions of epidemiological studies regarding past exposures and dose–response relationships.

In the face of uncertainties that produced risk estimates which varied by orders of magnitude for even the most thoroughly researched chemicals with long commercial histories, industry-sponsored studies that were publicly released could often be counted on to provide low-end estimates. The complexities and uncertainty of quantitative risk assessment, particularly when combined with its increasing and controversial regulatory application in association with formal cost-benefit analysis, left the practice of quantitative risk-assessment–based regulation subject to continuous legal challenge. Advanced under the mantle of "good science," it often served to function as a tool for *de facto* deregulation.[27]

The various applications of industrial toxicology that emerged during the late 1970s and 1980s (seeking a more effective early warning system while alternately challenging and exploiting agency risk assessment practices) also reflected the fact that industry-based toxics research tended to remain driven by regulation and prospective regulation, a basic research counterpart to the engineering of new pollution control technologies and other compliance-related mechanisms established during this period.

Industry-based toxics research and risk analysis also tended to be limited in their potential to become integral to any broader prevention-oriented efforts within companies. Instead of designing toxicity and risk-related criteria to guide product development and process decisions in advance of the decisionmaking process at the department or division level (e.g., a production "design for the environment" framework), industry-initiated toxics research and risk analysis has continued to remain a tool for assessing regulatory compliance. A prevention-oriented focus for toxicological and risk-related research has yet to be established as a fundamental component of environmental management at either the facility, company, or sectoral levels.

Environmental Audits and Life Cycle Analysis

Another environmental management tool that emerged in response to the regulatory and liability concerns of the 1970s and 1980s was the environmental audit. First employed in the early 1970s by a handful of companies in order to assess compliance with the Clean Air Act and Clean Water Act, the environmental audit became more widely used during the late 1970s and early 1980s as a result of the passage of RCRA and Superfund (and their provisions for waste tracking and corporate liability), and in response to a variety of environmental crises leading to new legislative initiatives such as TSCA and CERCLA. AlliedSignal Inc., for example, established an internal Environmental Audit Program in 1978. A plaintiff in a number of law suits, AlliedSignal had signed a consent decree with EPA in response to a devastating release of a highly toxic pesticide, kepone, from its Hopewell, Virginia manufacturing site, that had created significant occupational, community, and environmental exposures.[28] The audit program was established in part to assure the company's board of directors and top management that an independent internal review process existed to assess compliance with laws and regulations and with company policy and standards, and to function as a mechanism helping advise higher management promptly of any "adverse situation."[29] Similarly, Union Carbide, in the wake of the Bhopal tragedy, established audit procedures consisting of informal surveillance, location compliance reviews performed by independent corporate auditors, independent reviews of subsidiary programs, and participation in subsidiary process safety reviews. Within a few years, the company would employ up to eighteen full-time auditors, including a number of retired Union Carbide managers.

By the early 1980s, many of the largest oil and chemical producers, particularly those concerned with the joint and several liability ("deep pocket") provisions of Superfund, also began instituting environmental audit programs. A.D. Little, one of the earliest consulting firms to conduct environmental audits for its clients, undertook as much as 80% of the audits of chemical and petroleum-based companies during the early 1980s. By 1991, the environmental audit (by then a $1 billion business involving outside consultants) had become a widely accepted practice in the oil and chemical industries, and had also begun to be adopted by companies from other industries involved in the use and release of toxic substances.[30] EPA began to require that companies conduct facility audits as part of specific administrative orders and/or consent decrees that were used for regulatory purposes, especially for TSCA noncompliance. Environmental audits had also become a standard operating procedure for many banks, insurance companies, and other financiers concerned about industrial, commercial, and even residential site histories in relation to their own liabilities. This concern was magnified after a U.S. District Court ruling extended liability to the Maryland Bank & Trust Company for cleanup of a hazardous waste site, although the site had been contaminated prior to its acquisition by the bank.[31]

As it evolved during the 1980s and 1990s, the environmental audit (also known as the Environmental, Health and Safety Audit or EHS) came to be defined as a "formal method of measuring compliance and the effectiveness of our environmental and safety management systems," as a United Technologies executive put it. It is often performed by a contracted auditor, such as A.D. Little, although it has been increasingly identified (partly to save money) as a function for internal audit groups, most often consisting of employees from various divisions who are joined together for purposes of the audit.[32] Several companies have established a combined approach, including Union Carbide, which reserved the use of its external auditors in the wake of its Bhopal disaster for its most sensitive activities considered to have the potential for "episodic catastrophic release." In some cases, states and federal agencies have developed variants of environmental auditing programs, either focusing on the activities of agencies [as in the case of the Waste Reduction Evaluations at Federal Sites (WREAFS) program jointly conducted by the EPA and the Department of Defense], or where technical resources are made available for audits of small and medium-sized manufacturers (for example, the city of Los Angeles' Hazardous and Toxic Materials program, with its use of retired engineers to perform specific facility audits for companies that might not otherwise have the resources or inclination to undertake such activities).[33]

In sum, audits can be structured to function as compliance tools that are waste- or pollutant-specific; to measure company performance against established quantitative goals (e.g., voluntary or mandated emission reductions); to evaluate standards and performance on environmental objectives in comparison with other companies and in relation to their own internal standards (especially relevant for companies with global operations); to identify weak or missing program areas and to assist management in identifying priorities for allocating resources and special emphasis programs; to identify potential cost savings by examining operations with respect to alternative processes or procedures; and/or to identify potential targets at a facility level for pollution prevention approaches.

Given its range of possibilities and interpretations, the environmental audit has evolved into a loosely defined review process of any company activities that have environmental implications. One 1993 survey of environmental policies among large companies revealed that more than 80% of the respondents had developed an environmental auditing program, though the nature of the programs varied widely both in terms of content and procedures.[34] But while the audit concept has become broader and looser in its application, most likely to be used as a regulatory compliance and early warning or liability avoidance tool, it has also demonstrated some modest potential for identifying opportunities for changing behavior in advance of or independent of specific regulations; that is, as a mechanism to develop targets and establish procedures for pollution prevention. Audits, for example, have on occasion been championed by practitioners for their ability to help define a proactive environmental philosophy and to help demonstrate a commitment to a form of environmental citizenship at both the facility and company level.[35]

This more expansive role for auditing, however, has been confounded by a number of organizational barriers, most notably by issues of confidentiality. Reflecting its roots as an early warning tool for regulatory compliance, most company officials have sought to ensure that the environmental audit itself not increase corporate liability. In the 1993 survey noted above, for example, only 6% of the companies with auditing programs made the summary results of the audit available to shareholders. AlliedSignal, as another example, has developed a strong auditing program and emphasizes a system of open reporting and correction of deficiencies, yet nevertheless stipulates, for liability purposes, that all rough notes and draft reports from an audit be destroyed three years after they have been put on paper. Law firms have also advised their corporate clients to employ an outside attorney to contract with an auditor, in order to maintain attorney–client confidentiality throughout the entire audit process. Such an attorney–client approach, as one industry auditor has remarked, emphasizes "confidentiality, less than full disclosure, a focus on wrong-doing, and sometimes a concept of fault-finding rather than problem-solving."[36]

Another application of environmental auditing which has emerged in recent years are those cases in which the audit functions as a review mechanism used by "outsider" analysts who are seeking to identify opportunities for improvement within a given industry sector or at the facility level (and who may or may not have the cooperation of the company or trade associations). INFORM's widely touted 1985 study of the waste and discharge problems at 29 different chemical plants, *Cutting Chemical Wastes* (and its subsequent 1992 follow-up survey *Environmental Dividends: Cutting More Chemical Wastes*), became a model for this kind of outside environmental audit.[37] Similarly, the study by UCLA graduate students of environmental problems at the UCLA campus became the prototype for the "campus environmental audit," widely initiated during Earth Day 1990 events and subsequently developed by students as both a tool for environmental education and as a tactic to pressure for environmental change at the facility level.[38] Movie studios, partly in response to such criticisms as the absence of recycling procedures for movie set materials, have also turned to more advocacy-oriented auditors to identify possible changes, especially in the areas of solid waste generation and energy use, but including toxics-related issues as well.[39]

The emergence of these "outside" audit approaches has itself further intensified the debate over the purpose and role of the company environmental audit and the related analytical tools of environmental impact analysis. It has done this by highlighting differences between types of audits (e.g., who conducts the audit, its primary purpose, and the level of public disclosure involved). It also points to the concept of environmental evaluation of industry activity embedded in proactive production design or planning, a more open-ended process of review and assessment that industry groups and facilities generally do not pursue, even though they might have the technical knowledge, resources, and community obligation to undertake a more proactive review. Structuring the audit as an evaluative tool could include more direct opportunity evaluations for pollution prevention, community reviews of industry activities, or specific pollution prevention studies with direct relevance to industrial restructuring activities.

A major offspring of this more open-ended process of environmental review is the concept of "life cycle analysis" (LCA). The methodology used in life cycle analysis was in fact developed partly to address shortcomings in environmental audit procedures which generally failed to consider environmental impacts beyond the facility level.[40] Life cycle analysis (similar to quantitative risk assessment, another modern derivative of formal systems analytic methodologies) essentially proposes to assess the full range of environmental impacts of a product, from raw materials extraction and processing stages, through manufacturing, transportation and distribution, to use and disposal. This approach seeks to examine a network of both materials and energy inputs and outputs, and could thus, presumably, identify a range of impacts above and beyond those that involve regulated activities or products, or which present specific liability concerns for a particular company or industry. In this way, a life cycle assessment has been defined by the Society of Environmental Toxicology and Chemistry (SETAC) as:

> ...an objective process to evaluate the environmental burdens associated with a product, process, or activity by identifying and quantifying energy and materials used and wastes released to the environment, to assess the impact of those energy and material uses and releases on the environment, and to evaluate and implement opportunities to affect environmental improvements. The assessment includes the entire life cycle of the product, process, or activity, encompassing extraction and processing of raw materials, manufacturing, transportation and distribution, use/reuse/maintenance, recycling, and final disposal.[41]

Clearly, such analyses are not in fact fully "objective." Initial choices to evaluate one product and not another must be made, but these are based primarily on funding priorities, public perceptions, or individual experience and intuition. Hence, findings are biased from the outset. Similarly, all analyses must be bounded in some way, again influencing results.

The roots of modern life cycle analyses can be traced to studies undertaken during the 1960s of the material and energy requirements of large industries such as chemical manufacturing, steel, pulp and paper, and petroleum refining. Later, efforts were undertaken to model the effects of population growth on global demands for raw materials and energy, and "fuel cycle" studies were used to estimate the costs and environmental consequences associated with alternative energy sources.

Until recently, there has been little or no incentive for industry and policy decisionmakers to examine the entire life cycle—and institutional constraints to such holistic assessments still remain. Life cycle analysis thus has tended to be precluded by the very nature of most media-specific regulatory decisionmaking procedures and consequent industry interest in it as an evaluative tool. However, interest in life cycle analyses began to grow during the past decade, primarily in response to public demands for more complete information about the environmental impacts of consumer goods. Certain business decisions were also shaped by life cycle analyses as industry began to try to market "green" products and realized it had to incorporate into manufacturing decisions concerns about environmental regulations that held it liable for wastes generated years after disposal.

Three interdependent components of life cycle analyses have been identified by LCA practicitioners: the inventory, the impact analysis, and the improvement analysis. Life cycle inventories have been designed to contain data on the energy and raw materials required to manufacture, use, and dispose of a product. They have also included information available regarding air emissions, waterborne effluents, solid and hazardous wastes, and other health or environmental impacts associated with each process in the life cycle, including occupational and product use risks.

Like its analytical cousin, quantitative risk assessment, upon which it is partly reliant for inputs, life cycle analysis has been plagued from the outset by (and abused as a consequence of) difficulties in bounding the "system" to be analyzed, by a wide variety of poorly defined parameters for which generalizations and assumptions and predictions must be made, and ultimately by the sheer complexity of the undertaking and the corollary opportunities for significant assumptions to be buried in a blizzard of data in the technical appendices. Although perhaps less subject than risk assessment to the phenomenon of the *cordon sanitaire* (in which a problem is defined as "scientific" and/or "technical" irrespective of its embedded social and political content and thus removed from the purview of ordinary citizens), life cycle analysis nevertheless has shared the same characteristic of quantitative risk assessment in the difficulty of being able to deconstruct and evaluate the process assumption by assumption. Even the comparatively simple problem of measuring on-site energy consumption, for example, has been treated in a variety of ways yielding significantly different results, as indicated by attempts to identify the relative energy consumption of recycled versus virgin paper production. Some analysts have used "electricity purchased" or "energy (including fuels) purchased" as the measure of energy consumption, which has drastically understated the gross energy consumption of virgin mills that burn wood bark and other residues to supply more than half of their energy requirements.[42]

Although promising in its stated goal to systematically expand understanding of environmental impacts, life cycle analysis, in its initial applications during the late 1980s and early 1990s, became a controversial tool used to compare environmental impacts between competing products, such as paper and plastic bags, or cloth (reusable) and paper/plastic (throwaway) diapers. Consulting firms like A.D. Little were hired by industry groups or specific companies to defend their products or at least to challenge the inconclusive nature of available comparisons between products, thus at times deflecting highly visible public campaigns targeting the product in question (e.g., throwaway diapers).[43] Many of LCA's initial applications were thus undertaken for public relations or marketing rather than pollution prevention or environmental design purposes.

By the early 1990s, concerns over the abuse of life cycle analysis had led to recommendations, by both the EPA (through its Life-Cycle Assessment Peer Review Group), and SETAC, to redefine life cycle analysis as an internal evaluation tool (parallel to the environmental audit) rather than as an external product evaluation device, and to extend the analysis beyond a simple inventory of impacts to include both impact and improvement analysis (that is, what was the nature of the problems and how could they be addressed). The difficulties of identifying, much less systematically quantifying, impacts and risks also echoed problems that came to be identified in the environmental audit process with respect to appropriate accounting procedures.

In terms of corporate accounting, it has long been recognized that product prices and corporate profits do not reflect the true "costs" of environmental depletion and degradation. While they have been marginally "internalized" by companies and society through the corporate and public costs of pollution control, among other mechanisms, the complex and protracted problems of increasing degradation of the environment, impacts on human health, or resource depletion, combined with the legacy of irreversible damage, indicates that the effect has been relatively negligible. While there may be increasingly widespread agreement that ecological and public health values have failed to be internalized within either corporate or national accounting practices, there have been different approaches concerning how to address the problem associated with different regulatory scenarios.

As one approach, some industry leaders have begun to publicly advance an interpretation of "full cost accounting" as a pricing practice that incorporates the environmental costs of goods and services in the market incentives tradition, although it has also been used to refer to allocating environmental costs within a firm's cost accounting procedures rather than having such costs figure as overhead. As the chairman of Dow Chemical describes it, "a key tool in initiating full-cost accounting will be life cycle analysis," and a key advantage will be to eliminate the need to employ "counterproductive" (overly broad) instruments such as environmental taxes. "By building environmental costs into a product's price, consumers will no longer need to rely on 'green' advertising, seals and guides. Consumers can objectively choose the best priced product and be confident that they are making the best choice for both their wallet and the world."[44]

Another approach criticizes the premise that tools such as life cycle analysis in conjunction with full-cost accounting can deliver an exclusively market-based solution, unfettered by extensive social and political analysis and debate. This approach, which more directly relies on community and workplace input in identifying and addressing the issues involved, generally advances various forms of precautionary regulatory intervention, including minimum standards, product and substance bans, various forms of environmental taxes, and, more broadly, alternative forms of economic, social, and industrial policy.

While some of the basic premises of full-cost accounting and life cycle analysis are crucial to any assessment of reduction opportunities (e.g., the proposition that products do not reflect their true environmental costs), it is clear that, given the latitude in interpretation, both the details of definition and application and the relationship between full-cost accounting, life cycle analysis, and regulation leave much to be addressed. What, for example, is the life cycle of a basic organic chemical product that can be variously created as a product of oil refining, natural gas production, coal processing, or botanochemical processes, and that provides the molecular building blocks for a range of other industrial sectors, which in turn provide products (such as various synthetic materials) used by every sector of society? How do we quantify the ecosystem services lost when wetlands, for example, are polluted beyond recovery by multiple point and nonpoint sources, and to which products do we attribute the cost? The idea of LCA, as currently formulated, can easily become a caricature of the problems that must be addressed, with such examples as Monsanto's imposition of a deposit charge on the containers it uses for distribution. The Monsanto application, similar to the approach taken by a number of other toxic generators, assumes a central role to solid waste disposal concerns within the life cycle trajectory, often minimizing the focus on a company's toxic releases and generation of toxic products for use downstream. Given its various constraints and interpretations, life cycle analysis has nevertheless begun to emerge as a leading decision tool in both national and international policy arenas and in the corporate search for public credibility, and will be an increasingly key element of the corporate and public agenda for some time to come.

Green Marketing and Labeling

During the 1980s and 1990s, the notion of a "green product" was introduced in relation to a wide range of product developments and industry activities. These developments were primarily stimulated by consumer-driven concerns over excess packaging, hazardous household products (e.g. insecticides, cleaning agents, automotive products), and particular product ingredients (most notably CFCs in aerosols). The issue of a company's environmental identity also tied into this green consumerism matrix, influenced by the negative perceptions stemming from major environmental disasters (e.g., the kepone episode for AlliedSignal, Bhopal for Union Carbide, the *Valdez* oil spill for Exxon). Corporate debates about appropriate environmental strategies (much of which was regulation-driven) began to expand beyond the regulatory domain to include questions of marketing and public relations. Reacting to specific campaigns initiated to stimulate product boycotts (many of them related to solid waste issues) as well as product or substance bans, a number of companies began to explore counter initiatives, designed to demonstrate the "greenness" of particular products or of the companies themselves. As a consequence, green marketing emerged as a tool both to deflect environmental criticism of industry activities, and, for some companies, as a new device to expand market share.

But what constituted a green product (or a green company) and how the claims of "greenness" were to be evaluated became crucial questions for both policymakers, product manufacturers, and environmental critics alike. In response to the proliferation of these green marketing claims, several organizations were established during the early 1990s (some broadly seeking to duplicate more elaborate European or Canadian programs) in hopes of initiating or influencing the development of a green labeling code for "environment friendly" products and companies. Many of these efforts were also seen as a way of creating incentives for corporations to explore more efficient or environmentally benign technologies and to reduce environmental impacts, as well as to enhance consumer education (particularly in the period prior to Earth Day 1990 when the concept of "individual responsibility" for the environment was widely promoted by the media, policymakers, and environmental groups).[45]

Much of the initial corporate activity regarding green consumerism was defensive in nature, often involving attempts to demonstrate a concern for the environment, as evidenced by the corporate signature ads of oil companies during the energy crisis period of the 1970s. By the 1990s, however, it had also become clear to several companies, particularly high profile consumer product companies, that marketing factors needed to be considered as well. A number of opinion polls undertaken in the period prior to Earth Day 1990 pointed to significant concerns about the environmental impacts of products and a willingness by consumers to pay higher prices for more environmentally oriented products.[46] In turn, a number of companies sought to isolate particular sets of consumer concerns (e.g., product biodegradability) and develop new "green" product lines based on claims regarding that concern. Such green marketing strategies were, however, subject to abuse, both in terms of the range of other impacts they failed to address as well as the very claims that were being made. Mobil Oil, for example, introduced a "biodegradable" Hefty trash bag which it subsequently withdrew after its claims of degradability in landfills were widely criticized as misleading.[47] Along these lines, Minnesota State Attorney General Hubert Humphrey III warned that "some environmental claims are confusing and vague—consumers can't tell from reading the labels just how these products are better for the environment. Some claims are simply trivial, offering no environmental benefit of any consequence. And some claims are downright misleading and fraudulent."[48]

Partly as a consequence of these misleading claims and the often vague yet increasingly prolific environmental labels that began to be attached to a wide range of products, the Federal Trade Commission in 1992 established guidelines addressing such concerns. The guidelines themselves did not become legally enforceable, nor did they provide language identifying appropriate environmental labels, but they did seek to provide a broad-based representation regarding a number of prevalent claims, such as degradable, biodegradable, photodegradable, compostable, recyclable, recycled content, source reduction, refillable, and ozone safe and ozone friendly.[49]

Green marketing claims also extended to company approaches regarding their environmental identity, particularly for the high profile, consumer product companies. During the late 1980s, for example, the McDonald's corporation became the focus of a "McToxics campaign," a wide-ranging protest effort initially focused on the fast food chain's use of polystyrene foam containers made with CFCs. As the campaign increased in scope beyond the CFC issue, McDonald's entered into an agreement with the Environmental Defense Fund (a mainstream environmental group which had not participated in the original McToxics Campaign) to undertake a joint environmental audit of various operations within the company, including packaging practices. Although much of the media attention focused on McDonalds' decision to substitute a paper wrapping for its foam containers, the audit in fact served to highlight a range of other environment-oriented actions taken by McDonald's, such as its increased use of recycled products and various changes to promote solid waste reduction (e.g., the use of dispensers instead of individual serving packages for ketchup and relish). Ultimately, McDonalds' changes became part of its own overall green marketing campaign.[50]

McDonalds' activities, particularly with respect to solid waste issues, paralleled the approach taken by a number of other companies subject to specific product criticisms and sensitive to the broader effects of green consumer awareness and activity. Proctor & Gamble, the largest consumer products company in the country and one of the two largest manufacturers of disposable diapers (with approximately 45–50% of the market share), felt particularly vulnerable regarding the controversies concerning that product. This vulnerability was underlined by the actions of a number of states and communities seeking to explore policy options (including product bans) to discourage throwaways in favor of reusable cloth diapers. To counter those initiatives, P & G hired the A.D. Little consulting firm to undertake a life cycle analysis of environmental impacts and economic comparisons between disposable and cloth diapers, a study subsequently criticized both for its methodology and assumptions. At the same time, especially in light of its substantial European operations, Proctor & Gamble became concerned that the development of green labeling policies, such as Germany's "Blue Angel" and the Nordic Council's "Environment Mark" programs, could have a significant adverse effect on its markets. Although environmental design criteria had never previously been incorporated into the company's substantial research and development activities, P&G decided, as part of its green marketing counteroffensive, to initiate new research efforts to identify possible packaging and materials use innovations to be marketed for their environmental benefits. As a consequence, P&G was able to launch, with much fanfare during the early 1990s, several new "green" product initiatives (e.g., a liquid concentrate in reusable containers and a new disposable diaper with recyclable components) which in turn became part of its overall green marketing approach.[51]

The development of green products and green labeling procedures also became the focus of several new organizations established in the wake of Earth Day 1990, an event which had itself provided a major focus on green consumer awareness. The most prominent of these organizations, Green Seal (founded by Earth Day 1990 organizer and promoter Denis Hayes), sought to develop a standards-based approach to product labeling that utilized "Environmental Impact Evaluations" for specific products. These highlighted what the organization considered the most important impacts in the product life cycle (as distinct from a more comprehensive—and

more expensive to undertake—life cycle analysis). Green Seal also established an "Environmental Partners Agreement" with companies that basically resembled a purchased logo. As part of the Partners Agreement, a
company would agree to purchase Green Seal–certified products, complete
an annual questionnaire to be used in Green Seal reports and promotional
literature, recycle their office materials, provide Green Seal with professional expertise for establishing product standards, and appoint a liaison to
the program. In exchange—at a cost of $150 to be paid to Green Seal—
they would receive a Green Seal Environmental Partners logo and advice
from the organization concerning environmentally responsible procure-
ment. Over time, the development of Green Seal standards and
Environmental Partners Agreements were seen as encouraging the development of more environmentally friendly technologies and green practices
and consciousness among companies.[52]

Despite its visibility, the Green Seal program has been limited in its
actual achievements. By 1994, Green Seal had developed only six standards
covering about 35 product categories such as light bulbs, refined motor oil,
tissue paper, paper towels and napkins, printing and writing paper, and
water efficient fixtures, among others. Although the organization encouraged feedback from industries and trade associations such as the Chemical
Manufacturers Association, it distinguished its efforts—as a third party
independent evaluator—from a "consensus" process that required industry
acceptance of the standard under consideration or from government programs that might lack the specificity and explicit environmental incentive
objectives of the private labelers. At the same time, Green Seal from the
outset concentrated its efforts solely on environmental and not occupational or product safety considerations, arguing that existing regulations in
these areas were already in effect.[53]

The third party environmental certification programs (or ECPs as they
are called) such as Green Seal or Green Cross have been criticized for their
own lack of accountability and difficulty in measuring program effectiveness. Among ECPs, there have emerged three distinctive types of programs:
(1) seal-of-approval programs which "identify products or services as being
less harmful to the environment than similar products or services with the
same function" (e.g., Green Seal); (2) single attribute certification programs
to validate environmental claims made by a manufacturer; and (3) report
card programs about products or a company's environmental performance,
such as for shareholders. Each of these programs is designed to provide a
positive label to encourage a green approach by companies, an approach
that broadly corresponded to the more official, government-sponsored
certification or labeling programs that seek to create a single, common ref-

erence point. Such programs, like those developed for the European Community, try to overcome the problems created by competition among the ECPs (as of 1993, there were at least 13 ECPs in operation in as many as 21 countries) by essentially adopting a baseline for positive green labels.[54]

Such positive-oriented programs contrast significantly with the "negative" or critical labeling programs that seek to discriminate among products (and also thereby provide incentives to change) by identifying their negative impacts. Similar in intent to one of the first of such programs, California's Proposition 65,[55] the "negative" label is often more sharply criticized and resisted by industry groups already fearful of the loss of control of their production processes and marketing decisions associated with the ECPs. One such local program strongly opposed by some industry groups was the city of Santa Monica's Hazardous Household Products Labeling Ordinance which sought to directly establish a link between green consumer awareness and pollution prevention opportunities. The Santa Monica ordinance was designed to heighten consumer awareness of such toxic products as paints, aerosols, and various cleaning products (products that also required disposal at the city's Household Hazardous Waste facility). The motivation for the city was financial: by operating a Household Hazardous Waste facility, it was incurring significant costs of disposal that, as with aerosol products, exceeded the cost of the product itself. Despite its clear intent as a consumer education program, however, industry groups, led by the Chemical Specialty Manufacturer's Association, the California Grocers Association, and the California Department of Pesticide Regulation, orchestrated a campaign to stop the ordinance on the basis that the city had no powers to influence the sale of toxic products![56]

In general, the rise of green labeling, often limited by its focus on a single environmental aspect of product use, has had little to show by way of measurable pollution prevention outcomes, with the important exception of California's Proposition 65 hazard warning provision which helped stimulate a number of process and product changes. At the same time, nearly all the industry claims targeting environmentally discriminating consumers initiated during the late 1980s and early 1990s tended to focus on municipal solid waste concerns and less on pollution prevention, playing to public familiarity and the positive identification with recycling efforts, while mostly avoiding the complexities and negative associations of toxic chemical and industrial process issues. Green marketing strategies as a whole, above and beyond the green label issue, have thus largely failed to directly incorporate pollution prevention criteria into the product development and process design stages, although some innovations have been introduced *ex post facto*, either to meet a perceived market opportunity, or to forestall potentially negative impacts affecting market share.

Broadly defined, green marketing has primarily evolved into a form of corporate advertising. As a nonregulated activity, green marketing has stretched the definitions of "greenness"; definitions often subject to exaggeration and contradictory information. In this context, the green product has become something of an oxymoron, given the absence of environmental criteria in actual product design. "There is no such thing as a 'green product'; it's really just a perception issue, a matter of marketing," argues investment analyst Jeffrey Cinci, underlining an oft-repeated industry perspective.[57]

Green product design remains an area to be explored, distinct from the biases and interpretations that have plagued its development to date. Such design factors clearly evolve by establishing new relationships between product and environment, built into the strategic planning process for any given production system. Today, those relationships are at best *ad hoc* and short term, primarily reactive to either regulation or public relations concerns. Even labeling programs, seeking to establish demand-side influences, tend to create awareness about specific concerns, such as excess packaging, recyclability, or energy content or use. Broader, more comprehensive programs, particularly among the ECPs or government-based programs emphasizing positive labels or approvals, have had difficulty establishing successful criteria that directly address toxics impacts. The negative labeling efforts, on the other hand, tend to have greater success in creating direct incentives for product and process changes. Ultimately, the influence of these kinds of programs or more broadly of green product innovation is going to require greater environmental literacy at both the designer and consumer level, an expertise of the environment in product design.

Efforts at establishing such literacy, like Patagonia's decision to undertake product life cycle analyses to make its entire operations more environment-friendly,[58] have reflected an (often unique) environmental consciousness at the executive level but not at the system or product design level. To establish such a production shift will require greater influences throughout the product decision chain, influences that will undoubtedly remain external (that is, demand and/or regulatory driven) until the reigning conceptual framework within industry decisionmaking ultimately allows for the common ground between environment and product. At the same time, the issue of product *use*, that is, how any given product, including "green" products, meets specific needs, raises larger and more generic concerns about production choices and the markets products serve and/or create. The relationship of environment and product then can be seen as a question of how products are produced as well as why they are produced in the first place.

Environmental Citizenship

During the past two decades, a number of environmental laws have been passed in response to environmental disasters, such as Love Canal (CERCLA) and Bhopal (SARA). Similarly, these events have created pressure on both policymakers and advocacy groups to establish new criteria for "environmental citizenship," a concept broadly corresponding to the term "social responsibility" that had been applied to corporate and investment activities since the late 1960s. The negative public perceptions generated by these disasters have also, in turn, led a number of companies and industry groups to adopt and publicize new internal procedures, such as the environmental audit, which demonstrate a new commitment to responsible environmental citizenship. Several of these factors became especially prominent in the reaction to the massive oil spill in Alaska's Prince William Sound in 1989, a disaster caused by the grounding of the Exxon *Valdez* oil tanker. One of the more immediate and visible outcomes from the Exxon *Valdez* episode was an effort by institutional investors to establish a code of environmental conduct for companies as a means by which the concept of good environmental citizenship could be formally evaluated.

Initially modeled after the "Sullivan Principles" (established in the early 1980s as a guide for businesses operating in South Africa to link their business decisions with efforts to end apartheid), the ten *Valdez* Principles for corporate environmental conduct were drafted by the Coalition for Environmentally Responsible Economies (CERES), a group of investment fund advisors and environmental and social justice advocates. CERES was itself a project of the Social Investment Forum, a national association of more than 350 institutional investors (including the New York City and state of California pension fund managers) who controlled more than $150 billion worth of investments. Unlike previous efforts to develop environmental conduct criteria for industry, such as the campaigns initiated in the 1970s advocating environmental representatives on company boards of directors, the campaign to obtain corporate signatories to the "*Valdez*" or "CERES" Principles" was backed by the potential power of the institutional investors involved in the effort, and thus represented a significant broadening of "outsider" claims on industry behavior.

The original CERES Principles included provisions for an annual envi-

ronmental audit and the disclosure to CERES of environmental performance. It also outlined broad principles of conduct governing energy use,
public disclosure, damage compensation, and sustainable use of natural
resources, while calling for environmental representation on boards of
directors and among top management. Three provisions with potential
pollution prevention implications were included in the principles: reduction and safe disposal of waste, especially hazardous waste; biosphere protection by eliminating the release of any pollutant "that may cause environmental damage to the air, water, or earth or its inhabitants"; and
occupational and community-focused risk reduction programs.[59]

Similar to the Green Seal approach, the Principles were developed independent of a "consensus" process with industry, although efforts were made
to solicit industry feedback. However, the CERES Principles, initially
issued in September 1989, failed to include either explicit compliance criteria for corporate signatories, or direct methods for translating the principles into uniform standards applicable across industries. When the Sun
Company (or Sunoco) became the first Fortune 500 company to endorse
the CERES Principles in February 1993 after lengthy negotiations, it did
so on the basis of identifying, with modifications, the category of *progress*
toward compliance, to accommodate Sun's continuing manufacture of
products (e.g., gasoline) which largely precluded a zero emissions goal, an
underlying though unstated intent of the Principles. Similarly, when
General Motors established an agreement in March 1994 to partially abide
by the Principles (e.g., public disclosure of environmental progress, recycling and waste reduction measures, and the use, where possible, of renewable resources) it was characterized by CERES members as "not an agreement to agree on every issue," but rather "a forum for discussion and
moving forward."[60] The primary process established by CERES to validate
compliance with the Principles was in fact limited to a public information
effort in the form of a 34-page "self-appraisal" manual, designed to inform
shareholders, investors, and the general public about the environmental
progress of the signatories and the specific programs that had been established.

Despite the caveat about environmental progress, the CERES Principles
were viewed from the outset by nearly all major toxics generating industry groups and companies as controversial and "interventionist." By 1994,
just seventy-five companies had adopted the Principles, and, of those, only
GM and the Sun Company could be considered major toxics generators.
Industry groups argued that conduct codes should be an internal industry
function (although, as one industry auditor put it, that required it to be a
"line responsibility" in order for it to be effective, an issue largely ignored

when "voluntarist" approaches were advocated). Industry groups were also especially wary of the potential new alliance between investors and environmental advocacy groups that could conceivably bring effective "outside" pressures into the sphere of industry decisionmaking. At the same time, they pointed to already existing internal conduct codes as more viable alternatives to the CERES approach, such as the International Chamber of Commerce's Principles of Environmental Management, and especially the Chemical Manufacturers Association's (CMA) Responsible Care program which had emerged during the late 1980s and early 1990s as a centerpiece of corporate environmental voluntarism.[61]

As early as 1983, CMA had begun to establish its own guidelines on how the chemical industry should conduct its business and relate to the public. After Bhopal, the organization expanded this effort to introduce a new, voluntary program called Community Awareness and Emergency Response (CAER). A Canadian initiative called Responsible Care was subsequently brought to the attention of CMA's "Public Perception" Committee, and in 1988 CMA announced its own Responsible Care program, adopting the CAER initiative as the first of six codes of practice. Other codes developed included pollution prevention, process safety, distribution (reducing transportation and storage risks), employee health and safety, and, most notably in terms of its approach, product stewardship (addressing the design, manufacture, handling, and use of chemical products by employees and contract manufacturers). In advance of Earth Day 1990, CMA launched a multimillion dollar advertising campaign highlighting the Responsible Care program—and by 1992/1993, the program's advertising budget had reached as high as $9 million. Described by CMA (and Dow Chemical) chairman Frank Popoff as the chemical industry's "strategy for survival," the program has also been widely criticized by environmental and public interest advocates as a public relations ploy. Critics have raised concerns about the absence of mechanisms for measuring performance and compliance with the codes, and on the disjuncture between the stated goals of Responsible Care and CMA's other activities.[62]

While the pollution prevention goals are to be measured by the Toxics Release Inventory (generally a viable approach for the chemical industry, although the list of chemicals has been criticized as inadequate) mechanisms for assessing performance in other areas do not exist, and CMA efforts, which have focused on self-evaluation by members, have been generally hostile to proposals for third party evaluations. CMA has also advanced, as a mechanism for disclosure, the formation of Citizen Advisory Panels within the communities in which its members operate. However, these company-appointed groups have often been dominated by company interests, denied information, and have been closed to technical experts representing the community. Moreover, community "tracking" programs have been limited to evaluations of RCRA-defined wastes and thus have remained simple extensions of regulatory compliance programs rather than new definitions of environmental citizenship.[63]

While publicizing its commitment to "responsible care," CMA has simultaneously been active in opposing public right-to-know legislation. This opposition dates back to the debates over EPCRA in the mid 1980s, and has continued with respect to the proposed Right-to-Know More Act (the most detailed and expansive of current TRI-related initiatives which, in its earliest versions, had provisions setting toxics use reduction performance standards), which CMA has called "a radical form of industrial policy in the guise of environmental protection."[64] Critics have pointed out that it is only right-to-know legislation that has given the public the ability to track the industry's performance (responding to the CMA slogan "track us, don't trust us"), and that CMA opposition to the Right-to-Know More legislation directly violates the presumed spirit of Responsible Care, and further undercuts its legitimacy. Ultimately, the concept of environmental citizenship remains contested terrain, both in terms of what constitutes "citizenship" and "responsibility," as well as how such citizenship is to be determined.

Decisionmaking and Production Outcomes

The distinctions and the debates surrounding the value and efficacy of the CERES and Responsible Care programs, a debate in part over "outsider" versus "internal" or "voluntary" efforts aimed at changing industry organization and management behavior, provide yet one more example of the need to carefully situate the analytic context for evaluating industries with respect to pollution prevention. The questions posed must not only reflect upon *what* a facility or an industry produces and how it gets produced, but also *why* it is produced, how it came to be produced in the first place, and who else might be vested in its production. It becomes crucial to examine the linkages between any particular industry and the broader economy, and the roles of particular companies or facilities within that industry, in order to meaningfully evaluate both the opportunities for and the barriers to pollution prevention. In this context, pollution prevention policy can be considered a form of economic development or industrial policy, including the need for public input into industry decisionmaking, an approach powerfully resisted by most industry groups.

Any pollution prevention analysis of industry activities must necessarily be concerned with what gets produced and how it is produced, with a specific focus on how production decisions are made and how they can be influenced. Such an analysis may focus on mechanisms of public disclosure, environmental auditing, and the development of standards and operating principles, while also considering the organizational mechanisms by which decisions are made and the extent to which environmental design criteria are included. This form of analysis may often be instructive in suggesting operational and product design changes companies can make, how they can accomplish such changes, and, ultimately, how such changes can be both evaluated and institutionalized.

Most discussions of "corporate environmentalism" have, essentially by definition, focused on questions of industry compliance with certain internal, industry-wide, or regulatory requirements or codes of conduct, ignoring broader questions of product and process development and purpose. Thus, much of the discussion about industry decisionmaking tends to get deflected into sometimes superficial debates over "voluntarism" versus outside intervention and regulation. Critics of voluntarism have argued that most such efforts have amounted to a form of "greenwashing," employed to disguise corporate responsibility for pollution and environmental degradation, and to evade further regulation. Critics of outside intervention, on the other hand, have argued that industry knows itself best, and that existing internal efforts have been substantial and far-reaching, and have thus transformed groups like the chemical industry into "a part of the solution and not the problem," as a Responsible Care slogan has suggested. But what is perhaps most significant about this debate is its recognition of the increasing importance that environmental factors generally—and toxics generation, use, and disposal issues specifically—have become and will increasingly become in relation to overall production and public policy decisions.

The threshold questions for pollution prevention (how, what, and why are specific production decisions made) are in fact directly related to the kinds of questions that emerged in our historical case study: that is, how to situate the decisions that were made concerning the introduction and continuing use of tetraethyl lead. In examining those decisions, a pollution prevention approach requires an understanding—and a plan of action—with respect to how such decisions could have been made differently. What social and industrial relationships, for example, were involved (e.g., between automobile manufacturers, the chemical and oil industries, and the nation's transportation needs) and what core technologies were relied upon (e.g., the internal combustion engine)? How were these factors addressed during the evolution of TEL use and its eventual decline, and how could they be addressed differently today? What were the key forces that influenced organizational choices and behavior and what innovations could be introduced today which might modify such choices (e.g., different kinds of research design, objective evaluations, a new definition of the "consumer" and his or her "needs," a strengthened precautionary approach to environmental risk by researchers, designers, and policymakers, a new overall corporate culture for decisionmaking, and so forth). The answer to such questions, whether in relation to the historical example of TEL or in relation to the reduction and/or elimination of both present and future environmental hazards, will only effectively emerge when such questions can be situated directly within our understanding of production decisions and their environmental outcomes.

Notes

1. Charles Kettering, a key figure in the development and marketing of tetraethyl lead, described the "solution of the problem of knock in automobile engines" as also having been made possible by "the hearty cooperation of both [the petroleum and automobile] industries." Cited in *Prophet of Progress: Selections from the Speeches of Charles F. Kettering*, edited by T.A. Boyd, (New York: E.P. Dutton & Co, 1961), p. 165.

2. The Sloan quote is cited in "'A Gift of God'?: The Public Health Controversy over Leaded Gasoline during the 1920s," David Rosner and Gerald Markowitz in *Dying for Work: Workers' Safety and Health in Twentieth-Century America*, David Rosner and Gerald Markowitz, eds. (Bloomington: Indiana University Press, 1989), p. 122.

3. TEL consumption would in fact increase by more than a factor of 8 in less than twenty years after that first plateau of 60 million pounds had been achieved in 1938. See "Estimated Domestic Tetraethyl Lead Consumption in Millions of Pounds, 1924-1958," Table 1, cited in "Public Health Aspects of Increasing Tetraethyl Lead Content in Motor Fuel," Public Health Service Publication No. 712, 1959, p. 8.

4. Du Pont official W.F. Harrington in fact argued at a 1925 conference on TEL that Du Pont's long history in the "manufacture of dangerous chemicals" gave it the ability to manufacture TEL safely and without consequence. In *Proceedings of a Conference to Determine Whether or Not There is a Public Health Question in the Manufacture, Distribution, or Use of Tetraethyl Lead Gasoline*, Public Health Bulletin No. 158, (Washington D.C.: Government Printing Office, 1925), pp. 11-12.

5. *Professional Amateur: The Biography of Charles Franklin Kettering*, T.A. Boyd (New York: E.P. Dutton, 1957), pp. 147, 152.

6. Production levels at Du Pont's TEL pilot plant in Deepwater, New Jersey increased to 700 gallons per day within the first year alone, considered at the time a phenomenal growth rate for the new product, exceeding the company's own expectations. Cited in *Science & Corporate Strategy: Du Pont R&D, 1902–1980*, David A. Hounshell and John Kenley Smith, Jr., (Cambridge: Cambridge University Press, 1988), p. 152.

7. U.S. Public Health Service, 1926, *op cit.*; *New York Times* October 31, 1924.

8. The Bureau of Mines study also played a central role in seeking to develop a "scientific consensus" that there was "complete safety" in the use of TEL as an additive. See, for example, the "Ethyl Gasoline" editorial in the *American Journal of Public Health*, Vol. XV, No. 3, March 1925, pp. 239–240; and "Tetraethyl Lead and the Public Health," J.H. Shrader, in the same issue of the *AJPH*, pp. 213–216. On the Bureau of Mines study, see the testimony of Bureau of Mines official Dr. R. R. Sayers in the Surgeon General's Conference proceedings in Public Health Bulletin No. 158, pp. 25–31.

9. Charles Kettering's biographer noted how Midgley and Kettering argued at the time that the TEL fatalities "had been caused by the heedlessness of the workers and that ethyl was harmless when properly handled." See *Boss Ket: A Life of Charles F. Kettering*, Rosamond McPherson Young, 1961, pp. 162–163. Both Midgley and Kettering in fact identified their research as corporate-driven, that is, industrial research designed to meet the product and process requirements for particular companies and industries. As a consequence, both men also saw their role as corporate leaders as well as researchers and, with respect to leaded gasoline, were given high positions in the company and served on the board of directors of the newly formed Ethyl Corporation which marketed the product. See "Thomas Midgley and the Politics of Industrial Research," Stuart W. Leslie, *Business History Review*, Vol. LIV, No. 4, Winter 1980, pp. 480–502; Midgley's testimony cited above can be found in the proceedings of the Surgeon General's Conference in Public Health Bulletin #158 (1925), pp. 12–13.

10. The definitiveness of proof was also seen as requiring a standard separate from the (presumed to be) inconclusive results from animal testing, a position (innocent until proven guilty) that would prevail among industry advocates for more than another half century. See the discussion on this issue in an *American Journal of Public Health* editorial, "The Washington

Conference on the Ethyl Gasoline Hazard," Vol. XV, No. 7, July 1925, pp. 632–634.

11. Testimony of Mr. Frank A. Howard, representing the Ethyl Gasoline Corporation in Public Health Bulletin No. 158, pp. 105–106.

12. Hamilton's position about potential environmental impacts, ultimately borne out by later studies concerning ambient lead exposures, was contested at the outset by the scientists and engineers like Midgley and Kettering associated with TEL development. At a 1924 conference of the American Chemical Society in Baltimore, Midgley presented a paper on toxicity issues with respect to TEL and argued that the "actual hazard involved in the general program of treating gasoline with tetraethyl has been found to exist only in the manufacture and handling of the concentrated material." Hamilton's testimony at the Surgeon General's Conference is in Public Health Bulletin No. 158, pp. 98–99. Her position advocating government intervention regarding interstate commerce is also argued in "Investigation of Ethyl Gas," *American Journal of Public Health,* Vol. XV, No. 5, May 1925, p. 484.

13. The Committee's proposed regulations covered the conditions for the manufacture of TEL and its blending in the production of ethyl gasoline (and included a maximum concentration level of 3.0 ml/gal for TEL in commercial gasolines); the mixing and distribution of the product; and specific precautions regarding automobile garages, repair shops, service stations, and filling stations. Much of the focus of these recommendations evolved around core control techniques such as ventilation requirements. See "The Use of Tetraethyl Lead Gasoline and Its Relation to Public Health," Public Health Bulletin No. 163, 1926.

14. "It remains possible," the Surgeon General Committee's report noted, "that, if the use of leaded gasoline becomes widespread, conditions may arise very different from those studied by us which would render its use more of a hazard than would appear to be the case from this investigation." The committee's warnings, however, became forgotten in the subsequent rush to production. More than thirty years later, when the Ethyl Corporation sought to increase the maximum concentration of TEL in gasoline by 25%, it again approached the Surgeon General to establish a committee to determine whether such an increase represented a public health hazard. This 1958 committee, primarily consisting of or dependent upon industry researchers or advocates, also argued that it did not have sufficient medical data to make such a determination. "It is regrettable," this 1958 Surgeon General committee noted, "that the investigations recommended by the Surgeon General's Committee in 1926 were not carried

out by the Public Health Service." Although acknowledging the absence
of such crucial information even as "some authorities believe that the tol-
erable limit of lead absorption is being approached," the 1958 committee
still recommended approval of the increase in concentration levels, and
urged that future health-based studies be undertaken "to assure the valid-
ity of the present decision." Such an "innocent until proven guilty" framework remained the rule rather than the exception for at least another
decade. See *Public Health Aspects of Increasing Tetraethyl Lead Content in Motor
Fuel*, Public Health Publication No. 712, 1959, p. viii.

15. See the testimony of Yandell Henderson and Grace Burnham in
Public Health Bulletin No. 158, 1925, *op. cit.*

16. The figures for Du Pont's net earnings are cited in *Du Pont and the
International Chemical Industry*, Graham D. Taylor and Patricia E. Sudnik
(Boston: Twayne Publishers, 1984), p. 85. In terms of the concept of the
timing of a chemical's "innocence" or "guilt," some public health officials
did argue at the time of the TEL events that the TEL episode "called attention to the fact," as Henry Field Smyth stated at the annual meeting of the
American Public Health Association, "that when manufacturing exists
which is constantly producing new poisonous substances, we have no
machinery for evaluating their dangers, until much harm may have already
been done." Speech reproduced as "Recent Developments in Industrial
Hygiene," Henry Field Smyth, *American Journal of Public Health*, February
1926, Vol. XVI, No. 2, p. 129; see also Hounshell and Smith, p. 555.

17. Coleman Du Pont's remarks are cited in Taylor and Sudnik, p. 84.

18. The issue of the incompatibility of leaded gasoline with the catalytic
converter had already emerged as a significant concern during the late
1950s but only became a factor with the 1970 Act's mandated emission
levels for criteria pollutants.

19. Hounshell and Smith, p. 584.

20. See Barry Commoner's *New Yorker* article, "The Environment," June
15, 1987, pp. 46–71.

21. See *Ethyl: A History of the Corporation and the People Who Made It*,
Joseph C. Robert, (Charlottesville: University Press of Virginia, 1983), pp.
295–310.

22. See Henry F. Smyth, Jr., "Toxicology of Industrial Chemicals,"
Archives of Environmental Health, March 1964, pp. 384–392; Hounshell and
Smith, pp. 555–558.

23. Alice Hamilton, *Exploring the Dangerous Trades: The Autobiography of
Alice Hamilton, M.D.*, (Boston: Little, Brown, 1943), p. 4; Barbara
Sicherman, *Alice Hamilton: A Life in Letters*, (Cambridge: Harvard Uni-
versity Press, 1984).

24. William Chambless, *Fifty Years of Research and Service: Haskell Laboratory for Toxicology and Industrial Medicine*, (Wilmington, Delaware: Du Pont, 1985), p. 6.

25. Hounshell and Smith, pp. 563, 566. Parallel to the development of company-based industrial toxicology programs, some of the early academic research efforts in this area sought to deal with hazard issues as a clinical issue, distinct from its industrial implications. A Harvard University team in the 1920s, for example, which undertook lead and manganese studies funded by companies with lead and manganese occupational hazard problems, pursued its research with the understanding that its investigation would approach the question of lead poisoning "neither as an industrial hazard nor in the light of preventive medicine, but with the desire to understand more fully the chemistry, physiology, and clinical aspects of the disease itself." From the David Edsall Papers, Harvard Medical School, cited in "The Public Health Service's Office of Industrial Hygiene and the Transformation of Industrial Medicine," Christopher Sellers, *Bulletin of the History of Medicine*, Vol. 65, No. 1, Spring 1991, p. 66.

26. See Sheldon Hochheiser, *Rohm and Haas: History of a Chemical Company*, (Philadelphia: University of Pennsylvania Press, 1986); Andrea Hricko and Daniel Pertschuk, *Cancer in the Workplace: A Report on Corporate Secrecy at the Rohm and Haas Company, Philadelphia, Pennsylvania*, (Washington D.C.; Health Research Group, October 1974).

27. There is a voluminous literature on the politics of risk assessment that burgeoned in the 1970s and continues today. For a sample of interesting discussions see Howard Latin, "Good Science, Bad Regulation, and Toxic Risk Assessment," 5, *Yale Journal on Regulation* 89 (1988); Howard Latin, "The 'Significance' of Toxic Health Risks: An Essay on Legal Decisionmaking Under Uncertainty," 10, *Ecology Law Quarterly* 339 (1982); "The Risk Wars: Assessing Risk Assessment," Daniel Wartenberg and Caron Chess, New Solutions, Winter 1993, pp. 16–25; William Rogers, "Benefits, Costs, and Risks: Oversight of Health and Environmental Decision-making," 4, *Harvard Environmental Law Review* 191 (1980); and Brian Wynne, *Risk Management and Hazardous Waste: Implementation and the Dialectics of Credibility* (1987).

28. See Christopher Stone, "A Slap on the Wrist for the Kepone Mob," *Business and Society Review*, No. 22, (Summer 1977), pp. 4–11; Marvin H. Zim, "Allied Chemical's $20-Million Ordeal with Kepone," *Fortune*, Vol. 98, No. 5, September 11, 1978, pp. 82–91.

29. See "Corporate Health, Safety and Environmental Audit Standard Operating Procedures," AlliedSignal, 1994.

30. See *Green is Gold: Business Talking to Business About the Environmental*

Revolution, Patrick Carson and Julia Moulden, (Toronto: HarperBusiness, 1991).

31. *United States v. Maryland Bank & Trust Co.* [632 F. Supp 573 (D. Md. 1986)].

32. Cited in *Beyond Compliance: A New Industry View of the Environment,* Bruce Smart (editor), (Washington D.C.: World Resources Institute, 1992), p. 117; see also "Standards for Performance of Environmental, Health, and Safety Audits," (Morristown, N.J.: Environmental Auditing Roundtable, Inc., 1993).

33. "Waste Minimization at Selected DOD Facilities," James Bridges, in Environmental Protection Agency, *Proceedings of the International Conference on Pollution Prevention: Clean Technologies and Clean Products,* Washington D.C., (EPA/600/9-90/039) 1990; "Waste Minimization Assessment Centers," William Kirsch and G.P. Lobby in Clean Technologies and Clean Products Proceeedings; presentation by Donna Chen, Hazardous and Toxic Materials Department, City of Los Angeles, at UCLA, May 2, 1994.

34. *1993 Corporate Environmental Profiles Directory: Executive Summary,* (Washington D.C.: Investor Responsibility Research Center, 1993), pp. 43–45.

35. One of the more striking examples of a company seeking a "proactive" approach is Patagonia, an outfitter company dominated by its founder and chief executive officer, Yvon Chouinard. Yet the Patagonia effort—which included the use of life cycle analysis to determine how to reduce energy use and toxic releases as well as active efforts to expand the use of recycled PET as a fiber source—was significantly linked to the personal environmental convictions of Chouinard, who maintained control of this privately held corporation. See *Patagonia: Transportation and Environmental Decisions,* Lynn Hopkins, Pollution Prevention Education and Research Center, UCLA, June 1994; "Patagonia's Unorthodox Corporate Philanthrophy," *The Chronicle of Philanthrophy,* June 1, 1993.

36. Background comments by an auditor with a Fortune 500 firm, February 1994.

37. M.H. Dorfman, W. Muir, and C.G. Miller, *Environmental Dividends: Cutting More Chemical Wastes,* (New York: INFORM, Inc., 1992); Dorfman et al., *Cutting Chemical Wastes,* (New York: INFORM Inc, 1985).

38. See *In Our Backyard: Environmental Issues at UCLA, Proposals for Change, and the Institution's Potential as a Model,* Tamra Brink et al., UCLA Urban Planning Program, Comprehensive Project, June 1989; "Campus Environmental Audits: The UCLA Experience," April A. Smith and Robert Gottlieb, in *The Campus and Environmental Responsibility,* edited by David

J. Eagan and David W. Orr, New Directions for Higher Education, No. 77, (San Francisco: Jossey-Bass, 1992).

39. Personal communication with April Smith, President, Rethink, Inc., September 1993.

40. During the 1970s, various government agencies, including the Bureau of Mines and the Department of Energy, undertook what were called "inventory analyses" (with broad similarities to life cycle analysis) to seek to identify the energy requirements of major industries. Similarly, in 1976, an interdepartmental materials inventory which was largely energy-related was published to help identify potential stresses in terms of materials use (both in relation to solid waste and energy considerations). This study was broadly parallel to the grandfather of inventory studies, the President's Materials Policy Commission study (*Resources for Freedom: A Report to the President,* Washington D.C., 1952) which linked the inventory exercise to questions of resource availability in the context of Cold War politics.

41. Fava, James A., Richard Denison, Bruce Jones, Mary Ann Curran, Bruce Vigon, Susan Selke, and James Barnum (eds.), 1991. *A Technical Framework for Life-Cycle Assessments* (Workshop Report), Society of Environmental Toxicology and Chemistry, p. xvii.

42. See "Life-Cycle Assessment: Proceed with Caution," Wilfred Cote *et al.*, cited in *Recycling versus Incineration: An Energy Conservation Analysis,* Jeffrey Morris and Diana Canzoneri, (Seattle: Sound Resource Management Group, September 1992).

43. Arthur D. Little, "Disposable versus Reusable Diapers: Health, Environmental and Economic Comparisons," (Cambridge: Arthur D. Little, 1990); "Environmental Labeling: Life Cycle Analysis Approach to Product Evaluation and Comparison," Abby Gayle Goldenberg, University of North Carolina at Chapel Hill, 1990.

44. "Full Cost Accounting," Frank Popoff and David Buzell, *Chemical and Engineering News,* January 11, 1993, pp. 8–10.

45. The term "environment friendly" was itself a term of controversy as first applied for environmental labeling programs in West Germany and Canada. A number of environmental advocates pointed out that the term was misleading since no manufactured product could be truly friendly to the environment. As a consequence the wording in such programs was changed to simply indicate environmental "advantage" or an environmental "choice." See Tom Watson, "Product Labelling Efforts Are on the March Worldwide," *Resource Recycling,* October 1989; see also Goldenberg, 1990.

46. See "Leading the Crusade into Consumer Marketing," *Fortune,*

February 1990, pp. 44–52; "A Bill of Goods: Green Consuming in Perspective," *Greenpeace,* May/June 1990, pp. 8–12.

47. *Breaking Down the Degradable Plastics Scam,* Anita Glazer Sadun, Thomas F. Webster, and Barry Commoner, (Flushing, New York: Center for the Biology of Natural Systems, March 1990).

48. "The Green Revolution: An Opportunity Too Important to Waste," Hubert H. Humphrey III, *Pollution Prevention News,* U.S. Environmental Protection Agency, June 1990.

49. FTC guidelines are described in *Status Report on the Use of Environmental Labels Worldwide,* United States Environmental Protection Agency, Office of Pollution Prevention and Toxics, September 1993.

50. "McDonald's Says No to Foam: Why and How the Environment Benefits," Richard Denison, (Washington D.C.: Environmental Defense Fund, 1990); "McDonald's Decision on Polystyrene: Cooperation Instead of Confrontation," *Oil and Environment,* December 4, 1990; "Packaging and Public Image: McDonald's Fills a Big Order," John Holusha, *New York Times,* November 2, 1990, p. 1; "Theater of the McServed," Art Kleiner, *Garbage,* September–October 1991, Vol. III, No. 5, pp. 52–56.

51. The liquid concentrate concept in fact was a mirror image variation of earlier marketing-oriented innovations associated with the introduction of larger containers or excess packaging designed to create the (misleading) impression for consumers of greater product bulk. Interviews with Daniel Briggs, Sue Hale, Tina Berry (1988); *War on Waste: Can America Win Its Battle With Garbage?,* Louis Blumberg and Robert Gottlieb, (Washington DC: Island Press, 1989).

52. Environmental Partners Program: Memorandum of Understanding, Green Seal, 1993; see also, "The Green Police," Hannah Holmes, *Garbage,* September–October 1991, Vol. III No. 5, pp. 44–51.

53. In its cleaning products standard, the organization notes in describing the limitations it imposes on the "purpose" of its standards, that provisions for product safety are not included because "government agencies and other national standard-setting organizations establish and enforce safety requirements," *Environmental Standard for Household Cleaners,* Green Seal Standards GS-8, November 2, 1993; personal communication with Norman Dean, 1993.

54. See *Status Report on the Use of Environmental Labels Worldwide,* U.S. EPA, 1993.

55. Proposition 65, passed in 1986, with its provisions for providing "clear and reasonable warning" of potential exposure to toxic substances (including those in consumer products), derived more directly from a right-to-know approach than from green marketing or green consumer

interests. Proposition 65 was vigorously opposed by certain industry interests, notably oil and chemical companies, partly on the basis of its enforcement mechanisms that included stiff fines and a citizen-enforcement provision which allowed any individual to prosecute a violation in the public
interest. Proposition 65, however, was also designed to intersect with the
more market-related green consumer issues of product labeling and consumer choice. *The Implementation of Proposition 65: A Progress Report,*
California Environmental Protection Agency, Office of Environmental
Health Hazard Assessment, July 1992; see also "California Spurs
Reformulated Products," Randolph B. Smith, *Wall Street Journal,*
November 1, 1990.

56. See Chapter 5.36, Article V of the Santa Monica Municipal Code to
Require Labeling of Shelves Where Toxic and Hazardous Household
Products are Sold or Distributed; Beth Beeman, California Grocers
Association to Brian Johnson, Environmental Programs Coordinator, City
of Santa Monica, December 13, 1993; Stephen Kellner, Chemical
Specialties Manufacturer's Association to Brian Johnson, City of Santa
Monica, December 1, 1993; Victoria Gall, California Department of
Pesticide Regulation to Brian Johnson, City of Santa Monica, January 31,
1994.

57. Interview with Jeffrey Cinci (1993).

58. "Patagonia's Approach to Greener Retailing," presentation of
Michael Brown, Director of Environmental Assessment, Patagonia,
Pollution Prevention Forum Series, UCLA, April 18, 1994. See also *The
Ecology of Commerce: A Declaration of Sustainability,* Paul Hawken (New York:
Harper Collins, 1993).

59. *Valdez Principals: Statement of Intent,* Coalition for Environmentally
Responsible Economies, (San Francisco: Sierra Club Books, 1989); see also
"What Does it Mean to be Green?," Art Kleiner, *Harvard Business Review,*
July–August 1991, pp. 38–47.

60. Cited in "GM Signs On to Environmental Code of Conduct,"
Michael Parrish, *Los Angeles Times,* March 4, 1994, Section D1.; see also
"General Motors Endorses CERES Principles," *Business and the
Environment,* February 1994, p. 6; "Environmentally Committed and Doing
Something About It," Sun Co., 1993.

61. See *Responsible Care: A Public Commitment,* (Washington D.C.:
Chemical Manufacturers Association, December 1993); *Improving
Performance in the Chemical Industry: Ten Steps for Pollution Prevention,*
Chemical Manufacturers Association, (Washington D.C.: CMA, September
1990); *The Business Charter for Sustainable Development: Principles for
Environmental Management,* (Paris: International Chamber of Commerce,

1991); "Proactive Environmental Management: Avoiding the Toxic Trap," Christopher Hunt and Ellen R. Auster, *Sloan Management Review,* Winter 1990, pp. 7–18; "Assessing Corporate Environmental Policies: Origins and Strategic Implications," Monika Winn, paper presented at the Second International Conference of the Greening of Industry Network, "Designing the Sustainable Enterprise," Cambridge, MA, November 14–16, 1993.

62. Cited in "Chemical Makers Pin Hopes on Responsible Care to Improve Image," Lois Kimber, *Chemical and Engineering News,* October 5, 1992, pp. 13–39.

63. See "New Approaches Show Promise," *Working Notes on Community Right-to-Know,* January–February 1993.

64. The language was contained in a letter signed by CMA and other trade groups, and sent to all members of the House of Representatives, see Lois Kimber, 1992.

7

The Chemical Industry: Structure and Function

Maureen Smith
Robert Gottlieb

Introduction

The chemical industry represents an obvious starting point in considering, from a pollution prevention perspective, what industries *do* as well as how they are *structured*. The chemical industry, for one, has become central to toxics issues via any number of entry points, including its position as the largest industrial source of toxic chemical pollution, its historical role in the introduction of toxic substances to the production process, and as the most visible and prominent industry seeking to influence the definition of pollution prevention as a type of voluntary management prerogative.

At the same time, the structure and activities of the chemical industry illustrate the complexities involved in forming and implementing pollution prevention policies in an industrial setting. There are questions of appropriate industry definitions and analytic boundaries, as well as the availability and interpretation of data sources that help us situate some of the structural considerations involved in any assessment of the opportunities for pollution prevention in the chemical industry. These will be discussed in this chapter. Chapter 8 will focus on particular chemical products and processes—activities and choices within the chemical industry—that also describe the context for pollution prevention. Taken together, these two chapters make clear that structure and activity in the chemical industry form a complex whole, part of the larger set of relationships between and among industries. The two chapters also shed light on the chemical industry's place within the overall context of economic development activities, for which pollution prevention ultimately remains a crucial though underexamined subtext.

Engine of Growth/Toxic Generator

Historically, the chemical industry in the U.S. has been the country's largest consumer and generator of highly toxic substances (with the possible exception of the federal defense and energy complex when the legacy of impacts from weapons testing, production, storage, and destruction or deployment are included).[1] Simultaneously, it can be seen as the locomotive of the domestic and global economies, having laid the groundwork for much of the evolution of industrial activity during the past two centuries. As one example, the development of the alkali industry in the early nineteenth century underlines an intersection of industrial evolution and environmental impact. Often identified as the foundation of the modern chemical industry and, indeed, of the larger industrial revolution remaking Europe and the United States, the early technologies involved in the production of alkali also generated substantial wastes, created extreme hazards for its workforce and nearby communities, and had devastating effects on the natural environment. One nineteenth century government inspector monitoring emissions levels at an alkali plant in Widnes, England, commented that anyone entering the town where the plant was located would likely experience "a certain awe and horror, at least on calm, damp days, and wonder if life can be sustained there."[2] Community protests, including landowner complaints from surrounding areas, eventually caused the British House of Lords to pass the Alkali Act of 1863, one of the first pieces of legislation to address toxics issues. This legislation required that facilities capture up to 95% of the emissions of hydrochloric acid gas, the primary waste stemming from alkali production. Industry responses to the legislation included efforts to develop uses for waste byproducts, the development of control technologies for capturing and condensing gaseous emissions into liquid form, and the construction of tall smokestacks which allowed the gas to be dispersed more widely, with each approach anticipating by more than one hundred years industry responses to modern pollution control legislation such as the Clean Air Act.[3]

The expansion and consolidation of the chemical industry in explosives, synthetic dyes, pharmaceuticals, and, after the 1920s, in petrochemical sectors, and the accompanying diffusion of chemical industry products into other industrial sectors, paralleled the emergence of toxics issues in modern industrial societies. These developments occurred at a scale and pace unprecedented in the history of industrial change. As economists and other industrial analysts have long observed, the idea that particular sectors have the ability to transmit growth impulses to other branches of the economy has become central to the concept of manufacturing as an "engine of growth."With respect to the chemical industry's role, it has been described as "essentially a supplier of intermediate products to other sectors," enabling it to become "a vital element in a virtuous circle of economic growth created by the mutually reinforcing effects of changes in technology and demand."The petrochemical industry, in particular, can be seen as "central to a chain of economic events in the post-war period which seem to qualify as a technological revolution."[4]

However, the dynamics of technological innovation and diffusion, so central to the growth of the chemical industry and its propulsive effects on other sectors, also led to the severe problems of toxic pollution, problems that preoccupied nineteenth and twentieth century policymakers and citizens alike. This expanding circle of chemical pollution and toxic chemical dependency has thus from the outset shadowed the "virtuous circle" of economic growth propelled by the chemical industry.

The early debates over tetraethyl lead (see Chapter 6), became representative of the way toxics issues were addressed by the chemical industry and its critics. These debates, which situated the chemical industry as the primary promoter of the "engine of growth" concept against public health and worker rights advocates, anticipated later conflicts over hazardous and toxic consumer products during the 1930s, the battles over whether to regulate food additives during the 1950s, subsequent scandals over hazardous drugs later in the decade, and, ultimately, the intense debates during the 1970s and 1980s over toxic chemicals and wastes. Each of these conflicts contributed in turn to the evolution of the contemporary environmental policy system. A pivotal factor has been the dual role of the chemical industry as both developer/vendor of toxic chemical *products,* and environmental point source of toxic chemical *pollution,* although it is only the latter role that has received significant attention.

While both public attention and industry response have long been driven by dramatic chemical accidents and highly publicized chemical waste tragedies in various communities, the chemical industry's role as a point source of chemical pollution was first quantitatively suggested at a national scale by the Resource Conservation and Recovery Act (RCRA) hazardous waste data that became available in the mid 1980s. This information was in turn sharply magnified by Toxic Release Inventory (TRI) reports filed under EPCRA beginning in the late 1980s. Despite limitations in using TRI data discussed earlier,[5] it is nevertheless inescapably significant that the chemical industry, as narrowly defined by SIC code 28, continues to account for close to half of all reported releases and transfers of TRI chemicals. In 1990 the industry reported nearly 2.1 billion pounds, or about 44 percent of the 4.8 billion pounds reported nationally. States with a large concentration of petrochemical manufacturing capacity, particularly Louisiana and Texas, continued to be the most actively polluted in the nation (the two states together accounted for almost a fifth of total chemical releases and transfers reported nationally). Chemical manufacturing facilities also dominate individual facilities top-ranked for largest total emissions (in 1991 the top 50 facilities—more than two-thirds of which were related to the chemical industry—accounted for almost 40 percent of total releases and transfers). Leading chemical manufacturers Du Pont, American Cyanamide, and Monsanto represented three of the top five parent companies ranked by total releases and transfers (together responsible for more than 10 percent of the total in 1991).[6]

At the same time, the environmental impact of the chemical industry's far more complex role as the primary producer/vendor of toxic chemicals is suggested by chemical industry production data. Table 7.1 lists the leading commodity chemicals as defined by *Chemical and Engineering News'* annual review of the chemical industry. Most are manufactured in the U.S. at levels in excess of one billion pounds per year (up to tens of billions of pounds in a number of cases). Of the chemicals included, 21 are inorganic and 45 are organic. Among the latter, basic and intermediate petrochemical building blocks, such as benzene, ethylene, propylene, ethylene dichloride, etc., account for most of the production numbers. Moreover, many are used (though not exclusively) as feedstocks in the production of others (e.g., ethylene for ethylene dichloride, ethylene dichloride for vinyl chloride, and so on).

As is evident from the number of key toxic chemical regulatory lists on which these products appear, almost all have been prominent subjects of pollution control efforts. More than 90 percent of the organic chemicals appear on one or more of the 15 regulatory lists explored here (which variously emphasize both environmental and health concerns), while most appear on at least 5 and as many as 10 lists. A number of these organics, such as vinyl chloride and benzene, are also well-known carcinogens. Only 8 such chemicals do not appear on the TRI list of toxic chemicals. These organic chemicals, the foundation of essentially all other chemical industry activities and central to a number of other economic sectors, are in turn the source of the immense toxic chemical pollution problem that plagues modern industrial societies. When environmental advocates and other analysts speak of a "toxics economy," they are referring largely to this chemical infrastructure.

Table 7.1 contrasts production levels and reported TRI releases and transfers of these chemicals between the years 1989–1990 as the most prominent available markers of the passage of toxic substances through the economy and environment. The association is not intended to suggest that such markers are directly comparable; that we should, for example, simplistically expect increased domestic production to be directly mirrored in increased TRI emissions. What it does suggest, however, is that the exploration of whether and how such markers are associated (including where those 99.9 percent—by production level—of specific chemicals that do not show up in TRI reports ultimately go) can help illuminate the network of relationships between chemical production and chemical pollution.

From the chemical production side of the equation, we would not expect a simple correspondence with TRI release over time, given the impact of different import and export scenarios; that is, some chemicals might show net exports, while others might represent net imports. For example, domestic production of a particular chemical could remain constant, while releases could increase as a function of increased imports. In general, international trade in chemical products is extremely large. In 1990, chemicals accounted for more than 10 percent of all U.S. exports (valued at almost $39 billion), and 5 percent of all imports (valued at $22 billion).[7] Exports have in fact long provided a growth market for toxic chemical products banned or regulated in the U.S. due to environmental impacts (e.g., the pesticide "circle of poison" in which the banned substance, manufactured here, is exported and used elsewhere, and finds its way back to the U.S. as residue on imported agricultural commodities).

A simple correlation between production levels and total toxic releases is also not likely, due to the efficiencies of chemical use (or the inefficiencies with respect to environmental release). The relative efficiencies might depend on whether substances are used as feedstocks, process aids, or for end uses such as cleaning and pest control, with the probability of proportionately higher releases generally increasing in end use applications. (Typically, in the cases of both pesticides and cleaners, *all* of the product is released to the environment in end use). The levels of benzene release, for example, could be a function of different production processes, such as cyclohexane production (for which benzene is a feedstock), other manufacturing operations (such as oil refining) that could yield fugitive emissions of benzene, or in relation to the end use of benzene as a solvent. Production of a chemical could increase, with a relatively negligible effect on reported emissions, if both production and the dominant use of a chemical involved very high efficiency closed processes.

In addition, simple correlations should not be expected given all the limitations of the TRI (prominently, the exclusion of many industrial sectors with high levels of chemical use as well as the exclusion from TRI reporting of a number of significant toxic chemicals), the efficiencies of

Table 7.1 Commodity Chemicals and TRI Totals, 1989–1990[a]

Commodity Chemical Products[b]	1989 TRI Total (lbs)	1990 TRI Total (lbs)
Organic Chemicals		
Acetone	255,502,080	220,985,437
Acrylonitrile	12,280,895	9,281,687
Aniline	7,000,181	5,349,153
Benzene	28,591,407	28,669,739
Bisphenol A	NL	NL
1,3-Butadiene	6,136,125	5,321,454
1-Butanol (*N*-Butyl Alcohol)	NL	NL
Caprolactum	NL	NL
Carbon Tetrachloride	4,607,809	2,829,825
Chloroethane (Ethyl Chloride)	5,255,383	4,414,679
Chloroform	27,325,508	24,864,365
Chloromethane (Methyl Chloride)	9,279,868	8,258,055
Cumene	4,819,808	4,838,536
Cyclohexane	19,750,323	18,967,658
2-4-D (Acetic Acid)	373,947	85,658
1,2-Dichloromethane (Ethylene Dichloride)	9,509,848	10,128,782
Dichloromethane (Methylene Chloride)	130,355,581	103,318,608
N-Dioctyl Phthlate	719,442	232,520
Ethanol (Synthetic)	NL	NL
Ethanolamines[1]	4,077,078	5,092,018
Ethylbenzene	13,304,664	11,546,766
Ethylene	41,802,964	38,787,732
Ethylene Glycol	57,972,359	39,349,923
Ethylene Oxide	3,447,067	2,798,920
2-Ethylhexanol	NL	NL
Formaldehyde[2]	30,042,348	30,051,781
Isobutylene	NL	NL
Isopropyl Alcohol	7,664,243	4,294,608
Maleic Anhydride	1,914,385	1,996,552
Methanol	408,119,083	400,709,225
Methyl Ethyl Ketone (2-Butanone)	156,992,642	141,020,100
Methyl Methacrylate	7,392,226	3,609,270
Phenol	24,963,185	23,915,709
Phthalic Anhydride	4,444,673	3,049,966
Propylene	30,615,459	26,409,981
Propylene Glycol	NL	NL
Styrene	41,169,973	43,617,539
Terephthalic Acid	NL	NL
Tetrachloroethylene (Perchloroethylene)	30,058,581	26,395,306
Toluene	322,521,176	275,862,754
1,1,1-Trichlorethane (Methylchloroform)	185,026,191	162,697,721

1989 Prod. (mil lbs)	1990 Prod. (mil lbs)	1989 TRI Total (% prod.)	1990 TRI Total (% prod.)	TRI Annual Growth (%)	Prod. Annual Growth (%)	California and Federal Regulatory Lists[c]
2,524	2,329	10.12	9.49	(13.5)	(7.7)	d, g, m, n
2,362	2,676	0.52	0.35	(24.4)	13.3	a, b, d, e, g, j, k, l, m, n
1,016	989	0.69	0.54	(23.6)	(2.7)	d, e, g, j, k, m, n
1,631	1,699	1.75	1.69	0.3	4.2	a, b, c, d, f, g, i, j, k, m, n, o
1,241	1,149	NL	NL	NL	(7.4)	
3,121	3,088	0.20	0.17	(13.3)	(1.1)	d, g, i, k, m, n
1,751	1,269	NL	NL	NL	(27.5)	d, g, m, n
1,307	1,379	NL	NL	NL	5.5	g, j, m, n
271	413	1.70	0.69	(38.6)	52.4	b, c, d, f, g, i, j, k, m, n, o
162	149	3.24	2.96	(16.0)	(8.0)	b, c, d, g, k, m
588	484	4.65	5.14	(9.0)	(17.7)	b, c, d, e, g, i, k, m, n, o
461	772	2.01	1.07	(11.0)	67.5	b, c, d, g, j, m, n
4,426	4,311	0.11	0.11	0.4	(2.6)	d, g, j, m, n
2,273	2,460	0.87	0.77	(4.0)	(8.2)	d, g, m, n
3,294	3,751	0.01	0.00	(77.1)	13.9	m, n
13,383	13,849	0.07	0.07	6.5	3.5	b, c, f, g, j, k, m, n
482	461	27.04	22.41	(20.7)	(4.4)	b, c, d, g, h, i, j, k, m, n, o
306	310	0.24	0.08	(67.7)	1.3	
562	546	NL	NL	NL	(2.8)	c, m
667	727	0.61	0.70	24.9	9.0	m, n
9,235	8,369	0.14	0.14	(13.2)	(9.4)	g, j, m, n
34,988	36,467	0.12	0.11	(7.2)	4.2	d, g, m
5,461	5,070	1.06	0.78	(32.1)	(7.2)	c, d, g, j, m, n
5,031	5,355	0.07	0.05	(18.8)	6.4	a, d, e, g, i, j, k, m, n
612	650	NL	NL	NL	6.2	
5,893	6,720	0.51	0.45	0.0	14.0	a, d, e, g, h, k, m, n
1,193	1,212	NL	NL	NL	1.6	
1,474	1,456	0.52	0.29	(44.0)	(1.2)	d, g, m, n
475	424	0.40	0.47	4.3	(10.7)	d, g, j, m, n
8,167	8,344	5.00	4.80	(1.8)	2.2	d, g, j, m, n
450	465	34.89	30.33	(10.2)	3.3	c, d, g, j, m, n, o
1,161	1,182	0.64	0.31	(51.2)	1.8	d, g, j, m, n
3,806	3,538	0.66	0.68	(4.2)	(7.0)	b, c, d, e, g, h, j, m, n
917	940	0.48	0.32	(31.4)	2.5	d, g, j, m, n
20,571	21,846	0.15	0.12	(13.7)	6.2	d, g, m, n
805	754	NL	NL	NL	(6.3)	m, n
8,337	8,017	0.49	0.54	5.9	(3.8)	d, g, m, n
8,426	7,773	NL	NL	NL	(7.7)	g
481	372	6.25	7.10	(12.2)	(22.7)	b, c, d, f, g, i, j, k, m, n, o
5,846	861	5.52	32.04	(14.5)	(85.3)	b, c, d, g, h, j, k, m, n, o
783	803	23.63	20.26	(12.1)	2.6	b, c, d, f, j, m, n, o

continues

Table 7.1 *continued*

Commodity Chemical Products[b]	1989 TRI Total (lbs)	1990 TRI Total (lbs)
Vinyl Acetate	7,138,898	9,213,468
Vinyl Chloride	1,363,697	1,278,984
o-Xylene	2,242,661	2,417,775
p-Xylene	4, 811, 223	5,996,420
Inorganic Chemicals		
Aluminum Sulfate (17%)	NL	NL
Ammonia	377,248,848	616,411,010
Ammonium Nitrate[3]	73,313, 949	62,727,721
Ammonium Sulfate[3]	750,649,064	84,449,603
Chlorine	141,428,470	108,497,625
Hydrochloric Acid	495,609,047	298,785,788
Hydrogen	NL	NL
Hydrogen Peroxide	NL	NL
Nitric Acid	74,861,200	70,781,062
Nitrogen Gas	NL	NL
Oxygen Gas	NL	NL
Phosphoric Acid	98,660,456	148,248,123
Phosphorus[4]	3,400,677	2,232,300
Sodium Chlorate	NL	NL
Sodium Hydroxide (Caustic Soda)	NL	NL
Sodium Phosphate	NL	NL
Sodium Silicate	NL	NL
Sodium Sulfate	NL	NL
Sulfuric Acid	318,395,014	267,366,707
Titanium Dioxide	NL	NL
Urea	NL	NL

Sources: Chemical and Engineering News, June 24, 1991; EPA, *1990 Toxics Release Inventory: Public Data Release;* EPA, *Toxics in the Community: 1989 National and Local Perspectives;* California EPA, *Chemical List of Lists* (May 1992).

[a]NL=not a listed TRI chemical.

[b]TRI data is not comparable to production data because: [1]TRI reports only diethanolamine, C&EN data includes mono-, di-, and tri-ethanolamine; [2]C&EN reports formaldehyde 37% by weight; [3]TRI reports chemical in solution; [4]C&EN reports phosphorus (yellow/white, red), TRI reports yellow/white only.

1989 Prod. (mil lbs)	1990 Prod. (mil lbs)	1989 TRI Total (% prod.)	1990 TRI Total (% prod.)	TRI Annual Growth (%)	Prod. Annual Growth (%)	California and Federal Regulatory Lists[c]
2,552	2,659	0.28	0.35	29.1	4.2	d, e
10,135	10,623	0.01	0.01	(6.2)	4.8	a, b, c, d, f, g, i, j, k, m, n
983	943	0.23	0.26	7.8	(4.1)	d, h, j
5,344	5,200	0.09	0.12	24.6	(2.7)	d, h
2,486	2,454	NL	NL	NL	(1.3)	
35,724	33,592	1.15	1.83	63.4	2.7	d, e, g, m, n
15,742	14,162	0.47	0.44	(14.4)	(10.0)	d, g
4,694	5,078	15.99	1.66	(88.7)	8.2	d, g
22,830	23,620	0.62	0.46	(23.3)	3.5	d, e, g, j, m, n
6,354	6,026	7.80	4.96	(39.7)	(5.2)	d, g, m, n
208 bcf	148 bcf	NL	NL	NL	(28.8)	m, n
816	476	NL	NL	NL	(41.7)	e, m, n
16,698	15,998	0.45	0.44	(5.5)	(4.2)	d, e, g, l, m, n
53,910	56,230	NL	NL	NL	4.3	m
37,420	40,480	NL	NL	NL	8.2	
23,474	24,068	0.42	0.62	50.3	2.5	d, g, m, n
706	692	0.48	0.32	(34.4)	(2.0)	d, e, g, j, m, n
580	694	NL	NL	NL	19.7	
20,982	24,060	NL	NL	NL	14.7	g, m, n
1,220	992	NL	NL	NL	(18.7)	
1,666	1,632	NL	NL	NL	(2.0)	
1,510	1,572	NL	NL	NL	4.1	
86,602	88,088	0.37	0.30	(16.0)	1.7	d, e, g, m, n
2,202	2,154	NL	NL	NL	(2.2)	m
15,926	16,240	NL	NL	NL	2.0	

[c]Regulatory status: (a) California OSHA carcinogen user register chemicals; (b) EPA list of priority pollutants; (c) California AB 1803—well monitoring chemicals; (d) SARA section 313 toxic chemicals (TRI); (e) SARA section 302 extremely hazardous substances; (f) MCL (maximum contaminant levels) list of chemicals; (g) California AB 2588—air toxics "hot spot" chemicals; (h) California drinking water action levels; (i) California AB 1807—toxic air contaminants; (j) NESHAP (National Emission Standard for Hazardous Air Pollutants) chemicals; (k) California Proposition 65 chemicals; (l) DOT inhalation hazard chemicals; (m) permissible exposure limits for chemicals; (n) California OSHA hazardous substance list; (o) EPA 33/50 program chemicals.

various control technologies, and the importance of byproduct formation of chemicals. Releases of chloroform as a byproduct of various processes, for example, could decline as a function of declining chlorine production and use, while both chloroform production and related TRI-reported releases remained constant.

The absence of a simple correlation with TRI figures does not suggest, however, that there is a weak relationship between chemical production and chemical pollution. Nor is decreasing chemical pollution simply a function of improved efficiency and better control technology on the part of manufacturers, as the Chemical Manufacturers Association's director of communications has implied, citing "a 35 percent reduction in [TRI emissions] in four years [ending in 1990], at a time when production was going up 10 percent."[8] Rather, the lack of correlation suggests a highly complex relationship between chemical production and pollution, dependent on structural factors not simply revealed through existing databases.

One of the most interesting examples of the significant impact that reduction activities can have on chemical production levels can be found in the modern history of chlorine production and use.[9] One of the early expansions of chlorine applications, beyond its use as a bleach, came in the early 1900s as a disinfectant for public drinking water. The truly dramatic expansions in chlorine consumption and production, however, did not occur until after World War II, when the manufacture of chlorinated organic derivatives (prominently including plastic resins, pesticides, and chlorinated solvents) rose sharply. Chlorinated intermediates also found increased application as agents in the manufacture of a variety of chemicals (significantly including the use of methyl and ethyl chloride in the manufacture of tetraethyl lead).[10] The environmental effects of both chlorine and various chlorine derivatives, however, came under fire beginning in the late 1950s, and concerns have escalated ever since. Focal points have included chlorinated pesticides in the 1960s, CFCs during the late 1970s and again in the late 1980s, and, more recently, dioxins and furans. These latter substances are potent carcinogens which are produced as chlorine byproducts (though the degree of potency is contested) and have been strongly associated with the use of chlorine in pulp bleaching processes. Even the use of chlorine as a water disinfectant has been increasingly threatened, due to rising concerns over trihalomethane (THM) formation and similar byproducts of the chlorine treatment process.[11]

Domestic chlorine production peaked in 1979, but, despite heroic efforts at damage control by chlorine producers on a wide variety of fronts (largely coordinated by the Chlorine Institute in Washington, D.C.), production has fallen by more than 8 percent since then, significantly influenced by declines in domestic demand due to increasing environmental constraints.[12] The use of chlorine in pulp bleaching, for example, which accounted for approximately 15 percent of domestic chlorine consumption in 1990 (and for which alternatives exist), is expected to decline by at least half during the 1990s, and may eventually be phased out entirely by regulatory action (as in Canada, where several provinces, beginning with British Columbia, have set aggressive standards requiring the phase out of both chlorine and chlorine dioxide as bleaching reagents by dictating that all organochlorines be eliminated from mill effluent).[13] Various other end-use applications of chlorine and derivatives are also under fire, including methylene chloride (for paint stripping and plastics processing); perchloroethylene (dry cleaning); and methyl chloroform (circuit board cleaning). Chlorine thus represents a case where the production level itself, adjusted to reflect net trade or more precisely, the evolving structure of chlorine consumption by broad category (e.g., vinyl chloride, other organic chemicals, pulp bleaching), can serve as a very good indicator for monitoring pollution prevention progress. It can be argued that this presents a substantially more accurate way to measure such progress (rather than tracking TRI emissions and other pollution data sources) because a vast array of toxic chlorine derivatives are unlisted, and many are released as byproducts in comparatively small amounts.

Linking pollution prevention to a phaseout of particular chemical products such as chlorine and chlorine derivatives can generate powerful opposition from industry and legislators and even the press. This was seen in the firestorm of criticism during the 1994 Clean Water Act reauthorization debates when EPA Administrator Carol Browner proposed an EPA study on the feasibility of a chlorine phase out. In countering Browner, the chlorine industry argued that, in contrast to declines serving as a measure for pollution prevention, it would be more justifiable to measure the *benefits* of chlorine's various end uses, which in turn could serve as a proxy for the benefits of chlorine production as a whole. Phase out of chlorine products, the industry argued, not only represented job loss but major economic decline, borrowing liberally from long-standing assumptions of the "engine of growth" represented by chemical industry production. Critics of chlorine use, however, countered with arguments that challenged the economic (and job loss) assumptions, pointing to potential economic benefits and job gain opportunities on the basis of product and process substitutions related to various end uses (e.g., substituting for perchlorethylene in dry cleaning).[14] More directly, critics insisted that the economics of chlorine production and use were disguised by the multiple costs of associated hazards, which were increasingly identified through a variety of risk analyses at both upstream and downstream locations.[15] Ultimately, the chlorine debates serve to situate the issue of pollution prevention as significantly representing issues of industry structure (how has the chlorine industry been organized, including its downstream applications) and function (how have markets been established for chlorine products, and could such uses find successful substitutes) as one crucial direct route for identifying opportunities for pollution prevention.

Establishing an Analytic Framework

The production and ultimate environmental fates of commodity chemicals must be viewed within a complex industrial infrastructure that includes relationships among chemical industry sectors, and between the chemical industry and other sectors. In addressing the potential for pollution prevention, it is also necessary to establish a definitional framework for the chemical industry within the rest of the economy.

Generally, an analysis of the chemical industry requires (and can be organized by) looking at three different sets of structural issues: its sectoral organization; the structure of the leading chemical producers; and the structure of product relationships both within and outside the chemical industry. The task, with respect to pollution prevention approaches, is to highlight impediments and define opportunities which arise out of the infrastructure and interdependencies within and among these areas. In this context, measurement of pollution prevention will range from the efficiencies of product and process improvements associated with chemical production (as described in Chapter 8) to the actual chemical industry production data.

There is, interestingly, a relative dearth of broad analyses of the chemical industry. Much of the existing information lies in corporate histories, primary reference material from the Department of Commerce and Census Bureau surveys and analyses of U.S. industries, recent materials on global industrial competitiveness and technological innovation, or a wide range of relatively narrow topical analyses of various sector-specific issues. More comprehensive analyses of the chemical industry (such as William Haynes' multivolume *American Chemical Industry*)[16] have tended to be limited to the period prior to World War II and the rise of the international chemical cartels that dominated production in various sectors. While there are various contemporary efforts to bound the industry, these remain incomplete or inadequate in relating the structure of the industry to questions of toxics generation and use, and characteristically relegate environmental issues to minor footnotes. For example, Keith Chapman's analysis of the geographic evolution of the petrochemical industry, *The International Petrochemical Industry: Evolution and Location*,[17] devotes within the entire text just one paragraph to discussing the "externalities" (pollution) of chemical production. (It should be noted, however, that this absence of any consideration of environmental factors may accurately reflect the degree of impact that environmental concerns have in fact had on the evolution of the industry.) Several broad analytic frameworks for discussing the industry, each of which illustrates certain points useful to a pollution prevention perspective, are considered below.[18]

Generally the question of how to comprehensively describe the organization of the chemical industry is approached in one of two ways: by starting with "the economy," or with "industry," and working in, or by starting with commodity (large volume) chemical production and working out. The former tends to provide a slightly better reflection of corporate organization, the latter to better reflect product relationships and dependencies. Both approaches frequently make use of the concept of the "chemical *processing* industries" (CPI), rather unhelpfully defined as all industries in which a chemical reaction takes place, or in which chemistry is used and chemicals are produced. One definition of the CPI has included the following SIC codes: 20 (Food and Related Products), 26 (Paper and Allied Products), 28 (Chemicals and Allied Products), 29 (Petroleum and Coal Products), 30 (Rubber and Miscellaneous Plastic Products), 32 (Stone, Clay, and Glass), and 33 (Primary Metals Products).[19]

No approach satisfactorily defines the absolute limits of "the chemical industry"—perhaps there are none—and national and international industrial classification schemes differ. Areas where the boundaries are particularly confused include the interface between raw materials suppliers (such as petroleum refiners, natural gas producers, minerals mining, and some agricultural sources), and chemical producers, since in many cases activities in both areas are integrated within the same corporation (Occidental, Tenneco, Shell, Phillips Petroleum, etc.), and even within individual facilities. Although the petroleum refining industry is customarily viewed as distinct from the chemical industry, refineries in fact are chemical processing industries that produce chemicals, and the distinction is largely one of convention. Similarly, metals can be thought of as chemicals since their production makes extensive use of chemical processing (and many metals figure prominently on regulatory lists of toxic chemicals), but they are, by tradition, classified within the primary metals industry.

The Encyclopedia Britannica, one important reference source for the description of the chemical industry, has placed its definition within the broad framework of chemical processing industries (CPI), subdivided into "heavy chemical industries" (which generally correspond to the basic chemicals sectors engaged in manufacturing the products listed in Table 7.1), and "light chemical industries," which are clustered according to families of end products. The latter include soaps and detergents, dyes, pharmaceuticals, explosives, rubber, plastics and resins, manmade fibers, paints and varnishes, and the paper industry. This approach, however, also situates organic industrial minerals production (mining) and processing (primarily associated with fertilizer production) within the chemical process industries, while metal and other nonorganic minerals mining and processing, and oil, coal and gas production and processing are situated within "primary extractive industries."[20]

Another organizing device frequently employed describes the chemical process industries' conversion of raw materials into primary, secondary, and tertiary products, based on the remoteness of the product from the end consumer. In this context, primary products are the most remote (again subsuming both sectors that clearly are part of "the chemical industry" as well as those that are not). Pharmaceuticals and household cleaners are tertiary products, while most of the chemicals in Table 7.1 are primary and secondary products (although many, such as chlorine and various solvents, also have tertiary applications). An advantage of this scheme is that it begins to suggest the significance of the chemical industry's large-scale consumption of its own (mainly primary and secondary) products; the industry is, in fact, its own best customer. As has also been pointed out, it is simultaneously its own biggest competitor, since many of its products can be made from different raw materials and feedstocks, each typically associated with different and multiple potential production processes.

One of the better known efforts aimed at broadly evaluating the chemical industry has been the McGraw-Hill chemical engineering series first established in the 1920s. The series has included several overview analyses of the industry, including *The Structure of the Chemical Processing Industries,* written in 1979 by two chemical engineering professors and an official of Union Carbide.[21] This text explores a variety of approaches employed to classify CPI products (which in turn roughly characterize sectors), each emphasizing different characteristics such as volume of production, functional characteristics ("catalysts," "pigments"), level of product formula differentiation (chlorine, for example, is an undifferentiated product, while "paints" may be highly differentiated), market value, and chemical composition (such as organic versus inorganic) or derivation (such as "petrochemicals" or "botanochemicals"). In their own classification, the authors distinguish CPI products by four categories according to volume and formulaic differentiation: *true commodities* (high volume/undifferentiated), generally characterized by chemicals such as those in Table 7.1; *fine chemicals* (low volume/undifferentiated), including aspirin, citric acid and vitamin C; *pseudocommodities* (high volume/differentiated), including synthetic fibers such as nylon, plastic resins, and carbon blacks; and *specialty chemicals* (low volume/differentiated), such as adhesives, dyes, catalysts, and diagnostic aids. Each area implies different market strategies for producers, emphasizing price and reliable delivery for true commodities, and advanced research and customized performance design for highly differentiated products.

The U.S. Standard Industrial Classification codes associated with the "Chemicals and Allied Products" industry provide the basis for national economic accounting of the industry, and are generally reflected in the *Chemical & Engineering News* (C&EN) reporting scheme discussed below (although not in all cases; for example, pesticides production is reported by C&EN, but cannot be isolated by SIC code). The 1990 value of shipments by SIC code-defined chemical industry sectors is listed in Table 7.2. The "true commodities" (or "heavy chemical" sectors, SIC 281, 286, and 287) account for about 38 percent of total value, the "pseudocommodities" (SIC 282) account for 18 percent, and the "tertiary" products (SIC 283, 284, 285, and 289) account for about 44 percent.

SIC codes also provide the basis for national chemical pollution accounting representations, such as the TRI, various data sources on chemical exposure (e.g., the OSHA IMIS system), the RCRA biennial reports on hazardous waste, and so forth. Their utility for linking specific forms of chemical pollution with either chemical or other industrial production is, however, strongly limited by their inability to accurately reflect the realities of integration within individual facilities. In TRI reporting, for example, the EPA, evaluating industries only at the major industrial sector (2-digit) level, has nevertheless had to make use of an anonymous "multiple SIC code" category to accommodate cases where facilities reported activities that not only crossed the 3- and 4-digit levels, but even major industrial sectors (for example, petroleum refining in SIC 29 and chemical production in SIC 28 are often integrated within refineries). As an example of this problem, an Arthur D. Little analysis (for EPA) of the chemical industry (on the industry impact of TSCA premanufacturing notification requirements) required a more expansive classification scheme which incorporated additional industry groups located in SIC 2911 (petroleum refining).[22]

Most analysts who have attempted to evaluate toxics data by SIC code have acquired their own favorite examples of why they are inadequate.

Table 7.2 Chemicals and Allied Products, Value of Shipments, 1990

SIC	Description	1990 Value of Shipments (mil $)	%
28–	Chemicals and Allied Products	268,104.1	100.0
281–	Inorganic Chemicals	22,347.3	8.3
2812	Alkalies and chlorine	3,206.7	1.2
2813	Industrial gases	3,013.0	1.1
2816	Inorganic pigments	3,318.0	1.2
2819	Industrial inorganic pigments	12,809.6	4.8
282–	Polymers: Plastic, Rubber, Fiber	48,447.6	18.1
2821	Plastic materials and resins	33,037.6	12.3
2822	Synthetic rubber	4,219.1	1.6
2823	Cellulosic man-made fibers	1,445.1	0.5
2824	Man-made organic fibers, noncellulosic	9,745.8	3.6
283–	Drugs and Pharmaceuticals	47,830.6	17.8
2833	Medicinals and botanicals	5,789.0	2.2
2834	Pharmaceutical preparations	35,279.0	13.2
2835	Diagnostic substances	4,234.0	1.6
2836	Biological products, except diagnostics	2,528.6	0.9
284–	Soaps, Detergents, and Toiletries	38,634.1	14.4
2841	Soap and other detergents	11,860.4	4.4
2842	Polishes and sanitation goods	5,530.7	2.1
2843	Surface active agents	3,877.0	1.4
2844	Toilet preparations	17,366.0	6.5
285–	Paints and Allied Products	13,680.7	5.1
2851	Paints and allied products	13,680.7	5.1
286–	Organic Chemicals	61,811.0	23.1
2861	Gum and wood chemicals	767.3	0.3
2865	Cyclic crudes and intermediates	14,763.4	5.5
2869	Industrial organic chemicals, n.e.c.	46,280.3	17.3
287–	Agricultural Chemicals	16,770.6	6.3
2873	Nitrogenous fertilizers	3,356.5	1.3
2874	Phosphatic fertilizers	4,462.0	1.7
2875	Fertilizers, mixing only	1,671.7	0.6
2879	Agricultural chemicals, n.e.c.	7,280.4	2.7
289–	Miscellaneous Chemical Products	18,582.2	6.9
2891	Adhesives and sealants	5,402.6	2.0
2892	Explosives	867.9	0.3
2893	Printing ink	2,758.2	1.0
2895	Carbon black	691.9	0.3
2899	Chemical preparations, n.e.c.	8,861.6	3.3

Source: U.S. Bureau of the Census, *Annual Survey of Manufacturers.*

Within the paper industry, for example, integrated facilities engaged in both pulp (2611) and paper (2621) production will usually report activities under 2621, making even a rough representation of the aggregate contribution of pulping to toxic chemical pollution difficult. At the same time, the production of silvicultural (or wood-based) chemicals (2861) is also sometimes integrated with pulp and paper manufacturing, compounding these reporting problems. The increasing emphasis on conducting toxics analyses that integrate occupational and environmental health concerns also raises another set of problems. In the case of OSHA inspections, for example, inspectors who evaluate specific operations within large manufacturing complexes may be able to select 4-digit SIC codes that accurately describe the targeted operations, but do not accurately describe the primary activity at the facility, making it difficult to establish correlations with broader environmental pollution patterns.[23]

In sum, the outcomes derived from the use of SIC codes thus far have pointed to the difficulty of accurately and comprehensively associating chemical pollution with specific types of industrial activity, including chemical industry production in various sectors, beyond either a very specific level (focused research efforts that develop their own emissions or exposure data, for example), or a very broad level (such as the still inadequate 2-digit SIC level). While the SIC system is the only scheme currently available for anchoring comprehensive chemical pollution data, it is inadequate for discussing the actual organization of the industry in relation to toxics generation and use issues.

Chemical and Engineering News, a publication of the American Chemical Society and the most important trade journal in this area, uses the following categories in its annual report on "Facts and Figures" for the chemical industry: organic chemicals, inorganic chemicals, minerals, synthetic fibers (noncellulosic such as polyester; and cellulosic such as rayon), synthetic rubbers, plastics (by major resin categories), fertilizers, pesticides (by broad categories including fungicides, herbicides), coatings, and aerosols (by end-use category such as personal products, and insect sprays). The C&EN approach does not include primary petrochemical feedstocks such as butane and ethane since they are defined as "products of oil companies." It also distinguishes between certain minerals such as lime, which is considered a chemical product ("because it is processed and has many chemical and industrial applications"), and those minerals which are seen as having little or no chemical industry application. At the same time, the term "mineral chemicals" is also used to identify specific chemical industry mineral groups.[24]

C&EN also provides production data on "markets for the chemical

industry," a term used to designate chemical industry customers outside of
the chemical industry itself. The major markets identified include: housing,
motor vehicles, tires and tubes, paper, floor coverings, major home electrical appliances, textile mills, steel, agriculture, and furniture and fixtures.
While the analysis of "chemical markets" is used primarily to provide a
broad indicator of chemical industry prospects ("softness in the overall
economy" translates into "declines in the markets for chemicals" due to the
chemical industry's "vast array of products"), it can also be useful from
other perspectives. In particular, highlighting the chemical industry's view
of its markets also helps to emphasize a concept that is integral to structurally focused pollution prevention analysis: each of these "markets" is
subject to its own varied set of toxics concerns (those also reflected in the
other 50% of TRI releases for which the chemical industry is not directly
responsible). Yet in evaluating potential solutions to these concerns, it must
be recognized that many of these sectors themselves constitute a chemical
industry market.

The chlorine example again comes to mind. For example, when the first
concerns over dioxin and other byproducts of chlorine pulp bleaching surfaced, Scandinavian paper producers responded by seeking ways to eliminate the use of chlorine, and have since led the progress during the past
decade in developing alternative chlorine-free technologies through
improved hydrogen peroxide, ozone, and oxygen bleaching processes,
among others.[25] However, in the U.S.—the largest paper producer in the
world, but also the largest chlorine producer—the focus of efforts has been
on control technologies, such as improved wastewater treatment, greater
efficiency in chlorine use, and the use of chlorine dioxide, rather than on
more benign substitution opportunities. Chlorine producers, who refer to
"captive uses" of the product (traditionally including pulp bleaching) led
the way in collaborating with the U.S. paper industry on research in these
pollution control approaches.[26] Although, in this case, their efforts have
failed to forestall rising public and regulatory interest in preventative
approaches, the industry's power to respond to threats to the various "captive uses" of its products should not be underestimated. It is noteworthy
that the search for more substantial alternatives to the use of particular
toxic substances appears to occur in countries where the offending substance (or its chemical parent) is not produced at economically significant
levels.

At the same time, it is also worth reflecting on such phenomena as the
"sick building syndrome" that has come under increasing scrutiny in recent
years. In this instance, the use of synthetic textiles and building products is
heavily implicated in this new type of environmental illness, even as the use

of these products is continually increasing (a situation that has certain parallels with the case history of tetraethyl lead).[27] As with tetraethyl lead, it is critical to evaluate who is directing and/or funding the major research efforts focused on these problems. Are the problems to be addressed only case by case, or material by material as they arise (as in the case of urea formaldehyde foam insulation and formaldehyde exposures), or is it possible to address them further upstream? In the case of chlorine, a critical mass of information and attention eventually built up from a variety of problems affecting widely different areas of the environment and society, and finally pointed to a clear target located well upstream of many of the specific problems. However, it took about a century to clearly isolate the root problem, while it began to be an area of focus for possible policy interventions only in the last few years, despite the long-term and severe legacy of impacts. In the case of building products and synthetic textiles, the range of environmental problems that have recently been noted (including EPA's prominent placement of "indoor air pollution" as a severe environmental hazard requiring immediate attention) has yet to translate into a direction for policy intervention and/or regulatory incentives requiring industry to respond from a prevention perspective.

In distinguishing, then, between chemical product users and chemical producers, a structural approach ultimately seeks to demonstrate where and how a producer or a user becomes constrained in the choices available for a pollution prevention approach. In terms of producers, it helps identify ways in which producer activities involve highly mature processes (generally with significant capital investment that producers are disinclined to scrap) and highly integrated products relative to other chemical user sectors. But the distinction between producers and users becomes murkier when identifying toxics data points (TRI emissions, product-to-waste ratios, toxic ingredients in products themselves, release mechanisms), or in relation to either broad industry data points (production levels, historical development, etc.), unit process descriptors (feedstock/byproduct relationships, efficiency criteria, etc.), or product data points (toxic constituents, toxics use, etc.). A more viable set of definitions (in relation to toxic issues) needs to sort out the differences between the structure of product relationships, the various industry sectors, and various corporate organizational forms.

Differences can also be identified with respect to chemical industry relationships to other industries which use toxic substances. On the one hand, pollution prevention approaches often focus on different ways a product could be manufactured through process changes, raw materials substitutions, greater efficiencies in use such as closed loop recycling, and so forth.

Such an approach, however, might also necessitate a reduction or halt in production of certain of the industry's products, reductions which might be driven primarily by diminished downstream demand and/or by stringent regulatory action against specific chemicals (e.g., TEL, CFCs). In this way, diminishing production totals, as discussed earlier, can become the proxy for measuring reduction.

This can be clarified by looking at the "structure of consumption" for specific commodity chemicals such as the primary and intermediate petrochemical products, and some inorganics such as chlorine. Thus, for chlorine (as elaborated earlier), primary uses include the plastics sector of the chemical industry (specifically vinyl chloride—24%) and the inorganics sector of the industry (8%), but also include significant uses by other industries, including paper (14%) and water treatment (5%).[28] Ethylene glycol consumption, as another example, can be broken down primarily into final consumer product markets. Approximately 39% of total production is for use in antifreeze and 26% for polyester fiber. PET plastic bottle and film comprise 9% and 5% (respectively) of its uses. The remainder is exported and used by other industries.[29]

A conceptual approach that accounts for such distinctions needs to shift from a chemical users framework to one that distinguishes between the kinds of chemical markets that had been discussed in C&EN. As part of that evaluative framework, major chemical markets can themselves then be broken down into specific categories.

Ultimately, this effort at classification divides the chemical industry (by SIC code) into raw materials and feedstock suppliers (which are also chemical markets), by SIC 28 (chemicals and allied products), and by major chemical industry markets in addition to feedstock suppliers and the chemical industry itself. Overall, the structure of the chemical industry's output consumption then can be divided broadly as follows (a division which in turn situates the variety of end uses of toxic chemicals in the economy).

50%	All Manufacturing
22%	Service Industries, Extractive Industries, Agriculture (pesticides)
9%	Agriculture (fertilizers)
15%	Personal Consumption
4%	Net Exports

In summary, evaluating the potential for pollution prevention in the chemical industry can begin with a structural analysis of the industry itself as well as a discussion of chemical markets that elaborate questions of

industry function. These elaborations in turn help to identify and target
where the potential for pollution prevention might exist, while also suggesting which economic forces within the industry might directly present
barriers to prevention. These economic forces can best be identified in the
context of the industry-to-industry, market and raw materials dependencies that are less visible but directly shed light on the industry-to-end user
relationships that prevail throughout our chemical-dependent economy.
The process of discovering those linkages directly involves a structural
analysis of the chemical industry, including the intrinsic upstream/down-
stream relationships. At the same time, the chemical industry, as defined by
that analysis, can also be seen as the starting point for identifying the flow
of toxic chemicals through the economy and the environment. At the end
point of such an analysis are the decisionmaking processes within and
among the industries identified as generators and users of toxic chemicals—that is, the complex of chemical industry producers and markets
described above. And it is these decisionmaking points, which include the
types of technologies, products, and processes used, that primarily define
the contemporary discourse around pollution prevention both within the
chemical industry and out into the general economy. Engine of growth
and leading polluter, the chemical industry situates pollution prevention
opportunities at their source.

Notes

1. It should be noted that other industrial sectors, such as mining and
agriculture, have also played significant roles in generating and intensifying
the occupational and environmental hazards of production through technological innovations introduced during the nineteenth and twentieth
centuries. The introduction of the pneumatic drill at the turn of the century, for example, while dramatically increasing mining productivity, also
sharply increased the level of dust emissions in silicate mining, resulting in
the widespread occurrence of silicosis in the mines and surrounding communities in eastern, midwestern, and southwestern states. Similarly, the
introduction and use of metal-based insecticides such as lead arsenate,
which became prominent in the late nineteenth and first half of the twentieth century, generated significant occupational, environmental, and consumer hazards, and played an important role in the development of chemical hazard-related legislation in the 1930s and 1940s, well in advance of
the introduction of agroindustrial chemicals such as DDT and other
organic pesticides. The historical role of the chemical industry, however,

was different both qualitatively and quantitatively in its impact on the development of the new and extensive hazards of production and technology that later emerged.

2. Davis, Lee Niedringhaus. *The Corporate Alchemists: Profit Takers and Problem Makers in the Chemical Industry,* (New York: William Morrow and Company, 1984) p. 48.

3. "Industrial Air Pollution: Health and Safety, 1982" (London: Her Majesty's Stationery Office, 1984), The Health and Safety Executive of HM Alkali and Clean Air Inspectorate, p. 18.

4. Chapman, Keith. *The International Chemical Industry: Evolution and Location* (Oxford: Basil Blackwell Ltd., 1991), p. 14.

5. For the chemical industry, TRI reporting limits have primarily included the rather narrow and idiosyncratic list of reportable chemicals, extremely high reporting thresholds, SIC code problems, and the exclusion of important sectors such as mining, agriculture, and, until 1993, federal agencies, which have in turn represented significant chemical markets for the industry.

6. *1991 Toxic Release Inventory Public Data Release,* United States Environmental Protection Agency, Washington D.C., EPA 745-R-93-003, May 1993, pp. 57–58

7. *Survey of Current Business,* Bureau of Economic Analysis, U.S. Department of the Census, (Washington D.C.: U.S. Department of the Census, August 1991).

8. "Chemical Makers Pin Hopes on Responsible Care to Improve Image," Lois Kimber, *Chemical and Engineering News,* October 5, 1992, pp. 13–39.

9. There is a vast and wide-ranging literature on chlorine and its derivatives going back at least three decades, focusing on both policy and technical issues. Interest in chlorine use comes from many different sectors, including environmental organizations, regulatory agencies, and corporations and trade associations. These groups have variously focused on chlorine-related issues including pesticides, solvents, CFCs, and the paper industry. This discussion is broadly informed by this literature, as well as by the last several years of discussion and debate in various trade journals, including *Chemical and Engineering News, Chemical Business, Chemical Engineering, American Papermaker, Pulp and Paper, Pulp and Paper Canada,* and various environmental publications, including *Greenpeace* magazine. This discussion is also elaborated on in *The Paper Industry and Sustainable Production: An Environmental Argument for Industrial Restructuring,* Maureen Smith (Cambridge, MIT Press, in press).

10. The MIT/Norwegian Chlorine Policy Study published by MIT's

Program in Technology, Business, and Environment, MIT Center for Technology, Policy and Industrial Development, March, 1993.

11. See *Thirst for Growth: Water Agencies as Hidden Government in California*, Robert Gottlieb and Margaret FitzSimmons, (Tucson: University of Arizona Press, 1991).

12. For an example of how chlorine producers are fighting back, see the special advertising supplement "Can Chlorine and Caustic Recycle the Good Times" in *Chemical Business* (Sept. 1990), pp. 23–35.

13. "British Columbia Regulations to Eliminate Adsorbable Organic Halogens from Pulp Mill Effluents," Ann Hillyer, pp. 225–228 in "Proceeds of International Symposium on Pollution Prevention in Manufacturing of Pulp and Paper: Opportunities and Barriers," U.S. Environmental Protection Agency, Feb. 19, 1993, EPA-744-R-93-002.

14. See *Coming Clean: The Potential for Toxics Reduction in the Garment Care Industry*, Elizabeth Hill, Pollution Prevention Education and Research Center, University of California at Los Angeles, February 1995.

15. Kriz, Margaret, "Clashing Over Chlorine," *National Journal*, Vol. 26, No. 12 (March 19, 1994):659; Heylin, Michael, "Time Out!" (on relations between the EPA and the chemical industry), *Chemical and Engineering News*, Vol. 72, No. 7 (February 14, 1994):3; MacKenzie, Deborah, "Clinton backs call to ban chlorine," *New Scientist*, Vol. 141, No. 1912 (February 12, 1994):10.

16. William D. Haynes, *American Chemical Industry*, Vol. 1–4, (New York: D. Van Nostrand Co., 1945).

17. Chapman, *op cit.*, 1991.

18. In the past couple of years, the development of "industrial ecology" within the chemical engineering discipline has become a more expansive analytic entry point into the issues of chemical flows and life cycle analysis, seeking to identify industry interrelationships along a production chain in the context of environmental impacts at each point along that chain. See for example the MIT/Norwegian chlorine study. See also Chapter 8 for an "industrial ecology" approach to the chemical industry.

19. Wei, John, T.W.F. Russell, and M.W. Swartzlander, *The Structure of the Chemical Processing Industries* (New York: McGraw-Hill, 1979).

20. *Brittanica* 1990, pp. 251–253.

21. Wei, *op cit.*, 1979.

22. A.D. Little, "Impact of TSCA Proposed Premanufacturing Requirements," U.S. Environmental Protection Agency, Office of Planning and Management, EPA 230/2-1278-005, Dec. 1978.

23. Froines, J., Smith, M., and Cisternas, M., "Industries with Increased Risk of Occupational Disease in California," prepared for the California

State Compensation Insurance Fund #C7007939100, Center for Occupational Health, UCLA School of Public Health.

24. *Chemical and Engineering News,* "Facts and Figures for the Chemical Industry," p. 28, July 4, 1994.

25. For discussion of Scandanavian paper bleaching innovations see Chapter 3 in *The Paper Industry and Sustainable Production,* Maureen Smith, *op. cit.*

26. Smith, Maureen, *The Paper Industry and Sustainable Production, op cit.*

27. There is an extensive literature on this subject. For a current overview of the issue and clinical research see Mendell, Mark, J. and Lawrence Fine, "Editorial: Building Ventilation and Symptoms, Where Do We Go from Here?" *American Journal of Public Health,* Vol. 84, No. 3 (March, 1994) p. 346; Jaakkola, Jouni J.K., Tuimaala, Pekka, and Seppanen, Olli, "Air Recirculation and Sick Building Syndrome: A Blinded Crossover Trial," *American Journal of Public Health,* Vol. 84, No. 3 (March, 1994), p. 422.

28. MIT/Norwegian study, *op. cit.,* p. 17, Figure 2.5.

29. Ethylene glycol uses include antifreeze, polyester fiber, and PET bottles, *Chemical Marketing Reporter,* Jan. 22, 1990.

8

The Chemical Industry: Process Changes and the Search for Cleaner Technologies

David Allen

Clean Technology and the Chemical Industry

The chemical industry, as noted in the previous chapter, is a significant component of the domestic economy. It generates over $250 billion in sales, while creating a trade surplus of over $15 billion annually. But the industry is also a major source of industrial waste and the dominant source of hazardous waste in the United States. As a consequence, it spends billions of dollars annually on managing pollutants and has hundreds of billions of dollars invested in pollution control equipment. The costs of these pollutant controls have escalated dramatically over the past 20 years and there is growing concern that these expenditures will erode the industry's worldwide competitive position.

Within the industry, it is increasingly argued that the dual goals of global competitiveness and successful environmental management can be met with chemical processes that generate less wastes and emissions than their predecessors. Such prevention approaches may involve both evolutionary process and product changes and revolutionary designs. This chapter describes some of the evolutionary methods that have become available, and also assesses the extent to which industry has embraced cleaner technologies.

In terms of this analysis, clean technology is defined broadly as a product or a chemical process that generates less waste or emissions than the norm. Any more specific definition invariably creates controversy, centered on three types of issues.

The first involves the question of system boundaries. As shown in Figure 8.1, which is reproduced from the Office of Technology Assessment report on "Green Products by Design" (U.S. Congress OTA, 1992), the most

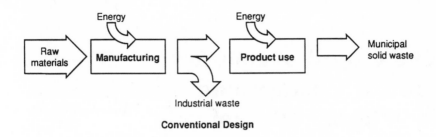

Conventional Design

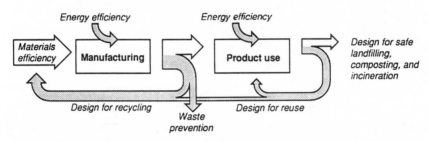

Figure 8.1 Life cycle framework for clean technology and green design (from 1992 OTA report on "Green Products by Design").

global view in assessing chemical technologies includes raw material extraction, manufacturing, product use, and product disposal. This cradle to grave or life cycle mapping of the material and energy flows required for products is conceptually attractive but introduces a number of difficulties. Assembling the data necessary to perform such studies presents a number of problems, and some of the emissions may be beyond the control of a single chemical manufacturer attempting to implement a clean technology approach. Perhaps most importantly, our current structure of environmental regulation focuses on the manufacturing step, largely neglecting product use and disposal issues. Balancing these disadvantages are a number of advantages to the life cycle approach. The expense and time required for data collection can sometimes be offset by the cost reduction opportunities that the life cycle data may reveal. Collecting information about raw material suppliers and product users can also be beneficial. For the purposes of this chapter, the focus is the chemical manufacturing industry and thus the definition of clean technology is restricted to the chemical manufacturing process.

A second issue involves situating the concept of clean technology as equivalent to waste minimization, to source reduction, or to toxics use reduction. These differentiated though related terms reflect different approaches to constructing a waste management hierarchy, as stipulated, for example, in the Pollution Prevention Act of 1990. While this Act defines a hierarchy of approaches to managing wastes, ranging from source reduction to disposal, it is not clear where clean technology fits. Depending on who is defining the term, clean technology may mean only source reduction or source reduction and recycling, or it may encompass the entire waste management hierarchy, from prevention to secure disposal as well as traditional control technologies. Still other advocates of clean technology discard the hierarchy as defined in the Pollution Prevention Act and situate clean technology within a toxics use reduction framework, where the focus is on reducing or eliminating toxic chemicals throughout a production cycle, both in terms of worker and consumer exposures as well as community and environmental hazards.

A third issue involves the selection of wastes and pollutants for reduction. Hazardous wastes, nonhazardous wastes, post-consumer wastes, releases of toxics, releases of priority air pollutants, and even the release of carbon dioxide can be used to judge the cleanliness of a technology. Here, the focus will be primarily on hazardous wastes and compounds reported through the Toxic Release Inventory, since the data on these wastes and materials are more comprehensive than any equivalent toxics release data set.

Clean Technology Options

As noted by the National Research Council (NRC, 1992), chemical manufacturing specifically and the chemical industry in general constitute a major driving force in our economy. This "engine of growth" (see Chapter 7) can be identified by the following features:

- U.S. chemical industry sales in 1990 were $268 billion. The chemical process industry, representing a broader range of chemical-related industries sold $432 billion worth of goods in the same year.

- The U.S. chemical industry added about $153 billion in value to the approximately $137 billion worth of raw materials it processed in 1990.

- The U.S. chemical trade balance, which has been consistently positive in the last decade, grew to a surplus of $19 billion in

1991; by contrast, the United States had a net trade deficit of more than $65 billion in that same year.

The largest domestic chemical manufacturers are also some of the largest chemical producers in the world. Of the top ten chemical manufacturers, ranked by chemical sales, three are U.S. firms, three are German, and none are Japanese; of the top twenty worldwide, five are based in the United States, four are German, and two are Japanese (*Chemical and Engineering News*, August 5, 1991). Large companies account for the bulk of domestic chemical sales. In the United States, the largest 50 companies account for 85% of total chemical sales (*Chemical and Engineering News*, May 11, 1992). These large companies consistently invest an average 9% of their sales in capital spending (*Chemical and Engineering News*, June 19, 1992).

The chemical industry, dominated by large companies, clearly plays a significant role in domestic and international economic activity and commerce. But the segregation of the industry into a number of major sectors such as basic (commodity) chemicals, specialty chemicals, pharmaceuticals, and agricultural chemicals also reveals that the patterns of product manufacture, use, and disposal in each of these sectors are themselves markedly different. For example, the manufacture of pharmaceuticals, usually done through relatively low-yield batch processing, generates significantly greater waste per unit of product in the manufacturing step than most continuous chemical manufacturing operations. Similarly, the majority of environmental releases associated with agricultural chemicals are associated with the application of the chemical to land (i.e., the use step in the product life cycle). A third example involves the use of basic (commodity) chemicals, such as ethylene, which often find their way into plastics such as polyethylene. In this case, a major environmental concern becomes the disposal stage of the product life cycle.

Given the vastly different life cycles of chemical products, it is clear that different segments of the chemical industry may vary in their efforts to identify cleaner chemical products. The pharmaceutical industry, for one, may seek to improve yields or recycle byproducts in the manufacturing step. Basic chemical manufacturers, on the other hand, may marginally improve process efficiencies or use recycled raw materials such as waste plastics. A single, uniform approach to clean technology in the design of chemical products and the choice of the chemical industry's raw materials is thus infeasible. In contrast to this variable situation for *product* design, the elements of chemical *processes* are relatively consistent throughout the industry.

Process–Related Wastes and Emissions

A starting point to understanding the options available for cleaner chemical processes is a review of the current state of process-related emissions and waste generation. In most analyses, this review of waste generation is simply a recitation of a few coarse yet very unsettling statistics. For example, as shown in Table 8.1, the chemical manufacturing industry generates more than 1.5 billion tons of hazardous waste and 9 billion tons of nonhazardous waste annually. To put these rates of waste generation in perspective, consider that the annual rate of production of the top 50 commodity chemicals is 0.3 billion tons and the rate of municipal solid waste generation is 0.2 billion tons per year. In addition, the chemical industry is frequently cited as the dominant industrial sector in waste generation. Roughly half of all releases and transfers reported through the Toxic Release Inventory (TRI) and 80–90% of hazardous waste generation reported through the Resource Conservation and Recovery Act (RCRA)

Table 8.1 Waste Generation in the Chemical Industry (millions of tons)[a]

Waste Management Method[b]	Nonhazardous		Hazardous[c]	
	Wastewater	Other[d]	Wastewater	Other[d]
Material recovery	7	0.68	<1	1.01
Burning/energy recovery	6	0.35	<1	1.27
NPDES facility[e]	7802	0.26	945	0.07
Publicly owned treatment works	726	<0.01	710	<0.01
Incineration	<1	0.41	<1	1.26
Land treatment	5	0.93	<1	0.01
Underground injection	34	0.29	22	0.78
Landfill	<1	22	<1	0.75
Other	569	3.48	3	0.12
Storage at year end[f]	18	13.8	<1	0.05
Total waste generated	9169	42.2	1681	5.32

Source: Chemical Manufacturers Association; *Chemical and Engineering News,* 1992
[a]Note that the vast majority of the waste is in the form of wastewaters.
[b]Generally last used on waste, therefore pretreatment or other steps not reflected.
[c]No distinction made for methods that rendered waste nonhazardous and those where it remained hazardous.
[d]Includes solids, semisolids, liquids, and gases.
[e]Treatment in National Pollutant Discharge Elimination System permitted facility.
[f]Includes surface impoundments and waste piles.

are due to chemical manufacturing (U.S. EPA, 1993; Allen and Jain, 1992). These figures imply great waste of raw materials and inefficient processing, but such data can also be somewhat deceptive. As portrayed in Figures 8.2 and 8.3, a number of other industrial sectors generate significant quantities of waste. Some of these sectors (e.g., mining, petroleum production, electric power generation) have been granted exclusions from the hazardous waste provisions of RCRA and are not required to report through the Toxic Release Inventory (TRI). Thus, when hazardous waste data are defined in terms of RCRA and TRI reporting, the chemical industry dominates all other industrial sectors. However, when the entire spectrum of industrial waste generation is considered, chemical manufacturing is a large, but not the dominant, waste generator.

Another cause for misinterpretation of waste generation data is the confusion of wet and dry bases. As reported in Table 8.1 and as documented in other public and trade association waste inventories (Allen and Jain, 1992), most of the waste generated by the chemical manufacturing industry is waterborne. Since almost all of our data on the mass of waste generated include the mass of the water (wet basis), as well as the mass of the contaminants, total reported rates of waste generation are staggering. The data would be more useful if, in addition to reporting the rate of waste generation, there was a measure of the concentration and the total level of contaminants in the waste streams (dry basis). Such data are in exceedingly short supply, although an analysis of production data for the chemical industry can lend some insight. Listed in Table 8.2 are the quantities of raw materials required in the production of basic chemicals. The data are reported as yields, where a 95% yield indicates that 1 ton of raw material is required to generate 0.95 tons of product. Also listed in Table 8.2 are estimated rates of byproduct and waste production, assuming that all of the raw materials that do not form products wind up as byproducts or wastes. A brief examination of Table 8.2 reveals a number of key points:

- Overall yields for basic chemicals average over 90%. By this measure, the chemical industry can be viewed as quite efficient in its use of raw materials. Increasing efficiencies to near 100% will pose significant engineering challenges.

- Processes that have low overall yields can be viewed as targets of opportunity for innovative technology. It must be noted, however, that yield data sometimes do not reflect rates of waste generation. For example, in the manufacture of 1,3-butadiene, the yield of butadiene is quite low, but most of the byproducts can be used directly as fuel gas and therefore cannot be

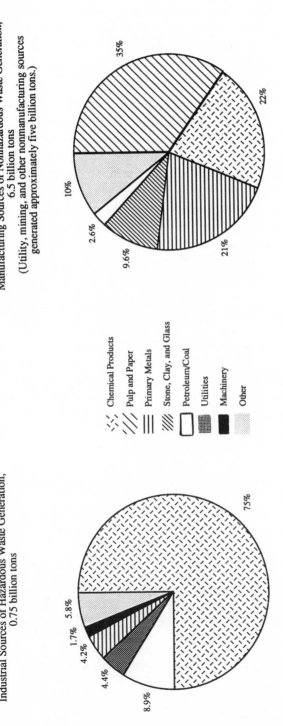

Manufacturing Sources of Nonhazardous Waste Generation,
6.5 billion tons
(Utility, mining, and other nonmanufacturing sources
generated approximately five billion tons.)

35%
22%
10%
2.6%
9.6%
21%

Chemical Products
Pulp and Paper
Primary Metals
Stone, Clay, and Glass
Petroleum/Coal
Utilities
Machinery
Other

Industrial Sources of Hazardous Waste Generation,
0.75 billion tons

5.8%
1.7%
4.2%
4.4%
8.9%
75%

Figure 8.2 Waste generation by U.S. industry as compiled by the Department of Energy's
Office of Industrial Technology (1991).

regarded as wastes. Thus, some caution must be used in attempting to estimate waste generation from yield data. In addition, some low volume, highly toxic wastes may be of more concern than high volume but relatively benign wastes.

Thus, the wastes generated by chemical manufacturing, when reported on a dry (water-free) basis, are a small percentage of the total amount of material used in and produced by chemical manufacturing. On the other hand, when viewed on a wet basis, the quantities of waste generated by chemical manufacturing are enormous. This paradox points clearly to one mechanism for cleaner chemical manufacturing—lower water usage. To gain more insight into the technologies required for cleaner chemical manufacturing, it is necessary to examine the nature and sources of waste streams generated by chemical manufacturing.

The Department of Energy's Office of Industrial Technologies has compiled extensive data on waste generation in the chemical industry and how these generation rates compare to other industry sectors. Summaries of some of the data are shown in Figures 8.2 and 8.3. Within the chemical industry, data from the National Hazardous Waste Survey (U.S. EPA, 1991) presented in Table 8.3, indicate that hazardous wastes from just a few sectors of the chemical manufacturing industry dominate industry totals. Further elaboration of this point is provided by Figure 8.4, which illustrates the astounding fact that the top 10 facilities manage more than 50% of the nation's total hazardous waste. In the chemical industry, according to a

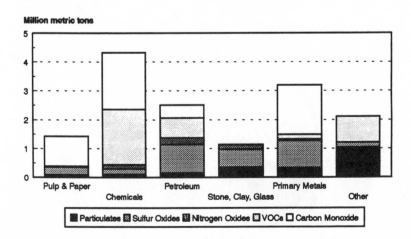

Figure 8.3 Air emissions by U.S. industry as compiled by the Department of Energy's Office of Industrial Technology (1991).

Table 8.2 Average Process Yield Data for the Chemical Industry and Estimates Based on Those Yields[a]

Chemical and Production Process	Annual Production (1000 tons)	Yield(%) Calculated[b]	Yield(%)[c]	Waste and Byproduct Generation (1000 tons)
Acetic Acid	2,728			
1. Carbonylation of Methanol		92	—	237
2. Air Oxydation of Acetaldehyde		99	95	28–143
3. Oxidation of n-Butane		71	—	1114
4. Oxidation of n-Butylenes		80	—	682
Acetone	1,910			
1. Dehydrogenation of Isopropanol		95	90	101–212
2. Oxidation of Propylene		89	—	236
Acrylonitrile	2,182			
1. Ammoxidation of Propylene		65	53	1175-1935
2. Cyanation/Oxidation of Ethylene		76	85	385–689
Aniline	824			
1. Reduction of Nitrobenzene		99	93	8–62
2. Ammonolysis of Cyclohexanol		78	—	232
3. Reaction of Phenol & Ammonia		98	—	17
Benzene	1,362			
1. Hydrodealkylation of Toluene		99.6	96	5–57
2. Disproportionation of Toluene		92	—	118
Bisphenol-A	956			
1. Reaction of Phenol & Acetone		92	94	61–83
1,3 Butadiene	2,546			
1. Dehydrogenation of n-Butylenes		64	70	1091–1432
2. Oxidative dehydrogenation of n-Butylenes		87	74–90	283–895
3. Dehydrogenation of n-Butane		42	57–63	1495–3516
1-Butanol	881			
1. Oxygenation of Propylene		72	76	37–278
2. Propylene using Cobalt–Phosphine catalyst		93	—	66
3. Propylene using Rhodium catalyst		95	—	46
Caprolactam	1,109			
1. Via Hexahydrobenzoic acid		67	—	546
2. Nitric oxide reduction process		77	—	331
3. Phenol process		89	81	137–260
4. Photonitrogenation of Cyclohexane		86	80	180–277
5. Cyclohexanone & Hydoxylamine		93	—	123
Carbon tetrachloride	627			
1. Carbon disulfide & Chlorine		—	88	86
2. Methane & Chlorine		—	95	33

continues

Table 8.2 *continued*

Chemical and Production Process	Annual Production (1000 tons)	Yield(%) Calculated^b	Yield(%)^c	Waste and Byproduct Generation (1000 tons)
Chloroform	**422**			
1. Methane & Chlorine		—	95	22
2. Methyl alcohol via Methyl chloride		—	91	42
Cumene	**3,745**			
1. Benzene & Propylene		94	82	239–822
Cyclohexane	**2,070**			
1. Hydrogenation of Benzene		99	100	0–21
Dioctyl phthalate	**296**			
1. Iso–octyl acohol & Phthalic anhydride		—	95–98	6–16
Ethanol, synthetic	**529**			
1. Hydration of Ethylene		90–95	92	29–59
Ethanolamines	**543**			
1. Ethylene oxide & Ammonia		—	92	47
Ethylbenzene	**9,020**			
1. Alkylation of Benzene		99	97	91–279
Ethyl Chloride	**164**			
1. Ethane & Chlorine		—	95	9
2. Ethyl alcohol & Hydrogen		—	95	9
3. Ethylene & Hydrogen Chloride		—	90	18
Ethylene	**32,859**			
1. Cracking of n-Butane		—	34–41	47285–63785
2. Cracking of Ethane		—	81	7708
3. Cracking of Propane		65	17693	—
Ethylene dichloride	**12,940**			
1. Chorination of Ethylene		94	90	826–1438
Ethylene glycol (Ethanediol)	**4,771**			
1. Hydration of Ethylene Oxide		98	89	97–590
2. Oxidation of Ethylene		93	—	359
Ethylene oxide	**5,430**			
1. Oxidation of Ethylene		72–79	63	1443–3189
2. Chlorohydration of Ethylene		92	80	340–1358
2-Ethylhexanol	**571**			
1. Propylene by oxo process		86	—	93
Formaldehyde, 37%	**5,549**			
1. Oxidation of Methanol		96	98	113–231

Table 8.2 *continued*

Chemical and Production Process	Annual Production (1000 tons)	Yield(%) Calculated[b]	Yield(%)[c]	Waste and Byproduct Generation (1000 tons)
Isobutylene	1,124			
1. Hydration of *tert*-Butyl alcohol		—	82	247
2. Di-*tert*-Butyl *para*-Cresol & *p*-Cresol		—	84	214
Isopropyl alcohol	1,301			
1. Hydration of Propylene		88–98	82	27–286
Maleic anhydride	359			
1. Oxidation of Benzene		39	60	239–562
2. Oxidation of *n*-Butane		48	27	389–971
Methanol, synthetic	7,205			
1. From Methane		99.2	—	58
2. Hydrogenation of Carbon monoxide		98–99	—	73–147
Methyl Chloride	605			
1. Chlorine & Methane		—	95	32
2. Hydrogen chloride & Methyl alcohol		—	91	60
Methyl ethyl ketone	600			
1. Dehydrogenation of *sec*-Butanol		96	88	25–82
2. Oxidation of *n*-Butylenes		96	—	25
Methyl methacrylate	943			
1. Acetone Cyanohydrin process		90	81	105–221
2. From Isobutylene via Methacrylic acid		57	—	711
Methyl chloroform	652			
1. Chorination, Dehydrochlorination, & Hydrochlorination of Ethylene chloride		—	90	72
Methylene chloride	566			
1. Chlorination of Methane		—	95	30
Perchloroethylene	414			
1. From Acetylene via Trichloroethylene		—	92	36
2. From Tetrachlorodifluoroethane via Hexachloroethane		—	90	46
3. From Trichlorotrifluoroethane via Hexachloroethane		—	90	46
Phenol, synthetic	3,115			
1. Oxidation of Cumene		93	90	234–346
2. Dehydrochlorination of Chlorobenzene		99	95	31–164
3. Alkaline Hydrolysis of Chlorobenzene		94	—	199
4. Sulfonation of Benzene		—	75	1038

continues

Table 8.2 *continued*

Chemical and Production Process	Annual Production (1000 tons)	Yield(%) Calculated[b]	Yield(%)[c]	Waste and Byproduct Generation (1000 tons)
Phthalic anhydride	**863**			
1. Oxidation of o-Xylene		77	60	258–575
2. Oxidation of Naphthalene		69	73	319–388
Propylene	**16,522**			
1. Chemical grade Propylene from Refinery grade Propylene		99	—	167
2. Polymer grade Propylene from Refinery grade Propylene		98	—	337
Propylene glycol	**573**			
1. Hydration of Propylene oxide		99	90	6–64
Styrene, monomer	**7,888**			
1. Dehydrogenation of Ethylbenzene		96	90	329–876
2. Ethylbenzene by Hydroperoxide process		86	85–88	1076–1392
Terephthalic acid, dimethyl ester	**6,257**			
1. Bromine promoted air Oxidation of p-Xylene		95	80	329–1564
2. Purification of crude Terephthalic acid		99	95	63–329
3. Oxidation of p-Xylene		90	95	329–695
4. Reaction of p-Xylene & Acetaldehyde		81	—	1468
Vinyl acetate	**1,710**			
1. Reaction of Ethylene & Acetic Acid		94–97	95	53–109
2. Reaction of Ethane & Acetic Acid		90	92	149–190
Vinyl chloride	**8,439**			
1. Chlorination & Oxychlorination of Ethylene		96	86	352–1374
2. Dehydrochlorination of Ethylene Dichloride		98	95	172–444
p-Xylene	**5,035**			
1. Isomerization of m-Xylene (Aromax-isolene)		87	—	752
2. Isomerization of m-Xylene (Parex-isomar)		88	—	687

[a]The implied total waste and byproduct generation (dry basis) is of order 50 million tons per year.

[b]Calculated using data reported in "Petrochemical Technology Assessment," by D.F. Rudd, S. Fathi-Afshar, A.A. Trevino, and M.A. Stadtherr, John Wiley & Sons, 1981.

[c]Erskine, M.G., "Chemical Conversion Factors and Yields," Chemical Information Services, Stanford Research Institute, 1969.

Table 8.3 Distribution of Hazardous Waste Generation in the Chemical Industry

SIC[a]	Description	Quantity Managed (million tons)	Percentage of Total Quantity for Industry (SIC 28)	Number of RCRA TSDRs[b]
2869	Organic Chemicals	103.4	48.0	171
2800	General Chemical Manufacturing	50.7	23.5	31
2821	Plastics	14.9	6.9	62
2892	Explosives	12.4	5.8	25
2816	Inorganic Pigments	8.1	3.8	11
	All Other Chemical Products Industries	25.9	12.0	346
	Total Industry	215.4	100.0%	646

Source: National Hazardous Waste Survey, EPA, 1991.
[a]SIC = Standard Industrial Classification
[b]RCRA TSDR = Resouce Conservation and Recovery Act Treatment Storage and Recycling facility.

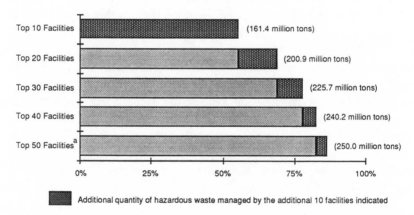

Figure 8.4   Waste management in hazardous permitted facilities in 1986. (National Hazardous Waste Survey, EPA, 1991). The top 50 facilities represent the top 2% of the 2509 RCRA TSDR facilities. These 50 facilities managed 86% of the total quantity of hazardous waste managed throughout RCRA TSDR units.

Chemical Manufacturers Association Survey (CMA, 1990), approximately 10% of the facilities responding to a waste survey generated approximately 95% of the wastewater. Generalizing from these data, it can be seen that the chemical industry's waste generation (hazardous and nonhazardous) is dominated by a relatively small number of facilities. And while the waste generation data have not been normalized by production, it is reasonably safe to presume that some of these mega-generators are large, integrated chemical manufacturing facilities containing many individual chemical processes.

Control and Management Technologies: Costs and Trends

The technologies that the chemical industry uses to manage its wastes fall into four broad categories: recovery, incineration/reuse as fuel, wastewater treatment, and land disposal (Figure 8.5). It is these end-of-pipe management technologies that cleaner process technologies will displace. As was shown in Table 8.1, wastewater treatment dominates current waste management, if only because of the vast quantity of wastewaters generated in chemical manufacturing. As seen in Figure 8.5, however, the use of incineration is on the rise, due in part to bans on the land disposal of untreated wastes.

Estimating the costs incurred in managing wastestreams in the chemical industry is difficult. One source of difficulty is the fact that over 90% of the wastes generated in chemical manufacturing are managed on-site (U.S. EPA, 1991; Chemical Manufacturers Association, 1990). Costs for the operation of on-site wastewater treatment facilities, incinerators, and other waste management technologies are not easily separated from other operating costs. In spite of these difficulties, the Department of Commerce attempts to estimate the capital and operating costs expended for pollution abatement by domestic manufacturers. For the chemical industry these expenditures totaled $6.1 billion in 1991 (U.S. Department of Commerce, 1994). This was the largest total for any industrial sector and the expenditures as a fraction of U.S. Gross National Product are increasing steadily (Figure 8.6 and Table 8.4). According to the Chemical Manufacturers Association, approximately $2.6 billion of chemical industry expenditures on pollutant control go for capital equipment (U.S. Department of Commerce, 1994), with pollution abatement capital expenditures constituting roughly 12% of total capital expenditures.

Another way to consider the costs of managing wastes from chemical manufacturing is to consider the total capital invested in waste management infrastructure, as opposed to annual expenditures. In terms of the costs of wastewater management, for example, a large-scale industrial wastewater facility can be constructed at a cost of $5–10 million per million gallons per day of capacity. Coupling these data with the rates of

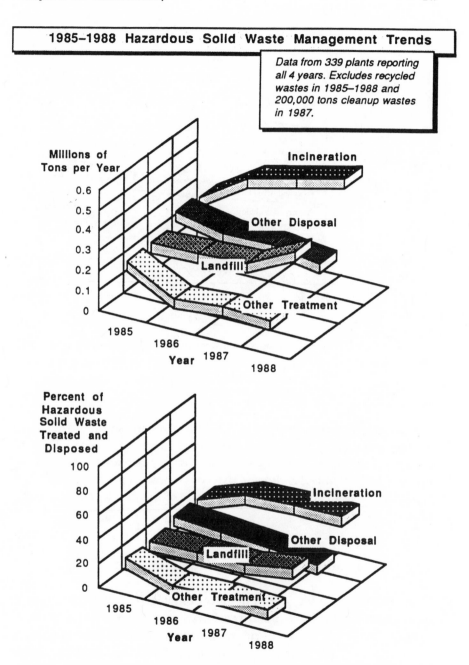

Figure 8.5 Hazardous waste management in the chemical industry (CMA, 1990).

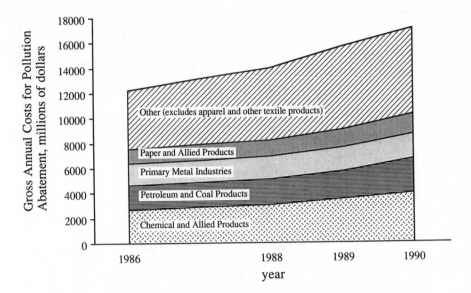

Figure 8.6 Capital and operating costs for pollution abatement (Department of Commerce, 1990, 1992).

wastewater generation reported in Table 8.1 gives an estimate of $30 billion to $60 billion invested in wastewater treatment capital. Thus it becomes clear that investment and annual costs associated with waste management are extensive. Although the cost estimates presented here are crude, they give an appreciation of the order of magnitude of waste management investments.

The Opportunities for Cleaner Technologies

Over the past five to ten years, a number of strategies for reducing the rate of waste generation in chemical processes have emerged. Some of these strategies are simply good housekeeping, maintenance, and operating practices. Frequently characterized as "low-hanging fruit," such methods have been extensively exploited in many major chemical manufacturing operations. A second tier of strategies involves relatively simple process modifications, employing currently available technology. Many of these approaches to waste reduction are still underutilized; some process modi-

Table 8.4 Employment in and Revenues of the Environmental Services Industry

	'91 Revs.[a]	Employees	Rev. Growth '91–'95	New Jobs by '95	New Jobs by '95 in CA
Solid Waste	28	185,000	14	64,000	13,000
Resource Recovery/Recycling	17	95,000	15	83,000	20,000
Water Treatment/Equipment	14	88,000	8	40,000	8,000
Hazardous Waste Mgt.	13	93,000	12	75,000	18,000
Engineering/Consulting	12	120,000	13	118,000	32,000
Private Water Utilities	11	55,000	3	15,000	3,000
Pollution/Waste Mgt. Equip.	10	62,000	6	30,000	6,000
Air Pollution Control	5	31,000	5	31,000	7,000
Asbestos Abatement	4	27,000	1	7,000	1,000
Analytical Services	2	25,000	1	12,000	2,000
Instruments	2	13,000	1	6,000	1,000
Alternative Energy	2	20,000	1	10,000	3,000
Total	**120**[b]	**814,000**[c]	**79**	**491,000**	**114,000**

Source: Environmental Business Journal (San Diego, CA).

[a]Revenues in billions

[b]$120 billion represents 2.9% of GNP.

[c]814,000 represents 0.7% of the U.S. employed workforce of 116 million or 1 out of 143 workers.

fications for reducing waste require technological innovation and are just beginning to be explored. Finally, product reformulation and raw material substitution have occasionally been used to reduce wastes. The DOE's Office of Industrial Technologies has summarized these approaches in the matrix of Table 8.5.

These strategies for reducing wastes can be divided into two broad categories: process modifications and product design/raw material substitution. To provide a logical structure to the process modifications, the waste reduction methods can be grouped by using a unit operations approach. This approach, which is the design method used in the chemical industry, recognizes that most chemical processes consist of a common sequence of steps or unit operations—raw material storage, reaction, separation and purification of products, heating and cooling of process streams, and product storage. The design methods for a given unit operation (e.g., chemical reactors) will be similar for many processes. Waste reduction methods can then be grouped according to the unit operation to which they apply. Thus, a matrix of approaches to waste reduction in the chemical industry can be identified (Table 8.6). The rows of the matrix will be common unit operations such as storage, pipes and valves, reactors, heat exchangers, and separation equipment. The columns of the matrix will separate the methods into changes in operating practices, currently feasible changes in process technologies, and process changes requiring technology breakthroughs. By presenting process modifications for waste reduction in this way, the notion that clean technologies are always process specific can be dispelled. Each of these process change opportunities are described below.

The first area involves the abundant and often relatively simple methods for reducing tank bottom wastes, fugitive emissions from tanks, residuals in shipping containers, and even the shipping containers themselves. Tank bottoms, which are solids or sludges that accumulate at the bottom of large storage vessels, are typically composed of rusts, soil contaminants, and heavy feedstock constituents. If the tank bottoms are composed primarily of heavy feedstock constituents (e.g., heavy oil components in an ethylene manufacturing facility that uses a naphtha feedstock), then mechanical mixers can often be used effectively (API, 1991). Emulsifying agents can also be used to solubilize tank bottoms, but care must be exercised in making sure that the emulsifier is compatible with downstream processing.

Fugitive emissions from tanks can be reduced by using fairly simple technologies. Floating roofs, insulated walls to prevent temperature and pressure swings, walls designed to withstand higher pressure (which reduce the need to vent) and vapor condensation and recovery systems can all be employed. Many of these technologies are expensive, however, and the amount of material that is saved by the tank design change will not always cover all the capital costs.

The next area involves the approaches available for reducing the wastes associated with the containers used to ship reactants and products (rail cars, drums, and other packages). Proper location of drainage valves can often reduce the amount of residual material in storage vessels. Storage drums dedicated to a specific use can reduce clean-out wastes and product storage containers compatible with the end use of the product (e.g., water soluble, biodegradable packages for water soluble pesticides, can reduce packaging wastes). One example of container waste reductions involved Chevron's efforts to address its monthly production of 10,000 oil samples, each of which needed to be contained in a glass vial. The used vials, considered hazardous waste, had been landfilled until Chevron developed a recycling operation for both the glass and the traces of oil left in the vials. The cost of the recycling system was recouped in less than a year. (Cairncross, 1992).

More sophisticated solutions to reducing storage wastes generally involve designing out the need for storage. For example, the release of methyl-isocyanate (MIC) that killed thousands in Bhopal was from a storage vessel. The MIC, which is a chemical intermediate in the manufacture of an agricultural chemical, is now no longer stored. The MIC is created on-demand in the chemical reactor that consumes the MIC, thus eliminating the need for storage.

Reducing wastes from piping and valves represents another category of low hanging fruit opportunities. The most significant environmental problem associated with valves, pumps, compressors, flanges, and other pipe fittings are fugitive emissions, which represent between 500 and 1500 pounds of material lost per million pounds of chemical production. (Berglund and Hansen, 1990). Typically, the vast majority of fugitive emissions from a chemical manufacturing operation are associated with a small percentage of process components that are actively leaking. If these leaking components are detected and repaired or replaced, then fugitive emissions can be dramatically reduced. Chemical manufacturing operations that have aggressive leak detection and repair (LDAR) programs (often due to the toxicity or other hazardous properties of the chemicals involved), have in fact identified substantially lower rates of losses due to fugitive emissions. In 1,3-butadiene manufacturing, for example, loss rates are estimated at 450 lbs per million lbs of product; for ethylene oxide, the rate is 35; for acrolein, the rate is 0.5 and for phosgene, the rate is 0.1 (Berglund and Hansen, 1990). The exceptional leak-free performance of ethylene oxide, acrolein, and phosgene manufacturing is mainly due to aggressive leak

Table 8.5 Strategies for Cleaner Technologies

Strategies	Housekeeping Measures	In-Process Recycling	Process Redesign	Input Substitution	Product Changes
Timing of Impacts	Near-Term	Near- & Mid-Term	Mid- & Long-Term	Near- & Mid-Term	Long-Term
Capital Cost	Low	Varies	High	Low	Moderate to High
Operating Cost	Low	Low to Moderate	Low	Moderate to High	Varies
Industry Incentives	High	Moderate	Low	Moderate	Low
Energy Saving Potential	Moderate	Moderate	High	Varies	High
Characteristics of Industries where Application is Possible	All industries	All industries except those with very stringent or high quality demands	Frequently changing, high-tech industrial products;	Frequently changing, high-tech industrial products;	Large-scale manufacturers of consumer goods

				Some commodity goods; Consumer goods manufacturers	Job shops for industrial processes; Some commodity goods; Consumer goods manufacturers
Industry Examples	Rubber, Electroplating, Textiles, Chemicals	Electronic Components, Chemicals, Appliances	Steelmaking, Medical, Chemicals Equipment, Automobiles	Electronic Components, Foundries, Printing, Paints, Chemicals	Consumer electronics, Chemicals
Possible Federal Contribution	Information Transfer, Assessments	R&D, Assessments	R&D	Assessments, Information Transfer	Assessments

Source: DOE Office of Industrial Technology, 1991.

Table 8.6 Reducing Wastes from Unit Operations in Chemical Processes[a]

	Changes in Operating Practices	Currently Process Feasible Modifications	Process Modifications Requiring Technology Development
Storage Vessels	Use of mixers to reduce sludge formation	Floating roof tanks, high pressure tanks, insulated tanks	Process-specific changes to eliminate the need for storage, particularly of intermediates
Pipes and Valves	Leak detection and repair programs for fugitive emissions	"Leakless" components	Process designs requiring the minimum number of valves and other components
Heat Exchangers	Use of antifoulants; innovative cleaning devices for heat exchanger tubes	Staged heat exchangers and use of adiabatic expanders to reduce heat exchanger temperatures	Heat exchanger networks to lower total process energy demand
Reactors	Higher selectivity through better mixing of reactants, elimination of hot and cold spots	Catalyst modifications to enhance selectivity or to prevent catalyst deactivation and attrition recycle reactors for catalyst recycling	Changes in process chemistry; integration of reaction and separation units
Separators	Reduce wastes from reboilers	Improvements in separation efficiencies	New separation devices, efficient for very dilute species

[a]Examples of process modifications for waste reduction.

detection and repair, careful equipment installation practices, critical evaluation of equipment vendors, and the design of process units for rapid start-up and shutdown (many leaks occur during the rapid changes in process operation that occur during start-up and shutdown). Expensive leakless equipment is used only sparingly.

While simple, the reduction of fugitive emissions is not inexpensive. In a case study involving ethylene oxide manufacturing, $1.5 million was spent over 2 years, with 55% spent on materials, 30% spent on labor, and 15% spent on a study of equipment leak rates. Just the labor involved in regular monitoring of the status of thousands to tens of thousands of pieces of equipment can be expensive. Added to that are the costs of replacement and repair, and where appropriate, expensive leakless components. In a fugitive emission reduction project for a moderately sized petroleum refinery (Klee, 1992), an LDAR program was estimated to have an annual cost of $150,000, largely due to labor. The program was projected to reduce emissions by 705 tons per year, yielding a cost per ton recovered of $213.00.

A long-term solution to fugitive emissions is the design of processes with a minimum number of pumps, valves, flanges, and other components. While minimizing the number of components is attractive for reducing fugitive emissions, safety concerns dictate that some redundancy be designed into chemical manufacturing systems.

Yet another area for reduction-related process changes involves reactor technologies. Reactors are a key element in any chemical manufacturing process, and are particularly important in waste generation. The reactor is, after all, the unit in which most of the undesired byproducts that will eventually make up the wastestreams are created. In examining reactor designs for waste reduction potential, several factors need to be considered. The first involves selectivity; that is, does the reactor produce the maximum amount of product and the minimum amount of byproduct (which may become waste) per unit mass of feed material. The tools for optimizing selectivity are well known to chemical reaction engineers and have been continuously incorporated into chemical reactor designs for several decades. Evidence of the high levels of selectivity already achieved in chemical manufacturing is given in Table 8.2, which shows that typical yields are over 90%. It is therefore unlikely that dramatic waste reductions will occur exclusively from reactor design changes to improve selectivity. In some rare cases waste reduction may require different reaction conditions than those that maximize selectivity, but in general the only changes in reactor design likely to result in waste reduction involve recycle reactors (Figure 8.7).

A second factor relates to the role of trace contaminants. For example, if a reactor produces a byproduct stream that is only considered a waste because it contains a trace of a chlorinated dibenzodioxin, then eliminating the trace level of dioxin may allow the byproduct stream to be used productively. Eliminating the production of very hazardous trace level

CONVENTIONAL RECYCLE REACTORS

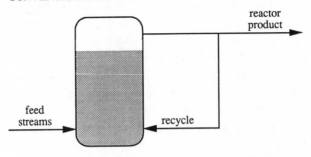

ALTERNATIVE RECYCLE REACTOR CONFIGURATIONS

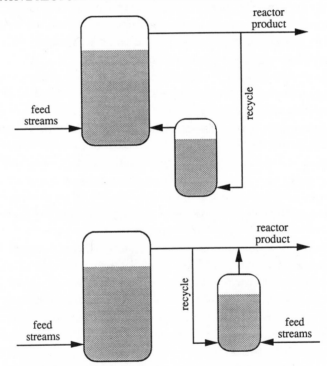

Figure 8.7 Recycle reactor configurations.

components may involve far different reactor designs than those used for maximizing selectivity. These types of improvements are still in their infancy and will require significant fundamental research to become practical.

A third factor involves reconsidering reaction chemistry, which may mean the use of different precursors or the use of a different catalyst. For example, throughout the late 1970s, the manufacturing of linear polypropylene generated nonlinear polypropylene waste amounting to 7–10% of the total product. The nonlinear polypropylene was generally landfilled or used as an auxiliary fuel. In 1980 the total quantity of nonlinear polypropylene generated was 200 million pounds. After a number of years, process research into the chemistry of propylene polymerization led to a new catalyst which reduced rates of nonlinear polypropylene (waste) generation by 90%. This example alone illustrates the huge potential for new catalytic technologies in reducing waste (U.S. Department of Energy, 1991a).

Another factor identifying opportunities for waste reduction in reactors focuses on spent catalyst wastes where recycling, controlling attrition, and limiting deactivation may reduce wastes. For example, hydroprocessing catalyst wastes are extensively recycled to recover cobalt, molybdenum, nickel, vanadium, and alumina (*Chemical and Engineering News,* October 26, 1992, page 20). More than a third of the domestic demand for vanadium is met via these recovery processes (*Chemical and Engineering News,* November 23, 1992, page 2).

Finally, integrating chemical reaction and separation in a single vessel offers opportunities for waste reduction. An example of this strategy is the synthesis of methyl-*tert*-butyl ether (MTBE). Two processes are common in industrial synthesis of MTBE from methanol and isobutylene. In one process, a series of fixed-bed catalytic reactors send a mix of product, unreacted methanol, and unreacted isobutylene to a series of separation devices. In an alternative process, the feed materials are sent to a distillation column that contains a series of catalytic beds. The processes are contrasted in Figure 8.8. There are several advantages to the catalytic distillation configuration:

- Because the less-volatile MTBE product moves down the distillation column, away from the reaction zone as it is produced, thermodynamic limitations to conversion are reduced.

- The simpler catalytic distillation design involves fewer valves, flanges, and components that can be a source of fugitive emis-

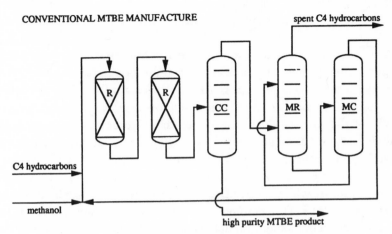

CONVENTIONAL MTBE MANUFACTURE

R: reactors   CC: C4 column   MR: methanol recovery   MC: methanol column

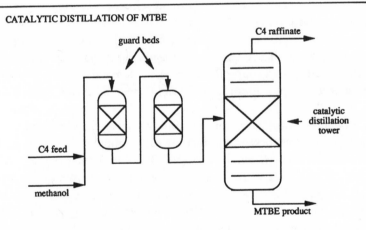

CATALYTIC DISTILLATION OF MTBE

Figure 8.8 Integration of reaction and separation (e.g., catalytic distillation) in a single vessel can reduce waste; shown are the conventional and catalytic distillation processes for manufacturing methyl-*tert*-butyl ether.

sions; it requires fewer heat exchangers which can generate wastes (see below) and capital costs are lower.

Catalytic distillation and other process configurations that combine reaction and separation in a single vessel are relatively new. Currently, MTBE is one of a few commodity chemicals manufactured using catalytic distillation. This is not attributable to a lack of versatility of this design concept, but, rather, reflects the timing of process selection. The choice between process configurations that are as different as fixed-bed reactors and catalytic distillation is generally made when a plant is initially built; retrofitting existing plants this drastically is not generally feasible.

Another area of opportunity for reduction involves heat exchange processes. Heat exchangers can be a source of waste when high temperatures in the exchangers cause the fluids to form sludges. These sludges reduce the effectiveness of the exchanger and therefore must be periodically removed. Methods for reducing wastes from heat exchanger cleaning fall into two major categories. One approach is to alter the cleaning process, which often involves blasting with high pressure steam, a method that generates significant quantities of wastewater. Alternatives include sandblasting with recyclable sand and blasting with dry ice. Another approach attempts to reduce the generation of sludges by injecting antifoulants or by reducing the temperatures used in the heat exchangers. Most of these approaches are relatively simple, with the exception of the use of temperature reductions. Temperature reductions in heat exchangers can be accomplished by considering design. In order to accomplish a given amount of heat exchange, a process designer attempts a compromise between the temperature driving force for heat exchange and the area available for the heat transfer. For example, the designer could choose a relatively low temperature difference between process fluids, then contact those fluids over a large surface. The same amount of energy transfer could also be achieved by imposing a large temperature difference over a much smaller area. The low temperature difference/high area alternative will generate less heat exchanger waste, but in general has been avoided for two reasons. Capital costs, for one, are greater for a large surface area exchanger than a smaller one. Secondly, in many large chemical process facilities, heat is supplied by steam, which generally is available at a set of fixed temperatures. The designer, confronted with heating a process fluid from 200 to 350°F, may be forced to choose between steam at 275° (30 psig) and high pressure steam at 400°F (235 psig). Clearly the low pressure steam is inadequate to do the job, but the high pressure steam may generate significant sludges. An alternative to choosing only the low or high pressure steam is the adiabatic expander shown in Figure 8.9. This low cost device can mix the low and high pressure steam to achieve the optimal heat transfer temperature (Nelson, 1990).

Another set of waste reduction methods involves separation equipment. Separation equipment can be regarded as both generator and minimizer of waste. An effective separation technology can be used to recycle materials within a chemical process. For example, solvent emissions are a significant problem in some sectors of the chemical industry (e.g., pharmaceuticals). Cost effective condensers to separate evaporating solvent from an air stream can be used to economically recycle these emissions (see, for example, the case study of Brayton-Cycle Solvent Recovery, U.S. DOE, 1991a). On the other hand, separation devices can be a significant source of waste. Since separation units are designed to generate pure products and isolate contaminants, they are by nature waste generating. The amount of waste generated can be minimized by performing clean separations (i.e., leaving the smallest possible amount of product in the separated contaminants). For some separation devices, such as distillation columns, this can be accomplished by varying the operating conditions of the separation unit (e.g., the reflux ratio), but such improvements are difficult to generalize.

A relatively simple example can illustrate the complexity of the issue. Consider the acetone recovery system shown in Figure 8.10. Acetone in a gas stream is removed by scrubbing with water; the water is sent to a second separation column where pure acetone and water are recovered. The water in the second column contains some acetone and some fraction of

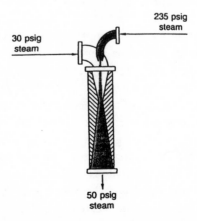

Figure 8.9 Use of an adiabatic expander can allow the designer to precisely control the temperature of steam used in a heat exchanger; if lower temperature can be used, wastes can often be reduced (Nelson, 1990).

a) ACETONE RECOVERY SYSTEM

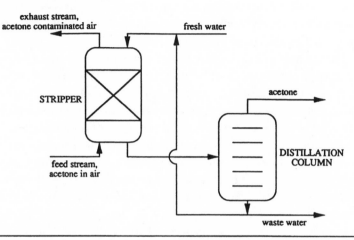

b) COST RECOVERY RELATIONSHIP FOR ACETONE IN AIR

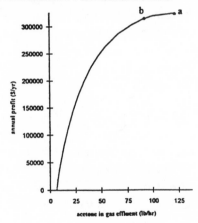

Figure 8.10 Acetone recovery system. (a) Flow diagram of the system; note there are two wastestreams: wastewater and an air stream contaminated with acetone. Complete recycle is possible and economical for the wastewater but not for the air stream. (b) Costs for recovering acetone from the air stream increase dramatically as the percent recovery increases (Ciric and Jia, 1992).

this water may become waste. The other potential wastestream for this process is acetone in the air which exits the scrubber. A complex optimization of the design parameters for these columns reveals that it is not economical to generate any wastewater and that the cost of the acetone recovery is a highly nonlinear function of the amount of acetone in the gas escaping as waste (Ciric and Jia, 1992).

This example suggests that one of the wastestreams can be completely eliminated economically. The other wastestreams may be reduced economically (from point a to point b in Figure 8.10), but complete elimination is not economically feasible. This type of case is not unusual and illustrates that for some wastestreams, complete elimination is possible; for others, some reductions, but not complete elimination, is possible. A more straightforward way to minimize wastes from separation devices is to focus on the heat exchange equipment associated with the units. Methods, such as those described above for heat exchangers, can also be effective for reboilers and condensers.

In sum, the variety of process changes described here, from those involving heat exchangers to separation equipment, are, in many cases, both widely available and potentially significant in addressing the issue of waste generation in chemical manufacturing.

Restructuring Processes

The analysis presented in the previous examples focused exclusively on reducing wastes from individual unit operations. This approach implicitly assumes that a process with an established sequence of unit operations exists. Another set of methods for waste reduction involves completely reconfiguring the entire process flowsheet. Such dramatic process modifications are only rarely done, but this section will examine the potential of a few simple cases.

One set of processes that might benefit from a dramatic process restructuring are those that involve direct contacting of process fluids with steam. One example involves the cracking of hydrocarbon gases and petroleum naphtha to form ethylene, one of the largest volume production processes in the chemical manufacturing industry. Ethylene plants that produce billions of pounds of product per year are currently in operation. In the cracking reactor, reactant concentration is controlled by adding steam as a relatively inert diluent. Such direct mixing of hydrocarbon and water unavoidably leads to the generation of wastewaters. Steam could be replaced by another recyclable diluent such as nitrogen; the substitution would be complex since the water has a different effect in the reactor than would nitrogen.

Another set of processes that might benefit from restructuring are those that use scrubbers and water absorption. These unit operations are extensively used in chemical manufacturing to remove contaminants from gaseous and occasionally liquid process streams and they are responsible in part for the vast quantities of wastewater generated in chemical manufacturing. For example, the treatment of sulfur dioxide wastes by aqueous scrubbers, which generate an acidic wastewater, can be avoided by hydrogenating and recovering the sulfur as a product.

Alternative process chemistries can also be considered. In the manufacture of vinyl chloride, waste in still bottoms can be catalytically converted to HCl and hydrocarbon reactants, some of which can be recycled (Kalnes and James, 1988).

Reductions in energy requirements in chemical manufacturing processes can also be considered as a method for reducing nitric oxide and sulfur oxide wastes. Methods of heat integration match process streams that need to be cooled with process streams that in turn need to be heated to reduce energy loads. These and other methods for promoting energy efficiency can be very attractive economically. Dow Chemical's Louisiana division has had an energy efficiency program for over a decade where an average of 60 projects per year have been implemented. The projects had an average return on investment of almost 200%, and generally improved process yields in addition to increasing energy efficiency (Nelson, 1989).

Product Redesign and Raw Material Substitution for Waste Reduction

It is far more difficult to describe generic methods for raw material substitution and product redesign than it is to identify process modifications to reduce waste. In chemical industry case studies reported by INFORM (Dorfman et al., 1992), little use was made of raw material substitution/product redesign (see Figure 8.11) and the only recurring material substitution was for solvents; in the rare instances of product change reported by chemical manufacturers, no recurring patterns could be identified.

While it is difficult to generalize about raw material substitution and product reformulation, some chemical manufacturers have developed aggressive and systematic efforts to identify productive uses for wastestreams. For example, Du Pont found a market in the pharmaceuticals and

coating industry for hexamethyleneimine, a byproduct of nylon manufacturing. The market is now so strong that demand exceeds supply and, in
1989, Du Pont had to find a way to intentionally manufacture what had
formerly been a waste. A Chevron subsidiary sends caustics to nearby pulp
and paper manufacturers and Dow has set up a formal program to find uses
for byproduct streams (Cairncross, 1992). Waste exchanges to facilitate
these transfers are emerging across the country.

Are these productive exchanges of wastes aberrations or are many wastes
really raw materials inappropriately labeled? This question has been
addressed by comparing the concentrations of metals in hazardous wastestreams to the concentrations usually required for economical extraction of
raw materials. For the 16 metals studied (reported in Table 8.7), in principle over 90% could be recovered, although, on average, only 15% are actually recycled.

The waste reduction measures described above appear, in many cases, to
be relatively simple and easy to implement. Have they been broadly implemented by the chemical industry? The answer is not entirely straightforward.

Chemical industry sources argue that releases and off-site transfers of the
320 "core" chemicals that have been listed every year in the Toxic Release
Inventory (TRI) have been continually reduced (e.g., by 47% from 1987
to 1990; Chemical Manufacturers Association, 1992). A number of large
companies such as Dow, Du Pont, 3M, and Monsanto have widely publicized waste reduction programs that describe successes in making chemical manufacturing technologies cleaner. Yet, this self reporting of the adop-

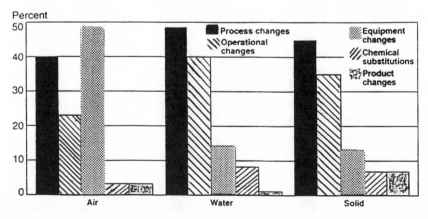

Figure 8.11 Distribution of approaches used in reducing wastes in the chemical industry
(INFORM, 1992).

Table 8.7 Analysis of the Potential for Metal Recovery from Hazardous Wastestreams

Metal	Minimum Concentration Recoverable, from Sherwood Plot (mass fraction)	Percent of Metal, Theoretically Recoverable (%)	Percent Recycled in 1986 (%)
Sb	0.00405	74–87	32
As	0.00015	98–99	3
Ba	0.0015	95–98	4
Be	0.012	54–84	31
Cd	0.0048	82–97	7
Cr	0.0012	68–89	8
Cu	0.0022	85–92	10
Pb	0.074	84–95	56
Hg	0.00012	99	41
Ni	0.0066	100	0.1
Se	0.0002	93–95	16
Ag	0.000035	99–100	1
Tl	0.00004	97–99	1
V	0.0002	74–98	1
Zn	0.0012	96–98	13

Source: Allen and Behmanesh, 1992.

tion of cleaner technology by the chemical industry creates much skepticism. Critics of the industry contend and often successfully document that many of the TRI reductions are the result of changes in emission estimation procedures or are the result of actions such as plant closings (see *Chemical and Engineering News*, December 14, 1992, p. 16). Further, the documentation of isolated success stories does not provide an industry-wide audit of the extent of adoption of clean technologies. Perhaps the best approximation of an independent audit of the chemical industry's adoption of clean technologies can be found in a pair of reports issued by INFORM. Entitled "Cutting Chemical Wastes" and "Environmental Dividends: Cutting More Chemical Wastes," these studies, published in 1985 and 1992, focused on 29 chemical manufacturing facilities in California, Ohio, and New Jersey. The plants selected were broadly representative of the wide diversity of facilities across the organic chemical industry, both by size, age, and types of products produced and processes used (batch or continuous; Dorfman *et al.*, 1992). By examining the use of source reduction in these facilities in both 1985 and 1992, INFORM effectively measured, albeit for a relatively small sample of facilities, the adoption of clean technologies by the chemical industry. Among the conclusions reached by the INFORM team about the advantages of source reduction were the dramatic reductions in toxic releases, the low costs and large savings from such programs even at plants with a long history of implementing source reduction approaches, the short implementation times required, and the accessible nature of such approaches. Nearly all of these (as much as 87%) involved process changes, operations changes, and equipment changes. In contrast, the more complex, yet crucial product changes and chemical substitutions accounted for only 13% of the source reduction activities in INFORM's study.

In examining INFORM's study, one is left with the impression that the chemical industry is successfully adopting cleaner technology. Source reduction measures at these facilities can be calculated to have led to a 33% reduction in the releases and off-site transfer of TRI chemicals (Dorfman et al., 1992, p. 89). The INFORM authors also conclude that "managers of waste-generating facilities can continually find many low-technology, efficiency-oriented source reduction opportunities when they look for them." INFORM president Joanna Underwood is quoted in *Chemical and Engineering News* (November 16, 1992) as saying that "source reduction is an essential key to economic competitiveness as well as an environmentally sound future." However, as noted by Dennis Redington, Monsanto's director for regulatory management, this view is not entirely shared by industry. "I would like to be able to say that we knew how to get financial payback, but we have not worked out how to make this all a positive return on investment... some of the individual projects will be cost effective, but in the aggregate, it is going to be hard, if not impossible, to achieve [pollution prevention]... with projects that yield enough savings to make the whole program [economically] positive" (*Chemical and Engineering News*, November, 16, 1992).

At one level, the chemical industry has clearly begun to introduce cleaner technologies and substantially lower emissions. But while some individual projects are acknowledged to be cost effective, when viewed in the aggregate, questions are raised whether a chemical manufacturing operation employing cleaner technologies is indeed more economically efficient than its competitors. Put another way, the question is whether a cleaner process technology is a more competitive way to address strict environmental regulations than conventional clean-up technologies. In fact, there are relatively few comprehensive case studies that address these issues.

The economic analysis of cleaner chemical manufacturing technologies is complex, largely because of uncertainties in the quantitative evaluation of the associated benefits. A number of studies have outlined accounting methods for evaluating the economic benefits of clean technologies (for a comprehensive review, see Tellus Institute, 1991). Most of these methods include the same basic features. They divide costs and benefits into a number of categories, ranging from the readily quantifiable to the inestimable. The most readily quantified costs are those associated with equipment, labor, and material expenses required for the new technology. Readily quantified benefits can include reduced raw material costs and avoided waste treatment and disposal costs. If these are the only costs and benefits considered in the economic analysis of clean technologies, then relatively few will have a positive rate of return. There are, however, other potential, quantifiable benefits associated with cleaner technologies that can be categorized under the general heading of "hidden costs." Tables 8.8 and 8.9 list just a few of the "hidden" costs associated with the generation of wastes. To the extent that clean technologies avoid the generation of wastes, they reduce these costs. Cleaner technologies can also reduce costs associated with permits, fees, and licenses. All told, these "hidden" costs can be quite significant, but they can be equally difficult to evaluate.

Another type of benefit associated with clean technology is the avoidance of long-term remediation liability. Stated simply, if no wastes are being sent to landfills, then no additional remediation liability is being incurred.

Table 8.8 Hidden Labor Costs Associated with Pollution Treatment[a]

Time to fill drums or storage tanks with waste
Time to properly label waste drums
Time to move waste drums within the plant
Time to load waste drums for shipment
Time to pump out drums or empty a storage tank
Time to schedule waste transportation
Time to fill out waste manifests
Time to file and record manifests
Time to cut checks for waste disposal and transportation firms
Time for waste information training
Time to approve waste disposal invoices
Time to supervise personnel engaged in waste-related activities
Time to select disposal facilities, transporters, consultants, laboratories, etc.
Time to inspect disposal rate site or sites
Time to obtain waste samples
Time for learning regulatory compliance requirements
Time for all other waste-related activities

Source: Waste Advantage, Inc., 1988.
[a]Clean technologies avoid some of these costs.

Table 8.9 Fifty Environmental Compliance Activities: Hidden Compliance Costs[a]

1. Title III—Emergency planning	26. Scheduling waste shipments
2. Title II—Emergency notification	27. Handling rejected waste shipments
3. Title III—Community right-to-know reporting	28. Air quality permits
4. Title III—Toxic chemical release reporting	29. Approve invoices
	30. Hire consultants
5. Waste generator biennial reports	31. County reporting requirements
6. Apply for construction permits	32. D.O.L. waste handling requirements
7. Apply for operating permits	33. D.O.T. waste shipping requirements
8. Compliance scheduling	34. Annual reports for exporting waste
9. Conduct testing and monitoring	35. Report waste information to management
10. Underground tank requirements	36. Mailing waste manifests
11. Self-monitoring requirements	37. Modeling requirements
12. Waste generator surveys	38. Selection of laboratory(s) for waste analysis
13. Recordkeeping requirements	39. Waste sampling
14. Contingency plan	40. NPDWR permit
15. Episode plan	41. NPDES permit
16. Pollution incident prevention plan	42. Read and understand new regulations
17. Employee waste training programs	43. Attend regulatory seminars
18. Federal inspections	44. CERCLA activities
19. State inspections	45. Inspect waste disposal facilities
20. Noncompliance reporting	46. Inspect waste transporters
21. Fire Marshall inspections	47. Inspect laboratories
22. Completing waste manifests	48. Evaluate bids and proposals
23. Disposal facility(s) selection	49. Manifest exception reporting
24. Waste transporter(s) selection	50. Supervise waste-related activities
25. Waste container labeling	

Source: Waste Advantage, Inc., 1988.
[a]Clean technologies may avoid some of these costs.

While clear in principle, accurately quantifying the reduced liability benefits of clean technology is difficult. No responsible company intentionally sets out to create a Superfund site. Instead, these sites are created by the failure of disposal technologies, and the rate of these failures can only be estimated probabilistically. Thus, the potential benefits can only be expressed as a highly uncertain expected value, based on an assumed rate of disposal site failure. A final set of benefits associated with clean technologies is even less quantifiable. Potential benefits include company image with customers, stockholders, and employees, and achieving targets associated with voluntary emission reduction programs.

In the face of these quantifiable, semiquantifiable, and inestimable costs and benefits, how do companies determine whether or not to proceed with a particular clean technology project? The most common procedure involves a semiquantitative estimate of a set of clean technology benefits. One such set, taken from a study by Amoco Oil Corporation, is given in Figure 8.12. The project evaluation criteria are grouped into three major categories: risk reduction, technical factors, and cost factors. In a joint study with the U.S. EPA, Amoco evaluated over a dozen clean technology options for its Yorktown, Virginia refinery and ranked them based on these criteria (Klee, 1992). The highest rated projects tended to score well in all of the areas. The implementation costs ranged from under $150,000 to over $30 million. Only a few of the projects generated a positive rate of return, although the source reduction projects were generally more economical than treatment and disposal options. The source reduction options had an average cost of $650/ton of pollutant recovered while the other options (largely treatment and disposal) had an average cost of $3200/ton, nearly five times higher (Klee, 1992).

To summarize, companies are proceeding with the implementation of clean technologies based on a number of quantifiable and semiquantifiable costs. In the limited number of comprehensive analyses available, relatively few of the possible clean technology projects can be economically justified based only on the value of recovered materials. Source reduction options seem to be more economical than treatment and disposal based on the Amoco case study. To justify many source reduction projects, however, "hidden" costs must be exposed and subjective issues such as avoided liability costs and the value of corporate image must be addressed.

Potential for Cleaner Technologies—Industry-Wide Perspectives

The chemical industry is a complex network of chemical processes which transform raw materials into thousands of organic chemicals for commercial use. The technologies used to accomplish this transformation have been selected, over the past several decades, on the basis of their economic and environmental performance. Yet many of these individual technologies may not result in the cleanest possible chemical industry overall. A chemical industry that is as clean as possible, viewed holistically, may still retain some individual chemical processes that generate significant quantities of waste. Further, a systems analysis of the chemical industry may reveal critical chemical processes that generate significant wastes and for which there is no current technological substitute.

Unfortunately, such systems analyses for the chemical industry are not

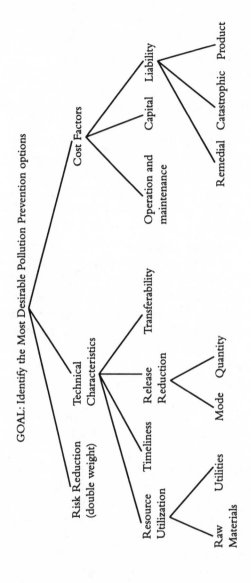

Figure 8.12 Criteria used in evaluating clean process technologies (Klee, 1992).

simple because most products are not produced in a single step and multiple technologies are available. For example, methyl-*tert*-butyl ether (MTBE), an oxygenated additive to gasoline that is being produced in large quantities to satisfy the provisions of the 1990 Clean Air Act Amendments, is produced by reacting methanol with isobutylene. There are two processes in common use. The methanol fed to the process can be made from methane, via carbon monoxide or via fermentation. The isobutylene can be made by cracking petroleum, by isomerizing butenes, or by dehydrogenating butanes. These alternatives lead to more than a dozen routes from raw materials to MTBE. Each route will have different energy requirements and rates of waste generation. Selecting the cleanest route is a difficult proposition. It is made even more difficult when we realize that our selection of a particular process may influence the rates of waste generation in the rest of the chemical industry. For example, if we choose to produce methanol via carbon monoxide, carbon monoxide may be generated through partial oxidation of a material that is currently wasted. On the other hand, to convert the carbon monoxide into methanol requires hydrogen, which is an energy intensive material.

Only a few comprehensive analyses of the technological structure of the chemical industry have been performed and most of these studies were done during the energy crises of the late 1970s and early 1980s. Their focus therefore tended to be on the role technology selection could play in improving the energy efficiency of the chemical industry. Wastes and emissions were not explicitly considered. One of the few studies available on the impact that technology selection can have on the environmental performance of the chemical industry was published in 1985 by a group at UCLA (Fathi-Afshar and Yang, 1985). This study examined the mix of technologies that would result in the minimum cost of production for 124 chemical products and would also result in the lowest gross toxicity of the chemical intermediates used in the synthesis. The results are summarized in Figure 8.13. The point labeled *A* in Figure 8.13 corresponds to the cost of production of the 124 chemicals if the sole criterion for process selection is the toxicity of the intermediates required. Point *C* corresponds to the total cost of chemical production if cost is the only criterion used in selecting technologies. The line connecting points *A* and *C* is the collection of possible technology mixes. The ideal point is *B* which represents the lowest possible cost and the lowest possible toxicity of intermediates, but which is not obtainable using current technologies. Clearly, a mix of technologies located somewhere near point *D* represents the best compromise between economics and environmental objectives. In addition to selecting desirable mixes of technologies, this type of analysis can help to

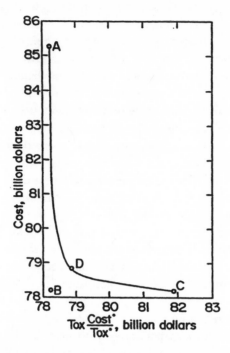

Figure 8.13 Tradeoffs between cost and the use of toxic intermediates in the chemical industry. Point *A* is the lowest toxicity route currently feasible but it comes at greater cost than the most economical approach (Point *C*). Point *B* (low cost, low toxicity) is not currently technologically feasible.

identify critical areas for technology improvement. If, for example, we were to select a mix of technologies that resulted in the lowest total cost of chemical production, we could then identify the chemical intermediates that contribute to toxicity. Such an analysis is presented in Figure 8.14 and reveals that just a few chemical intermediates dominate the toxicity of the entire system. In this example, toluene diisocyanate, phosgene, and methylene diphenylene dominate. Finding technological alternatives to these intermediates could dramatically reduce overall toxicity.

The examples described above also demonstrate the utility of structural analyses of the chemical industry. Similar studies should be done, examining the tradeoffs between economics, energy consumption, and waste generation. Unfortunately, no such studies, to date, have been initiated.

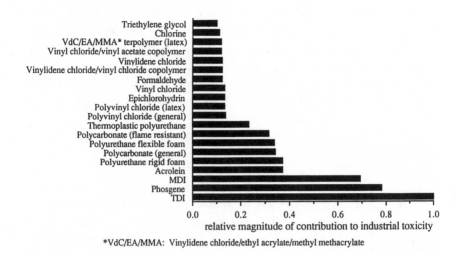

*VdC/EA/MMA: Vinylidene chloride/ethyl acrylate/methyl methacrylate

Figure 8.14 Major contributors to the total toxicity of the chemical intermediates industry.

Conclusion

Ultimately, this analysis has sought to demonstrate that clean technology has the potential to offer the chemical industry a more cost-effective mechanism to meet environmental objectives than the treatment and disposal of wastes. A number of clean technologies have developed over the past decade, and their focus has been evolutionary changes—modifications to existing processes that reduce wastes and emissions. Evolutionary changes with positive rates of return may have reached their limits (as currently cited by the chemical industry) or they might be exploited for several more years (as suggested by INFORM). Eventually, however, revolutionary changes in feedstocks, in product design, in the molecular understanding of chemical processes, and in the fundamental structure of the chemical industry will be required. Unfortunately, critical technologies required for these revolutionary changes have not been identified. Indeed, some of the most pressing needs for analysis, identified by chemical industry representatives (U.S. Department of Energy, 1991b), are the ranking of wastestreams and the identification of critical technologies. For clean technologies to continue to move forward, a comprehensive effort to identify critical technologies must be initiated. At the same time, systematic studies of technology needs are also of value, using a framework similar to that presented in the "opportunities" review described earlier. Without such analyses and technology assessments there will be no vision for a more environmentally benign chemical industry. And without a clear vision, both the evolutionary changes currently being aggressively implemented and the more complex arena of product redesign are likely to fall short of long-term public, industry, and environmental advocacy group goals.

References

Allen, D. T., "The Role of Catalysis in Industrial Waste Reduction," in Industrial Environmental Chemistry: Waste Minimization in Industrial Processes and Remediation of Hazardous Wastes, A. E. Martell and D. Sawyer, eds., (New York: Plenum, 1992) pp. 89–98.

Allen, D. T., and Behmanesh, N., "Wastes as Raw Materials," in The Greening of Industrial Ecosystems, B. R. Allenby and D.J. Richards, eds., National Academy Press (1992).

Allen, D. T. and Jain, R., eds., Hazardous Waste and Hazardous Materials, Volume 9(1), 1–111 (1992).

American Institute of Chemical Engineers, U.S. Environmental Protection Agency, National Science Foundation, "Workshop on Waste Minimization Research Needs," published by the Gulf Coast Hazardous Substance Research Center, 1989.

American Petroleum Institute (API), "Waste Minimization in the Petroleum Industry," API Publication 849-00020 (1991).

Berglund, R. L. and Hansen, J. L., "Fugitive Emissions: An Untapped Application for TQC," ASQC Quality Congress Transactions, San Francisco, CA (1990).

Byers, R. L., "Regulatory Barriers to Pollution Prevention," Journal of the Air and Waste Management Association, 41, 418–422 (1991).

Cairncross, F. "Costing the Earth," Harvard Business School Press, Cambridge, 1992.

Chemical Manufacturers Association, "CMA Hazardous Waste Survey '88," Chemical Manufacturers Association, Washington, D.C., August 1990.

Chemical Manufacturers Association, "Preventing Pollution in the Chemical Industry 1987–1990," Chemical Manufacturers Association, Washington, D.C., 1992.

Ciric, A. R., and Jia, T., "Economic Sensitivity Analysis of Waste Treatment Costs in Source Reduction Projects: Continuous Optimization Problems," University of Cincinnati, Cincinnati, OH, October 1992.

Cohen, Y., and Allen, D. T., "An Integrated Approach to Process Waste Minimization Research," Journal of Hazardous Materials 19, 237–253 (1992).

Cusumano, J. A., Chairman of the Board of Catalytica, Inc., "Designer Catalysts: Hastemakers for a Clean Environment," in Proceedings of Pollution Prevention in the Chemical Process Industries, April 6–7, 1992, Compiled by McGraw Hill, 1992.

Dorfman, M.H., Muir, W.R. and Miller, C.G. "Environmental Dividends: Cutting More Chemical Wastes," INFORM, Inc., New York, 1992.

Fathi-Afshar, S. and Yang, J.C., "Designing the Optimal Structure of the Petrochemical Industry for Minimum Cost and Least Gross Toxicity of Chemical Production," Chemical Engineering Science, 40, 781–797 (1985).

Freeman, H., Harten, T., Springer, J., Randall, P., Curran, M.A. and Stone, K., "Industrial Pollution Prevention: A Critical Review," Journal of the Air and Waste Management Association, 42, 618–656 (1992).

General Accounting Office, "Toxic Substances: Advantages of and Barriers to Reducing the Use of Toxic Chemicals, GAO/RCED-92-212 (1992).

Hagh, B., and Allen, D. T., "Catalytic Hydrodechlorination," in Innovative Hazardous Waste Treatment Technology, Volume 2, Physical/Chemical Processes, H. M. Freeman, ed., Technomic, Lancaster, PA, 1990, pp. 45–54.

Kalnes, T. N. and James, R. B., "Hydrogeneration and Recycle of Organic Waste Streams," Environmental Progress, 7(3), 185–191 (1988).

Klee, H., "Executive Summary of the AMOCO/EPA Pollution Prevention Project," Copies available through American Petroleum Institute, Washington, D.C. (1992).

NACEPT (National Advisory Council for Environmental Policy and Technology), "Improving Technology Diffusion for Environmental Protection," EPA 130-R-92-001 (1992).

National Research Council, "Critical Technologies: The Role of Chemistry and Chemical Engineering," National Academy Press, Washington, D.C., 1992.

Nelson, K. E., "Are there any energy savings left?," Chemical Processing, January 1989.

Nelson, K. E., "Use These Ideas to Cut Wastes," Hydrocarbon Processing, March (1990).

Rudd, D. F., Fathi-Afshar, S., Trevino, A. A. and Stadtherr, M. A., "Petrochemical Technology Assessment," Wiley, New York, 1981.

Tellus Institute, "Alternative Approaches to the Financial Evaluation of Industrial Pollution Prevention Investments," prepared for the New

Jersey Department of Environmental Protection Project P32250 (1991).

U.S. Congress, Office of Technology Assessment, "Green Products by Design: Choices for a Cleaner Environment," OTA-E-541 (Washington, D.C: U.S. Government Printing Office, October 1992).

U.S. Department of Commerce, Bureau of the Census, "Manufacturer's Pollution Abatement Expenditures and Operating Costs" MA200(88)-1 (1990).

U.S. Department of Commerce, Bureau of the Census, "Manufacturer's Pollution Abatement Costs and Expenditures," (MA200-90-1) April 1992.

U.S. Department of Energy, Office of Industrial Technologies "Industrial Waste Reduction Program: Program Plan" 1991a.

U.S. Department of Energy, "Report of the CWRT Workshop on: Waste Reduction R&D Opportunities in Industry," DOE/CE/40762T-H4, September 1991b.

U.S. Environmental Protection Agency, "Compilation of Air Pollutant Emission Factors," 4th ed. with Supplements A–D, Research Triangle Park, NC, Publication AP-42 (1985).

U.S. Environmental Protection Agency, Office of Research and Development, "Pollution Prevention Research Plan: Report to Congress" 1989.

U.S. Environmental Protection Agency, "Environmental Investments: The Cost of a Clean Environment," Office of Policy, Planning, and Evaluation, November 1990.

U.S. Environmental Protection Agency, Office of Solid Waste and Emergency Response, "National Survey of Hazardous Waste Generators and Treatment, Storage, Disposal and Recycling Facilities in 1986: Hazardous Waste Management in RCRA TSDR Units," EPA/530-SW-91-060 (1991).

U.S. Environmental Protection Agency, "National Biennial RCRA Hazardous Waste Report," Office of Solid Waste, EPA/530-R-92-027, February 1993.

Waste Advantage, Inc., "Industrial Waste Prevention," Waste Advantage, Inc., Southfield, MI (1988).

Working Notes on Community Right to Know, U.S. Public Interest Research Group Education Fund, 215 Pennsylvania Avenue, S.E., Washington, D.C. 20003 (1991).

9

Pollution Prevention for Emerging Industries: The Case of Electric Vehicles

Julie Roque

Separating Industrial Design and Environmental Management

Currently in the United States, sources of industrial pollution and hazards are assessed only after specific plans for new facilities are proposed. Under state and federal laws and regulations, developers usually are required to submit applications for construction and/or operation to governmental agencies charged with protecting the environment. These applications detail anticipated releases of toxic or hazardous materials to the air, water, or land. Occupational hazards are not characterized in such applications, and are evaluated only after manufacturing operations are underway. Consumer hazards are assessed only in certain circumstances when approval for marketing products is required (e.g., for pharmaceuticals or food additives).

Our entire environmental regulatory system is based upon a premise that some level of pollution and risk is unavoidable and "acceptable." For the most part, industries that use, generate, or dispose of hazardous materials are allowed to operate if they are able to meet *de minimis* standards for ambient discharges, and occupational and consumer hazards. Proposals for new projects are not evaluated and compared against competing proposals to weigh the economic benefits they promise with the deleterious public health and environmental risks they may pose. In short, economic development decisions rarely incorporate health and environmental concerns. New industries are identified and encouraged to develop while health and environmental issues are dealt with after the fact by separate governmental agencies that are responsible for regulating them. This process establishes, for the environmental considerations associated with the development of new industries, the rough equivalent to the pollution control framework itself;

namely, management after the fact, separating production design and development decisions from environmental management.

To some degree, the dichotomy between industrial development and environmental management is inevitable, at least within our current economic and governmental systems. Development decisions generally are made on a grander scale, with planning agencies involved in encouraging growth of whole industrial sectors within large regions. The environmental impacts of industrial activities, on the other hand, are exceptionally site-specific and dependent on the microstructures of the processes they involve.

Separate institutions have been established to deal with industrial development, with environmental quality, and with public health. Local economic development agencies and regional coalitions of city governments usually take the lead in attempting to attract new businesses, and their primary concerns are to increase tax bases and to create new jobs. Environmental management, on the other hand, generally is the domain of federal and state governments. Most programs enacted by state environmental agencies work under the delegation of authority of the federal government to implement and enforce federal legislation such as the Clean Air and Clean Water Acts, although a number of states have enacted parallel or additional and more stringent environmental legislation. Similarly, occupational and consumer hazards often are regulated at the state level. And while larger states may have regional offices for implementing these and other programs, industrial siting decisions, discharge permitting procedures, and the adoption of other environmental policies usually remain centralized at the state level.

To maximize economic benefits without sacrificing public welfare, however, it is imperative that industrial development and environmental decisions be linked. Adoption of the "cleanest" production processes possible can be encouraged most effectively at the planning stages of new facilities and industries. For public officials to weigh explicitly the economic gains of new businesses against potential environmental costs, analyses of emerging industries must be performed before development decisions are made. In other words, health and environmental assessments must become part of the development process.

Electric Vehicles: "Clean" Products?

This chapter examines the potential environmental consequences associated with proposals for an emerging industry: the manufacture of electric vehicles (EVs). EVs provide an unusually interesting case study because they are being promoted as "clean" technologies and one solution to regional air quality problems. As "zero emission vehicles" (ZEVs), EVs do not discharge the hydrocarbons and the nitrogen oxides emitted by conventional cars and trucks that form smog. And, as a number of researchers have illustrated, even the air pollutants from stationary sources (i.e., power plants) that produce the electricity required to recharge EVs are not likely to offset the benefits gained in air quality from driving EVs. Some researchers have also pointed out that energy security in the United States would be enhanced by shifting to EVs powered primarily by domestic fuels. Almost half of the gasoline used in the United States currently is imported, while only about 5% of the electricity used in the United States today is generated from imported fuels (Mader, 1991).

Although Europe and other regions of the United States probably will begin to shift toward some reliance on EVs, it is most likely that California will be the first major market for these products. In 1991, the California Air Resources Board adopted a rule that requires, by 1998, at least 2% of the cars and trucks marketed in California by major automobile manufacturers to be ZEVs. That percentage is to rise to 5% in 2001 and to 10% in 2003, with only EVs defined as meeting the "zero emission" definition (CARB, 1991). The CARB upheld its EV rule in 1994. As a result, there may be over 500,000 EVs on the road by the year 2003 (SCE, 1991), or up to 1.2 million by the year 2010 (Cone, 1992). Yet the question remains: what will be the public health and environmental impacts associated with building these vehicles? Clearly, almost all manufacturing carries with it some costs. The crucial issue is to what degree these costs offset some of the benefits captured in shifting toward driving EVs.

Defining products as "clean," "green," or environmentally sound is not a straightforward problem. Methods for analyzing the total environmental costs throughout the entire lifecycle of a product are not well developed, but a proposed framework for characterizing and assessing the environmental impacts of various stages in the lifecycle of consumer products such as EVs will be outlined as a starting point in discussing this intersection of environment and industrial development. Such an assessment is limited primarily because of the lack of data concerning EVs—products and an industry that do not yet exist. Therefore, lessons are drawn from existing industries that might manufacture certain components of EVs. Projections of the number of EVs that will be built and how the industry might develop also are relied upon for rough estimations of what environmental costs might be incurred in this process. Issues that are raised by the EV assessment, and improvements in manufacturing processes relevant to EVs that would enable the EV industry to develop "cleanly," are also discussed.

This case study seeks to analyze the public health and environmental implications of the *entire* EV lifecycle within a pollution prevention framework. While the titles of some previous studies have sought to describe specific environmental effects or lifecycle costs of EVs, the process of examining multiple impacts from all stages of manufacturing, as well as operation and final disposal, has only just begun. This gap appears to be indicative of the lack of information about all of the possible production steps for EVs, of how complicated such an analysis would be to complete, and, especially, how researchers draw boundaries for their work that reflect a piecemeal, but detailed and technical, approach to managing new sources of wastes and hazards. In contrast, a general framework for analyzing emerging industries of many types needs to be developed.

Analyzing Industrial Processes: Using Lifecycle Analysis

The term "product lifecycles" refers to all stages of manufacturing consumer goods, the use of those goods, and their ultimate disposal. The production of most consumer goods requires a number of different inputs, and involves multiple stages of manufacturing and processing. Further, products can be used and disposed of in many different ways. A simplified depiction of a product lifecycle is presented in Figure 9.1.

Lifecycle analyses or assessments have been proposed to evaluate all of the potential human health and environmental impacts associated with consumer products. In general, materials and energy are inputs at each stage of a product's lifecycle. Wastes also are generated at each stage, which then are released into the environment or recycled back into the manufacturing stream for the same or other products.

A lifecycle approach can enable decisionmakers to identify the most important issues of concern and helps to force analysts to make explicit all of their assumptions. Such analyses map out all of the processes that lead to the manufacture of a product, its use, and its disposal or reuse. And unlike media-specific environmental assessments, lifecycle analyses include wastes released to all environmental media (air, water, or land) throughout the product's lifecycle. They also should characterize other hazards posed during the manufacture of the product (e.g., occupational risks) and to consumers during use of the product.

The use of lifecycle analysis, however, has not been constructed as an environmental design tool. If standards for levels of risk considered "acceptable" are met, permission is granted for construction, operation, or marketing. Further, full lifecycle analyses cannot be performed until detailed proposals for new facilities, operating processes or products are

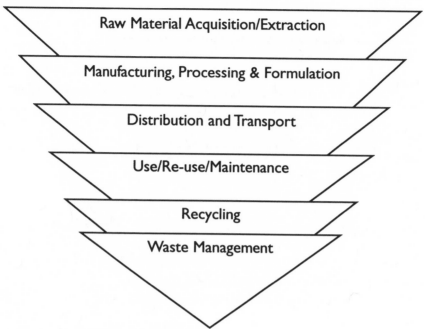

Figure 9.1 A simplified product lifecycle.

made because many health and environmental effects are dependent on geography, meteorology, and specific operating, workplace, or product use conditions.

Before a lifecycle analysis can be performed, boundaries around the analysis must be drawn. Many consumer products are composed of multiple components, and therefore the manufacturing steps of each component must first be examined independently. Assessments of these processes then should be aggregated, and linked with an analysis of their assembly into the final product; packaging, transport, distribution, and use all may be viewed as additional lifecycle steps. If the product is disassembled after use, yet another step must be added to the lifecycle to characterize that process and the hazards it may present. Finally, the ultimate treatment and/or disposal of each component must be included. Figure 9.2 illustrates one possible configuration of a lifecycle for a product composed of several components made through multiple manufacturing steps.

While mapping in detail the full lifecycles of complex products obviously can become very complicated, the difficulty in identifying and evaluating impacts at each point in the product lifecycle also grows with the

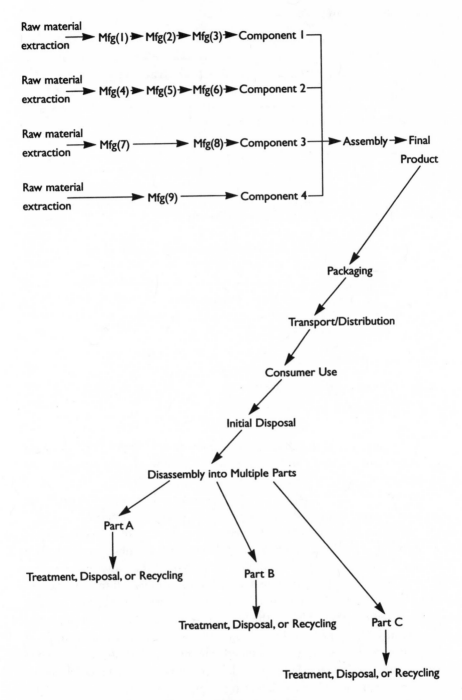

Figure 9.2 Lifecycle for a product of multiple components.

degree of precision and the inclusiveness of the analysis. At each point in the lifecycle, materials and/or energy may be added, wastes may be generated and other hazards may be posed. Because such analyses can quickly grow out of hand, it becomes imperative that assessments be bounded. Boundaries most often limit the number and types of impacts measured, or the parts of the lifecycle assessed.

The Manufacture of Electric Vehicles

How then might a lifecycle approach be applied to electric vehicles? According to a major advocate for EV manufacture, the Electric Power Research Institute (EPRI), a lifecycle comparison needs to begin with "a full accounting of all of the emissions sources for each vehicle type." But EPRI, in its own accounting, identified the "total emissions profile for a vehicle" as the "operating emissions plus all those emissions linked with its energy source." Thus, EPRI included only the operation of the vehicle and omitted all other steps in the lifecycle: both upstream (from extracting the raw materials to produce each component to their manufacture and assembly) as well as downstream (disassembly and disposal).

Other researchers have performed studies to estimate the environmental effects of EVs, but, despite the usage of the term "lifecycle" in several papers, almost all the reports examined only impacts associated with the operation of EVs (DeLuchi, 1991; Dowlatabadi et al., 1990; EPRI, 1989; Finson et al., 1992; Fischetti, 1992; Ford, 1992; Gordon, 1991; Lloyd & Leonard, 1992; Lloyd et al., 1991; LA DWP; Mader, 1991; O'Connell, 1990; SCE, 1991; Sperling, 1991; Sperling et al., 1991; Wang et al., 1990; Wuebben et al., 1990). These authors defined "lifecycle" costs only as the environmental costs associated with driving and recharging EVs throughout those vehicles' lifetimes; none attempted to provide a full accounting of the additional health and environmental costs associated with manufacturing and disposal.

Some studies began to account for full lifecycle costs by comparing lifetime dollar costs of EVs to conventional vehicles (CVs) (Bevilacqua-Knight, 1992; DeLuchi et al., 1989). These costs, including vehicle purchase prices, presumably represent some of the different potential effects posed by EVs and CVs. Other reports simply compared the dollar costs of manufacturing batteries for EVs against other fuels (CARB, 1990a; CARB, 1990b). Clearly, such analyses provide an extremely weak basis for comparison because most environmental impacts are not internalized.

One exception to these operation-focused studies was a report prepared for the U.S. Department of Energy in 1980 by Singh *et al.* Here, the authors suggested that the impacts of manufacturing EVs (particularly local air emissions, wastewater loadings, solid waste, and occupational hazards) would increase, possibly outweighing the benefits gained from driving EVs. They also claimed that while EVs would save petroleum, they would require more total energy for production and operation. Their results, however, were based on proposals for EVs that are no longer current. (They assumed, for example, that these vehicles would operate with DC motors and outdated battery technology.) A more recent report, *Methodology For Analyzing the Environmental and Economic Effects of Electric Vehicles: An Illustrative Study,* prepared for the U.S. EPA's Office of Mobile Sources, did mention that manufacturing hazards should be accounted for, but did not attempt to evaluate them (ICF, 1991).

Operating Costs

Almost invariably, studies that have examined the environmental conse-quences associated with EV operation (which is essentially emission-free), compared those impacts to tailpipe emissions from CVs. These studies found that an overall improvement in air quality could be obtained, even after accounting for additional emissions from increased electrical genera-tion by stationary power plants. The degree to which increased stationary source emissions are offset by decreased vehicle tailpipe emissions, how-ever, varies with the time of day an EV is recharged (peak hour charging would increase emissions more than offpeak charging) and the fuel gener-ating mix used to produce electricity. The generation of nitrogen oxides can be most sensitive to the time of day that EVs are recharged, and their net production (from CV tailpipes versus stationary sources) could increase or decrease depending on the assumption of the analysis (Lloyd & Leonard, 1992).

The burning of fossil fuels to generate electricity produces most of the same air pollutants as those emitted from CVs: nitrogen oxides, hydrocar-bons and volatile organic gases (VOCs), carbon monoxide, carbon dioxide, particulates, and some air toxics (e.g., benzene, formaldehyde). In addition, power plants emit sulfur oxides, an acid rain precursor associated with the burning of high sulfur coal in the eastern United States. Of course, the generation of air pollutants from stationary sources depends upon the type of fuel used. The average generating mix used to make electricity in the United States is 55% coal, 7% oil, 7% natural gas, and 31% nuclear and renewable fuels. According to EPRI, with this average fuel mix, the recharging of EVs would result in only 5.2% of the nitrogen oxides; 0.03% of the carbon monoxide; 0.04% of the nonmethane organic gases (hydrocarbon precursors to smog); and 0.50% of the particulates emitted by an equivalent number of CVs. A different author reported that recharging EVs would release 25% less carbon dioxide (Fischetti, 1992).

Other researchers examined regional scenarios and agreed that shifting to EVs would drastically reduce hydrocarbons, carbon monoxide, and benzene with any energy generating mix. They did not draw any conclusions about particulates and sulfur dioxide, however, noting instead that regional acid deposition could increase or decrease, depending on power sources. Some predict slight increases in nitrogen oxide emissions on a national scale, and significant local increases in particulates and sulfur dioxide near power plants (ICF, 1991). Producing the power to recharge EVs would emit less greenhouse gases nationwide, particularly carbon dioxide, unless coal is used to generate electricity (DeLuchi, 1991; Dowlatabadi et al., 1990).

In short, shifting to EVs will decrease total air emissions, unless they are powered primarily or entirely by coal-fired plants. The use of EVs powered by electricity generated from coal would increase greenhouse gases, including carbon dioxide, nitrogen oxides, hydrocarbons, carbon monoxide, sulfur oxides, and other air toxics such as formaldehyde and benzene (Gordon, 1991). Further, increased reliance on EVs shifts the location of air emissions, because CVs emit pollutants during operation, primarily in urban areas, while stationary sources are often in more rural areas. The timing of air emissions also may change as CVs pollute mainly during morning and evening rush hours. EVs, on the other hand, are primarily expected to be recharged overnight, where the added demand for electricity would then be experienced (ICF, 1991). (Location and timing are especially important variables in the production of ozone from nitrogen oxides and hydrocarbons in urban areas.)

To obtain the greatest air quality improvements, the most polluting (and most heavily used) vehicles should be targeted first for substitution with EVs. Automobiles are the largest source of air pollution; in California, for example, they produce 24% of the nonmethane hydrocarbons, 27% of the nitrogen oxides, and 55% of the carbon monoxide emitted into the air. Researchers from the California Bureau of Automotive Repair and the California Air Resources Board have found that just 7% of the cars on the road emit 50% of the total carbon monoxide, while 50% emitted only 0.3%; 6% of all vehicles emitted 50% of the hydrocarbons, while 50% emitted 3% (California Senate Office of Research, 1991). Pulling the most polluting cars off the road and replacing them with EVs would optimize the tradeoffs between tailpipe emissions and the environmental effects of operating EVs.

An ideal assessment of EVs would consider all other steps in the lifecycle in addition to operation. Such an analysis would require that a complete list of the components of EVs be obtained, and the health and environmental impacts of each component's manufacture be characterized. The assembly of these components would be evaluated, as would their disassembly and disposal. Assumptions about what an EV would be, and about how and where the industry would develop, however, must be made.

Current proposals for EVs include converted CVs, hybrid electric/gasoline powered vehicles, and vehicles specially designed to maximize speed, acceleration, and/or vehicle driving range while relying completely on batteries. Some of these types of vehicles are in operation, while others remain in a prototype stage or even on the drawing board. Yet, some assumptions must be developed for a lifecycle assessment as each of these different types of vehicles would pose different environmental consequences. Batteries for EVs may be composed of different substances with different lifespans and different types of hazards in their manufacture, use, and disposal. Similarly, different materials (especially aluminum and plastics) may be used to produce certain components. And various proposals for EVs have projected different vehicle lifespans that would determine manufacturing and waste generation rates.

There are numerous possibilities for how and where an EV industry might develop, and these factors will determine the nature, the magnitude, and the geographic and social distributions of detrimental health and environmental impacts. Although some scenarios may be more plausible than others, it is not yet obvious where different components will be manufactured and subsequently shipped for assembly. Each location scenario suggests different impacts: producing more components in one area could result in higher process discharges, but shipping them will result in greater transportation-related pollution.

The location of specific sources is important because certain environmental effects (e.g., smog) are geographically specific, and because some airsheds and wastewater treatment systems are already heavily burdened with industrial wastes and may not be able to accommodate increased pollutant loadings. The siting of new pollution sources in such areas may have adverse effects, while discharging wastes in less sensitive environmental regions or to facilities with greater treatment capacities available may enable hazardous materials to be managed effectively. In addition, economies of scale usually can be captured by traditional pollution control

devices and techniques which operate more efficiently on highly concentrated wastestreams. Thus, small manufacturing firms may pollute more per
unit of production in comparison with larger firms that are able to finance
capital intensive—but cleaner—operations. If linear relations between production rates and hazardous exposures or discharges are assumed, extrapo-
lations may be overestimates if the increased production of components is
accommodated by existing manufacturers. They may be underestimates, on
the other hand, if small firms are created to meet added demands.

Clearly, some boundaries must be drawn for the performance of a lifecycle assessment. First the data needs for performing a full lifecycle evaluation must be identified. For this study, five specific aspects of the production of EVs are examined: substitutions of aluminum for steel or iron
components; the manufacture of plastic components and their disposal;
electric motor production; electronics production; and the manufacture
and recycling of lead-acid batteries. These topics were selected because
they are most likely to differ significantly from parts found in conventional
automobiles in terms of the types and/or quantities of raw materials used.
It was assumed that other parts (e.g., the vehicle interior, bumpers, tires,
windows, accessories) would be more similar to those in CVs. An abbrevi-
ated lifecycle diagram of an EV is illustrated in Figure 9.3.

Data Needs and Gaps

To project EV manufacturing impacts, some measure needs to be developed of the health and environmental costs per unit of production for each
industrial sector that would contribute to an EV industry. These 'hazard
indices' then could be multiplied by anticipated production rates (for each
sector) to calculate the needed resources, the environmental discharges, and
other risks that might be incurred from various levels of production.
Although such indices would not be linear, but would indicate the functions of the size and structure of manufacturing processes, they could provide an initial glimpse into which operations are likely to be the most
detrimental to public health and the environment.

Table 9.1 lists three categories of environmental impact to assess each
step of the EV lifecycle. All potential impacts at each stage of the lifecycle
step should be accounted, including those associated with acquiring raw
materials, transporting materials or components, and generating the energy
required at each step. Some of the measures of production levels that might
be used as a denominator for hazard indices include units of production
(numbers of motors, batteries, etc.), numbers of employees, total sales, or

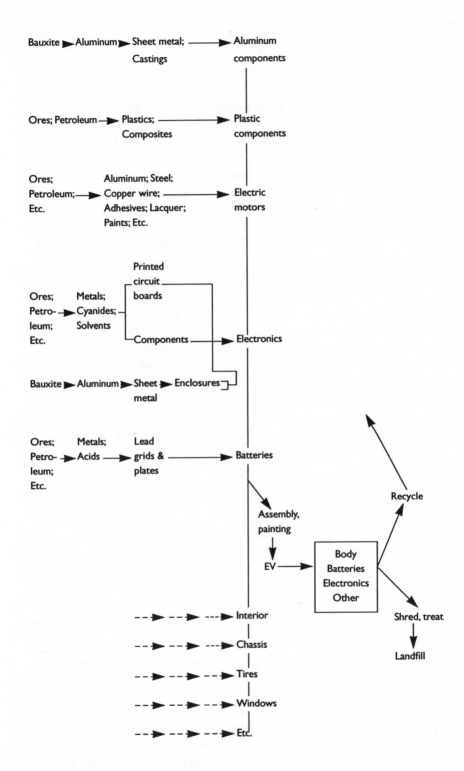

Figure 9.3 The lifecycle of an electric vehicle.

Table 9.1 Potential Environmental Impacts of Manufacturing and Maintaining Electric Vehicles

Resources: Material and Energy Use	Environmental Impacts (routine and accidental releases)	Direct Injuries
Renewable resources Nonrenewable resources	Air emissions Water discharges Hazardous wastes Solid wastes Other (noise, ecological impacts, aesthetics, etc.)	Occupational risks Consumer hazards Other environmental damage

value added. While actual units of production would be most accurate, such data are often not available even on an aggregate level from the Census of Manufacturing. Other variables measure production rates indirectly, and their accuracy probably varies from industry to industry. For example, numbers of employees reflect how labor intensive an industry is, and may vary by facility depending on whether production is automated.

The following section is based on general information obtained from a number of sources: emissions permits for particular firms; self-reported discharge data; waste audit manuals; and industry, governmental, and environmental publications. Table 9.2 summarizes the specific environmental data that are available for firms that discharge toxic or hazardous chemicals and that could potentially contribute to the development of hazard indices. As noted, however, there are severe limits to all of the data collected by governmental agencies.

Methods for developing hazard indices are discussed, as are the limits to the data collected for this report. Analogies to the production of similar products can be drawn to assess the environmental impacts of manufacturing components that are not being made in large quantities today. Some processes, however, present special problems. For example, some of the new plastic composites that may be used in EVs may be composed of very different materials, and produced by very different processes, than those used currently in other applications. The electronics industry, on the other hand, actually is a conglomeration of many businesses that produce various components and employ a wide variety of manufacturing processes.

Measuring Wastes and Hazards

To extend driving range and increase acceleration, EVs need to be lighter in weight than CVs to offset the mass of the batteries they carry. Most EV

Table 9.2 Major Sources of Environmental Data

	Toxics Release Inventory (TRI)	Hazardous Waste Manifests & Biennial Reports	Air Emission Permits	Wastewater Discharge Permits
Releases	Multi-media	Hazardous wastes	Criteria air pollutants, some air toxics + misc.	Priority pollutants + other toxics
Authority	Superfund Amendments & Reauthorization Act (SARA)	Resources Conservation & Recovery Act (RCRA)	Federal & state Clean Air Acts	Federal & state Clean Water Acts
Who Collects	State agencies & U.S. EPA	State agencies	Regional air quality agencies	Regional & local agencies
Data	Releases of 320 listed chemicals	Wastes treated or disposed of on land	Maximum allowed emission rates	Maximum allowed discharge rates and concentrations
Limits	Releases reported in ranges; high reporting thresholds	Single medium; waste codes usually do not describe chemical composition of waste precisely	Single medium; max emissions rather than actual quantities	Single medium; max discharges rather than actual quantities

designs currently propose the use of aluminum bodies; the GM Impact, for example, will be built with aluminum (Fischetti, 1992; D. Hill, *pers. comm.,* 9/9/92). Plastics also could enhance energy efficiency, and several automobile manufacturers have produced body panels composed almost entirely of composite plastics (Bleviss, 1989). Although manufacturers do not appear to be planning to produce all-plastic bodies in the near future, it is likely that EVs will contain greater percentages of plastics than vehicles on the road today (Winfield, 1992).

Up to 1990, most CVs were approximately 68% iron or steel by weight, 5% aluminum, and 7.5% to 12% plastics and plastic composites. The remaining weight of vehicles is attributable to other metals, rubber, glass, fluids, and lubricants. Aluminum can be substituted for certain steel or cast iron parts and reduces the weight of those parts by 40 to 50%. Sheet or wrought aluminum is used for body panels, vehicle doors, hoods, deck lids, and fenders. Other applications of aluminum are in suspension systems, various engine components, drive shafts, radiators, frames, brake pedal arms, wheel rims, and other body reinforcements and brackets. Aluminum alloys are used for interior and exterior trim, grilles, wheels, air conditioners, intake manifolds, water pumps and automatic transmissions (The Aluminum Association, 1992; Corcoran, 1992; Parker, 1992; SMC Automotive Alliance, 1992; Winfield, 1992; Wolfson, 1992).

The production of aluminum vehicle components is a multistep process. As illustrated in Figure 9.3, these processes include mining, the extraction of primary aluminum from ore, the fabrication of sheet metal or ingots, and the final formation or casting of components. Downstream manufacturing steps do not pose significant hazards to the ambient environment, although metal working may pose occupational risks through exposures to dusts and fumes, spot welding, and the use of adhesives for assembling aluminum parts and frames. These hazards, however, are generally controllable with protective equipment in the workplace. The major environmental impacts associated with the production of aluminum components arise in earlier steps in the manufacturing chain, particularly mining and the extraction of primary aluminum, both of which are highly polluting and energy intensive.

While the United States is one of the world's leading producers of aluminum, 90% of the bauxite consumed is imported from Australia, Guinea, Jamaica, Brazil, and other nations. The predominant domestic sources of alumina are central Arkansas, and, to a lesser degree, Alabama and Georgia (The Aluminum Association, The Story and Uses of Aluminum). In 1991, transportation (including commercial and military aircraft) accounted for 16.5% of the total shipments of aluminum in the United States. A 10% penetration of EVs, even into the nation's vehicle fleet, should, therefore, not significantly increase the national demand for aluminum.

The extraction of aluminum most often is performed by passing electricity through bauxite, reducing aluminum oxides to aluminum metal. Byproducts from this process include red mud wastes that are difficult to dewater and must be allowed to settle for years in slurry lakes, during which caustic effluent may leak. Dust from these impoundments may be a problem if they are not covered with water. Dust problems also occur with the handling of alumina and the coke that is burned as fuel.

The major hazardous waste from primary aluminum smelting operations is the cyanide-containing potliner. Fluoride emissions from smelting cells, hydrocarbons evolved during anode baking, and particulates emitted into the air from refinery stacks may present significant local environmental concerns. Pollution control devices (e.g., electrostatic precipitators, dry scrubbers) are relatively effective in capturing these pollutants, but are costly. Water effluent from secondary smelters and fabricators contains oils, graphite, and chemical contaminants (Kirk–Othmer, 1979; McCawley & Baumgardner, 1985; Singh et al., 1980). And generating electricity required to produce aluminum inputs produces a variety of air pollutants which may have local, regional, and/or global effects on the atmosphere, depending on the fuel mix.

While the production of iron, steel, and aluminum all involve highly polluting and energy intensive processes, some of the environmental impacts associated with their production can be offset with recycling. Currently, over 11 million vehicles are recycled in the United States each year, supplying 37% of all ferrous scrap (Automotive Dismantlers & Recycling Association). The use of scrap iron and steel to produce new steel reduces air pollution from mills by 86%, water pollution by 76%, and solid wastes by 105%. (The reduction in solid waste is obtained by the recovery of both consumer wastes and wastes from processing virgin ore.) In addition, recycling iron and steel scrap reduces the use of virgin materials by 90%, water by 40%, and mining wastes by 97% (Institute of Scrap Recycling Industries). Similar benefits are gained from recycling aluminum. In 1991, some 2,425,000 tons of aluminum scrap were consumed in the United States—over 31% of the domestic supply (Parker, 1992). Sixty percent of the aluminum in vehicles today comprises recycled scrap; and more than 85% in junked cars is reclaimed and recycled (The Aluminum Association, 1991).

In comparison with steel, the production of aluminum from virgin ore is both more polluting and energy intensive. Reductions in particulate emissions and the energy required to produce an equivalent amount of aluminum, however, can be achieved by producing ingots from recycled scrap. (Because aluminum is lighter than steel or iron, the weight of vehicle components made of aluminum is cut approximately in half: one pound of aluminum replaces roughly two pounds of steel.) Table 9.3 summarizes particulate emissions from the production of steel using two different processes and three combinations of virgin and recycled inputs; two scenarios for aluminum production are presented, one with 100% virgin ore and the other with 100% recycled scrap. The reductions in particulate emissions gained by switching from each steel process to the production of aluminum from virgin ore and from recycled scrap are reported in Table

9.4. Shifting from the production of steel to the production of primary aluminum increases particulate emissions in each scenario. Replacing steel with secondary aluminum, on the other hand, reduces particulate emissions in all cases. Table 9.5 compares water usage, other air emissions, water pollutants, and solid wastes for producing steel and aluminum from virgin and recycled inputs.

The production of primary aluminum is far more energy intensive than the production of steel, but net energy savings from the use of aluminum can be realized with improved fuel economy and reductions in the energy needed to fabricate parts. Lifecycle energy requirements to produce steel and aluminum vehicle components are compared in Table 9.6. Further

Table 9.3 Particulate Emissions from Steel and Aluminum Making

	Process	Effluent Discharge[a]
Steel	BOF/Virgin Ore	9,697
	BOF/10% Auto Scrap, 30% Home Scrap, 60% Virgin Ore	8,394
	Electric Furnace/70% Auto Scrap, 30% Home Scrap	1,009
Aluminum	Standard Process/Virgin Ore	36,654
	Standard Process/100% Auto Scrap	1,166

Source: Purcell, 1978, p. 47.
[a]Molton ingot stage, in grams per metric ton, for uncontrolled effluent.

Table 9.4 Change in Particulate Production in Producing One Ton of Aluminum in Place of Two Tons of Steel

Steel Process	Aluminum Process	Change[a]
All virgin—BOF	All virgin—Standard	+17,260
All virgin—BOF	All recycled cast auto scrap	-18,228
10-30-60—BOF	All virgin—Standard	+19,866
10-30-60—BOF	All recycled cast auto scrap	-15,622
70-30—Elect furnace	All virgin—Standard	+34,636
70-30—Elect furnace	All recycled cast auto scrap	-852

Source: Purcell, 1978, p. 47.
[a]In grams per two metric tons of steel ingot replaced by one ton of aluminum ingot.

Table 9.5 Environmental Impacts of Steel and Aluminum Production[a]

	Steel		Aluminum	
	Virgin materials/ BOF	30% home scrap, 70% obsolete/ electric furnace	Virgin materials	Secondary smelter w/ auto scrap
Water Discharged (liters)				
Process	76,597	683	160,266	4,193
Mine drainage	360	63	1,091	5
Air Emissions (grams)				
Particulates	9,697	1,009	36,654	1,166
Sulfur oxides	3,033	2,875	88,603	662
Carbon monoxide	963	3,103	34,684	3,475
Hydrocarbons	1,785	1,732	86,804	5,205
Nitrogen oxides	1,844	3,549	138,628	6,751
Aldehydes	24	29	611	40
Organics	8	26	265	58
Ammonia	63			
Fluorides			1,050	
Chlorides				1,000
Water Pollutants (grams)				
Suspended solids	27		1,595	875
Dissolved solids	1,114	277	18,567	2,544
BOD	4		150	
COD			1,093	
Oil and grease	2	2	327	
Iron	2		14	
Phenols	0.2		77	
Sulfide	0.2		10	
Ammonia	5		15	
Cyanide	0.1		3	0.1
Fluoride	11		1,000	
Chloride				1,700
Cadmium				0.02
Lead				0.04
Manganese				0.045
Solid Wastes (kilograms)				
Overburden	6,665	1,216	28,800	218
Process	4,841	105	15,478	295
Postconsumer		-889		-1,149

Source: Niemczewski, 1984, pp. 33–34.

[a]Per metric ton carbon steel and one half metric ton aluminum.

energy savings can be captured with recycling. Recycling iron and steel consumes just 26%, and aluminum only 5%, of the energy required to produce those materials from virgin ore—reducing the depletion of nonrenewable fuels and the pollution from their combustion. Table 9.7 compares the energy requirements for vehicles with steel, primary aluminum, and secondary aluminum components.

Table 9.6 Lifecycle Energies for Steel and Aluminum Parts

	Steel part	15,450 Btu/lb
	Aluminum part	55,040 Btu/lb
	Gasoline energy	130,500 Btu/lb

	Steel part (20 lbs)	Aluminum part (10 lbs)
Energy to produce part (Btu)	309,000	550,400
Lifetime fuel consumed (Btu)	2,610,000	1,305,000
Total Btu's	2,919,000	2,855,400

Source: The Aluminum Association, 1991.

Table 9.7 Energy Comparison of Aluminum in EVs versus Steel in ICE Vehicles

	lb/car	Btu/lb[a]	Btu/car
'85 ICE			
Steel[b]	1,716	15,450–20,100	26–34M
Cast iron[b]	450	10,300	4.6M
Subtotal	2,166		31M–39M
EV (aluminum)[c]	1,083	65,500–105,000	71M–114M
EV (recycled Al)[c]	1,083	3,275–5,250	3.5M–5.5M

[a]Ranges of Btus/lb from SMC Automotive Alliance, 1992, and The Aluminum Association, 1991.

[b]Weights of steel and iron parts for a 1985 internal combustion engine vehicle from Niemczewski, 1984, p. 30.

[c]Weight of aluminum parts in 1992 and beyond EVs assumes substitution for all iron and steel parts with a 50% reduction in weight.

Plastic Components

Like aluminum, the substitution of plastics for certain components will reduce vehicle weight and increase driving range, speed, and acceleration. Automotive plastics often are composite blends of resins, fiberglass or other fiber substrates, metals, and plastics, or thermosets. Thermosets provide greater strength and durability by undergoing molecular cross-linking reactions during molding. Both composites and thermosets essentially are nonrecyclable; composite mixtures of materials cannot be separated and thermosets, when heated, degrade rather than melt. A second class of plastics is thermoplastics which, in contrast to thermosets, can be melted and remolded into the same or other products. Nylon, acrylic, polyvinyl chloride, polyethylene, polypropylene, and polyester all are thermoplastics. Chemical reagents added to plastics to obtain desired characteristics, however, may affect their recyclability.

It is most likely that the specific plastics to be used in EVs will at least resemble those already in use in CVs today. The manufacture of chemical precursors and the formulation of plastics involve the use of hazardous and toxic chemicals. Plastics are produced from hydrocarbons such as ethane, ethylene, propylene and styrene obtained from petroleum refining. Emissions of many of these materials present both acute and chronic health hazards such as organ damage and cancer; styrene, for example, is flammable and oxidizes readily to glycols, benzaldehyde, and/or benzoic acid, all of which pose human health effects. (Glycols are associated with reproductive disorders and benzaldehyde is a suspected carcinogen.) Styrene also combines with ozone to yield benzaldehyde and formic acid, and in chlorinated water it will react to form chlorohydrin. Chemical fumes may be released when plastics are heated for molding into components or for recycling, posing toxic occupational exposures as well as environmental impacts. A variety of hazardous solvents such as acetone, methyl ethyl ketone (MEK), methanol, methylene chloride (MC), trichloroethylene (TCE), xylene, and toluene are used as carriers in reinforced plastics (e.g., fiberglass), and evaporate during the formation of products. Some of these chemicals are associated with a range of human health effects, including cancer, neurological disorders, and organ damage (CA DHS, 1989; Radian Corporation, 1990).

In addition to the hazardous materials used to produce plastics themselves, an assortment of glues and other adhesives are used in the manufacture of plastic products. Adhesives often contain 70% or more solvents which evaporate when they set. These solvents include aliphatic hydrocarbons (e.g., hexane and heptane), ketones (acetone, MEK), or alcohols, all of which contribute to the formation of smog. Many of these materials also are flammable and toxic. Aromatic hydrocarbons, such as xylene and toluene, are sometimes used as carriers, as may be 1,1,1-trichloroethane (TCA) or other chlorinated solvents. TCA and MC may be used as cleaning solvents in the application of adhesives (SRRP, 1991a).

The production of plastic products also is energy intensive. As shown in Table 9.8, however, plastics can save energy in comparison to steel and aluminum throughout the lifecycle of a component. The energy requirements for the manufacture of an intermediate-sized vehicle hood from steel and from aluminum are compared to one made of sheet molding composite (SMC). Similar calculations are available for other types of plastics. The total embodied energy content of 73 million kilograms of reaction injection molding (RIM) and polyurethane/ABS materials, for example, is equivalent to 183 million liters of oil, while the same parts in steel would require 194 million liters of oil. In addition, 33 million liters of oil energy could be saved by reduced fuel requirements with plastic parts (*Automotive Engineering*, 1991).

Automobile manufacturers already are substituting plastics in CVs to increase fuel economy. Plastics accounted for 2.9% of the weight of cars in 1973 and 7.5% in 1989 (Wolfson, 1992); another source reports that in 1991 plastics comprised 13% of the weight of new cars (Jones, 1992). The substitution of plastics for certain components in EVs, however, should not increase the production and use of these materials significantly in compar-

Table 9.8 Energy Needs for the Manufacture of Intermediate-Sized Vehicle Hoods

	Part weight (lb)	Material energy needs (Btu/lb)	Energy to produce (M Btu)	Energy savings (M Btu)
Steel	33.5	20,100	1,090	base
Aluminum	14.2	105,000	2,400	–1,310
SMC	22.0	24,700	640	+450

Energy Savings Relative to Steel

	Weight difference (lb/hood)	Lifetime energy savings (M Btu)	Mfg savings (M Btu)	Total Energy Savings	
Material				M Btu	Gallons of fuel
Steel	base	base	base	base	base
Aluminum	19.3	2,328	–1,310	1,018	6.8
SMC	11.5	1,387	+450	1,837	12.2

Source: The SMC Automotive Alliance, 1992.

ison to the national demand for a huge variety of plastic products (Singh et al., 1980).

Two concerns over the increasing percentages of plastics in automobiles are the energy requirements for their manufacture and their solid waste impacts. Both of these issues could be addressed with recycling; the use of recycled plastics saves more than 80% of the energy required to produce the same components from virgin plastics (Institute of Scrap Recycling Industries). Plastics, however, are difficult to recycle. Unlike mixed metals, minimal levels of contamination will ruin entire batches (Wolfson, 1992).

More than eight million automobiles are junked each year, and 75 to 80% of vehicle parts are already recycled. The remainder, however, of which approximately half is plastics, must be landfilled. In 1988, only 1.1 tons of the 14.4 tons of automotive plastics generated were recovered from the solid wastestream. New recycling processes for plastics are being developed, but there may be sixty or more different types of plastic in a single vehicle and sorting them for recycling is too expensive to be worthwhile. Further, certain components such as dashboards and steering wheels often contain a combination of different plastics that cannot be separated for recycling. As a result, an estimated three million tons of shredded auto parts end up in landfills each year (Corcoran, 1992; Finson et al., 1992; Jones, 1992; Environmental Vehicles Review, 1991a; SMC Automotive Alliance, 1992; Wolfson, 1992).

Electric Motors

An electric motor usually consists of two metal parts, one which fits inside the other. An electromagnetic field, generated by power supplied through bands of copper wire wrapped around the outer part (the stator), causes the inner part (the rotor) to spin. The rotor and stator generally are made of cast metals (aluminum and steel or alloys). The copper wires are coated with organic lacquers, and motors may be painted with oil-based finishes. Other hazardous materials which can be used in the manufacture of electric motors are resins in solvent carriers, cutting and lubricating oils, acetylene (for welding), acids, and cleaning solvents. Electroplating that may be performed involves the use and discharge of toxic metals such as chromium.

A full lifecycle assessment would account for the production of all inputs to electric motor manufacturing. This section, however, is narrowed to downstream manufacturing processes, the most likely to be expanded with a growing market for EVs. The amounts of metals and other materials consumed in the production of electric motors is negligible in comparison to all other uses. In comparison to internal combustion engines, the solid waste impacts of electric motors are much smaller. They are far simpler to disassemble for recycling, and do not contain the oil and other fluids that internal combustion engines do.

The metal working processes (casting, cutting, welding, etc.) in building electric motors pose occupational hazards that are generally controllable. The use of organic solvents, paints, lacquers, and toxic metals, can also present serious risks to workers and nearby residents if they are not handled and managed properly. Styrene and other hazardous organics may be emitted from ovens used to dry finishes, and extremely toxic metals (e.g., chromium VI) can be emitted from plating processes. The human health effects associated with such materials include skin irritations, neurological effects, and cancer risks. The discharge of volatile organic compounds also will contribute to the formation of smog. The air emissions (organic gases, nitrogen oxides, sulfur oxides, carbon monoxide, and particulates) of a medium-sized electric motor manufacturer are summarized in Tables 9.9 and 9.10.

Table 9.9 Air Emissions from the Manufacture of Electric Motors[a]

	Organic gases	Nitrogen oxides	Sulfur oxides	Carbon monoxide	Particulates
General fuel burning	79.31	1,472.90	9.40	396.55	84.98
I.C. fuel burning	267.26	447.58	1.13	415.38	16.10
Use of organics	37,698.35	0	0	0	0
Process emissions	0	0	0	0	609.81
Total (lb/yr)	38,044.92	1,920.48	10.53	811.93	710.89
Total (ton/yr)	19	0.960	0.005	0.406	0.355

Source: Reuland Electric, facility emission summary form.
[a]Pounds per year, operating 24 hr/day × 5 days/wk × 52 wk/yr.

Table 9.10 Air Toxics from Electric Motor Manufacturing[a]

Xylene	437.68
Methylene Chloride	323.4
Styrene	5378.2
Toluene	961.71
Chromium VI	0.307

Source: Reuland Electric, facility emission summary form.
[a]Pounds per year.

Electronics

To power the electric motors now used in all proposed models, EVs
depend on inverters composed of electronic components that convert from
DC to AC the electrical current from the batteries. Electronics are also
used to match and control the power supply from the batteries needed by
the motor under different driving conditions. Electronics consist of both
printed circuit boards and electronic components.

The manufacture and assembly of electronic components involves wafer
fabrication (growing crystals from silicon, gallium arsenide, or other materials); wafer assembly (cutting wafers into chips); printed circuit board fabrication (electroplating, etching, and cleaning); and assembly (attaching and
soldering components onto boards and removing excess flux). These
processes rely upon a variety of hazardous materials that include gases such
as arsine and phosphine which are more toxic than those used by any other
industry in the United States. They also use heavy metals in plating baths
(copper [see Table 9.11], tin, lead, nickel); strong acids, TCA, and chlorofluorocarbons (CFCs) for etching; acid and alkali cleaning agents, detergents and organic solvent cleaners (many of which are chlorinated); and
solder and rosin fluxes for the assembly of components on boards. Fluoride
wastes that are generated in the electroplating and etching of printed cir-

Table 9.11 Estimated Copper Wastes from Printed Circuit Board Manufacturing

Operation	Small firm	Large firm
Board Production Volume (sq ft/day)	250	4,000
Water Usage (& Discharge) (gal/day)	12,500	200,000
Acid Copper Plating Tank		
Volume of drag-out (liter/day)	3	48
Copper metal produced (kg/day)	0.075	1.2
Copper metal (kg/year)	18.75	300
Percent of Total Acid Copper Wastes	10%	10%
Total Copper Sources		
Copper produced (kg/day)	0.75	12
Copper produced (kg/year)	187	3,000
Total copper in untreated waste	15 ppm	15 ppm
Sludge Generation (est. 3% copper)	6 tons/yr	100 tons/yr

Source: California Department of Health Services, 1987 (CA DHS, 1987b).

cuit boards, and waste oils from machinery, must be disposed of as hazardous wastes (CA DHS, 1987b; CA DHS, 1991a; SRRP, 1991b).

Solvents, metals, acids and alkalis from these processes generally are pretreated and then discharged into wastewater treatment systems, landfilled as hazardous wastes, or treated on land. Some of these wastes (waste oils and metal sludges, for example) can be contained effectively, but solvents and spent process baths can cause environmental problems at manufacturing facilities and in landfills or hazardous waste incinerators. Silicon Valley in Northern California, for example, contains more EPA Superfund sites than anywhere else in the country due to electronics firms there. The variety of RCRA-regulated hazardous waste produced by printed circuit board manufacturers is illustrated in Table 9.12. It is important to note the vague descriptions of many of these wastes provided by the manifest systems which limit the extrapolation of waste generation rates for new processes (CA DHS, 1987b; CA DHS, 1991a; Silicon Valley Toxics Coalition, 1992).

Volatile organics used primarily for cleaning in the electronics industry are emitted into the air routinely. Aliphatic hydrocarbon solvents (kerosene, mineral spirits, Stoddard solvent, heptane) are cleaners and degreasers that contribute to smog formation. Toluene, turpentine, and xylene are aromatic hydrocarbons with known toxicities including organ damage and cancer risks. Ketones such as acetone and MEK, used to remove paints, resins, and coatings, are toxic and also contribute to smog. Most of these nonchlorinated solvents have low flash points and are flammable, presenting significant occupational hazards.

The chlorinated solvents used most widely in the electronics industry are TCE, TCA, MC, perchloroethylene (PERC), and CFC-113 (see Table 9.13). Chlorinated solvents are safer to use but pose chronic health risks (including cancer) to both workers and local communities. In addition, some of the compounds used impact the global environment. Solvents such as TCE, carbon tetrachloride, and CFCs rise through the atmosphere and degrade the protective stratospheric ozone. Although they are being phased out by many larger firms, CFCs still are used for vapor degreasing and critical cleaning in some parts of the electronics industry because they provide good solvency, rapid evaporation, and dry with no detectable residue (Reinhardt et al., 1992; Silicon Valley Toxics Coalition, 1992).

Significant occupational risks are associated with the electronics industry. During soldering, for example, workers may be exposed to lead and other toxic metals (e.g., cadmium, arsenic, beryllium), organic solvents, and rosin fluxes that decompose to formaldehyde and other hazardous compounds (Lead Industries Association, 1990). Recent research has also pointed to links between exposures to the glycol ethers used in etching processes and reproductive effects in workers (Weber and Gellene, 1992).

Table 9.12 Hazardous Wastes from 57 Printed Circuit Board Firms

California Waste Code	Description	Tons Generated
111	Acid solution w/ metals	3847.53
112	Acid solution w/o metals	166.03
113	Unspecified acid solution	86.63
121	Alkaline solution w/ metals	4000.05
122	Alkaline solution w/o metals	61.00
123	Unspecified alkaline solution	204.58
131	Aqueous solution w/ reactive anions	635.24
132	Aqueous solution w/ metals	4628.18
134	Aqueous solution w/ organic residues <10%	70.26
135	Unspecified aqueous solution	242.90
141	Off-spec inorganically	52.72
151	Asbestos	64.38
171	Metal sludge	798.23
172	Metal dust	189.25
181	Other inorganic solid waste	450.86
211	Halogenated solvents	519.35
212	Oxygenated solvents	90.93
213	Hydrocarbon solvents	3.81
214	Unspecified solvent mixture	236.13
221	Waste oil and mixed oil	814.87
222	Oil/water separator sludge	107.11
223	Unspecified oil waste	406.61
241	Tank bottom waste	109.40
261	PCBs	15.20
271	Organic monomer waste	13.75
272	Polymeric resin waste	21.19
281	Adhesives	5.63
291	Latex waste	4.16
321	Wastewater treatment sludge	89.24
331	Off-spec organics	30.75
342	Organic liquids w/ metals	4.17
343	Unspecified organic liquid	124.75
351	Organic solids w/ halogens	21.43
352	Other organic solids	202.66
411	Alum and gypsum	1.67
421	Lime sludge	174.46
461	Paint sludge	95.07
491	Unspecified sludge waste	352.03
512	Other empty containers	348.02
513	Other empty containers <30 gal	460.28
541	Photographic chemicals	8.10
551	Lab chemicals	116.56
571	Fly ash, bottom ash, retort ash	10.96
611	Contaminated soil	75.49
711	Liquids w/ cyanides >1000 mg/l	9.74
723	Liquids w/ chromium (VI) >500 mg/l	12.51
741	Liquids w/ halogenated organics >1000 mg/l	4.17
	Total	19,988.14

Source: California Department of Health Services, 1987 (CA DHS, 1987b), p. 19.

Table 9.13 Solvent Use in the Electronics Industry

	Solvent				
	CFC-113	TCA	MC	TCE	PERC
Wafer fabrication	5.4	0.3	1.3	2.2	0.5
Wafer assembly	2.1	1.1	0.5	0.3	—
Board fabrication					
Dev'g photoresist	—	8.0	—	—	—
Stripping photoresist	—	—	13.8	—	—
Board assembly					
Primarily defluxing	25.6	6.6	0.7	0.5	0.5
Critical cleaning	9.2	—	—	—	—
In-situ generation					
of etchants	0.2	0.2	—	—	—

Source: Source Reduction Research Partnership, 1991b.

Batteries

Alternative fuel cells that would provide greater driving ranges between charges, be more compact, and have longer lifespans have been proposed to power EVs (Bates, 1992; DeLuchi *et al.*, 1989; O'Connell, 1990). The primary battery technologies promoted for future EV production have been the nickel–cadmium and lead-acid batteries, either alone or in tandem with a "range-extender." Of these, the lead-acid battery continues to be the primary candidate for substantial increases in production, and, as such, introduces significant health and environmental impacts. The lead industry is committing major resources to improving the lead-acid technology in an attempt to increase their markets through EVs (The Advanced Lead-Acid Battery Consortium, 1992). Given these factors, this analysis only focuses on the potential health and environmental consequences of lead-acid batteries.

Increased use of lead-acid batteries leads to greater mining of lead and greater smelting, particularly by recyclers. The energy requirements for lead production (mining, concentration, smelting, and refining) are lower than those of other major metals, using 25% of what is required for copper, and less than one-half that for zinc. In terms of usage, lead ranks only after aluminum, copper, and zinc among the nonferrous metals (Woodbury, 1985).

The United States has some of the largest lead reserves in the world. In 1990, primary lead smelters produced approximately 400,000 tons of lead while secondary smelters produced about 900,000 tons, most (85%) of which came from spent automobile batteries. There are three primary lead smelters in operation in the United States: one in central Montana and two in southeastern Missouri. Since primary smelters are considered a part of an ore beneficiation process (they also mine zinc and copper), they are exempt from hazardous waste regulations under RCRA. In contrast, there are 23 secondary lead smelters in the United States, some owned by lead-acid battery manufacturers and others that are independent (U.S. EPA, 1992; Theodore Barry & Associates, 1989). Unlike primary plants, secondary smelters are subject to the full requirements of RCRA. Spent lead-acid batteries were declared hazardous wastes by the U.S. EPA in 1985, and many of the materials generated in the recycling process meet RCRA's definition of hazardous wastes (Apotheker, 1990; Gruber, 1991; Kafka, 1990; Singh et al., 1980).

Nearly two-thirds of all the lead produced in the United States in 1990 (800,000 tons) was destined for use in storage batteries. Batteries are produced for a variety of applications such as marine, industrial, stationary, military, and other mobile uses (e.g., golf carts, tractors, motorcycles), but automobiles clearly account for the majority. Roughly 72 million new car batteries were produced in 1990; that year original equipment and replacement batteries for passenger cars and for light commercial vehicles represented 72% and 78% of the total battery market, respectively (Battery Council International; Gruber, 1991; U.S. EPA, 1992; Wojton, 1990; Woodbury, 1985).

Until recently, batteries have been the bottleneck in the development of EVs. Technologies other than lead-acid are only now becoming commercially feasible, and the lead-acid batteries required to power an EV are so heavy that it has been difficult to obtain acceptable driving performances. Lead-acid batteries are also most likely to be the bottleneck in the development of an EV manufacturing industry because of the large numbers of batteries that will be required and the significant health and environmental impacts associated with their manufacture.

The increase in battery production and recycling that is expected to accompany the commercialization of EVs will pose extremely high impacts near manufacturing facilities, and extremely high occupational risks. Currently, there is not the capacity for managing and recycling the large numbers of batteries that would be generated by EVs, and it is unlikely that significant new capacity will be added soon (GNB, 1992).

The manufacture of new batteries, and the generation of spent ones, will rise exponentially if EVs enter the market as planned. Most EVs, including the GM Impact, the GM HX3, AC Propulsion's CRX, and the Opel Impuls 2, currently use 28 to 32 ten-volt lead-acid batteries with a total weight of between 850 and 1100 pounds (*Automotive Engineering,* 1992; Cone, 1992; Dunne, 1992; Fischetti, 1992; Mader, 1991; Reynolds, 1992). These EVs appear most likely to be marketed in the near future, although other proposed EVs would use as few as 18 batteries (Bates, 1992; Gay *et al.*, 1992). Designers and manufacturers predict that batteries might last two to three years, and would cost $1500 to $2000 to replace (Cone, 1992; Dunne, 1992; Fischetti, 1992; Reynolds, 1992).

A typical lead-acid battery contains 17.5 to 20 pounds of lead, 9 to 11 pounds of sulfuric acid, and 1.6 to 3 pounds of (polypropylene) for the case. In CVs, batteries have an average life of 3 to 4 years. The U.S. EPA recognizes an 80% recycling rate is being achieved for lead-acid batteries, while other sources have claimed rates of nearly 98% (Apotheker, 1990; Battery Council International; Finson *et al.*,1992; Gruber, 1991; Smith, Bucklin and Associates, 1992; Theodore Barry and Associates, 1989). These statistics are summarized in Table 9.14.

In the long run, however, spent batteries from a growing number of EVs will become a significant problem if EVs continue to rely on lead-acid batteries. EVs now require 28 to 32 batteries, in contrast to one in each CV, and these need to be replaced more often. Assuming 1.2 million EVs will be in use by 2010 and that each will rely upon 32 lead-acid batteries, as many as 37.2 million additional batteries—or over half of the total 72 million batteries already produced today—may be required to power EVs alone. (The 1.2 million batteries that would be used by an equivalent number of CVs were subtracted.) Because EV batteries might last only half as long before they have to be replaced, this value would have to be doubled to calculate the number of spent batteries generated. These calculations become more dramatic when examined in terms of impacts for California (the state primarily driving initial EV production). If 1.2 million of the

Table 9.14 Statistics for Lead-Acid Vehicle Batteries

Current production rate	72M/year (1990)
Current recycling rate	80–97.8%
Number of batteries/EV	28–32
Weight of batteries/EV	870–1100 lbs
EV battery lifetime	2–3 years
CV battery lifetime	3–4 years
Weight of lead/battery	17.5–20 lbs
Weight of acid/battery	9–11 lbs
Weight of polypropylene/battery	1.6–3 lbs
Total weight of battery	28–34 lbs

Sources: See text for citations.

eight million cars on the road in California were replaced with EVs with 32 batteries each, 45.2 million batteries would be in use at one time. If EV batteries were replaced every two years and CV batteries every four, 20.9 million spent batteries would be generated each year (assuming a steady state). In contrast, two million would be generated if EVs were not introduced. In other words, in just 17 years, over ten times as many spent lead–acid batteries could be produced with the introduction of EVs.

It is most likely, of course, that EVs will have to adopt alternative battery technologies to become marketable, particularly because of the high cost of replacing the entire battery pack and the limited ranges lead–acid batteries can offer. One lead–acid battery manufacturer, for example, predicted that demand will increase just four-fold over the next twenty years (rather than by a factor of ten) by assuming that half of EVs in the year 2010 will use other types of batteries. Under this scenario, approximately 47 million spent batteries will be generated each year, in contrast to the 10 million per year generated today (see Figure 9.4). It also must be noted that alternatives to lead–acid batteries potentially will pose significant, although different, health and environmental risks as well (ICF, 1991). The main source of toxic cadmium in landfills, for example, is rechargeable batteries (Reinhardt et al., 1992).

In addition to lead and sulfuric acid, the manufacture of lead–acid bat-

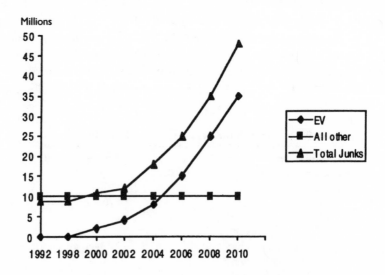

Figure 9.4 Spent batteries generated by California vehicles (GNB Incorporated).

teries involves the use of smaller amounts of other hazardous chemicals. These include organic solvents (in cooling towers and for cleaners); paints, enamels, and thinners; other acids; and metals such as antimony, arsenic, cadmium, copper, manganese, nickel, tin, and zinc to produce alloys for various applications. Fossil fuels that may contain impurities such as benzene, formaldehyde, and chlorine are also needed to melt lead and lead alloys for casting.

Figure 9.5 illustrates the recycling process for spent lead–acid batteries. Batteries are broken apart and the acid is allowed to drain. The acid from spent batteries is of low grade, and therefore is neutralized (rather than recovered) and discharged to wastewater treatment systems. Polypropylene battery cases are ground and recovered, and then sent to plastic recyclers who can reuse them to make new cases; polyethylene separators and other material become feed for the furnace. All lead scrap is melted, and slag, formed from lead sulfide in the furnace, must be disposed of as a hazardous waste. (The slag from primary smelters is exempt from RCRA regulations.) An average battery with 18 to 20 pounds of recyclable lead will produce roughly 2.2 pounds of silica-based slag that contains about 5 grams of lead. By weight, 98% of a spent battery can be recycled and only the equivalent of the lead in less than one battery is released to the environment from recycling facilities for every 24,000 recycled (EPRI; GNB Incorporated; Gruber, 1991; U.S. EPA, 1992).

The most obvious concerns with battery manufacturing and recycling are worker exposures to air emissions of lead particulates for which there are stringent occupational and environmental standards. Lead is a notorious toxin associated with a wide range of health impacts (see Chapter 10). Children and fetuses are especially susceptible to lead and no threshold is apparent for the neurobehavioral and developmental effects in children nor for cardiovascular effects in adults (ICF, 1991; Isherwood et al., 1988; U.S. EPA, 1991).

Lead bioaccumulates in the environment and chronic exposure may cause serious health effects at levels lower than those established for acute effects. The major pathways of exposure to lead are inhalation of particulates, and consumption of particles deposited on soil, vegetables, or in house dust. Workers in smelters and those who handle municipal solid waste (MSW) ash are at greatest risk of exposure in occupational settings. Leachate from landfills also may contain mobilized lead and has the potential to contaminate drinking water supplies. Of 786 National Priority List (Superfund) hazardous waste sites, 55 are listed with lead as a significant contaminant. It has also been estimated that 20% (120) of the companies or sites on the Superfund list in 1985 are former lead processing facilities

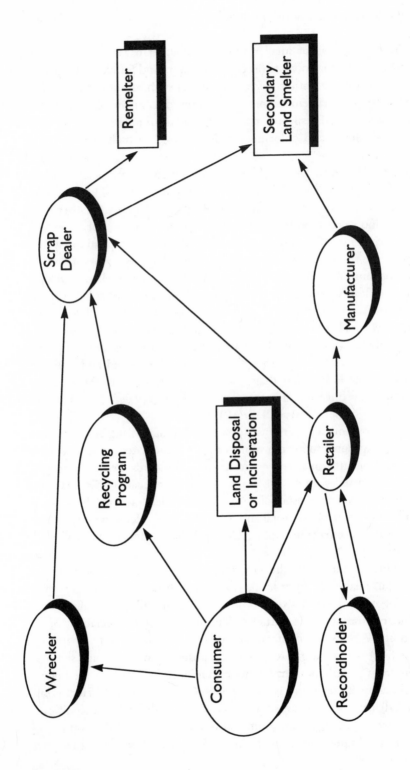

Figure 9.5 Simplified lead-acid battery recycling chain (U.S. EPA, 1992).

(battery breakers, secondary lead smelters, or scrap metal dealers) (Apotheker, 1990; U.S., EPA 1991).

EPA has developed emission factors for discharges of lead from primary and secondary smelters. Using the TRI data collected under SARA and by assuming a 95% recycling rate nationally, they calculated annual discharges of lead to the air, water, and land from primary and secondary smelters, and from MSW incinerators that receive unrecycled batteries. They also calculated the quantity of lead that ends up in MSW landfills. These estimates are summarized in Table 9.15.

EPA's emission factors and GNB's estimate that 47 million batteries will be generated each year to meet the 20% EV requirement can be used to estimate the additional lead that might be discharged from secondary smelters in California by the year 2010. If an average battery contains 18 pounds of lead and a 95% recycling rate is achieved, 72 tons of lead per year will be emitted into the air; 1,897 tons to land; and 2.2 tons to waterways. This is an increase over nationwide emissions from secondary smelters by 13% for air and 50% for land.

While lead is the most prominent concern in battery manufacturing, other pollutants may prove to be limiting factors to the expansion of production and recycling facilities. Air emissions of cadmium, for example, pose carcinogenic risks. Secondary smelters are also operating near capacity and some are unlikely to receive the necessary air emission permits for criteria pollutants (carbon dioxide and sulfur oxides) to build additional furnaces (A. Saldana, personal communication, 9/4/92).

The air emissions and hazardous wastes that would be generated by the year 2010 were extrapolated from the discharge data of one battery man-

Table 9.15 Lead to the Environment from Secondary Smelters

	Air Emissions (metric tons/year)	Land Discharges (metric tons/year)
Primary smelters	473	6,028
Secondary smelters	560	3,750
MSW incinerators	282	5,319
MSW landfills		76,618

Emission factors (in pounds per pound of lead produced) x 10,000:

	Air	Land	Water
Primary smelters	8.4	151.4	0.056
Secondary smelters	1.8	47.2	0.055

Source: U.S. Environmental Protection Agency, 1991.

ufacturing firm by assuming a linear relation between each pollutant and battery production. Annual emissions of various pollutants were divided by ranges of estimated battery production. These values were multiplied by the 47 million batteries expected to be consumed annually by the year 2010. The results of these calculations are summarized in Table 9.16. Table 9.17 contrasts the air emissions associated with manufacturing 32 batteries with the tailpipe emissions of a CV over a two year period (the assumed lifespan of EV batteries). While the increases in toxic lead and arsenic may pose significant local risks, the emissions of criteria pollutants from additional battery manufacturing are negligible in comparison with the reductions gained by replacing CVs with EVs.

Because huge numbers of spent lead–acid batteries most likely will be generated, it is imperative that an effective recycling system be established. Battery firms are exploring an electrolytic method of production (electrowinning) as a clean alternative, but the development of this process does not appear feasible in the near term without a sizeable public investment. Thirty four states have enacted battery recycling laws, and federal battery recycling legislation is being discussed as a means to stabilize the price of lead. Secondary smelters are especially susceptible to market fluctuations because, while they have to purchase scrap, primary smelters obtain it from ongoing, mixed metal mining operations. But even before it was mandatory, the rate of battery recycling was always 65% or higher. Secondary smelters were able to compete with primary smelters until they became subject to stringent hazardous waste regulations under RCRA, establishing economically unequal operating conditions (*Electrical Vehicle Progress,*

Table 9.16 **Increased Wasteloads from Battery Manufacturing Associated with EVs by 2010**

Air emissions (tons/year)	
Lead	6–10
Arsenic	.01
Methylene chloride	540–800
Organic gases	19–28
Nitrogen oxides	33–49
Sulfur oxides	0.1–0.2
Carbon monoxide	24–35
Particulates	1.4–2
Hazardous wastes	
Acid sludge/paste	94,000–141,000 gal/year
Epoxy resin/hardener	4,700–8,272 gal/year
Metal plating sludge	20,487–30,550 lbs/year

Table 9.17 EV Battery Manufacturing Emissions versus CV Tailpipe Emissions

	lb/EV (32 batteries)	CV (2 years)
Organic gases	.026–.038	105
NO_x	.045–.067	86
SO_x	$1.6–2.6 \times 10^{-4}$	4
CO	.032–.048	715
PM	$1.9–2.9 \times 10^{-3}$	11

Source: CV emissions, South Coast Air Quality Management District.

11/15/90; Motor Vehicle Manufacturers Association, 1992; Theodore Barry and Associates, 1989; U.S. EPA, 1992).

Air emissions are also probably going to be a limiting factor in expanding recycling facilities. The U.S. EPA's Office of Air Quality Planning and Standards is likely to lower the federal National Ambient Air Quality Standard for lead although most secondary lead smelters are not now in compliance with the current standard. A 1987 report prepared for the U.S. EPA found that roughly two thirds of the domestic secondary smelters operating in 1976 had closed by 1986 due to stringent environmental regulations and low lead prices. As a result, the national capacity for recycling lead dropped from 1.3 million metric tons in 1980 to 800,000 metric tons in 1986; it later rose to 930,000 metric tons in 1989, with the industry operating at 87% capacity (Battery Council International; Gruber, 1991; Smith & Daley, 1987; U.S. EPA, 1991).

Conclusion

Clearly, the largest barrier to completing a full analysis of complex products like EVs is the lack of data that reflect geographical variations and differences in specific manufacturing processes. Analogies to other industrial operations, however, can be drawn. And, although lifecycle analyses may raise more questions than they resolve, they can make assumptions explicit, illuminate surprises, and serve to identify during the planning process opportunities to improve production. Such an approach also may elucidate basic policy choices, and competing goals (such as health and economics) may become apparent when environmental analyses are incorporated into development decisions. A means to reduce occupational exposures and environmental emissions, for example, is to automate manufacturing processes. Automation, however, can reduce significantly the number of jobs that are created with new industries. For example, a Hughes facility automated their assembly of electronic components and decreased the number of employees they needed by a factor of at least forty (D. Hill, personal communication, 9/9/92).

As discussed earlier, a lifecycle analysis must be bounded in a way to limit data collection. Yet, these boundaries should not be so restrictive that the analysis no longer provides a full evaluation of the potential effects of all hazards in each environmental medium. It is also imperative that all potential impacts which might be imposed on various regions be identified. When analyses are bounded too narrowly, they fail to account for the fact that pollutants are transferred from one medium to another; that equally hazardous (but different) materials are substituted for others; that contamination might be diluted to minimize local effects but present worse regional problems; or that pollution simply is exported to other areas. Even once a lifecycle analysis is completed, defining a baseline for evaluating its results may not be a straightforward task and "better" choices should not be precluded. The conclusion that EVs are environmentally sound is based only on a comparison with CVs. Instead, EVs ought to be compared to other transportation and land use alternatives, a process never fully explored through the Clean Air Act.

Such a conclusion is also based on the assumptions that the tradeoff between smog and toxics such as lead is positive, and that our exclusive goal is to clean up the air in communities like Los Angeles. But the introduction of EVs, while lowering ozone levels in those communities, will cause dramatic increases in concentrations of lead and other heavy metals near battery manufacturers and secondary smelters. Whether this is an improvement depends on how such very different concerns are weighed. Further, batteries can be exported to other regions for recycling while most of the electricity used to recharge EVs may be generated elsewhere.

It is also important to note that the emissions of certain air pollutants from stationary sources may, in the aggregate, be greater than CV tailpipe emissions if coal is burned to produce electricity. It has been suggested that capturing the manufacturing of EVs in initial regional markets such as Southern California might be an important economic opportunity, given that other regions in the United States and other countries may provide sizeable markets in the future—indeed, EVs have been raced even around Katmandu (*Electrical Vehicle Progress*, 10/1/90)! Decisionmakers in these regions ought to consider their local circumstances, however, before policies to encourage EV use are adopted. The northeast United States and countries such as China, for example, rely primarily on coal for electricity, and increased power generation could lead to serious local and regional air quality problems (sulfates, particulates, acid rain) that might outweigh even the local benefits of EVs.

"Total" or Overall Impacts?

The results of a full lifecycle analysis are not unidimensional and should be presented in such a manner to preserve as much information as possible. With regard to the aggregation of environmental releases across media or chemicals, summing releases across different routes of exposure or different environmental media cannot be justified, as health and environmental impacts often vary with these factors. Summing effects experienced in different locales or different geographic regions also should not be done, as aggregate data will mask regional or site-specific variations in energy and material requirements, and in the types and magnitudes of hazard presented and pollution generated. And it clearly makes no sense to sum across potential impacts of different natures; risks of different types of health effects such as cancer and neurological damage, for example, clearly cannot be added, nor can such human health impacts be summed with ecological or other environmental consequences. Instead, the results of a lifecycle analysis might be presented in a multidimensional matrix, or as a collection of two-dimensional matrices cut along different axes. These two-dimensional matrices could describe the health and environmental impacts of concern along one axis, and each step in the lifecycle of one particular component in the final product along the other axis. Overlaying matrices for each component, and adding additional matrices for assembly and disassembly, would provide a third dimension to the results. Finally, the spatial distribution of each potential impact (by route of exposure and/or by region), or subdivisions within cells of the matrices, should be presented.

Although data are limited, the health and environmental impacts associated with the manufacture of EVs can be described qualitatively. It is apparent that overall, EVs can produce air quality benefits in a region like Southern California, given that most manufacturing, and certainly not the upstream processes (mining, primary smelting, chemical formulation), would not be undertaken in that region. EVs may, however, impose significant local environmental impacts, particularly in and near secondary lead smelters and battery manufacturers. Table 9.18 summarizes the major health and environmental impacts associated with the manufacturing processes described in the previous sections. These are ranked as negligible, low, moderate, and high in comparison to CVs (for operation) and other industrial processes in Table 9.19.

Table 9.18 Primary Health and Environmental Impacts Associated with EVs by Scale

	Individual (Occupational or Consumer)	Local and Regional	International/Global
Operation	Explosion hazards during battery recharging	Air pollution from power sources; spent batteries (air, water, and land pollution)	Acid rain, greenhouse gases from power generation; use of nonrenewable fuels
Aluminum Substitution	Mining hazards; smelter workers exposed to toxics; metal working risks	Hazardous mining wastes; air, water, and land discharges from smelting and component manufacturing	Significant energy consumption and associated pollution; transportation risks with Al importation
Plastic Substitutions	Exposures to hazardous organics	Nonrecyclable plastics to solid wastestream; air and land discharges of hazardous organics	Energy consumption and associated pollution; petroleum use

Electric Motors	Metal working risks; exposures to toxic metals and organics	Waste oils, etc.; air emissions of solvents and painting materials; wastewater discharges of metals and solvents	Emissions of stratospheric ozone depleters
Electronics	Worker exposures to reproductive toxins, carcinogens, and other hazardous chemicals	Air, water, and land discharges of toxic metals, solvents, acids, and alkalis; VOCs contribute to smog formations	
Lead-acid Batteries	Extremely high exposures of lead to workers	Extremely high local lead emissions; lead-bearing hazardous wastes; acid wastewaters; toxic metals and organics to air, water, and land; criteria air pollutants and air toxics from fuel burning	

Table 9.19 Ranking of Health and Environmental Consequences of EVs

	Consumer/ Occupational	Local	Regional	International/Global
Operation (battery recharging)	negligible	low/mod (depending on fuel mix and source)	low/mod (depending on fuel mix and source)	low/mod (assuming an average fuel mix)
Aluminum Substitutions				
Extraction/smelting	high	high	high	moderate
Metal work	low	low	low	negligible
Paint/lacquer	moderate	moderate	low	negligible
Plastic Substitutions				
Formulation	moderate	moderate	moderate	mod/low
Molding	moderate	moderate	low	negligible
Assembly	moderate	low	low	negligible
Electric Motors				
Metalwork	low	low	low	negligible
Paint/lacquer	moderate	moderate	low	negligible
Electronics	mod/high	mod/high	moderate	mod/low
Lead-acid Batteries (mfg/recycling)	high	high	moderate	low

Opportunities for Clean Manufacturing

The final component of a full lifecycle analysis is an improvement analysis, or an "...evaluation of the needs and opportunities to reduce the environmental burden associated with energy and raw materials use and environmental releases throughout the entire lifecycle of the product, process, or activity" (Fava et al., 1991, xviii). Once capital expenditures have been made, firms often are more resistant to changing their operations. The performance of a lifecycle analysis early in the planning stages of a developing industry, however, enables "clean" technologies to be incorporated into the design of manufacturing processes. In sum, strategies to reduce or minimize the environmental impacts of manufacturing EVs ought to be encouraged (or required) as the industry develops. All production processes should be reviewed to reduce the use of toxic or hazardous chemicals wherever possible.

In addition to introducing "clean" manufacturing techniques, it is important that opportunities to minimize the environmental impacts posed in other stages in the EV lifecycle also be identified and promoted. To minimize solid waste impacts and materials and/or energy use, for example, the potential for reuse and recycling needs to be considered in the design of EVs. Currently in the United States, an estimated $15 billion a year is saved by the recycling of used automotive parts compared with the cost of manufacturing new parts (Environmental Vehicles Review, 1991a). While one optimistic source reports that EVs may be up to 85% recyclable (Environmental Vehicles Review, 1991b), choices of materials for various components in EVs and the ease of disassembly will determine whether they can be recycled economically.

Automobile manufacturers in Europe have taken a lead in recycling that might provide valuable lessons for the United States. BMW (among others) established a pilot facility at their Landshut, Germany factory in June 1990 to improve methods and minimize the time and cost of disassembling old BMWs. They also are working to redesign BMWs so that they are more recyclable by making them easier to disassemble and by not manufacturing parts of mixed materials (e.g., plastics and metals). A Volkswagen "laboratory" in Leer, Germany has been successful in removing metals from bumpers and then grinding the plastic into pellets which are mixed with fresh resin to form new bumpers. Since May 1991, about 20% of the material in new bumpers came from old ones. The main limitation to this recycling has been the lack of a steady stream of scrap materials due, in part, to the fact that not all bumpers are made of the same materials. To ease the separation of plastics, Volkswagen is redesigning their cars so that

they will use fewer different plastics. The plastic tank in the VW Golf that
went into production in summer 1991, for example, has 11 fewer parts
than the previous design (BMW AG, 1991; Corcoran, 1992; Motor Vehicle
Manufacturers Association, 1992).

German manufacturers also are stamping government standardized
codes that identify different materials. Yet, these efforts still address only 30
to 40% of the thermoplastics typically found in cars. In the United States,
the Society for Automotive Engineers has issued a standard for labeling
various plastics used in cars. Automakers' recycling codes are different than
those for household plastics, however, and different collection systems are
needed. In addition, markets for postconsumer plastic auto scrap do not
exist currently (Corcoran, 1992; Wolfson, 1992).

Laws have been proposed in Europe that would make the complete
recycling of automobiles the responsibility of the manufacturers. Germany,
for example, is proposing to require auto manufacturers to take back cars
free of charge. Sweden charges a "scrapping premium" to help recycle cars,
and requires owners to prove they have responsibly disposed of a car before
it is removed from the tax rolls (Jones, 1992; Parker, 1992; Wolfson, 1992)

The Driving Force? Environment and/or Development

This chapter examined the potential health and environmental effects associated with the manufacture of EVs. During the course of research, however, a larger question has quickly emerged: namely, will industrial development initiatives like the current effort to promote EV manufacturing
determine the quality of the environment in specific regions or will environmental regulations ultimately shape the economic base of these
regions?

In terms of the battery issues alone, the capacity to manage the anticipated volume of lead-acid batteries that will accompany the introduction
of EVs just into the California automotive market does not exist currently.
Yet, battery manufacturers do not anticipate they will be granted air permits to expand their processes. It remains to be seen whether regional or
state officials will discover an environmentally sound means to manage the
spent batteries that will be collected once EVs are on the road. It is also
not clear which regions will ultimately bear the health and environmental
costs associated with EV manufacturing, nor where the economic benefits
of EV production will be captured. As the EV industry develops and policies to promote the use of EVs are debated, the lifecycle framework proposed here should be continually revisited, reworking assumptions upon
which a full assessment might be based. Beyond the specific comparison of

EVs to convention fuel vehicles, for which lifecycle analysis can appropriately be applied, also reside the larger questions of transportation planning and the crucial industrial and environmental issues associated with it. EVs, widely touted as the "no emissions" environmental technology of the future (EPRI, 1993), ultimately provide a mixed lesson for those seeking a place for "clean technology" as the building block for regional, national, and global economies. Clean yet dirty, creating winners and losers in their environmental impacts, EVs can be evaluated along a continuum of efforts to establish a different kind of framework for the introduction of new technologies.

References

The Advanced Lead-Acid Battery Consortium, International Lead Zinc Research Organization, Inc. (Research Triangle Park, NC), 1992. "Development of Rapid Charging Devices and Monitoring and Control Equipment for Electric Vehicles," a proposal submitted to the Federal Transit Administration, U.S. Department of Transportation. May 26, 1992.

Agarwal, J.C., 1991. "Minerals, Energy, and the Environment," in Jefferson W. Tester, David O. Wood, & Nancy A. Ferrari (eds.), *Energy and the Environment in the 21st Century,* MIT Press, pp. 389–395.

The Aluminum Association, 1991. Committee on Fuel Economy of Automobiles and Light Trucks, Report to the National Academy of Sciences.

The Aluminum Association (Washington, D.C.), 1992. Aluminum Statistical Review for 1991.

The Aluminum Association, The Story and Uses of Aluminum.

Apotheker, Steve, 1990. "Does battery recycling need a jump?," *Resource Recycling.* February 1990. pp. 21–23, and 91.

Atkins, Patrick R., Herman J. Hittner & Don Willoughby, 1991. "Some Energy and Environmental Impacts of Aluminum Usage," in Jefferson W. Tester, David O. Wood & Nancy A. Ferrari (eds.), *Energy and the Environment in the 21st Century,* MIT Press. pp. 383–387.

Automotive Dismantlers & Recyclers Association, "Facts About the Automotive Recycling Industry."

Automotive Engineering, 1990a. "Transportation Fuels and the Environment," Vol. 99, No. 1. January 1990. pp. 27–29.

Automotive Engineering, 1990b. "Selection of body panel materials," Vol. 98, No. 5. May 1990. pp. 55–60.

320   J. Roque

Automotive Engineering, 1991. "Plastics Recycling: Status," Vol. 99, No. 5. May 1991. pp. 21–25.

Automotive Engineering, 1992. "Battery and Electric Vehicle Update." September 1992. pp. 17–25.

Bates, Bradford (ed.), 1992. *Electric Vehicles: A Decade of Transition*, SAE International, Inc. (Warrendate, PA).

Batteries International, 1990. "Recycling Batteries: the EC Takes Action." December 1990.

Battery Council International (Chicago). *The Consumer's Guide to Lead Battery Recycling* (brochure).

Bevilacqua-Knight, Inc. (Oakland, CA), 1992. *1992 Electric Vehicle Technology and Emissions Update*, prepared for the California Air Resources Board.

Biviano, Marilyn & Judith Owens. *The Minerals Related Implications of a Direct Tax on U.S. Primary Lead Production and Primary Lead Imports*, U.S. Department of the Interior, Bureau of Mines.

Blelloch, R. Andrew (ed.), 1978. *Measurements of the Impacts of Materials Substitution—A Case Study in the Automobile Industry*, proceedings of the Winter Annual Meeting of the American Society of Mechanical Engineers, San Francisco, California, December 10–15, 1977. ASME (New York).

Blelloch, R. Andrew (ed.), 1984. *The Impacts of Material Substitution on the Recyclability of Automobiles*, American Society of Mechanical Engineers.

Bleviss, Deborah L., 1989. "The Role of Energy Efficiency in Making the Transition to Nonpetroleum Transportation Fuels," Chapter 18 in Daniel Sperling (ed.), *Alternative Transportation Fuels: An Environmental and Energy Solution*, Quorum Books (NY).

BMW AG, 1991. *Current Factbook: Recycling.*

CARB, 1990a. California Air Resources Board, *Proposed Regulations for Low-Emission Vehicles and Clean Fuels: Staff Report*. August 13, 1990.

CARB, 1990b. California Air Resources Board, *Proposed Regulations for Low-Emission Vehicles and Clean Fuels: Technical Support Document*. August 13, 1990.

CARB, 1991. California Air Resources Board, *Clean Fuels Regulations* (Amendments to the California Code of Regulations, Title 13). Adopted July 12, 1991.

CA DHS, 1987a. California Department of Health Services, Toxic Substances Control Division, Alternative Technology & Policy Development Section, *The Reduction of Arsenic Wastes in the Electronics*

Industry, prepared by Envirosphere Company and Hewlett-Packard Company. June 1987.

CA DHS, 1987b. California Department of Health Services, Toxic Substances Control Division, Alternative Technology, *Waste Reduction Strategies for the Printed Circuit Board Industry,* prepared by Cal-Tech Management Associates. October 1987.

CA DHS, 1988. California Department of Health Services, Toxic Substances Control Division, Alternative Technology & Policy Development Section, *The Reduction of Solvent Wastes in the Electronics Industry,* prepared by Envirosphere Company and Hewlett-Packard Company. June 1988.

CA DHS, 1989. California Department of Health Services, Toxic Substances Control Division, Alternative Technology Section, *Waste Audit Study: Fiberglass—Reinforced and Composite Plastic Products,* prepared by Woodward-Clyde Consultants (Oakland, CA). April 1989.

CA DHS, 1991a. California Department of Health Services, Toxic Substances Control Program, Alternative Technology Division, *Fact Sheet: Printed Circuit Board Manufacturers.* February 1991.

CA, DHS 1991b. California Department of Health Services, Toxic Substances Control Program, Alternative Technology Division, Technology Clearinghouse Unit, *Hazardous Waste Reduction Checklist & Assessment Manual for Printed Circuit Board Manufacturers.* May 1991.

California Electric Vehicle Task Force, 1989. *A California Plan for the Commercialization of Electric Vehicles.* November 3, 1989.

California Administrative Health & Safety Code, Ch. 209, Sec. 25215. *Management of Lead-Acid Batteries.*

California Senate Office of Research, 1991. *Reducing Automobile Pollution.*

Cone, Marla, 1992. "GM and the Juicemobile," *Los Angeles Times Magazine.* June 21, 1992. pp. 8–12, and 34.

Corcoran, Elizabeth, 1992. "Green Machine: Volkswagen gears up to recycle autos," *Scientific American,* January 1992. pp. 140–141.

DeLuchi, Mark, Quanlu Wang & Daniel Sperling, 1989. "Electric Vehicles: Performance, Life Cycle Costs, Emissions, and Recharging Requirements," *Transportation Research,* Vol. 23A, No. 3.

DeLuchi, M.A., 1991. *Emissions of Greenhouse Gases from the Use of Transportation Fuels and Electricity,* prepared for the U.S. Department of Energy. November 1991.

Dowlatabadi, Hadi, Alan J. Krupnick & Armistead Russell, 1990. *Electric Vehicles and the Environment: Consequences for Emissions and Air Quality in Los Angeles and U.S. Regions,* Resources for the Future (Washington, D.C.).

Dunne, Jim, 1992. "The Alternative Fuel Report: GM's Electric Car & Dodge's CNG Fueled Van," *Popular Mechanics.* October 1992.

EPRI 1989. Electric Power Research Institute, "Electric Van and Gasoline Van Emissions: A Comparison," *Technical Brief.*

EPRI, 1993. Electric Power Research Institute (Palo Alto, CA), *Electric Vehicles and the Environment* (brochure).

Electric Vehicle Progress (newsletter), 1993. Alexander Research & Communications, Inc. (New York).

Environmental Vehicles Review, 1991a. "Recycling Cars," Vol. 11, Issue 10. October 1991. p. 2.

Environmental Vehicles Review, 1991b. "Recycling II: Assessing the Potential,"Vol. 11, Issue 11. November 1991. p. 2.

Erlhoff, Michael, 1990. "Design and Ecology: A Marriage for Our Future," *Innovation,* Industrial Designers Society of America (Great Falls, VA). Summer 1990. pp. 6–8.

Farrissey, William J., 1991. *RIM Parts for Automobiles—Life Cycle Energy and Ecobalance in Designing for Recyclability and Reuse of Automotive Plastics* (SP-867). Society of Automotive Engineers, Inc. (Warrendale, PA). pp. 1–8.

Fava, James A., Richard Denison, Bruce Jones, Mary Ann Curran, Bruce Vigon, Susan Selke, & James Barnum (eds.), 1991. *A Technical Framework For Life-Cycle Assessments* (Workshop Report). Society of Environmental Toxicology and Chemistry.

Finson, Rachel, Veronica Kun & Chris Caldwell (NRDC, Los Angeles), 1992. "Comments of the Natural Resources Defense Council Concerning the Environmental Impacts of Electric Vehicles in Southern California," at the Electric Vehicle Forum, March 5–6, 1992.

Fischetti, Mark, 1992. "Here comes the electric car—it's sporty, agressive and clean," *Smithsonian.* April 1992. pp. 34–43.

Forcucci, Francesco & David Tompkins, 1991. "Automotive Interiors—Design for Recyclability," in *Designing for Recyclability and Reuse of Automotive Plastics* (SP-867). Society of Automotive Engineers, Inc. (Warrendale, PA). pp. 41–46.

Ford, Andrew (USC Institute of Safety and Systems Management), 1992. "The Impact of Electric Vehicles on the Southern California Edison System," report to the California Institute for Energy Efficiency, Lawrence Berkeley Laboratory.

Gavert, R.B., 1978. "The Resources to Meet the Needs of the Automobile Industry in 1985," in Andrew Blelloch (ed.), *Measurements of the Impacts of Materials Substitution—A Case Study in the Automobile Industry.*

Gay, E.C., C.E. Webster, F. Hornstra, N.P. Yao, D.O. Corp & E.R. Hayes, 1992. "Testing and Evaluation of EV-1300 Lead-Acid Modules for the Hybrid Vehicle Application," in Bradford Bates (ed.), *Electric Vehicles: A Decade of Transition*. SAE International, Inc.

GNB Incorporated. *Seizing the Environmental Initiative* (brochure).

GNB Incorporated, 1992. "Questions and Answers: Battery Recycling." September 18, 1992.

Gordon, Deborah (Union of Concerned Scientists), 1991. *Steering a New Course: Transportation, Energy, and the Environment*, Island Press (Washington, D.C.).

Gruber, William, 1991. "Lead-Acid Battery Recycling: Mandating Recycling in a Market-Driven Industry, *EI Digest*. January 1991. pp. 18–27.

Hardin, Charles, 1992. "Designing for Disassembly," *Automotive Recycling*, Vol. 12, No. 3. May/June 1992. pp. 18–20.

Hartt, George N. & Daniel P. Carey (SMC Automotive Alliance), 1992. "Economics of Recycling Thermosets," SAE Technical Paper Series, Society of Automotive Engineers.

Herridge, J.T. & R.W. Hale, 1978. "Energy Requirement for the Material Needs of the Automobile Industry in 1985," in Andrew Blelloch (ed.), *Measurements of the Impacts of Materials Substitution—A Case Study in the Automobile Industry*.

Hoechst Celanese, 1992. Advanced Materials Group (Chatham, NJ), "Designing With Plastic," *Design Manual* (TDM-1).

ICF Incorporated, 1991. *Methodology For Analyzing the Environmental and Economic Effects of Electric Vehicles: An Illustrative Study*, prepared for the U.S. Environmental Protection Agency, Office of Mobile Sources, Emission Control Technology Division.

Institute of Scrap Recycling Industries, Inc. (Washington, D.C.). "Recycling Scrap Materials Contributes To A Better Environment."

Isherwood, Raymond J., R. Craig Smith, Orville A. Kiehn & Michael R. Daley, 1988. *The Impact of Existing and Proposed Regulations Upon the Domestic Lead Industry*, U.S. Department of the Interior, Bureau of Mines. August 1988.

Jones, Tamara, 1992. "Is Your Car a Wreck? It Could Be Time to Reincarnate It," *Los Angeles Times*. September 1992.

Kafka, Alan S. (Manager, Base Metal Sales, ASARCO, Inc.), 1990. "Remarks," to the Fourth International Lead Zinc Research Organization Lead-Acid Battery Seminar (San Francisco). April 25, 1990.

Kirk-Othmer, "Aluminum and Aluminum Alloys," in *Encyclopedia of*

Chemical Technology, Volume 2, Third Edition, John Wiley & Sons (New York). pp. 129-188, 1979.

Kirk-Othmer, "Batteries, Secondary Cells, Lead-Acid," in *Encyclopedia of Chemical Technology,* Volume 3, Third Edition, John Wiley & Sons (New York). pp. 640-663, 1980.

Lead Industries Association, Inc. (New York), 1990. "Safety in Soldering."

Lloyd, Alan C., & Jon Leonard (South Coast Air Quality Management District), 1992. "The Role of Battery- and Fuel Cell-Powered Electric Vehicles in Air Quality Planning." Paper presented at the Transportation Research Board 71st Annual Meeting (Washington, D.C.). January 12–16, 1992.

Lloyd, Alan C., Paul Wuebben & Jon Leonard (South Coast Air Quality Management District), 1991. "Electric Vehicles and Future Air Quality in the Los Angeles Basin, Air Pollution Control (Equipment, Inspection, Maintenance, and Fuels), *Proceedings of the 84th Annual Meeting & Exhibition of the Air & Waste Management Association,* Volume 9b. June 16–21, 1991.

LA DWP. Los Angeles Department of Water & Power, *Going Electric* (brochure).

Mader, Gerald H. (Electric Vehicle Development Corporation, Cupertino, CA), 1991. "The Early 1990's: Laying the Foundation for Commercializing Electric Vehicles," Air Pollution Control (Equipment, Inspection, Maintenance, and Fuels), Volume 9b, *Proceedings of the 84th Annual Meeting & Exhibition of the Air & Waste Management Association.* June 16–21, 1991.

McCawley, Frank X. & Luke Baumgardner, 1985. "Aluminum," preprint from U.S. Department of the Interior, Bureau of Mines, Mineral Facts and Problems, Bulletin 675.

Motor Vehicle Manufacturers Association, 1992. *Post-Consumer Vehicle Recycling,* prepared by Phillip Townsend Associates, Inc. October 21, 1992.

Niemczewski, Christopher M., 1984. "The Changing Material Content of Automobiles," Chapter 1 in R. Andrew Blelloch (ed.), *The Impacts of Material Substitution on the Recyclability of Automobiles.*

O'Connell, Lawrence G. (Electric Power Research Institute), 1990. "Building an Electric Vehicle Future," in *Proceedings, 82nd A&WMA Annual Meeting, Air & Waste Management Association.* June 25–30, 1990.

Parker, David N., 1992. "Recycling push could mean more aluminum in cars," in "Automotive Aluminum," Supplement to the American Metal Market. September 10, 1992. p. 10A.

Peters, Anthony T., 1992. *Iron and Steel: Annual Report 1990*, U.S. Department of the Interior, Bureau of Mines.

Plunkert, Patricia A. & Errol D. Sehnke, 1992. *Aluminum, Bauxite, and Alumina:Annual Report 1990*, U.S. Department of the Interior, Bureau of Mines.

Purcell, A.H., 1978. "Materials Substitution in the Automotive Industry: Environmental Impacts," in Andrew Blelloch (ed.), *Measurements of the Impacts of Materials Substitution—A Case Study in the Automobile Industry*.

Radian Corporation (Research Triangle Park, NC), 1990. *Locating and Estimating Air Emissions From Sources of Styrene* (draft), prepared for the U.S. Environmental Protection Agency, Noncriteria Pollutant Programs Branch (Research Triangle Park).

Reinhardt, Andy, Ed Perratore, Andy Redfern & Rich Malloy, 1992. "The Greening of Computers," *Byte*, September 1992. pp. 147–158.

Reuland Electric Company, *Facility Emission Reports*, submitted to the South Coast Air Quality Management District, and *Hazardous Material Inventory*, submitted to the Los Angeles County Fire Department.

Reynolds, Kim, 1992. "AC Propulsion CRX: Harbinger of Things Electric," *Road & Track.* October 1992. pp. 126–129.

Schottman, Frederick J., 1985. "Iron and Steel," in *Mineral Facts and Problems, 1985 Edition*, U.S. Department of the Interior, Bureau of Mines. pp. 405–424.

Silicon Valley Toxics Coalition, 1992. "Celebrating a Decade of Progress" (announcement).

Singh, M.K., M.J. Bernard III, W.J. Walsh, R.F. Giese, J.R. Gasper & C.L. Saricks (Energy & Environmental Systems Division, Center for Transportation Research, Argonne National Laboratory), 1980. *Environmental Assessment of the U.S. Department of Energy Electric and Hybrid Vehicle Program*, prepared for the U.S. Department of Energy.

SMC Automotive Alliance, 1992. *Recycling of SMC—The Energy/ Environment Picture*, The Composites Institute of the Society of the Plastics Industry, Inc. (New York).

Smith, Bucklin & Associates, Inc. (Chicago), 1992. *1990 National Recycling Rate Study*, prepared for the Battery Council International (Chicago). May 1992.

Smith, R. Craig & Michael R. Daley, 1987. *Domestic Secondary Lead Industry: Production and Regulatory Compliance Costs*, U.S. Department of the Interior, Bureau of Mines.

SRRP, 1991a. Source Reduction Research Partnership (Metropolitan

Water District of Southern California & Environmental Defense
Fund), *Adhesives Manufacture: Source Reduction of Chlorinated Solvents*
(draft), prepared for the California Department of Health Services,
Toxic Substances Control Program, and the U.S. Environmental
Protection Agency, Office of Research and Development.

SRRP, 1991b. Source Reduction Research Partnership, *Electronic Products
Manufacture: Source Reduction of Chlorinated Solvents* (draft), prepared for
the California Department of Health Services and the U.S.
Environmental Protection Agency.

SRRP, 1991c. Source Reduction Research Partnership, *Solvent Cleaning:
Source Reduction of Chlorinated Solvents* (draft), prepared for the
California Department of Health Services and the U.S.
Environmental Protection Agency.

SCAQMD, 1991. South Coast Air Quality Management District & the
Southern California Association of Governments, *1991 Air Quality
Management Plan.*

SCE, 1991. Southern California Edison, *Electric Transportation.*

Sperling, Daniel, 1991. "The Future of the Car in an Environmentally
Constrained World," *Financial Times Conferences.* 11 & 12 September
1991. pp. 18.1–18.6.

Sperling, Daniel, Mark A. DeLuchi & Quanlu Wang, 1991. *Toward
Alternative Transportation Fuels and Incentive-Based Regulation of Vehicle
Fuels and Emissions,* California Policy Seminar Research Report,
University of California.

Theodore Barry & Associates (Los Angeles), 1989. *Electric Vehicle Battery
Pack Recycling and Disposal in Southern California,* A Study Performed
for Southern California Edison. December 1989.

Toensmeier, Patrick A., 1989. "Electric cars stage a comeback; lightweight-
ing makes them practical," *Modern Plastics.* September 1989. pp. 44–45.

Trojan Battery Company, (Santa Fe Springs, CA). Emission inventories,
hazardous waste permit applications, miscellaneous correspondence,
etc., submitted to the South Coast Air Quality Management District,
the U.S. Environmental Protection Agency and the California
Department of Toxic Substances.

Trojan Battery Company, 1984. "Hazardous Waste Personnel Training
Program and Hazardous Waste Emergency Plan," prepared by Francais
Engineering Corp. (Cypress, CA). June 1984.

U.S. DHHS, 1990. U.S. Department of Health & Human Services, U.S.
Public Health Service, Agency for Toxic Substances & Disease
Registry, *Toxicological Profile for Lead.*

U.S. DOI, 1988. U.S. Department of the Interior, Bureau of Mines,

Minerals Yearbook, 1986, Volume I: Metals and Minerals, U.S. Government Printing Office (Washington, D.C.).

U.S. DOI, 1992. U.S. Department of the Interior, Bureau of Mines, *Mineral Industry Surveys: Lead Monthly.* June 1992.

U.S. EPA, 1986. U.S. Environmental Protection Agency, Office of Research & Development, and Environmental Criteria & Assessment Office, *Addendum to Air Quality Standards Criteria for Lead.* September 1986.

U.S. EPA, 1990. U.S. Environmental Protection Agency, Office of Research & Development, and Environmental Criteria & Assessment Office, *Air Quality Standards Criteria for Lead.* August 1990.

U.S. EPA, 1991. U.S. Environmental Protection Agency, Office of Toxic Substances, *Lead Acid Battery Recycling Risk Assessment* (draft). September 1991.

U.S. EPA, 1992. U.S. Environmental Protection Agency, Office of Solid Waste & Emergency Response, and the Office of Policy, Planning and Evaluation, *States' Efforts to Promote Lead-Acid Battery Recycling.* January 1992.

Wang, Quanlu & Mark DeLuchi, 1992. "Impacts of Electric Vehicles on Primary Energy Consumption and Petroleum Displacement," *Energy,* Vol. 17, No. 4. pp. 351–366.

Wang, Quanlu, Mark DeLuchi & Daniel Sperling, 1990. "Emission Impacts of Electric Vehicles," *Journal of the Waste Management Association,* Vol. 40, No. 9. September 1990. pp. 1275–82.

Weber, Jonathan & Denise Gellene, 1992. "Job Hazards and Pregnant Women," *Los Angeles Times.* 5 December 1992. pp. D1 & 3.

Whitehead, Michael L., 1992. "A High Energy Tabular Battery for a 1800 kg Payload Electric Delivery Van," in Bradford Bates (ed.), *Electric Vehicles: A Decade of Transition.* SAE International, Inc.

Winfield, Barry, 1992. "Automotive plastics are tough and long lasting. That's the bad news, too," *Automobile Magazine.* September 1992.

Wojton, Donald A. (Battery Council International, & East Penn Manufacturing Co., Inc.), 1990. "Lead-Acid Battery Recycling," presented at the International Lead Zinc Research Organization, Inc. Fourth International Lead-Acid Battery Seminar (San Francisco). April 27, 1990.

Wolfson, Elissa (ed.), 1992. "Dawn of the Enviro-Mobile" (Currents), *E-Magazine.* May/June 1992. pp. 16–18.

Woodbury, William D., 1985. "Lead," preprint from U.S. Department of the Interior, Bureau of Mines, Mineral Facts and Problems, Bulletin 675.

Woodbury, William D., 1992. *Lead: Annual Report 1990,* U.S. Department of the Interior, Bureau of Mines.

Wuebben, Paul, Alan C. Lloyd & Jonathan H. Leonard (South Coast Air Quality Management District), 1990. *The Future of Electric Vehicles in Meeting the Air Quality Challenges in Southern California,* SAE Technical Paper Series, SAE publication #SP-817.

Contacts

The Aluminum Association
900 19th Street, N.W.
Washington, D.C. 20006
202/862-5100

Aluminum Recycling Association
1000 16th Street, N.W.
Washington, D.C. 20036

Richard C. Bower, Vice President, Marketing and Sales
Trojan Battery Company
12380 Clark Street
Santa Fe Springs, CA 90670
310/946-8381; 714/521-8215; 800/423-6569

Alan Cocconi
AC Propulsion, Inc.
462 Borrego Ct., Unit B
San Dimas, CA 91773
818/914-4415

Kyle Davis
Planning & Technology Advancement
South Coast Air Quality Management District
21865 East Copley Drive
Diamond Bar, CA 91765-4182
714/396-3258

Thomas Doughty, Director
Electric Vehicle Program
Department of Water and Power
City of Los Angeles
111 N. Hope Street, Room 1129
Los Angeles, CA 90012-2694
 213/481-4725

Electric Power Research Institute (EPRI)
3412 Hillview Avenue, P.O. Box 10412
Palo Alto, CA 94303
 415/855-2411

Bob Garino
Institute of Scrap Recycling Industries, Inc.
1325 G Street, N.W.
Washington, D.C. 20005
 202/466-4050

Daniel D. Hill, Project Manager
Hughes, Advanced Programs, Commercial Programs Division
Bldg. 237, MS 1524
P.O. Box 2923
Torrance, CA 90509-2923
 310/517-5858

Bill Huff
Reuland Electric
City of Industry, CA

Susan V. Huscroft, Chief
California Environmental Protection Agency
Air Resources Board, Mobile Source Division
On-Road Controls Branch
2020 L Street, P.O. Box 2815
Sacramento, CA 95812
 916/323-6169

Lead Industries Association, Inc.
295 Madison Avenue
New York, NY 10017
212/578-4750; 800/922-LEAD

Charles N. Pavia, Director of Marketing
Trojan Battery Company
12380 Clark Street
Santa Fe Springs, CA 90670
213/946-8381; 714/521-8215; 800/423-6569.

Carol Precobb, Manager
Electric Transportation Information Center
501 Fourteenth Street, Suite 210
Oakland, CA 94612
800/848-ETIC

Kristin Reade
Automotive Dismantlers & Recyclers Association
3975 Fair Ridge Drive, Suite 20
Terrace Level, North
Fairfax, VA 22033-2906
703/385-1001

Anthony C. Saldana, Director
Resource Recycling Division
GNB Incorporated
2700 Indiana Street
Los Angeles, CA 90023
213/262-1101

Silicon Valley Toxics Coalition
277 W. Hedding St., #204
San Jose, CA 95110
408/287-6707

Society of Automotive Engineers, Inc.
400 Commonwealth Drive
Warrendale, PA 15096-0001
412/772-7103

Society of the Plastics Industry, Inc.
355 Lexington Avenue
New York, NY 10017
212/351-5413

Nancy Steele, Hazardous Materials Specialist
California Environmental Protection Agency
Department of Toxic Substances
Region 3/Facility Management Branch
1405 N. San Fernando Boulevard, Suite 300
Burbank, CA 91504
818/567-3020

William D. Woodbury
U.S. Department of the Interior, Bureau of Mines
Division of Mineral Commodities, The Branch of Metals
810 Seventh Street, N.W.
Washington, D.C. 20241
202/501-9444

Christy R. Zidonis, P.E.
Engineer of Electric Transportation
Department of Water and Power, City of Los Angeles
Conservation and Planning Division
111 North Hope Street, Room 1141
Los Angeles, CA 90012-2694
213/481-5085

10

Substituting for Lead:
The Radiator Repair Industry

Tamira Cohen
Rania Sabty
John Froines

Resisting Change

Pollution prevention is often assumed to require a certain scale of production for its successful implementation, particularly in terms of "downstream" service industries, dependent on their "upstream" suppliers. In some cases, alternatives may be available to substitute for hazardous substances that impact downstream users, but replacement is frequently hindered by the resistance or inertia of such industries. The radiator repair industry, as an example of this type of resistance, has only minimally addressed lead-related occupational health issues, despite the presence of lead-free substitutes. The structure and dynamics of this industry, in addition to its dependence upon the larger, upstream radiator industry, has inhibited the effective implementation of specific pollution prevention strategies that might be immediately available.

The U.S. radiator repair industry consists of many small businesses distributed nationwide. The primary role of these radiator repair businesses, as their name suggests, is the repair of radiators (usually automotive) in order to extend their lifespans. This industry provides an interesting case study for pollution prevention for three compelling reasons: the clear nature of the hazard (occupational exposure to lead); the dynamics associated with a small, downstream-dependent service business; and the ready availability of alternatives that are capable of shifting the industry emphasis from control to prevention.

Occupational lead ailments have been recognized since the third or fourth century B.C. and have markedly increased over the last 250 years with the growth of lead consumption (Matte *et al.*, 1992). Lead, an ancient metal, has become one of the most useful metals in the industrialized world due to its many favorable properties. One of its many industrial uses, extensively utilized in the radiator manufacturing and repair industries, is in solder. The presence of lead solder in radiator repair has resulted in high levels of occupational lead exposure. Excessive blood lead levels and exposure-related lead toxicity have been identified in workers in the radiator repair industry. Airborne concentrations of lead above mandated levels in radiator repair shops has caused state health agencies to identify this industry as high-risk (Sheehy and Hall, 1991; Cooper et al., 1991).

Overall, the radiator repair industry is located nationwide, comprising primarily businesses employing small numbers of employees. It has been estimated that 88% of radiator repair workers are employed in shops with fewer than twenty employees (Rudolph et al., 1990). The industry comprises a medium-sized workforce of approximately 40,000 nationally and 5,300 in the state of California, which represents the largest statewide concentration of such businesses (Juchno, 1992; American Business Lists, 1992; Sheehy and Hall, 1991). Protection of workers in small businesses, as with other small business activities, is often overlooked by government regulatory agencies whose enforcement programs emphasize mid-size to large companies.

Highlighting this case study are the presence of well-defined functional alternatives available for the radiator repair industry. Substitutes with less toxic materials are already known to exist and, in some instances, are being used on a limited scale. The challenge presented to policymakers is not how to press for the creation of a pollution prevention strategy, but rather how to guide an economically sensitive industry, traditionally resistant to change, toward the use of less toxic substances that are immediately available.

This chapter broadly addresses the issue of the use of lead-based substances in radiator repair. The upstream radiator industry is crucial to illuminate the role and position of downstream radiator repair shops. The four main types of radiator and the radiator repair process will be described to identify the sources of occupational lead hazards. The resulting health problems will be examined through a discussion of lead toxicity and occupational exposures to lead followed by a discussion of the Occupational Safety and Health Administration's (OSHA) Lead Standard, the specific lead legislation directed at the protection of workers. The available control strategies for lead exposures in the radiator repair industry, the dominant strategies currently in use (e.g., engineering controls), will also be reviewed and evaluated. Finally, the chapter will seek to analyze the nature of the deterrents to use of lead-free alternatives and recommendations for an effective pollution prevention strategy.

Industry Background

The need for radiator repair quickly followed the production of the first motor cars in the late 1800s. General auto mechanic shops were the first to emerge, followed by the first radiator repair shops in the late 1910s (Larson-Struss, 1994). By 1954, the radiator repair industry was well established and manufacturers, shop owners, and suppliers formed the National Automotive Radiator Service Association to support and service the industry. A reversal of earlier trends was apparent, however, by the end of 1986. Many shops had expanded products and services in response to the heightened market pressures of the 1980s (*ACJ*, January 1994). Today, most shops offer auto air conditioning services in addition to radiator replacement and repair.

Radiators for automobiles are manufactured by two distinct segments of the market: the original equipment (OE) manufacturers and the after market (AM) manufacturers. Original equipment radiators are supplied to car manufacturers and some after market manufacturers. In contrast, the after market, as a distinct segment of the industry, furnishes radiators for replacement when original vehicle radiators are damaged beyond repair. The after market industry also manufactures radiator cores which can be fitted to existing tanks and thus reduce repair costs to the consumer. Thus, the radiator repair industry is specifically dependent on the after market for necessary replacements. In turn, the issue of occupational hazards due to lead exposure tends to be most directly influenced by the structure and operations of the after market. After market manufacturers continue to primarily supply copper/brass radiators and cores which are held together with lead-containing solders. Some AM manufacturers continue the older "island dip" practice of dipping the whole header into melted solder (Larson-Struss, 1994). These practices impede the progress toward a less toxic occupational setting for the radiator repair industry and necessitate costly expenditures on pollution control strategies (that is, by requiring engineering control devices).

The Standard Industrial Classification (SIC) code for "automotive repair shops, not elsewhere classified" is 7539 and includes radiator repair shops. This code, rather than identifying radiator repair shops as an exclusive, separate classification, lumps together all automotive repair shops such as air-conditioning repair, brake repair, frame repair, wheel alignment, and any other automotive repair industries. As a consequence, no independent data source specifically identifies radiator repair shops. The only extant estimate of the size of the industry comes from the National Automotive Radiator Service Association (NARSA) which identifies 10,000 radiator repair shops in the nation, with approximately 40,000 employees (NARSA, 1990). These shops are generally small and employ an average of four workers each.

Radiator Repair Process

A typical radiator consists of a core, tanks, headers, tubes, mounting attachments and fittings which are riveted, or otherwise held together to form the total radiator assembly (Figure 10.1). Four different types of radiator are presently being manufactured (Friand, 1992):

- Copper/brass radiator. The tanks and headers are made of brass (usually 30% zinc and 70% copper) and the core has copper fins and brass tubing. Solder is used for assembly. This type of radiator is used in automobiles, trucks, and commercial equipment.

- *Aluminum/plastic radiator.* The aluminum core is clamped to plastic tanks. This radiator is used predominantly in new automobiles and light trucks.

- *Steel/copper radiator.* The steel core fins are soldered to copper tubes, headers, and tanks. This radiator is used only in heavy industrial equipment.

- *Aluminum/aluminum radiator.* The aluminum core is joined to aluminum tanks in a single brazing operation, producing a stronger design at substantially reduced costs. These radiators cannot be separated for repair operations, which may present difficulties. Presently, this type of radiator is produced on a small scale and is still at the experimental stage for use in automobiles.

Copper/brass and aluminum/plastic radiators are the predominant types found in cars and trucks. Copper/brass radiators are of primary concern as a source of hazards since lead-based solders are used extensively in both their manufacture and repair. When the research for this chapter was initiated, it was assumed that workplace exposure to lead from lead solder used in radiators and the potential for eliminating lead from solder would be the principal issues to be addressed. However, the existence of nonbrass radiators and the availability of aluminum/plastic radiators (which have become increasingly prevalent in new cars and light trucks especially in Europe and

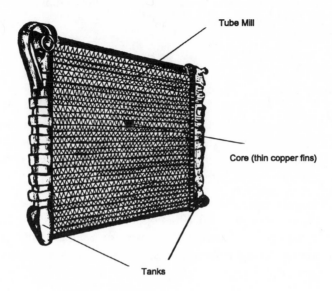

Figure 10.1 Typical copper/brass radiator.

North America) shifted in part the focus of the research to broader pollution prevention opportunities. These radiators have distinctive advantages over their copper/brass counterparts. They are lighter in weight, and have higher strength, longer life, better efficiency, cheaper manufacturing, and lower materials costs. These benefits have eased the replacement of copper/brass radiators as the preferred choice for auto manufacturers and shifted the trend toward aluminum/plastic radiators in the original equipment market, and thereby expanded the potential for reducing or eliminating lead exposures in the workplace (Hall, 1991).

Despite the entry into the market of aluminum/plastic radiators, approximately two-thirds of the cars and light trucks in operation today in the United States and Canada are still equipped with copper/brass radiators, thus requiring a continuing focus on the repair process and the hazards it can present. The typical radiator repair process for a copper/brass radiator consists of a series of steps, described below:

- *Boil Out:* The radiator is initially lowered into a hot caustic soda bath (180–190°F) for approximately 45 minutes in order to strip grease and paint from its surface, and then rinsed.

- *Leak Testing:* The radiator is submerged in a water bath and pressurized with eight to twelve pounds per square inch of air to check for leaks and total integrity.

- *Tear Down:* The radiator is disassembled by separating the top and bottom (or side) tanks from the core. This is accomplished by melting the old lead-based solder with a natural gas/oxygen or oxygen/acetylene flame torch set at 500°F. Melted solder drops into a tank or onto the floor and solder fume is emitted into the air.

- *Cleaning:* Radiator parts needing further repair are cleaned in an acid solution. Mechanical cleaning is also performed by a wire wheel, abrasive blasting, and/or wire brushing. Sand blasters are usually used for cleaning radiator headers, while bead blasters are used for cleaning tanks and other large radiator parts. These abrasive operations generate lead oxide dust. An additional operation which does not specifically result in lead emissions involves rodding out core tubes to clear blockages.

- *Tinning:* If a header needs repair, it is placed in a fuming bath of molten solder solution to yield a smooth surface to which solder can be applied.

- *Running the Header:* For 10–25% of header repair operations, solder is melted to increase strength. This process is time consuming, requiring one-half to two hours per header. Consequently, significant worker exposure to lead fumes can occur.

- *Repairing:* Leaks are patched with molten solder after a chloride flux (usually zinc chloride) is applied to surfaces for additional cleaning. Melted solder commonly drops into a test and repair tank above which the operation is performed.

- *Reassembly:* The radiator is reassembled by applying solder to the tanks and core ends around each tube as needed and then soldering the tanks to the core.

- *Leak Retesting:* The radiator is retested for leaks at the end of its repair.

- *Spray Painting:* The radiator is finished by spraying with black paint.

The main sources of lead exposure during the repair process are: (1) the generation of lead fumes when leaded solder is heated, and (2) the generation of lead oxide (Pb_3O_4) dust through the mechanical abrasion of lead-containing metals. A further source of lead exposure results from the reintroduction of settled lead particles into the air during general clean-up processes such as sweeping dry floors.

Lead in the Workplace: Exposures and Risks

The focus on lead in radiator repair is critical for a pollution prevention analysis, given the nature of the risks involved in occupational lead exposures, and the considerable literature on lead health effects that set the context for the discussion of alternatives.

Lead has two major routes of entry into the body: inhalation and ingestion. It is most efficiently absorbed into the body when inhaled. Particle size is a significant determinant of the respirability and hence absorption of lead into the bloodstream (FR, 1978; Davidson and Rabinowitz, 1992) The larger lead dust particles (>1-2 microns) generated by grinding operations are generally trapped by the upper respiratory tract and subsequently either expectorated or ingested. The smaller particles (e.g., lead fumes resulting from vaporized solder) reach the lower lung and are efficiently absorbed into the bloodstream (37–50%). Approximately 8% of ingested lead is absorbed through the gastrointestinal trait; however, children have a much higher gut absorption rate (up to 50%) (Davidson and Rabinowitz, 1992).

Once absorbed, lead is quickly cleared from the bloodstream and either undergoes urinary elimination or accumulation in other various body compartments. Bone represents the major storage depot for lead, with over 90% of the body lead burden and a high residence time of decades. Blood lead concentrations generally reflect recent lead exposures, whereas lead levels in bone reveal long term exposure histories. After a prolonged period of occupational lead exposure, blood lead begins to reflect both continuing exposure and resorption of lead from bone. Movement of lead from bone to blood is significant in older adults and may also be prominent in lactating and pregnant females (Mushak, 1992; Wedeen, 1992; Silbergeld et al., 1988). Subsequently, health risks for lead workers may continue long after retirement or change of careers and can easily be transmitted to developing fetuses or newborns.

Absorbed lead can result in a variety of adverse health effects through impacts on the hematopoietic, gastrointestinal, nervous, renal, and reproductive systems. A recent survey of radiator repair workers in New York City, with blood lead concentrations ranging from 6 to over 40 micrograms/dl, reported symptoms of appetite loss, constipation, abdominal pain, excessive tiredness, weakness, insomnia, headaches, dizziness, vomiting, clumsiness, nervousness, muscle aches and pains, joint pains, shaking, unintentional weight loss, and/or blurred vision (Nunez et al., 1993). If exposure to lead ceases, many of these symptoms and abnormalities could resolve over a period of time. The reversibility of these health effects is described as dependent on the intensity and duration of lead exposures.

The earliest effects of lead exposure are usually hematological and include inhibition of heme synthesis and shortened red blood cell destruction which can progress in a dose-dependent manner to anemia (NRC, 1993). While anemia only occurs at relatively high blood lead levels of 50 micrograms/dl and higher, inhibition of heme synthesis is observed at levels of 10–20 micrograms/dl (Moore and Goldberg, 1985; NRC, 1993). Anemia is widely recognized as one of the clinical signs of lead poisoning and its symptoms are weakness, fatigue, pallor, sallow complexion, headaches, and irritability. Depression of heme synthesis, which is indicative of lead impairment, usually proceeds without any apparent symptoms.

Neurological abnormalities involve both the central and peripheral nervous systems. Impairment of central nervous functions manifested by symptoms of diminished neuropsychiatric performance, fatigue, headaches, and irritability, may develop within 2 to 3 months after occupational lead exposure. Peripheral nerve deficits involving sensory or motor nerves can lead to pronounced motor dysfunction such as reduced motor conduction velocity, weakened parathesis of the extremities, and, in the extreme, wrist drop or ankle drop (Baker, 1988; NRC, 1993).

In contrast, permanent renal damage characteristically develops after a minimum of 5 years of occupational lead exposure and is often not detected until considerable damage has occurred (Baker, 1988; Lilis and Landrigan, 1988). Long-term exposure results in severe kidney damage, and, at lower levels of exposure, slow deterioration of renal function is seen to occur (Lilis and Landrigan, 1988; NRC, 1993). Kidney disease has historically been associated with hypertension. There is strong evidence provided by both animal and human studies demonstrating a correlation between hypertension and low blood lead levels (as low as 10 to 15 micrograms/dl in humans) (NRC, 1993; Wedeen, 1992).

The question of lead carcinogenicity has received increased attention during the past decade. Numerous animal studies have been conducted that provided evidence relating kidney cancer to relatively high doses of inorganic lead. In the late 1980s, several epidemiological studies of lead workers were conducted which suggested a renal-cancer risk. In response to the animal and human data, the U.S. Environmental Protection Agency in 1989 declared lead a probable human carcinogen (NRC, 1993; Silbergeld et al., 1991).

Low blood lead levels have also been found to profoundly affect reproductive functions in both males and females. Male workers with blood lead levels of 40 micrograms/dl and above have exhibited signs of decreased libido, impotence, decreased ability to produce healthy sperm, and sterility (FR, 1978; NRC, 1993). In females, lead exposure has been associated with abnormal ovarian cycles, menstrual disorders, sterility, spontaneous abortions, and stillbirths. Adverse impacts on fetal development such as retarded growth, preterm deliveries, and impaired cognitive development have been demonstrated from blood lead concentrations as low as 8 to 15 micrograms/dl (FR, 1978; NRC, 1993). These latter findings of fetal toxicity are attributable to the relative ease with which lead can cross the placental barrier to exert its effects.

Additional suspected fetal impacts, as observed in children, include damage to the central nervous system, the kidneys, and the blood-forming organs. Numerous studies have indicated that children are more susceptible than adults to these types of afflictions. Neurobehavioral and other developmental effects in children have been reported at blood lead levels as low as 10 micrograms/dl and found to worsen with increased blood concentrations (NRC, 1993; Bellinger and Needleman, 1992).

Lead toxicity research strongly underscores the growing recognition that adverse effects occur at blood lead levels previously considered safe and that lead is able to persist in the body through its accumulation in bone (Silbergeld et al., 1991; Matte et al., 1992). The suggestion that there may not be a threshold for lead toxicity has profound implications for the future of occupational health in the radiator repair industry.

Lead exposures in radiator repair shops occur during disassembly and reassembly of radiators. Tear down operations of incoming radiators contribute both lead fumes from melting existing solder and lead dust from abrasive cleaning of solder containing areas. Fumes are also introduced by new solder applications for the sealing of joints and other repairs.

In 1989, the California Department of Health Services implemented a Lead Poisoning Prevention Project as a result of data on lead exposure in the radiator repair industry which revealed substantial problems. Dozens of California radiator repair shops were found to employ one or more workers with dangerous blood lead levels of 40 micrograms/dl or higher (DHS, 1989). Fewer than 16% of radiator repair shops surveyed met OSHA requirements for tests and evaluation of workers' blood lead levels in 1989

(Sprinson, 1992). High blood lead levels have also been documented in other recent studies covering a number of states, including California (Table 10.1). In California, workers' blood levels have improved slightly since 1989; but, high levels are still reported to the California Department of Health Services as well as to other state health departments with disturbing frequency (Harrington, 1994; NRC, 1993).

Within the last decade, surveys of radiator repair shops have demonstrated numerous deficiencies in hazard controls. Two separate studies specifically mention the absence of proper work practices and education (Nunez et al., 1993; Goldman et al., 1987); and at least one study conducted for the National Institute of Occupational Health and Safety (NIOSH) contributed faulty engineering controls as the cause of high exposure levels (Sheehy et al., 1990). Engineering control devices are not always found in the repair shops, but even when used, they are often inadequate or ineffective. Improper work practices prevail in the industry, such as eating and smoking in the workplace and not washing or changing clothes after work,

Table 10.1 Blood Lead Levels in Radiator Repair Workers

Study Site: Key References	Number of Workers	Median/ Mean	Blood Lead Assessment
Boston Area: Goldman et al., 1987	56	Mn=37.1μg/dl	16% > 50 μg/dl 39% > 40 μg/dl
California, Colorado, Georgia (NIOSH Hlth. Haz. Evaluations): Gunter and Pryor, 1980 Gunter and Hales, 1990	46		26% ≥ 50 μg/dl 83% ≥ 30 μg/dl
Minneapolis-St Paul Metropolitan Area: Lussenhop et al., 1989	53		32% ≥ 40 μg/dl
Finland (mid '70s): Hernberg and Tola, 1979		Md=38μg/dl	40% > 40 μg/dl
New York City: Nunez et al., 1993	62	Mn=34μg/dl	24% > 50 μg/dl 68% > 25 μg/dl
Los Angeles and San Bernadino Counties (1990–1992): CA Dept. of Health Services, unpublished	246		1% > 80 μg/dl 6% > 60 μg/dl 22% > 40 μg/dl 60% > 25 μg/dl

and can be attributed to inadequate worker training and lack of appropriate facilities.

The Occupational Safety and Health Lead Standard

The Occupation Safety and Health Administration's (OSHA) Lead Standard of 1978 is very broad in scope and establishes multiple criteria and a comprehensive strategy for controlling work exposure to lead. It is one of the most progressive standards mandated by OSHA and requires employers to both monitor the airborne concentration of lead and to conduct biological monitoring of worker blood lead levels. Under the standard, employers must provide a safe work environment by ensuring adequate ventilation systems, proper housekeeping, separate lunchrooms and good personal hygiene. Health risks to employee families must also be minimized, by limiting the transfer of lead from work to home by requiring changing facilities and showers. Employee training, maintenance of records, and medical monitoring are also mandated (FR, 1978).

The standard outlines a series of steps designed to bring about these protective measures (see Figure 10.2). Radiator repair shops are required to make an initial determination of airborne lead for every workstation or shop operation where employee exposure may occur. If airborne lead concentrations are found to be below OSHA's Action Level, set at 30 micrograms/m³, no further action is required unless a relevant change in the shop's operation occurs. However, if airborne lead occurs at levels above OSHA's Permissible Exposure Limit (PEL) (both Action Levels and PELs represent time-weighted averages for 8-hour workdays and 40-hour work weeks), which is 50 micrograms/m³, the level of lead in the air must be measured quarterly, employees must be notified in writing of the air monitoring results and the course of actions that will be undertaken to reduce exposures, and respirators must be provided to employees until mitigation through the use of other controls has occurred. Finally, when airborne lead levels are above the Action Level but below the Permissible Exposure Limit, air measurements must be taken every 6 months, written notification must be given to employees, and a medical surveillance program as detailed in Figure 10.2 must be conducted if the Action Level is exceeded for more than 30 days each year (FR, 1978).

For any employee who has either been determined to have a blood lead concentration at or above 50 micrograms/dl (averaged over six months) or is recommended by a physician for removal from lead exposure, OSHA mandates a program known as Medical Removal Protection. This program

Initial Determination

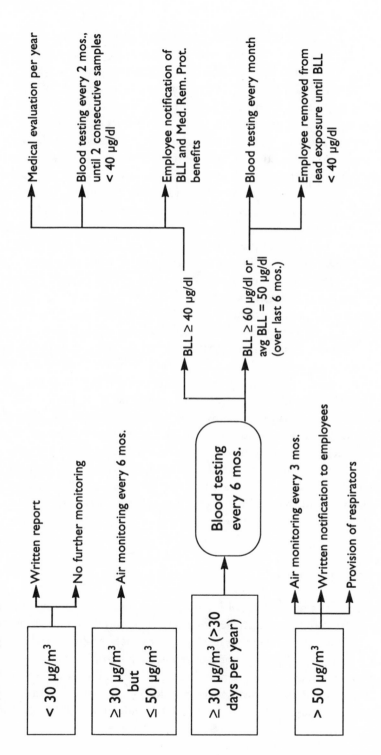

Figure 10.2 OSHA lead standard (BLL, blood lead level).

stipulates that workers identified for such protection must be removed
from any work areas that exceed the Action Level until blood levels drop
to below 40 micrograms/dl. The salary, benefits, seniority, and other
employment rights of the worker are protected during the removal period,
which may continue for up to 18 months.

Although the lead standard provides a stringent set of management tools
for the protection of worker health, numerous studies have shown that
considerable problems still pervade the radiator repair industry. Of the few
studies that have actually focused on radiator repair shops in this country,
most have shown one or more OSHA violations. The occurrence of health
problems, elevated blood lead levels, and excessive airborne lead concentrations are common in this industry and illustrate both a serious lack of
compliance and a continuing problem of high lead-related exposure levels.

Compliance difficulties in this industry have, at least in part, been attributed to OSHA's deficient enforcement capacity. OSHA inspections tend to
concentrate on the larger, more traditional lead-using industries and customarily bypass substantial portions of the radiator repair industry. This
tendency has even provoked an outcry from the National Automotive
Radiator Service Association (NARSA)—not for the lack of inspections
but for their uneven distribution which they believe creates equity problems that unjustly disadvantage some businesses and benefit others (*ACJ*,
March 1994). Overall, the lack of compliance presents an unfortunate situation for many radiator repair workers whose continued lead exposures
will eventually, if not already, manifest as adverse health impacts. It also
throws in relief the limits of a standard-based, control-oriented strategy,
even when such standards and recommended controls are considerably
protective of worker (or community and/or environmental) health, and
the separate, more compelling benefits that could be associated with a prevention-based framework.

Control Strategies

A variety of strategies are available for the purpose of reducing employee
exposure to lead. These strategies focus on: (1) controlling sources of lead,
which includes substitution to less toxic substances or process and engineering changes that reduce lead emissions; (2) controlling transmission of
lead which includes workplace ventilation, air dilution, isolation, or enclosure of the most hazardous processes; and (3) controlling lead–worker
interaction through the use of personal protective equipment and

improved work practices. Traditionally, health and safety professionals have ranked highest those control strategies capable of controlling hazards closest to the source. General acceptance has been achieved for a three-line defense system beginning with the preferred choice of engineering controls (including substitution, enclosure, isolation, and ventilation), which is followed by work practices, and then, as the last line of defense, personal protective equipment.

In the discussion of worker protection within the radiator repair industry, attention by most parties, including government agencies, has focused on only some engineering controls (including ventilation, isolation, and enclosure). Substitution of lead solder for lead-free solder has received little enthusiasm by the industry as a whole, and is discussed separately from the other control strategies, given its relevance to a pollution prevention framework.

Several control strategies have been developed to reduce workers' lead exposure in radiator repair shops. These control approaches consist of engineering controls (including ventilation systems and air cleaning devices), improved work and personal hygiene practices, and personal protective equipment.

Ventilation Systems

Several radiator repair shops control lead exposure by using wall- or roof-mounted propeller fans for general ventilation with or without electrostatic precipitators that remove airborne particles (*MMWR*, 1991). While this type of system reduces the concentration of lead in air, it does not eliminate exposure to workers, and is not appropriate for controlling toxic contaminants. Airborne lead levels as high as 500 micrograms/m^3 have been found in shops that rely on these methods (Goldman et al., 1987).

In 1991, NIOSH researchers evaluated the effectiveness of four local exhaust ventilation control systems, including ventilated booths, ventilated enclosures, movable exhaust hoods, and adjustable-arm elephant trunk systems for radiator repair shops, and recommended the first three for reduction of occupational lead exposure (Sheehy et al., 1990; Sheehy and Hall, 1991; Cooper et al., 1991; Goldfield et al., 1991). These systems were tested in radiator repair shops and the results are shown in Table 10.2. The three recommended systems were comparable in construction and materials costs ($1000–$1100 per workstation) and all achieved reductions of over 90% in radiator mechanics' lead exposures.

Table 10.2 NIOSH Evaluations of Four Local Exhaust Ventilation Systems

Study Site: Key References	Type of Ventilation Control	Mean Lead Exposure, with Control (µg/m³)	Mean Lead Exposure, No Control (µg/m³)	Percentage Reduction Exposure	Cost per Workstation (1990)
Denver, CO: Goldfield *et al.*, 1991	Ventilated Enclosure	10	453	98	$1000
Chamblee, GA: Cooper *et al.*, 1991	Ventilated Booth	9	98	91	$1100
Charlottesville, VA: Sheehy and Hall, 1991	Movable Exhaust Hood	13	193	93	$1000
? Sheehy *et al.*, 1990	Adjustable-Arm Elephant Trunk System	193	25	87	$2500

Sources: Sheehy, 1992; Sheehy *et al.*, 1990.

Abrasive Blaster

Another control strategy for radiator repair shops involves the use of abrasive blasters. Abrasive cleaning of radiator parts such as headers and tanks is required to remove any existing lead solder before any new soldering can take place. Wire brushing, which is usually performed to accomplish this task, not only generates a large amount of lead dust but also forces the mechanic to lean into the dust plume to view the work (Sheehy and Hall, 1991). Totally enclosing the process prevents exposure of workers to lead dust. Some radiator repair shops now use abrasive blasters which are essentially enclosed glove boxes with beads or sand used as the abrasive materials and a connected bag house to capture air emissions.

Personal Protective Equipment

Another standard control strategy is the use of personal protective equipment. Within the radiator repair operation, personal protective equipment (PPE) is worn at a minimum. The types of PPE that could be supplied by the employer at no cost to the employee are: goggles, steel-toed boots, disposable shoe/boot coverlets, rubber boots, gloves, aprons, cloth or Tyvek coveralls (full body clothing), and hard hats or other head coverings. PPE forms the last line of defense against worker lead exposure. Alone, it can never provide satisfactory protection, but used in combination with other control strategies it can help to modestly reduce lead exposures.

Respiratory Protection

Respirators provide temporary protection from airborne lead until levels can be reduced permanently. They are also useful for some infrequent hazardous jobs such as bag house cleaning. Respirators are not recommended as the sole control method and, under OSHA, can only be used for 4.4 hours per day, if required. They are recommended for use only when needed to supplement inefficient engineering controls until repair is possible. In order to provide adequate protection, respirators must be individually fit tested to workers, and equipped with correct filters.

Safe Work Practices

Safe work practices, such as more thorough clean up or improved personal hygiene practices, are other common control strategies. In terms of clean up, dry sweeping of radiator repair shop floors or blowing dust is a common practice that moves settled lead dust into the air. Special vacuums or wet mopping is the best method for removing lead dust from floors. Vacuums fitted with HEPA filters (High Efficiency Particulate Accumulator) collect very fine lead dust particles. Reduction of lead dust exposure is also accomplished by the simple practice of waiting for dust particles to settle in abrasive blasters before opening to remove radiator parts.

In terms of personal hygiene, employees can expose family members to workplace lead by carrying lead dust (on clothes, shoes, skin, etc.) into their cars and homes. This poses a particular danger to children at home, since they are more susceptible than adults to the effects of lead. Proper work practices include showering and changing clothes after a workday is complete. Equipment or clothing worn by the employee during the work shift and brought into the home poses an immediate danger to family members. Another simple practice of eliminating smoking or eating within the radiator repair area of the shop further reduces lead exposure.

Despite the multiplicity of control strategies that appear readily available, typical radiator repair shops often lack or inadequately utilize such strategies. In a revealing survey, the California Department of Health Services (DHS) revealed that 80% of radiator repair workers reported no ventilation system at work, 56% did not take showers before leaving home for work, and 44% did not change clothes before going home (*ACJ*, 1990). Another radiator repair shop survey in Los Angeles and San Bernardino counties, undertaken by the California DHS, revealed that only 46% of the shops were using any type of ventilation control (33% had bead blasters, 9% had ventilated booths, and 4% used local exhaust ventilation). Furthermore, most of the installed control systems were either functioning poorly or not used at all during lead generating operations (Sprinson, 1992). Control strategies thus ultimately suffer from both the failure to fully eliminate, or, even when those strategies are utilized individually, significantly reduce exposures, while the actual implementation of such strategies remains problematic.

Substitutions: The Primary Strategy for Prevention

A well-recognized but still poorly used approach in addressing exposure issues involves substituting toxic substances with less toxic or nontoxic substances. Indeed, the best method of reducing worker lead exposure in the radiator repair industry is to eliminate the use of lead. In particular, the use of lead-free solder and lead-free radiators has emerged as the industry's most effective and viable alternative.

Lead-Free Solder

Solder is a metal alloy that is available in varying compositions. The most common solder used in manufacture and repair of automotive copper/brass radiators is a lead-containing solder with 60% lead and 40% tin (60/40 lead/tin solder). Substituting lead-free solder in place of lead-containing solder greatly reduces lead exposure to workers and the environment that results from soldering operations and waste disposal in radiator repair shops. However, since radiator repair involves disassembly or "tear-down" operations, lead fumes and dust may still be generated from the original radiator solder. A complete removal of lead exposure in radiator repair shops would necessitate the use of lead-free solder in both the manufacture and repair of radiators.

Many tin-based lead-free solders have been introduced in recent years, but have had limited success due to the lack of economic incentives and legal requirements, their poor distribution, and the personal preferences of some radiator repair mechanics. At least two types of tin-based solders (i.e., those with no lead component) are used by some radiator repair shops: a 96% tin, 4% silver alloy; and the more popular 95% tin, 5% antimony alloy. Both types are substantially higher in cost than the common lead-containing solder. One solder manufacturer's (Kester Solder) competitive prices are $2.17 per pound for 60/40 lead/tin solder; $7.56 per pound for 96/4 tin/silver solder; and $4.03 per pound for 95/5 tin/antimony solder (Hoyt, 1994). The obvious economic choice for most radiator repair shops is the cheaper and more hazardous lead-containing solder, particularly when the external costs of exposure (or control strategies to reduce exposure) do not get factored into any price comparisons.

Although legislative efforts could force a switch to lead-free solders in this industry, such requirements are currently absent. From 1990 to 1993, several unsuccessful attempts were made to pass lead-banning legislation that would affect this industry (*ACJ*, Dec. 1993; *ACJ*, Jan. 1994). The advancement of such legal requirements in the near future is uncertain. So far, lobbying efforts have been successful in opposing legislative restrictions, and, in a letter dated January 12, 1993, the EPA indicated that as long as lead exposure appears to be on the decline, it would not pursue further attempts to restrict lead solder use in radiator repair (*ACJ*, Dec. 1993).

Another factor affecting the success of the tin-based solders is their poor distribution. They have not been well advertised and aggressively marketed, hence most local suppliers have chosen to remain with products that are familiar and known to their radiator repair clientele (*RR*, 1990).

Once tin-based solders find their way to the radiator repair shop, personal preferences may further affect their success. Some shops have reported inconveniences associated with the use of these solders. These solders melt at slightly higher temperatures than lead-containing solders, and flame adjustments and temperature increases between 60° and 100°F may be necessary to ensure good flow of the solder onto metal surfaces (*RR*, 1990; Minor, 1992; Beal, 1992). Tin-based solders have a thicker flow than lead-containing solders and have proved cumbersome for some shops. Other shops have found that this thicker flow contributes to a more efficient filling of joints.

In addition to providing a lead-free alternative, tin-based solders offer a few other advantages over lead-containing solders. Because they consist mainly of tin (over 90%), tin-based solders are lighter in weight than lead solders. This results in 20–25% more repairs possible compared with an equivalent weight of lead solder, and thereby effectively reduces the cost differences, although such reductions often do not factor into decisions that are based primarily on front-end costs. Tests have also demonstrated that tin solders are stronger than lead solders (shear strength of 9,000 psi compared with 5,000 psi at room temperature, respectively) (*RR*, 1990).

Another lead-free alternative, zinc-based solders, was specifically developed for radiator repair (Minor, 1992; Hall, 1994). These solders have significant advantages over their lead-based counterparts: (1) 63% less weight; (2) higher thermal conductivity, which means better performance during engine cooling; (3) increased strength—tensile strength is retained at 250°F without deterioration, while leaded solders lose significant strength at normal radiator-operating temperatures; and (4) better joint durability, as indicated by corrosion test results with common coolants.

A disadvantage of zinc solders is their high melting point (approximately 800°F). During repair with zinc solder, radiator metal is heated to temperatures around 800°F, which melts existing solder on the radiator. This may increase occupational lead exposure if lead solders are used in the original manufacture of the radiators. Overall, zinc solders provide a "realistic substitute" for tin/lead radiator solder alloys (Beal, 1992). They are lead free and generally a better and cheaper substitute than tin-based solders (Juchno, 1991; Minor, 1992). Their use in radiator manufacture has been recommended, but manufacturers would require an initial capital investment in the form of an upgraded core bake oven for their adoption. This economic constraint has prevented their commercial release. Amalgamated Technologies is one company that is continuing research for the production of a cost-effective zinc solder (Henderson, 1994).

Lead-Free Radiators

Since 1890, when the first motor car was produced, copper and brass have been the specified materials for automotive heat exchange. The aluminum/plastic radiator was first introduced to European car manufacturing in the early 1970s and began appearing in U.S. cars in the early 1980s. Since then, the use of aluminum/plastic radiators in new vehicles has steadily increased (see Figure 10.3) (Juchno, 1991; Hall; 1991; *MST*, Feb/Mar 1994). Aluminum/plastic radiators provide a range of advantages over the copper/brass designs. These radiators are substantially lighter (about 30%) which has helped automobiles meet the fuel economy regulations and demands. They are stronger, their heat dissipation performance is equal to or better than copper/brass, they have significantly lower manufacture failure rates, and they have a longer life of about 10 years (2 to 3 years longer on average). These features, in addition to the material and manufacturing costs, have collectively contributed to aluminum's success-

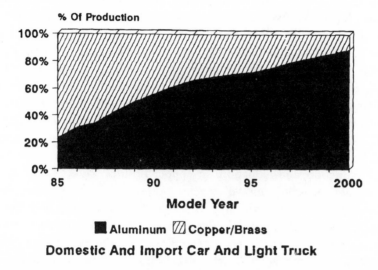

Model Year

■ Aluminum ▨ Copper/Brass

Domestic And Import Car And Light Truck

Figure 10.3 The total OEM use of aluminum radiators in new cars and light trucks has increased from 24% in 1985 to 56% in 1990. OEM usage of aluminum radiators was approximately 70% in 1993 and is expected to approach 90% by the year 2000. In the next 20 to 25 years, OEM usage of copper/brass radiators may be as rare as aluminum radiators were 20 to 25 years ago (*Modine Shop Talk*, 1994).

ful penetration into the original equipment radiator market (*MST*, 1994; Friand, 1992; Juchno, 1991; Minor, 1992; Hall, 1991).

Despite the remarkable advantages of aluminum/plastic radiators, copper-brass radiators still dominate in the after market. In 1990, the market for replacement radiators and cores in Western Europe was 26% aluminum, and 74% copper/brass. In North America, sales of aluminum cores and radiators represented less than 2% of the after market sales (Hall, 1991).

There are a variety of reasons for this apparent trend. Car manufacturers need to consider such factors as weight and warranty costs, whereas after market suppliers, which consist of many small companies, are primarily concerned with price comparisons (NARSA, 1988). Manufacturing of aluminum/plastic radiators requires major equipment and tooling changes, which are quite costly and financially constraining to smaller after market suppliers (Larson-Struss, 1994). Copper/brass radiators are becoming cheaper, lighter, and longer lasting as a result of various manufacturing and materials improvements. In an effort to keep copper/brass radiators alive, copper and brass material suppliers as well as a variety of organizations, including the Copper Development Association (CDA), the International Copper Research Association (ICRA), and the Improved Radiator Standards Association (IRSA), are providing radiator manufacturers with improved materials and technology, research, and funding to help them compete with the newer aluminum/plastic types. For example, IRSA has developed computer programs and a wind tunnel test facility to measure OE aluminum/plastic performance and aid in the design of copper/brass cores to meet or exceed such performance levels (Juchno, 1991; NARSA, 1988). New integrated production cycles have reduced manufacturing costs, the introduction of welded brass tubes has permitted at least a 12% weight reduction, and reductions in copper finstock gauges have further reduced radiator weight and volume and purportedly offer increased thermal and aerodynamic efficiency (Hall, 1991). In Europe and North America, plastic tanks from defective aluminum radiators are often reused by fitting with replacement copper/brass cores. These replacement radiators are much more readily available than aluminum cores and can usually perform as well as their aluminum counterparts at a substantially lower cost (Hall, 1991).

The capital investment required for equipment needed in aluminum/plastic radiator repairs (plastic tank radiator fixture, tools and materials for welding aluminum, epoxy, and a plastic–heat welder) serves as a deterrent to some radiator repair shops (RR, June 1990). In 1992, the cost of aluminum cores was nearly competitive with the price of completes (a difference of $9 to $10) which made repairs requiring recores difficult to justify for many shops (RR, Jan. 1992). Replacement of radiators in these instances is the more common practice. Although this trend is changing, the demand for after market copper/brass radiators remains high. The replacement rate of original aluminum/plastic radiators by copper/brass radiators was estimated at 50% by several radiator repair shops in 1993 (Bilodeau, 1993).

At the end of 1993, approximately 16% of the replacement market was held by aluminum replacement radiators. Several experts in the industry have predicted sharp increases in aluminum's market share (Anderson, 1992; Juchno, 1991; RR, 1992), including representatives of the Modine Aftermarket Division who also reported an expected increase to 52% (see Figure 10.4) (MST, 1994). The long life of aluminum radiators is increasingly affecting sales of replacement radiators in the aftermarket (Anderson, 1992; MST, 1994) and several U.S. aftermarket radiator manufacturers, including Modine Manufacturing Co., have increased production and stocks of aluminum radiator/plastic radiators for after market supply (MST, 1994). Copper/brass radiators remain a predominant presence in the radi-

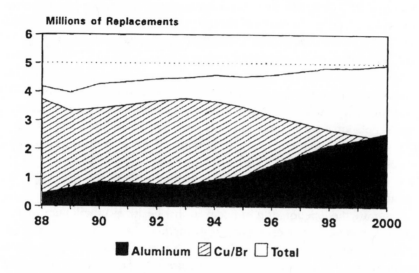

Figure 10.4 Total radiator replacements (completes and cores) for 1988–2000 for the United States and Canada. While the number of recores and replacements grows at a modest pace, the number of aluminum replacements accelerates quite rapidly. The 1993 level is approximately 16% of the total recore and replacement market or 720,000 aluminum radiator replacements. By the year 2000, the comparable numbers are expected to be 52% and 2.6 million aluminum radiator replacements. Clearly, aluminum replacements will be the only growing segment of the market (*Modine Shop Talk,* 1994).

ator repair industry; however, the undeniable trend is toward aluminum (*RR,* 1989; *MST,* 1994). Ultimately, the issue of substitution becomes one of timing, and the opportunities for facilitating substitution to address the continuing issues of risk and exposure.

Eliminating Risk: The Need to Intervene

The use of leaded solder has been emphasized in this chapter since it offers the radiator repair industry an ideal candidate for pursuing pollution prevention as a strategy for reducing or eliminating risk in the workplace. In contrast, the prevailing pollution control strategies, mandated under existing rules, have been largely ineffective in the elimination of lead-related health risks to workers. Reduction of health risks via engineering controls has had minimal success, given the nature of the industry and its broader interrelationships, which have made compliance with the OSHA Lead

Standard difficult for many radiator repair shops. The financial costs of air and blood testing, engineering control equipment, and potential medical removal benefits have served as effective deterrents to these small shops. The difficulty with these control strategies is in their focus on minimizing (with only limited success), but not eliminating, lead exposure. The role of lead as a causative agent in numerous health effects is not in question; however, the issue of the level of exposure at which workers are at risk has been raised. Policymakers are now not only concerned with the acute effects of high-level exposures, but also with chronic effects of continued low-level exposures.

If preventative measures such as substitutions do not get supported through policy initiatives and rely instead on a market whose outcomes are not certain, the amelioration of occupational health risks will necessitate a strict adherence to existing control methods and the OSHA Lead Standard, with revisions to the latter for more effective protection even possible. Such protections are expensive, assume a far greater enforcement capability, and underline the tension that often exists between government as regulator and small business as regulated entity. Yet occupational lead exposure will remain a powerful "toxics use" issue as long as copper/brass radiators containing leaded solder remain in use.

The availability of lead-free substitutes in this industry is well established; however, their implementation presents new sets of problems. Availability of lead-free tin-based solder is not widespread; zinc solder is still being studied; aluminum/plastic radiators are used in original equipment manufacturing, but are experiencing a very slow rise in the after market; and aluminum/aluminum radiators are still in an experimental stage. Preventative strategies will likely require some form of intervention, including the possibility of an industry-wide ban on lead-containing solders in order to effectively bring about change. In addition, incentive programs (e.g., tax credits for installing/retrofitting lead-free substitutions) could encourage more immediate substitutions, influencing timing factors which remain considerable, given the cumulative nature of the health risks. A reliance on market or incentives or change through "voluntary" initiatives, on the other hand, remains inadequate for an industry whose structure creates significant barriers and whose practices continue to counter or delay the achievement of pollution prevention as the clearest and most viable strategy for eliminating the risks at hand. The opportunities are available; the issue is when and how those opportunities can be realized.

References

American Business Lists. Personal communication, Omaha, NE, February 20, 1992.

ACJ (Automotive Cooling Journal). 1994. "Regulatory Watch, Unequal Enforcement: A Real Problem," March, 37(3):14.

ACJ (Automotive Cooling Journal). 1994. "NARSA: Celebrating 40 Years of Service to Each Other," January, 37(1):20–22, 26, 28–29.

ACJ (Automotive Cooling Journal). 1993. "Legislative Year in Review," December, 36(12):14–17.

ACJ (Automotive Cooling Journal). 1991. "Aftermarket Architect, Wynn Jacob," 34(10): 26–32.

ACJ (Automotive Cooling Journal). 1990. "Regulatory Watch, California Health Department Tackles Lead Threat," 33(10):10.

Anderson, W. 1992. Personal communication. *Cooling Systems and Flexibles*, Riverside, CA, March 19.

Baker, Edward L. Jr. 1988. "Neurologic and Behavioral Disorders." In: *Occupational Health: Recognizing and Preventing Work-Related Disease*, Barry S. Levy and David H. Wegman (eds.), Little, Brown and Company, Toronto, 399–414.

Beal, R.E. 1992. Zinc-Soldered Copper and Brass Radiators, Their Processing and Their Tests Results. *SAE Technical Paper Series*, Warrendale, PA.

Bellinger, David and Herbert L. Needleman. 1992. "Neurodevelopmental Effects of Low-Level Lead Exposure in Children." In: *Human Lead Exposure*. Herbert L. Needleman (ed.), CRC Press, Inc., Boca Raton, 191–208.

Bilodeau, Suzanne. 1993. Personal memo to Dr. John Froines. July 21.

Cooper, Thomas C., John W. Sheehy, and Charlie Sanders. 1991. In-Depth Survey Report: Control Technology for Small Business: Evaluation of a Ventilated Booth for Radiator Repair., NIOSH, Engineering Control Technology Branch, Cincinnati, Ohio, July. (Report No. ECTB 172-12a).

Davidson, Cliff I., and Michael Rabinowitz. 1992. "Lead in the Environment: From Sources to Human Receptors." In: *Human Lead Exposure*, Herbert L. Needleman (ed.), CRC Press, Inc., Boca Raton, 65–88.

DHS (Department of Health Services, State of California). 1989. Lead in the Workplace: A Guide for Employers and Health & Safety Trainers,

Suppl. (Manual developed by the California Occupational Health Program model project for radiator repair shops in Southern California).

FR *(Federal Register)*. 1978. Occupational Exposure to Lead, Final Standard. Department of Labor, Occupational Safety and Health Administration, November 14, Part IV.

Friand, C. 1992. Personal communication. Young's Radiators Repair Shop, San Fernando, CA, February 11, 18.

Goldfield, J., J.W.. Sheehy, B.J. Gunter, and W.J. Daniels. 1991. "Cost-effective Radiator Repair Ventilation Control. *Applied Occupational and Environmental Hygiene,* 6(11):959–65.

Goldman, R.H., E.L. Baker, M. Hannon, and D.B. Kamerow. 1987. "Lead Poisoning in Automobile Radiator Mechanics," *New England Journal of Medicine,* 317:214–218.

Gunter, B.J. and T. Hales, 1990. *Health Hazard Evaluation Report No. 89-232-2015,* NIOSH, U.S. Department of Health and Human Services, Public Health Service, CDC, Cincinatti, Ohio.

Gunter, B.J. and R.D. Pryor, 1980. *Health Hazard Evaluation Report No. HETA 80-89-723,* NIOSH, U.S. Department of Health and Human Services, Public Health Service, CDC, Cincinatti, Ohio.

Hall, Allan V. 1991. "The Growing World Acceptance of Aluminum Original Equipment Radiators" presented at the NARSA Convention, Reno, NV, March 14–16.

Harrington, David. 1994. Personal Communication. California Department of Health Services, April 8.

Henderson, Steve. 1994. Personal communication, Amalgamated Technologies, Inc., Scottsdale, AZ, April 13.

Hernberg, S. and S. Tola, 1979. "The Battle Against Occupational Lead Poisoning in Finland. Experiences During the 15-year period 1964–1978," *Scandinavian Journal of Work and Environmental Health,* 5:336.

Hoyt, Erin. 1994. Personal communication, Kester Solder, April 18.

Juchno, W. 1992. Personal communication, National Automotive Radiator Service Association, East Greenville, PA, February 15, 18; March 5.

Juchno, W. 1991. "Is Copper Still King?" *Automotive Cooling Journal,* 34(5): 12–26.

Larson-Struss, Carla. 1994. Personal communication, Modine Manufacturing Co., Aftermarket Division, Racine, WA, April 18.

Lilis, Ruth and Philip J. Landrigan. 1988. "Renal and Urinary Tract Disorders," In: *Occupational Health: Recognizing and Preventing Work-Related Disease,* Barry S. Levy and David H. Wegman (eds.), Little, Brown and Company, Toronto, 465–478.

Lussenhop, Daniel H., David L. Paker, Anita Barklind, and Chuch Mojiton, 1989. "Lead Exposure and Repair Work," *American Journal of Public Health,* 79(11): 1558–1560.

MST (Modine ShopTalk). 1994. TechTopics, Keeping Tabs on the Future of Aluminum Radiators. Modine Manufacturing Co., Feb/Mar, 6(6).

MMWR (Morbidity and Mortality Weekly Report). 1991. Control of Excessive Lead Exposure in Radiator Repair Workers., Centers for Disease Control, March 1, 40(8): 139–141.

Matte, Thomas D., Philip J. Landrigan, and Edward L. Baker. 1992. "Occupational Lead Exposure," In: *Human Lead Exposure.* Herbert L. Needleman (ed.), CRC Press, Inc., Boca Raton, 155–168.

Minor, Don. Personal Communication, Copper Development Association Inc., Birmingham, MI, February 20,21.

Moore, M.R. and A. Goldberg. 1985. "Health Implications of the Hematopoietic Effects of Lead," In: *Dietary and Environmental Lead: Human Health Effects. (Topics in Environmental Health; Vol. 7).* Kathryn R. Mahaffey (ed.), Elsevier Science Publishers, New York, 261–314.

Mushak, Paul. 1992. "The Monitoring of Human Lead Exposure," In: *Human Lead Exposure.* Herbert L. Needleman (ed.), CRC Press, Inc., Boca Raton, 45–64.

NARSA (National Automotive Radiator Service Association). 1990. "Statement on SB 2637 before the Subcommittee on Toxic Substances," Environmental Oversight, Research and Development of the Committee on Environment and Public Works United States Senate. The Lead Ban Act of 1990 and the Lead Exposure Reduction Act of 1990. 101 Congress, 2nd Session: 339–343.

NARSA. 1988. "Changing Role of Copper/Brass in Aftermarket," *NARSA Service Reports,* 2(4):1–5.

NRC (National Research Council). 1993. "Measuring Lead Exposure in Infants, Children, and Other Sensitive Populations." National Academy Press, Washington D.C.

Nunez, Carol M., Susan Klitzman, and Andrew Goodman. 1993. "Lead Exposure Among Automobile Radiator Repair Workers and Their Children in New York City," *American Journal of Industrial Medicine,* 23:763–777.

RR (Radiator Reporter). 1992. "PTRs Generate Opposing Viewpoints," January, 20(1):5–6.

RR (Radiator Reporter). November 1990. "Lead-Free Solder," November, 18(11):121–123.

RR (Radiator Reporter). 1990. "1990 Pricing Survey Results," June, 18(6):61–67.

RR (Radiator Reporter). 1989. "Winning the War Against Lead," July, 17(7):73–75.

Rudolph, L., D.S. Sharp, S. Samuels, C. Perkins, and J. Rosenberg. 1990. "Environmental and Biological Monitoring for Lead Exposure in California Workplaces," *American Journal of Public Health,* 80(8):921–925.

Sheehy, John W., 1992. "Getting the Lead Out!" *Automotive Cooling Journal,* 35(10): 14–27.

Sheehy, John W. and Ronald M. Hall. 1991. In-Depth Survey Report: "Control Technology for Small Business: Evaluation of Flexible Duct-Large Hood Ventilation for Radiator Repair," NIOSH, Engineering Control Technology Branch, Cincinnati, Ohio, May. (Report No. ECTB 172-14a).

Sheehy, John W., Thomas C. Cooper, Ronald M. Hall, and Richard M. Meier. 1990. In-Depth Survey Report: "Control Technology for Small Business: Evaluation of Flexible Duct Ventilation System for Radiator Repair," NIOSH, Engineering Control Technology Branch, Cincinnati, Ohio, February. (Report No. ECTB 172-11a).

Silbergeld, Ellen K., Philip J. Landrigan, John R. Froines, and Richard M. Pfeffer. 1991. "The Occupational Lead Standard: A Goal Unachieved, A Process in Need of Repair," *Scientific Solutions,* Spring: 20–30.

Silbergeld, Ellen K., Joel Schwartz, and Kathryn Mahaffey. 1988. "Lead and Osteoporosis: Mobilization of Lead from Bone in Postmenopausal Women," *Environmental Research,* 47:79–94.

Sprinson, Joan. 1992. Personal communication, California Department of Health Services, February 15 and 24.

Wedeen, Richard P. 1992. "Lead, the Kidney, and Hypertension," In: *Human Lead Exposure.* Herbert L. Needleman (ed.), CRC Press, Inc., Boca Raton, 169–190.

11

The Aerosols Packaging Industry: Product Concerns

Pamela Yates
Robert Gottlieb

Products as Hazards

Products sold for use in homes, businesses, and retail establishments contain literally thousands of different chemicals, many of which are toxic or otherwise pose dangers to people or the environment. Since the post World War II period, these toxic chemicals have become increasingly ubiquitous in consumer products, whether in the form of formaldehyde in products like pressed wood, as dyes in cosmetics that are both toxic and possibly mutagenic, in preservatives, in hundreds of products containing chlorinated solvents, as flammable ingredients, as sensitizers, as allergens, and in numerous other forms. Among these hundreds of types of product, many provide potential opportunities for pollution prevention, including one particular group reviewed here. This group is significant both in terms of how its markets have been established and expanded, the range of hazards such products represent, the regulatory issues they face, the evolution of the industry which produces them, and how to evaluate product need when a pollution prevention approach raises the possibility of a complete or partial product ban. These products are aerosols, linked together by their common delivery system that involves physical components (hardware) and by their mix of chemical components (solvents, active ingredients, propellants).

In technical terms, an aerosol is a suspension of solid or liquid particles in air or in some other gaseous phase. As a type of product, however, an aerosol can be defined as a package which holds its contents within a pressurized container, which can then be dispensed under pressure. Therefore, as discussed here, aerosols are simply a way of packaging and dispensing products, not distinctive as products in their own right.

In the context of pollution prevention, aerosol products offer a rich case study for several reasons. First, although aerosols have had a relatively short history of use, they are today widely sold in the U.S. and in other countries, and can be found in virtually every home. Since aerosols are largely consumer products used by millions of people in their homes and workplaces, they have come to represent a significant potential public health concern due to the effects of frequent, short-term exposure to product components that may occur repeatedly over many years. Not all aerosols necessarily contain toxic ingredients; yet, many types of aerosol products used in homes, shops, offices, retail establishments, hospitals, and schools do contain substances known to be flammable, carcinogenic, acutely toxic, respiratory irritants or sensitizers, ozone depleters, precursors to photochemical smog, or skin and eye irritants. Aerosols thus represent both a problem in terms of use, a hazard in terms of emissions, and a concern in terms of disposal.

For the aerosols industry in particular, there have been continuing problems associated with finding suitable substitute chemicals and alternative manufacturing processes that are themselves less toxic but which still leave the industry and its product base intact. This includes efforts at product substitution, which has often emerged as a primary method for regulatory compliance. This strategy may involve the use of substitute chemicals that themselves become subject to potential regulatory review. But product substitution can also involve manufacturing a different type of product in place of the one facing restrictions. For the aerosols industry, this may ultimately mean replacing aerosol products with products in other forms (liquids, powders, etc.). However, there are complexities associated with this approach to pollution prevention as well. In some cases, for instance, the toxic ingredients will remain in the product regardless of the form in which the product is sold.

There are other important aspects of the aerosols industry that make it worth studying. As with all consumer products, there are unique product requirements not encountered when manufacturing other kinds of products (e.g, industrial supplies, commodity and specialty chemicals, agricultural products). There are a number of federal and state agencies that have jurisdiction over different segments of the aerosols industry. And, as with certain other manufacturing sectors, there are also issues related to hazardous waste generation and disposal, indoor air pollution, solid waste generation and disposal (empty and rejected cans), and air quality problems caused by the release of volatile organic compounds into the atmosphere. Ultimately, given its use characteristics, aerosols may well represent a product where the most effective pollution prevention strategy should focus on the product itself, rather than specific parts or processes.

The Rise of the Aerosols Industry

The first aerosol spray product to be used in this country was an insecticide developed during World War II by the U.S. Department of Agriculture, although the original idea for an aerosol dispenser was conceived as early as 1935 with respect to greenhouse fumigation research. Called a "bug bomb," the USDA's pressurized aerosol pesticide was directly introduced for insect control purposes as a means of limiting the spread of insect-borne diseases, primarily malaria, among U.S. troops.[1]

The first commercial uses of aerosol products in the U.S. began to occur in the late 1940s, aided in part by a relaxation of the Interstate Commerce Commission's regulation regarding the allowable internal pressure in thin wall containers. The major breakthrough for the industry occurred in the early 1950s when Robert Abplanalp, a founder of the Precision Valve Corporation (the leading manufacturer of aerosol valves), designed the first workable plastic assemblage for an aerosol valve, thus significantly reducing the unit cost for the overall aerosol product. With a more competitive production cost, the industry was poised for expansion in a number of consumer product arenas.[2]

During the 1960s, aerosol packaging became the industry leader within several consumer product lines, particularly in the area of convenience products such as personal care applications (antiperspirants, hair sprays, etc.).[3] The number of aerosol units produced in the United States quickly increased, from five million in 1947 to 250 million in 1955 to nearly 2.5 billion by 1970 (itself a figure more than seven times greater than the number of units filled by the second largest producer of aerosols, West Germany).[4] Many of these products were specifically introduced as part of the development of new consumer products as well as through the construction of new consumer "needs." Aerosol deodorant sprays, for example, were first introduced in 1957. The product, which consisted of a germicide as the active ingredient, ethanol as a solvent, and a fluorocarbon as the propellant, failed to capture any significant market share in the personal care products area at the time. When aerosol deodorant sprays were reintroduced in the late 1960s, however, they became an immediate success. The major change in the product involved the substitution of an aluminum chlorohydrate compound for the germicide, although industry figures focused on the development of an "energetic and vigorous promotional marketing plan" as responsible for the establishment of a new market niche for aerosol deodorants.[5] "The simple message," one industry figure commented about such marketing efforts, "was that perspiration is offensive, to be dry is therefore a necessity to avoid giving unwitting offense, to avoid something of which one might be ashamed."[6] Another article in *Aerosol Age,* the industry's trade publication, put it this way: "Three years ago we were hard pressed to collect five hygiene sprays— in fact, they were scoffed at in many quite knowledgeable circles and laughed at in cartoons and not a few off-color jokes and puns." "But such is the American way of advertising, suggestion and persuasion," the commentator continued, "that even the best smelling ladies began to feel insecure and wonder if they were offending—and another new market was born!"[7] The key to the industry success, industry figures often noted, was its ability to meet "consumer perceived wants and needs."[8]

During this period of rapid growth, the industry also began to experience significant hazard-related problems. Flammable propellants (liquefied petroleum products) were both widely used and were largely responsible for a number of reports of product accidents in which the aerosol can exploded, or the emitted propellant caught fire, burning the user. Fires were a particular hazard when a flammable propellant was released near someone who was smoking.

During the late 1960s and early 1970s, partly in response to concerns about possible regulatory intervention regarding product safety, there was a move away from the flammable propellants in some personal care aerosols, particularly hairsprays, antiperspirants, and deodorants. Flammable propellants were also removed from many kinds of spray paints. The flammable propellants were primarily replaced by chlorofluorocarbon (CFC) propellants. Because of their low flammability, the use of chlorinated solvents increased as well. By 1974, about 70% of the country's fluorocarbon production was used for aerosol propellants, which accounted for 50–60% of all aerosol units sold (refrigerants, by way of contrast, accounted for 30% of the fluorocarbon market). Nearly all of the CFC aerosol units (over 90%) were in turn used for personal products, primarily deodorants and hair care products.[9]

The CFC issue, it turned out, represented the industry's greatest challenge and most protracted regulatory conflict. In 1974, two scientists from the University of California at Irvine, F. Sherwood Rowland and Mario Molina, published an article in *Nature* about the role of fluorocarbons in contributing to the depletion of stratospheric ozone.[10] The *Nature* article, and subsequent research by scientists at Harvard, the University of Michigan, and the National Center for Atmospheric Research, quickly touched off an intense debate over the use of fluorocarbons in aerosol propellants. Environmental advocates, led by the Natural Resources Defense Council (which filed a petition that same year with the Consumer Product

Safety Commission calling for an immediate ban on fluorocarbon propellants), were most focused on aerosols (as opposed to refrigerants, the second largest source of CFC use), since aerosol units were considered not available for recovery and reuse. A number of industry interests most directly associated with CFC production and use such as Du Pont (which had shortly prior to publication of the *Nature* article consolidated its CFC manufacturing capacity into a single integrated plant at Corpus Christi, Texas) strongly resisted any product ban on the basis of incomplete scientific evidence.[11] But a number of aerosol producers, such as the Johnson Wax company, immediately suspended CFC use in propellants in order to prevent any further erosion of aerosol markets on the basis of public concerns.[12]

Through the late 1970s, with public concerns about stratospheric ozone depletion intensifying, CFC aerosol propellant use became a prominent regulatory issue, reviewed simultaneously by EPA, FDA, and the Consumer Product Safety Commission. These three agencies, responding to the rising concern regarding stratospheric ozone depletion, decided to pool resources in order to develop a common regulatory approach. Subsequently, in March 1978, EPA, the lead agency on the issue, promulgated the rule which banned, with certain exemptions, all uses of CFCs in aerosols.[13]

For aerosols producers, the CFC debates came as a rude shock to an industry which had experienced several decades of rapid growth. For the first time in its history, aerosol production levels began to decline, while producers were forced to immediately explore various propellant substitutes. This search for substitutes was pursued not only in response to the CFC rule but in the hope of locating a more environmentally benign propellant that could help restimulate markets that had declined due to environmental concerns.

In this setting, several producers substituted methylene chloride (METH) for CFCs, especially in paints, in paint stripping agents, in hair sprays, in insecticides, and in certain cosmetic products. But methylene chloride also became subject to regulatory review from the CPSC and the Food and Drug Administration as well as by state and local agencies. This review process intensified after the National Toxicology Program reported in 1986 that high concentrations of methylene chloride caused an increased incidence of lung and liver tumors in mice. Soon after, the FDA banned the use of METH in cosmetic products, effective August 1989.[14]

Unlike the CFC debacle (with its concomitant market declines), the industry anticipated its METH-related problems, partly in response to consumer complaints about skin tingling and irritation from its use in personal products. This included a new round of propellant ingredient substitutions, most notably 1,1,1-trichloroethane (TCA), especially for industrial and insecticide aerosol products. Yet almost immediately, these substitution strategies, based as they were on the continuing use of VOC-related solvents, created another round of difficulties for the industry. For one, TCA became identified, by the early 1990s, as an ozone depleter, and thus found itself subject to new phase-out schedules in the wake of both the Montreal Protocol agreement of 1987 and the 1990 Clean Air Act Amendments.[15]

Thus, in each of these cases, the sequence of product substitutions further subjected the aerosols industry to substantial public (and consumer) criticism about the environmental hazards associated with aerosols production and use. And although modest growth levels for aerosol products had resumed by the mid 1980s after its years of declines, most increases took place within the industry's most secure market, personal care applications (e.g., hair sprays and antiperspirants). There was little market expansion, however, in new areas such as food aerosols, despite continuing efforts at product differentiation which remained the "true life blood" of the industry, as one consultant characterized the aerosols market.[16] This inability to enlarge markets underlined the industry's vulnerabilities. More than most product-based industries, aerosol packagers found themselves highly sensitive to consumer-based environmental concerns, whether CFCs (an issue retriggered in the late 1980s by the wide publicity given the Montreal Protocol) or VOC issues (e.g., smog formation, health impacts) regarding their use as propellants. Thus, while aerosol producers remained major players in the consumer products packaging area, their products had come to represent a controversial source of environmental hazards, subject to a multilayered and potentially far reaching process of regulatory action. This process in turn influenced both the nature of the product and the evolution of the industry itself.

The Structure of the Industry

Companies that manufacture aerosol products have generally fallen into two general categories. First, there are companies that produce either a variety of consumer or industrial products, or both, and package these products in more than one form. For instance, a paint manufacturer may purchase raw ingredients, make paint blends, and package the paints in gallon and quart size cans, and, in addition, package the paints in aerosol spray cans. A household products manufacturer might do the same, preparing cleaning compounds and packaging them in liquid or paste form as well as in aerosol containers. A company might have several packaging lines within a single facility, might locate its aerosol filling line in a separate plant, while still subcontracting some of the work to other fillers. For example, the 3M company, which produces a variety of products packaged in aerosol sprays, has long been an aerosols packager for several of its products, while also, in recent years, contracting out some of its production to smaller fillers.[17]

The second type of company that produces aerosols specializes in packaging the products of other manufacturers into aerosol cans. These custom fillers, as they are called within the industry, or subcontractors, package aerosol products according to their customers' specifications. In recent years, subcontracting to custom fillers has increased significantly as a way to reduce liability concerns of the larger product-based manufacturers, due to the additional regulations regarding VOC emissions and particular propellant ingredients. Custom fillers, in turn, consider highly proprietary the specific product-related requests involved in the subcontracting arrangements, including the name of the contracting entity, the type of product involved, and the specific ingredients used in the blend.

Aerosol manufacturers are also identified by the types of products they sell. Most companies specialize in one of eight product categories recognized by the industry itself (see Table 11.1), although some large companies manufacture products from more than one category. It is unlikely, though, that a company that makes household or automotive cleaning products, for example, also produces pharmaceuticals or food products. This is especially true of manufacturers who package their own products in aerosol cans. Custom fillers, on the other hand, often package many kinds of products in different plants, or in different filling lines of the same plant. Fillers have expertise in developing the right blend of active ingredients, solvents, propellants, and hardware that will yield the desired product spray characteristics and performance. Some fillers utilize this knowledge by contracting to do development work for their customers who have little or no knowledge in the special blends required to make aerosol products work.

Aerosol producers are identified by the Standard Industrial Classification code associated with the primary types of products they sell. Table 11.2 lists common SIC codes associated with products sold in aerosol form. Industries that sell the same type of product in nonaerosol form would be identified with the same SIC code. Various estimates have placed the overall number of companies in the U.S. with aerosol filling lines at about 200, with one Chemical Specialties Manufacturers Association (CSMA) survey reporting that 151 fillers represented 94% of all containers filled in the U.S.[18]

Aerosol companies range from multinational corporations with several

Table 11.1 Categories of Aerosol Products

Personal Care Products:
Hair care products including hair sprays and mousses; cosmetics; personal deodorants and antiperspirants; shaving lather; colognes, perfumes, and aftershaves; pharmaceutical and medicinal products; other personal products such as suntan preparations and breath fresheners

Paints and Finishes:
Lacquers; automotive paints; architectural coatings; varnishes; primers; paint strippers; graffiti removers; artificial snow and other decorative products

Automotive and Industrial Products:
Adhesives and sealants; mold release agents; lubricants; automotive products including brake, choke, and carburetor cleaners, engine degreasers, engine starting fluid, spray undercoating, refrigerants, windshield and lock spray de-icers, tire inflators; other miscellaneous cleaners

Household Products:
Laundry products including stain and spot removers, starch, pre-wash sprays; shoe polishes; water repellents for fabric and leather; cleaning products for fabrics, rugs and household surfaces; furniture polishes and waxes; room deodorants and disinfectants; air fresheners; anti-static sprays

Food Products:
Pan sprays; cheese; whipped cream; condiments

Pesticides and Insect Sprays:
Wasp and hornet killers; total release indoor foggers; personal repellents; crack, crevice, and surface sprays

Animal Products:
Veterinarian and pet care products, including shampoos, insecticides, repellents

Miscellaneous Products:
Nonclassified products

Source: Chemical Specialties Manufacturers Association, Annual Survey of Aerosol Pressurized Products Survey, 1988, 1992.

sites that do filling such as 3M or Colgate–Palmolive to small fillers that have 30 or fewer employees, a number of which are located in the South, primarily in the Carolinas and in the state of Georgia. A number of the small custom fillers do contract work for medium to large size companies, a trend related to the growth of subcontracting. Custom filling by small fillers is also largely decentralized and regionally specific (that is companies will custom order for specific regional markets) in order to reduce shipping costs and be able to meet specific state and local environmental regulations which have increased substantially during the past decade. The subcontracting that now occurs between the medium-sized companies

Table 11.2 SIC Codes Associated with Aerosol Fillers

2813 - Industrial gases	
2841 - Soap and other detergents	
2842 - Polishes and sanitation goods	
2844 - Toilet preparations	
2851 - Paints and allied products	
2879 - Agricultural chemicals (not elsewhere classified)	
2891 - Adhesives and sealants	
2899 - Chemical preparations (not elsewhere classified)	
2992 - Lubricating oils and greases	
5169 - Chemicals and allied products (not elsewhere classified)	
7389 - Business services (not elsewhere classified)	

(the "marketers" of the product) and the small custom fillers has, in turn, further reduced the overall capital commitments to aerosol production from both the multinationals and the medium-sized companies.[19] Some companies have also explored the possibilities of shifting production outside the U.S. as a means of shifting regulatory burdens.

Information about the structure of the industry has been limited by the lack of publicly available production and market share data. Although the CSMA undertakes an annual survey of container and valve manufacturers to determine the size and numbers of aerosol units filled, none of that information is made available regarding the market share among companies reporting such information. The submitted data is instead reviewed by a CSMA Aerosol Division Product Survey Committee consisting of about fifteen industry representatives which is responsible for the final report listing the number of units filled, the units filled by category of aerosol product, and the names of the fillers participating in the survey, while the specific figures per filler remain confidential. The strong bias against providing market share information by company—"nobody wants the competition to know their market share," argues CSMA official Paul Pierpoint—reduces the ability to analyze such organizational trends as the shift toward subcontracting and limits an analysis to interviews and first hand observations.[20]

The U.S. aerosols industry today is considered to be mature. Production levels had initially peaked in 1973 at 2.9 billion units filled but then began a period of decline (related initially to the CFC issue), with production bottoming out in 1982 at 2.1 billion units filled. During this period, however, production levels in Western Europe (which had not instituted a CFC aerosols ban) continued to rise, thus establishing a modest increase in production levels on a world-wide basis, some of which was also attributable to the overseas activities of U.S.-based multinationals.[21] Between 1982 and 1989, there was a modest growth of production volumes both within the U.S. and (with some variation)[22] worldwide, with the 1973 U.S. production peak of 2.9 billion units filled matched only in 1989 (a figure which then declined until 1992, when production levels increased again to slightly more than the 1973 and 1989 figures). Although limited in terms of facility and company-related information, the CSMA summary of U.S. aerosol production, based on its survey of domestic aerosol manufacturers, does provide information about certain industry trends. In 1992, for example, an estimated 2.989 billion aerosol units were filled, representing a 5.8% increase over 1991 production levels. That increase, however, had followed two previous years of decline, further underlining the limited recovery from the industry's previous period of decline in the late 1970s and early 1980s.[23] During the late 1980s and early 1990s, there had been a handful of new products in the personal care area that had provided some modest growth for the industry—antiperspirants, hair sprays, and eye care products. And while CSMA had argued during this period that such limited growth was a result of "continuing consumer confidence in aerosol products,"[24] the lack of product expansion into new categories of use demonstrated significant consumer ambivalence in other than established market niches.

Product Manufacture

Aerosols are best described as pressurized products. An aerosol product contains, generally, three constituents—an active ingredient (or mixture of active ingredients) selected to perform the desired function of the product, a propellant to deliver the product from the container, and a solvent (or mixture of solvents). The solvent component is necessary because active ingredients are often not directly soluble in the propellant. Since all the ingredients need to be released together, the solvent functions as a vehicle to insure that the ingredients release in the right proportions. Inside the can, the ingredients may be in the form of a liquid solution, a slurry or an emulsion. It is possible to dispense powders and other solids, foams, and pastes from a pressurized can. The other parts of the physical product include the container itself, and a valve system for dispensing the contents of the container.

The valve systems may contain seven or more different parts. The selection of the valve components is important in obtaining the desired spray pattern—in terms of (1) the size of the spray droplets, (2) the direction and distance of the propelled droplets, (3) the wetness or dryness of the spray, and (4) fast or slow evaporation. It is the right combination of the amount and blend of active ingredients, selection of solvent and propellant, container and hardware that, together, determine the characteristics of the spray. Inside the aerosol container, the propellants are stored under pressure. The dispensing valve opens when depressed, allowing the propellant to expand and flow from the container. The propellant carries the rest of the product blend with it. The difference between the pressure within the can and the ambient pressure when the valve is opened forces the product from the container.

Propellants most commonly fall into two types—compressed gases or liquefied propellants. The liquefied propellants in turn fall into two chemical classes—halogenated organics (which include the CFCs, HCFCs, HFCs, and chlorinated hydrocarbons) and petroleum hydrocarbons. By 1990, less than one percent of aerosol products still utilized CFC propellants. Chlorinated solvents are not used alone as propellants, although they are occasionally added to propellant systems to impart certain desired properties. There are three widely used liquefied petroleum propellants—propane, isobutane, and normal-butane. All three are extremely flammable, so flammability suppressants are added to aerosol formulations containing them.

The next key phase of aerosols production, the filling of containers, is a relatively simple and largely automated process. Propellants are delivered by tank car (rail) or by tank truck, and are either kept in the rail car for on-site storage or are off-loaded to bulk storage tanks. Solvents are usually delivered in drums or by tank truck for large volume customers. The formulation constituents are mixed together with solvent in a blending tank to form a concentrate. Empty cans, without valve hardware in them, are removed from pallets and placed on a conveyor belt that leads to a filling station.

Immediately after the filling station, the valve hardware is placed in the cans. Next, the containers go to the gassing room where propellant is added. When flammable propellants are used, this step must be done in a separate, explosion-proof room equipped with a ventilation system, and a monitoring/alarm system to warn for an explosive atmosphere.

The most significant source of toxic ingredients in product manufacture can be found in solvent usage, which might vary substantially from plant to plant, depending on the types of products filled and on operating practices. TCA, for example, a core ingredient in a number of propellant blends, can also be used to flush transfer lines and clean tanks. In an extensive survey of aerosol filler companies in the Southern California region undertaken by one of the authors of this chapter, TCA usage among chlorinated solvents was the highest overall for the facilities providing data (whose filling products included personal care products, automotive and industrial products, paintings and coatings, foods, household products, and insecticides). This was followed by perchloroethylene (PERC), methylene chloride (METH), trichloroethylene (TCE), and CFC-113. At the national level, TCA also represented the largest chlorinated solvent-based ingredient in the formulation of aerosols, with more than 34.5 thousand metric tons used in 1988, according to industry estimates, while METH use, the second largest ingredient, was estimated at 20.4 thousand metric tons.[25]

Environmental Exposures

Exposure to toxic chemicals from aerosol product manufacturing and use takes several forms. Aerosol production generates toxic chemical releases to air and water and in solid waste streams. Workers at filling plants are exposed to hazardous materials during production and clean-up operations. However, most of the toxic chemicals contained in aerosol products are released during product use, resulting in consumer exposures that have not been well characterized. While home use of aerosols is, for the most part, of short duration and intermittent, there are upwards of hundreds of thousands of workers in the U.S. who are exposed to toxic chemicals in aerosol products in the course of their work. Such exposures can range from one hour or less in a single work day to as much as a full eight-hour day. As with consumer exposures, these workplace exposures associated with aerosol products have not been well characterized, with the possible exception of chlorinated solvent exposures in certain limited cases. Both EPA and CPSC's interest in indoor air quality issues have yet to translate into specific exposure assessment studies characterizing aerosol use within the home, although the Agency has acknowledged the potential for such exposure associated with consumer products like aerosol spray paints containing methylene chloride. On a broader scale, EPA's Total Exposure Assessment Methodology studies have identified levels of various organic pollutants 2 to 5 times higher inside homes than outside in the ambient environment, regardless of location.[26]

In general, environmental releases from aerosol packaging plants are of three types—fugitive air emissions, solid and hazardous waste in the form of unusable products and cans, and waste water. In filler plants, there are no point sources of air contaminants (i.e., fillers do not install scrubbers or other pollution control devices). Fugitive emissions occur when chemicals are transferred from tank trucks or rail cars into on-site storage tanks.

Fugitive emissions can also occur through leaks in transport pipes and enclosed process vessels. At the filling station, where concentrate and solvents are fed into the aerosol cans, the injection nozzles and the cans are open to the atmosphere. During the short period of time before the valve hardware is placed onto the containers (on the order of a minute or two, sometimes less), the contents may volatilize from the can. Generally, there is no vapor collection device at the filling station, and vapors typically are released to the atmosphere.

Waste generation tends to be limited to a small percentage of the aerosol units filled, although there is significant controversy concerning the hazardous nature of the wastes involved. There are two sources of solid waste from packaging operations. Some cans are rejected from the manufacturing line due to leaks or other damage. Aerosol products are sometimes returned to the filler because their expiration date has been exceeded or as the result of a product recall. According to one industry source, the reject cans that become waste constitute about 0.5% to 1.0% of all containers filled. Using the CSMA's own figure of 2.989 billion units filled in 1992, this translates to between 15 and 30 million reject containers generated in a year.[27]

The containers and the product retained in them must be disposed of separately. There are devices available that are designed to puncture the cans, and capture and collect the liquid contents. When these devices are used, the gaseous component of the product (often the propellant) is released directly to the atmosphere. The liquid is either reused on site or sent offsite for recycling or for use as secondary fuel. The empty cans are crushed and are usually disposed of as waste. There is regulatory uncertainty as to whether waste cans need to be treated as hazardous or nonhazardous waste. Some fillers simply treat the crushed containers as nonhazardous solid waste. Other fillers believe that the containers should be treated as hazardous waste because they can be contaminated with residual amounts of flammable or otherwise hazardous chemicals. Empty metal cans are sometimes sent with other metals to local recycling stations, although some recyclers do not accept metal aerosol cans due to the hazard associated with the product under pressure.

There is a waste water stream from most packaging plants. When filled, sealed containers are leak tested in the hot water bath, and any chemicals that do leak will end up in the water. Depending on the size of the operation, the water may be continuously drained into an industrial waste water discharge line. Some smaller operations have reported that they do not replace the water bath, but just let the chemicals evaporate or periodically skim off any material that collects. At least one large filler installed a waste

P.Yates and R. Gottlieb

water pretreatment system to remove organics from the water stream prior to discharge. Other fillers claim this is not necessary because so little product is released from leaking cans (the leakers are removed from the bath as they are discovered).[28]

Eventually, all aerosol containers become solid waste. One industry source has estimated that aluminum and steel aerosol containers make up 0.08% (by volume) of U.S. consumer wastes.[29] Often, there is residual product contained in the cans when they are sent for disposal. The residuals may consist of any of the toxic, flammable or irritating chemicals used in the formulation of aerosol products. These chemicals end up either in solid waste landfills, or are burned in incinerators, where they may decompose to form other toxic or hazardous chemicals. The accumulation of aerosol containers also represents a potential safety concern for households, trash collectors, landfill and incinerator operators, and fire fighters, each of whom could be exposed to the problem of exploding aerosols where stockpiling of empty aerosol containers occurs. In general, empty aerosol containers have been defined by various state and federal regulations as a hazardous waste, although significant exemptions have been made (e.g., the California Department of Health Services allows farmers to throw emptied aerosol pesticide containers in the trash if they are properly rinsed and the rinsate is recycled).[30] And while emptied aerosol cans in household wastes are not currently treated as a hazardous waste, a number of cities encourage consumers to dispose of emptied aerosol containers at household hazardous waste collection centers or through hazardous waste collection roundups. Once collected in this manner, the cost per aerosol unit earmarked for hazardous waste disposal is as much as *$5 per can* when packed in 55 gallon drums and sent to an incinerator.[31]

A core environmental concern related to the use of aerosol products is the release of toxic compounds, notably volatile organic compounds, into the ambient environment. VOCs account for as much as an average of 75% of the weight of all antiperspirant aerosols and 95% by weight of aerosol deodorants, according to a study of the California Air Resources Board. That translates into an estimate of 1.2 tons of VOC emissions per day in California, a significant amount for a single product line.[32] The Toxics Release Inventory could provide another potential source of information regarding different environmental exposures from aerosol production, but is limited by two key constraints: large fillers often do not have a single packaging line in a single facility, thus precluding specific information about releases from that production source, while a number of small fillers are not required to report under TRI provisions due to the small size of the facility. Despite the absence of reported information, the volume of aerosol use and product hazards involved have still generated substantial regulatory interest in this area.

Occupational Exposures During Production

Aside from issues of waste generation and disposal and environmental releases, significant occupational exposures can also occur at aerosol packaging facilities. A 1987 study of worker exposures to methylene chloride at filling operations, for example, identified five process areas where workers are potentially exposed to hazardous chemicals.[33] One potential area for exposure not explored in this particular study is the materials handling area where chemicals are received, offloaded, and stored. The study data were further limited to METH exposure only, based on a review of monitoring data obtained at eight aerosol facilities in the years 1971–1987. Despite these omissions, the results of the study revealed that "directly exposed" employees were subjected to an average of 138 ppm METH, about 27% of the OSHA Permissible Exposure Limit (PEL) (500 ppm) at the time the study was undertaken. But those numbers are more than five times greater than the current PEL of 25 ppm. At the same time, exposures of "indirectly exposed" employees were estimated to be 69 ppm.[34]

A 1986 OSHA document on METH exposures in the workplace provides job specific exposure measurements for aerosol packing facilities. The results are listed in Table 11.3. The eight hour time-weighted average exposure for all job categories was estimated to range from 15 ppm to 635 ppm, which, in nearly all cases, exceeded the current PEL. Even the low end of

Table 11.3 Measured Methylene Chloride Exposures During Aerosol Filling Operations

Job Title[a]	Measured METH Exposure (ppm)[b]
Batch Mixer	15
Filler, Line Operator	29
Valve Dropper	49–635
Bath Cleaner	151

Source: OSHA Instruction, PUB8-1.2A, August 11, 1986.

[a]Average 8-hr time-weighted average exposures estimated to be 29 ppm to 540 ppm for all job categories.

[b]OSHA PEL (8-hr time-weighted average) for METH in 1986 was 500 ppm; present PEL is 25 ppm (8-hr TWA).

OSHA's estimated range is just slightly below (60%) the current PEL. If local exhaust ventilation or other engineering controls have not been installed, even these exposures would exceed the current PEL.[35]

An estimated average of 4.5 directly exposed workers and 3.2 indirectly exposed workers occurred at each site. Based on this estimate and a recently published survey of aerosol manufacturers based on earlier research by one of the coauthors of this study,[36] it is clear that while only a small number of workers are involved directly or indirectly in the filling process, they are subject to potentially significant and not well addressed hazards. Local exhaust ventilation is generally not used on filling lines, even though, were it installed, it would lower worker exposures to solvent vapors. At the same time, it is not possible to fully characterize the typical pattern of exposure in individual plants. Exposures are dependent upon the mix of products filled at a particular facility, how many of the products contain chlorinated solvent and in what proportions, how long the production runs are, and how often they occur. The difficulty in exposure characterization during filling operations extends to all toxic chemicals used in aerosol production. There is thus little information available regarding actual occupational exposures at aerosol filling plants, although the potential for significant occupational exposure remains high.[37]

This lack of information is compounded by the fact that a number of small fillers who employ only a few workers often function outside the purview of any regulatory authority. Given the relatively low tech, inexpensive nature of the filling process, a number of fillers literally operate out of garages, with their employees drawn from a low-paid, low-skilled work force. For example, one of the authors of this study visited more than a dozen fillers located in the Southern California region and encountered a high percentage of Spanish-speaking employees who were identified as part of the low-wage sector used by the industry in the region. Opportunities for exposure in these facilities, where ventilation and equipment problems could be clearly identified, were substantial.

Exposures from Product Use

The bulk of toxic chemical exposure from aerosol products occurs during product use, rather than during container filling operations. Consumer exposure, in the context of this analysis, refers to those exposures which occur when individuals use aerosol products in their homes, and can be contrasted with industrial product exposures that occur when workers use aerosol products in the course of their jobs. Such occupational exposures

are wide-ranging and potentially significant, given that many aerosol products are sold expressly for industrial use. Examples include automotive
cleaning products, mold release agents, industrial adhesives and spray
paints, some pesticides, and cleaning products for the electronics industry.

There have been few comprehensive studies conducted to quantify
exposures resulting from either workplace or household use of aerosol
products. The few older studies that do exist have primarily been designed
to estimate exposures to chlorinated solvents in specific workplace situations. In the 1987 study discussed earlier, occupational exposures to three
chlorinated solvents were estimated for two industrial use settings. The
results were extrapolated to predict chlorinated solvent exposures associated with the use of industrial aerosol products. The results of this study are
summarized in Table 11.4. During the year studied, an estimated 11 million cans of brake cleaner were used by 658,000 workers. They were typically exposed to predicted concentrations of 0.3 ppm perchloroethylene
(PERC) and 0.1 ppm 1,1,1-trichloroethane (TCA). The range of exposures was predicted to be 0.09 ppm to 35 ppm for PERC and 0.04 ppm
to 13 ppm for TCA. The predictions were based on one hour per day of
brake cleaner use, and the exposures were averaged over an eight-hour day
(known as 8-hr TWA). It was noted that duration of brake cleaner use
might actually range as high as eight hours per day, which would significantly increase the time-weighted average predictions. By comparison, the
OSHA PEL (8-hr TWA) was 100 ppm for PERC and 350 ppm for TCA.
In 1989, the PEL for PERC was lowered to 25 ppm.

The same kinds of predictions were made for exposures to TCA and
METH in mold release sprays, which are used in plastic molding operations and other industrial applications. Typical exposures were predicted to
range from 0.04 to 4.0 ppm for TCA and 0.09 to 9.0 ppm for METH.
These predictions were based on eight hours per day of use.

The above predictions were based on an assumed set of conditions. The
exposures will vary as conditions change, and are dependent on whether
the use occurs in a confined space, the adequacy of ventilation (the air
exchange rate), the presence of other toxic chemicals in conjunction with
the chlorinated solvents, and the quantity of aerosol product used.

Other reports of occupational exposure to solvents during aerosol use
are summarized below:

- METH exposures during thirty minutes of spray paint use
  were measured to be 75 ppm to 144 ppm;

- Dow Chemical Company measured average 15-minute
  METH concentrations of 102 ppm after five-second use of air

fresheners, antiperspirants, and hairsprays (METH is no longer
used in antiperspirants or most hairsprays);

- Beauty salon exposure to METH in aerosol products was measured to be 8 ppm (8-hr TWA) in one study.

Equivalent studies designed to measure potential consumer exposures
from product use over time are currently not available, despite the
increased concerns regarding problems of indoor air pollution and the
strong evidence of exposure of product use in workplace settings, as
described above. For example, EPA's Science Advisory Board, in its comparative risk analysis undertaken in 1990,[38] characterized indoor air pollution as a substantial risk often underrepresented in allocation of agency
resources (or potential regulatory oversight), yet failed to provide specific
direction in terms of risk evaluation for specific sources, such as continuous consumer exposure from aerosols use. Thus, while product use in
industrial settings indicates significant sources of exposure, the indications
of product use exposures and hazards to consumers remain only suggestive,

**Table 11.4 Estimated Exposure to Chlorinated Solvents Resulting from Use of
Industrial Aerosol Products**

Product Type	Chemical[a]	Number of Units Consumed per Year	Predicted Typical Exposure (ppm)	Predicted Range of TWA Exposure (ppm)
Brake cleaner	PERC	11 million[b]	0.3[c]	0.09–35
	TCA	11 million	0.1[c]	0.04–13
Mold release	METH	8 million	0.2[d]	0.09–9
	TCA	8 million	0.1[d]	0.04–4
All aerosol products	PERC	51 million	n/a[e]	0.09–35[d]
	METH	197 million	n/a	0.09–9[d]
	TCA	84 million	n/a	0.04–13[c]

Source: PEI Associates, Inc., Washington, D.C.

[a]PERC = Perchloroethylene, TCA = 1,1,1-trichloroethane, METH = methylene chloride.

[b]An estimated 658,000 workers were exposed to PERC in industrial brake cleaners in
1986.

[c]Predicted exposure is for 8-hr time-weighted average (TWA), based on one hour exposure per day; however, duration of exposure may actually range from one to eight hours per
day; the estimated frequency of exposure is 102 days per year.

[d]Predicted exposure is for 8-hr TWA, based on eight hours of exposure per day; the estimated frequency of exposure is 250 days per year.

[e]n/a = data not available.

and would clearly merit further investigation. The absence of a strong regulatory presence regarding product use issues (see Chapter 4) underlines this need.

Regulatory History

The regulations affecting the aerosols industry can be summed up in three areas—environmental protection, employee health and safety, and consumer (public) health and safety. In that regard, three key issues have emerged during the past two decades that have directly impacted aerosol packagers: ozone depletion/CFC issues; VOC regulations; and storage and safety concerns. In terms of these areas of concern, various segments of the industry are now required to report to a number of federal and state and local agencies. The Consumer Product Safety Commission is responsible for product safety in general. For the aerosols industry, this might include issues of product flammability and the presence of carcinogenic or otherwise dangerous chemicals in the product formulations. The Food and Drug Administration regulates food products, pharmaceuticals, and cosmetics. The Environmental Protection Agency has authority to regulate pesticides and disinfectants in aerosol (as well as nonaerosol) form. The Department of Transportation regulates the shipping of pressurized aerosol products. Local fire codes and industry standards (such as those from the National Fire Protection Association or NFPA) stipulate the manner in which aerosol products are stored in warehouses and in retail establishments. State and local environmental agencies such as the California Air Resources Board and the South Coast Air Quality Management District have established standards for specific consumer products such as aerosols in relation to VOC emissions and/or regulations concerning ambient ozone.

Among these concerns, CFC aerosol product regulations have remained, in both historical and contemporary terms, the most comprehensive arena for regulatory activity related to the nature and structure of aerosol industry activity. The high volume of CFC use for aerosol propellants during the mid 1970s (70–75% of all CFC use) decreased significantly by 1990 to only 13% of total use. These continued uses were for such exempted categories as safety and warning devices, release agents for plastic or other molded objects, certain pesticides, nonconsumer solvent, lubricant, or coating sprays for electrical/electronic equipment, and products necessary for safe aircraft operation or the defense of the United States. The FDA had also banned the use of CFCs in aerosol medical products, though it too had created exempted categories such as asthma inhalers or those cases where alternative drug delivery was unavailable or less desirable.[39]

Following the signing of the Montreal Protocols in 1987, EPA capped, in July 1989, the allowable production of fully halogenated CFCs at 1986 volumes. In each succeeding year, the production volume has been further reduced. By 1998, the regulations will have cut production to 50% of the 1986 volume. Perhaps more importantly, the major CFC producers have agreed to phase out production of the fully halogenated CFCs by the year 2000. At the same time, the 1990 Clean Air Act Amendments established an even more rapid acceleration schedule for both "Class 1" ozone depleting chemicals (CFCs, halons, 1,1,1,-trichloroethane, carbon tetrachloride) and a less rapid phaseout of "Class II" chemicals (primarily hydrofluorocarbons or HCFCs).[40] However, because the U.S. aerosols industry had largely eliminated CFC propellant use shortly after the 1978 rule was promulgated (though not for all Class I or Class II chemicals), the required production changeovers have not been as dramatic as the initial substitutions of the late 1970s. Nevertheless, it is still critical to note that the original 1978 CFC/aerosols rule and subsequent ozone depletion regulations have had a significant impact on the industry. This has been expressed both in terms of consumer dissatisfaction (a 1990 Roper poll discovered that 53% of U.S. consumers still believed aerosols harmed the ozone layer and 58% said they avoided buying aerosol products because of environmental concerns), and as the opening wedge in developing environmental regulations that potentially affect the very operations of the industry itself, an issue that has become even more prominent with the debates over VOCs and aerosols.[41]

While the Clean Air Act has most directly sought to address the issue of VOC emissions through consumer product regulation at the federal level, the most prominent efforts at public intervention in this area have occurred at state and local jurisdictions, particularly in California. During the late 1980s and early 1990s, both the California Air Resources Board and the Southern California-based South Coast Air Quality Management District sought to impose restrictions on VOCs in consumer products, including aerosols, by establishing a set of standards governing the quantity and type of chemical ingredients to be used in such products. The action by the California agencies was perceived by industry associations and a number of aerosol packagers as potentially threatening the very existence of the industry. These concerns included how stringent such standards would become, how wide a net they might cast in terms of products affected, the ease with which the regulations could be implemented (e.g., using such standards to force product changes or product phase-out), and the continuing threat of further tightening of such standards influenced by the level of public concern regarding VOC emissions.[42]

For example, with respect to aerosol disinfectants, although aerosols constituted only 1% of the combined retail and industrial and institutional markets for disinfectant products, they still contributed approximately 40% of the emissions from the entire disinfectant category. Thus, CARB imposed a standard of 60% by weight of VOC content, a measure that forced either direct reduction or substitution approaches by the companies involved. [43] The CARB actions were immediately perceived by the industry to threaten the nature of the product line itself, given its continuing dependence through the 1980s and 1990s on VOC propellant ingredients. Although aerosol producers had been able to negotiate some limited changes in the CARB rulemaking process, the final standards promulgated during the early 1990s were seen as further intensifying the shift to subcontracting as the most likely method of complying with (by escaping) regulation. At the same time, some of the largest subcontractors, such as CCL Laboratories, have explored the possibility of overseas production facilities, while defining their aerosol domestic production line as a potentially highly profitable, albeit short-term, source of activity.[44]

Another area of concern for the aerosols industry has been the flammability of product ingredients for propellants, particularly after the shift away from CFCs in the mid to late 1970s. During the late 1980s, a number of warehouse insurers began to identify aerosol products as contributing to the severity and extent of damage related to a series of large fires that took place at warehouses around the country. As a result, insurance rates began to increase substantially for warehouses storing aerosol products, with some warehouses refusing to accept specific aerosol products. Large retailers also expressed concerns about long-term storage of aerosol containers. This in turn increased the pressure on aerosol producers to potentially undertake another round of product substitutions away from the more flammable ingredients that had been introduced during the late 1970s and 1980s. These pressures were intensified by the development of several new flammability regulations, most notably a new fire protection code (the National Fire Protection Association Code 30B) governing the manufacture and storage of aerosol products, from the filler to the warehouse to the retail outlet.[45]

Cumulatively, these regulations have transformed the aerosols industry in the past decade from a largely unregulated consumer product and packaging industry to one of the more intensely regulated industries in existence. While the force of such regulations could be considered to have some significant pollution prevention implications, they have not fully suc-

ceeded in identifying a pollution prevention framework for product substitution, the most frequent approach utilized by the industry to comply
with such regulations. The breadth of regulations has also served to shift the
industry increasingly toward custom filling production, where the products
and ingredients are specified by the customer but the liabilities and the
thrust of the regulations are experienced by the fillers. Ultimately, pollu-
tant-based regulatory issues have emerged in recent years as the single
largest external factor influencing the structure and direction of the
aerosols industry as a whole. At the same time, the regulatory approach fails
to answer the central question in aerosols production, namely, whether the
most effective pollution prevention strategy is a specific standard or the
banning or phasing out or reconfiguration of the product itself, based on
an evaluation of its uses and the needs represented by such uses.

The response of the aerosols (and chemical specialty products) industry
to regulatory intervention in the solvents area demonstrates both the resistance to—and the potential of—developing a pollution prevention
approach. A commentary on the Montreal Protocols and the Clean Air Act
by Brad Lienhart of Dow Chemical is instructive in this respect. On the
one hand, Lienhart argued that the market for solvents, including those
subject to regulation, had not yet been fully tapped, particularly in a global
context where markets in Europe and especially in the newly industrializ-
ing countries offered significant opportunities for substantial growth for an
increasingly globalized company like Dow. Yet a company like Dow was
also subject to pressures—both from customers and from regulators—to
develop less toxic products, such as chlorine-free solvents. Dow, like other
companies, has thus begun to incorporate specific environmental design
criteria in the development of products to meet those market and regulatory demands. The ultimate issue for the company has become whether
such an approach also presents "a profit opportunity," a question that
extends beyond the specific problem of solvents.[46] What is absent from that
perspective, however, is how an environmental design approach can also
shed light on the value of the nature and uses of the product, given the
varying types of hazards represented by its manufacture, use (most notably),
and disposal.

These issues remain relevant in relation to nearly all aerosol markets,
including those often deemed more "essential," such as aerosol spray paints
and coatings. These particular products account for approximately 10% of
all aerosol products filled, as reported in recent CSMA surveys. Spray paint
products include traditional spray paints for both consumer and industrial
uses, primers, varnishes, rush inhibitors, wood stains, paint strippers, and
various decorative products. Spray paints consist of four general compo-

nents. Solid pigments provide the paint with its opacity and color, while a resin system, when dry, forms the continuous film coating in which the pigments are contained. There are also solvent and propellant components. Commonly used solvents include methylene chloride, methyl chloroform, alcohols, and water. METH especially had been used heavily in spray paint formulations, particularly for gloss paints that contain a higher concentration of the solvent in relation to the paint pigment. However, since the mid to late 1980s when METH became subject to increasing regulations (most notably at the state level), there has been a rapid substitution to new solvent blends such as acetone or combinations of acetone with TCA or an acetone/ester solvent. Some spray paints have been reformulated with water as the solvent, although water is generally not used alone, but in combination with other ingredients.[47]

Though substitution has become in recent years the dominant, regulatory-driven response by the industry to the problems of the use of METH, there has also been a clear downside to the approach, as revealed in the aerosol paints area. Some substitutes tend to be more flammable, less dense, and runnier on application. Questions regarding toxicity of acetone solvents have not been fully explored nor have wastewater concerns been fully addressed for water-based solvents, depending on the ingredients involved. For spray paints, the potential for eliminating the use of METH is substantial, but the pollution prevention outcomes remain problematic. The more generic issue of aerosol utility for paint application (in what settings is it used, how to evaluate such uses, and where such uses should be defined as "essential" as was done in relation to markets for CFC aerosols) also remains unexplored, both by packagers and by regulators. In this context, regulation continues to be a form of "crisis management," with industry decisionmaking a subtext of that approach.

Conclusion

The range of hazards related to the manufacture, use, and disposal of aerosols represents a set of problems for an industry that finds itself increasingly regulated, while it simultaneously evolves into a more segmented and differentiated organizational structure. During this period of regulatory oversight, the industry has witnessed both sharp declines and only modest recovery in several of its markets. Such trends have also been strongly influenced by consumer perceptions about the nature and degree of the industry's environmental problems. One key response of the industry—to seek product substitutions for regulated substances such as CFCs or METH—

has often compounded the environmental and regulatory issues while creating new manufacturing and market concerns. The regulatory process has itself been ad hoc and pollutant and media-specific, further limiting the ability to initiate pollution prevention approaches on an industry-wide basis.

The reasons underlying the origins and growth of aerosols packaging—constructing a new set of consumer "needs"—has also remained an area of vulnerability for an industry subject to the extent and breadth of environmental regulation that it is currently experiencing. Industry critics, meanwhile, have sought to describe aerosol packaging as "nonessential," a category utilized as part of the original CFC rule by EPA in 1978. The industry, in turn, has countered that argument by elevating preference for "convenience" as a "right," by suggesting that environmental concerns regarding the industry and its products are misplaced, and by seeking to limit the reach of regulation as an unwanted and unnecessary intrusion into the sphere of private decisionmaking and activity. With the continuing debates about appropriate strategies for pollution prevention and the limits of media-specific regulation, the aerosols industry represents a case where pollution prevention policy is likely to require a form of industry-specific regulation, whereby the industry's product becomes the focus of public debate and policymaking, and where the potential for prevention might ultimately be measured by the level of use of the product rather than by the specific toxic substance or toxic release currently regulated.

Notes

1. The "bugbomb" consisted of pyrethrum (a pesticide still in use today) and sesame oil in a liquefied propellant (dichlorodifluoromethane, also known as P-12). The mixture was contained in a steel canister, and was dispensed through a valve on the top of the container. When released from the can, the propellant was in the gaseous phase. This insecticide was a "true" aerosol in the sense that it was dispensed as a suspension of active ingredient particles in the propellant stream. See, Kirk-Othmer, *Encyclopedia of Chemical Technology*, Vol. 1, 1979; see also "Who's Who in the Aerosol Industry," *Aerosol Age*, July 1956, Vol. 1, No. 3, p. 44.

2. Aerosols, however, still tended to be priced higher than equivalent competitors given the overall percentage costs of the the packaging, which included the propellant, the container, and the valve system. "Of course, it is an article of faith with us in the aerosol industry that aerosols are more convenient to use, are often more economic in use than alternatives, but

the fact remains that in terms of first cost they are relatively expensive... more expensive than alternative forms of packaging," one industry figure commented in relation to the first twenty years of the industry. "The Aerosol Industry Up to 1970," J.P. Green, *Aerosol Age*, November 1971, Vol. 16, No. 11, p. 25. For background to the early history of the industry, see "History of Low Pressure Aerosols," Lyle D. Goodhue, *Aerosol Age*, August 1970, Vol. 15, No. 8, pp. 16–18; "Fred Lodes: Part of the Industry from the Beginning," *Aerosol Age*, December 1971, Vol. 16, No. 12, pp. 69–71. For background to Robert Abplanalp's role, see "The Aerosol World of Robert Abplanalp," *New York Times*, August 12, 1973, Section 3, p.1

3. Marketing strategies for convenience products were designed to appeal to the "lazy" consumer who welcomed easier ways of accomplishing household chores or "personal beautification." "People are always intrigued by something new and different, elements that aerosol products clearly possess," aerosol company official Eugene L. Rose predicted. Cited in "Aerosols Are Here to Stay!(?)," *Aerosol Age*, June 1956, Vol. 1, No. 2, p. 43.

4. The production numbers are from a table prepared by CMB Aerosols and reproduced in *Aerosol Review*, 1989/1990, p. 5.

5. "Aerosols and the Cosmetic Industry," John Sciarra, *Aerosol Age*, November 1970, Vol. 15, No. 11, p. 18; see also "The History of Antiperspirant Product Development," Herman E. Jass, *Cosmetics and Toiletries*, July 1980, Vol. 95, p. 26.

6. "The Aerosol Industry Up to 1970," p. 28.

7. The *Aerosol Age* quote is from "Sugar and Spice and Everything Nice," Jerome N. Michell, December 1971, Vol. 16, No. 12, p. 30.

8. Cited in "A Consumer Product Company's View of Aerosols," James A. Latty, *Aerosol Age*, January 1990, Vol. 35, No. 1, p. 19.

9. Industry figures, such as chief Du Pont toxicologist John A. Zapp, argued at the time that fluorocarbon propellants (primarily a blend of CFCs with vinyl chloride used for such products as deodorant aerosols) had no toxic effects, and were therefore capable of offsetting any environmental or public health concerns that were just then beginning to emerge. Zapp's comments were made at the Government/Industry Conference on Aerosols, June 21, 1971, reprinted in *Aerosol Age*, August 1971, Vol. 16, No. 8, p. 16.

10. "Stratospheric Sink for Chlorofluoromethanes: Chlorine Atom Catalyzed Destruction of Ozone," M. Molina and F.S. Rowland, *Nature*, Vol. 249, No. 5460, pp. 10–12.

11. Du Pont was already experiencing income loss from CFC production by 1976 despite CFC sales of more than $260 million. See, David A.

Hounshell & John Kenly Smith, Jr., *Science and Corporate Strategy: Du Pont R&D, 1902–1980,* (Cambridge University Press: Cambridge, 1988), pp. 584–585; "Why Aerosols Are Under Attack," *Business Week,* February 17, 1975, No. 2368, pp. 50–51.

12. On announcing their decision to eliminate CFC use, Johnson Wax chairman Samuel C. Johnson declared that "during a period of uncertainty and scientific inquiry," it was important to take such an action in order that its customers "may use our aerosol products with greater confidence." Johnson Wax, however, had the advantage of having already shifted production toward a range of other, non–CFC propellants prior to the eruption of the ozone layer controversies. See, S.C. Johnson Wax case history in Bruce Smart (editor), *Beyond Compliance: A New Industry View of the Environment,* (Washington D.C.:World Resources Institute, April 1992), p. 86.

13. Exemptions were based on the concept of "essential uses" and included nonconsumer articles used as cleaner solvents, lubricants, or coatings for electrical or electronic equipment, articles for maintenance and operation of aircraft, and uses deemed essential for "military preparedness," as determined by the EPA Administrator and the Secretary of Defense. See, "The Economic Impact of Regulating Chlorofluorocarbon Emissions from Aerosols: A Retrospective Study," Faith H. Ando & Charles R. Marshall, Office of Pesticides and Toxic Substances, USEPA, EPA 560/4-83-001, April 1983.

14. "Toxicology and Carcinogenesis Studies of Dichloromethane in Rats and Mice," National Toxicology Program, National Institute of Environmental Health Sciences, 1986; National Toxicology Program, "NTP technical report of the toxicological and carcenogenesis studies of DCM" (CAS No. 75-09-2); see also, the *Federal Register,* Vol. 56, No. 216, June 1991.

15. Cited in Title 42 § 7617.

16. "Things to Come," Montfort A. Johnsen, *Aerosol Age,* December, 1971, p. 86. Food aerosols have long represented a much desired but unattainable market for aerosol producers. Through the 1960s and 1970s and again in the late 1980s, food aerosol products were introduced without much success. For example, William H. Rorer Inc.'s "Maalox Whip," an antacid promoted for its "smooth creamy taste," was introduced with great fanfare in 1987/1988, but was already considered a failure by industry analysts within the year. Still, the year after Maalox Whip was introduced to market, more than 250 new products, with such names as "Easy Cheese" and "Malibu Musk," were introduced as well, but without consumer acceptance. See, "Aerosols Expand Into New Markets," Gretchen Busch,

Chemical Marketing Reporter, May 2, 1988; "Aerosols Fueled by Personal Care," *Chemical Marketing Reporter,* April 24, 1989; "Sixth Annual New Product Roundup," *Aerosol Age,* August 1989, Vol. 34, No. 8, pp. 21–34.

17. Interview with Arlene Mencke, Marketing Development Manager, 1993.

18. Chemical Specialities Manufacturers Association, Inc. "Aerosol Pressurized Products Survey United States 1992, (Washington D.C.: CSMA, 1993).

19. For example, one of the largest of the fillers, a medium–sized Canadian company named CCL Industries acquired in 1992 a subsidiary of Proctor & Gamble which had specialized in producing primarily Old Spice products. CCL would continue the production of those products under a contract with P&G. At the same time, however, CCL, recognizing the limited growth potential in the industry, was actively seeking to shift more production to custom fillers as part of its decision to "diminish its reliance on aerosols." See CCL Industries Inc., 1992 Annual Information Form, (Willowdale, Ontario: CCL Industries, 1992), p. 10.

20. 1993 Interview with Paul Pierpoint; see also *Aerosol Pressurized Products Survey, United States 1992,* Chemical Specialties Manufacturers Association, 1993.

21. The European producers of aerosols, themselves responsible for an even more substantial share of the CFC market than their U.S. counterparts, remained strongly resistant to eliminating the use of CFCs for propellants during the 1970s and early 1980s, and their resistance contributed to only limited action in those countries (e.g., 30% reduction from 1976 figures of CFCs for aerosols by a 1981 target date). Only after a major environmental campaign was launched in the late 1980s in light of new scientific evidence of an enlarged ozone hole did European producers agree to stronger limits and thus contribute to more significant declines of CFC use in aerosol products. See "The Political Economy of the CFC Phaseout: Learning the Right Lessons," Sanford L. Weiner & James H. Maxwell, in *Dimensions of Managing Chlorine in the Environment: Report of The MIT/Norwegian Chlorine Policy Study,* (Cambridge: MIT Technology, Business and Environment Program, 1993); *Ozone Diplomacy,* Richard Elliot Benedick, (Cambridge: Harvard University Press, 1991).

22. CFC production totals outside the U.S. actually declined sharply between 1987 and 1989 as a consequence of a change in approach by the European community toward mandating CFC reductions in aerosol use.

23. CSMA, 42nd Annual Aerosol Pressurized Products Survey—1992, April 1993.

24. CSMA, Annual Product Survey, 1988.

25. The survey was undertaken as part of an extensive review of the use of chlorinated solvents in the Southern California region and their potential impact on groundwater quality. The final report that was issued included 12 technical reports, including one on aerosols. See *Source Reduction and Recycling of Halogenated Solvents in the Aerosols Industry*, A Report on Research Performed by the Source Reduction Research Partnership for the Metropolitan Water District and the Environmental Defense Fund; prepared by the Jacobs Engineering Group, Pasadena, 1992. Draft report and industry survey undertaken by Pamela Yates, 1989–1990.

26. See, *The Inside Story: A Guide to Indoor Air Quality*, Environmental Protection Agency and Consumer Product Safety Commission, EPA, 402-K-93-007, September 1993.

27. See "Aerosol Recyclability," Montfort A. Johnsen, *Spray Technology and Marketing*, April 1991.

28. One of the coauthors of this chapter undertook several in-depth background interviews on these and other subjects of industry figures in the Southern California region for the SRRP study.

29. "Aerosol Recyclability," Montfort A. Johnsen, *Spray Technology and Marketing*, April 1991, p. 28.

30. See "Aerosol Containers: What Should I Do With Them When They're Empty?," (Hazardous and Toxic Materials Project, City of Los Angeles: Los Angeles, January 1990).

31. The cost figures were identified in a memorandum, "Introduction and First Reading of an Ordinance Requiring Retailers to Display Consumer Awareness Information Wherever Household Hazardous Products are Sold," to the Mayor and City Council of the city of Santa Monica from city staff, April 26, 1994. The figures were also confirmed in a personal communication with Brian Johnson, director of the city of Santa Monica's Environmental Services Division (and supervisor of the city's household hazardous waste facility where aerosols are collected and sent for disposal). See also, "Aerosol Containers: What Should I Do With Them When They're Empty?," (Hazardous and Toxic Materials Project, City of Los Angeles: Los Angeles, January 1990).

32. The CARB estimates can be found in the Technical Support Document for *A Proposed Regulation to Reduce Volatile Organic Compound Emissions from Antiperspirants and Deodorants*, State of California Air Resources Board, Stationary Source Division, September 1989, p. 26.

33. Job descriptions for these processes include: (1) mixer (loads ingredients into mixing tanks, may take quality control samples); (2) filler (monitors automated filling process); (3) valve dropper (either manually places valve hardware into filled cans or monitors an automated operation); (4)

gasser (either manually adds nonflammable propellant to containers, or monitors automated gassing of flammable propellants from outside the gassing room); (5) packer (removes cans from lines, cleans them as necessary, and packs them into boxes). The filler, valve dropper, or packer may also be responsible for removing dirty or reject (damaged, over- or underfilled) containers from the line if this step is not automated. See *Estimates of Worker Exposures for Aerosol Packing*, (Washington D.C.: PEI Associates, Inc., December 1987).

34. PEI, 1987, *op. cit.*

35. *Occupational Exposure to Methylene Chloride*, OSHA instruction, PUB 8-1.2 A, Washington D.C., August 11, 1986.

36. "Source Reduction and Recycling of Halogenated Solvents in the Aerosols Industry," Technical Support Document, *op. cit.*

37. *Product Survey*, Source Reduction Research Partnership, Los Angeles, 1989; see also *Occupational Exposure and Environmental Release Assessment of Methylene Chloride*, (Washington D.C.: PEI Associates Inc., 1985).

38. *Reducing Risk: Setting Priorities and Strategies for Environmental Protection*, United States Environmental Protection Agency, Science Advisory Board, SAB-EC-90-021, September 1990.

39. For FDA actions see "Use of CFC propellants in self-pressurized containers, Federal Register, Vol. 43, p. 11316 Subpart G §2.125 and Code of Federal Regulations, Vol. 40, p. 302. For EPA activities, see also "CFC's nonpropellant uses," Code of Federal Regulations, Vol. 40, p. 4676, 1986.

40. Clean Air Act Amendments Title 42 § 7617 (c–e).

41. The Roper poll information is reported in the November 1990 issue of *Aerosol Age* (p. 28). The CFC issue—among other regulatory and consumer perception concerns—continued to weigh heavily on the aerosols industry as a source of potential consumer backlash and market loss through the late 1980s and early 1990s, more than a decade after EPA's 1978 CFC aerosol action. As a consequence, the industry began to devote increasing resources to public relations, establishing in 1990 the Consumer Aerosol Products Council (CAPCO) as the centerpiece of the industry campaign. CAPCO in turn devised plans for an advertising "media blitzkrieg" to offset "lingering consumer misperceptions" about CFCs in aerosols in particular. See "Personal-Care Products Offset Gains in Aerosols," *Chemical Marketing Reporter*, May 4, 1992, Vol. 241, No. 18, p. 5; also, "Coping with Misinformation," *Aerosol Age*, December 1990, pp. 52–53.

42. SanGiovanni, Michael L., "Special Report: California—South Coast Regulates Spray Paints," *Aerosol Age*, Vol. 35, No. 12, December 1990, pp. 12–15; see also "California: CARB Revises Table of Standards on

Consumer Product VOC Emissions," SanGiovanni, M.L, *Aerosol Age,* Vol. 35, No. 10, October, 1990, p. 8.; "Calfiornia CARB/Industry Negotiates Consumer Product Regs," SanGiovanni, M.L., *Aerosol Age,* Vol. 35, No. 7, p. 22.

43. See "Proposed Amendments to the Statewide Regulation to Reduce Volatile Organic Emissions from Consumer Products: Phase II—Technical Support Document," State of California, Air Resources Board, Stationary Source Division, October 1991.

44. See CCL Industries, Inc., 1992 Annual Information Form, (Willowdale, Ontario: CCL Industries, 1992).

45. See "An Update on the Safe Manufacture, Storage and Display of Aerosol Products," Montfort A. Johnsen, *Aerosol Age,* December 1990.

46. "Chlorinated Solvents: Coping with Events after the Montreal Protocols and the Clean Air Act," Brad Lienhart, *Spray Technology and Marketing,* April 1991, Vol. 1, No. 1, pp. 50–58.

47. Interviews undertaken by Pamela Yates 1989–1990 for the "Paints and Coatings" component of the Source Reduction Research Partnership study, 1989–1990. See *Source Reduction and Recycling of Halogenated Solvents in Paint Stripping,* Technical Support Document, Source Reduction Research Partnership, (Los Angeles: Metropolitan Water District and Environmental Defense Fund, 1992).

12

Pollution Prevention Voluntarism: The Example of 3M

Peter Sinsheimer
Robert Gottlieb

Company with a Conscience

If there is a company most directly identified with a voluntary pollution prevention perspective, it is the Minnesota-based 3M corporation, a research-oriented, innovation and product-driven manufacturer and one of the largest generators of toxic substances in the country. Since initiating in 1975 its "3P" ("Pollution Prevention Pays") program, 3M has been continually singled out and praised for its commitment to a pollution prevention approach. The company has been identified by corporate analysts as the corporation with the greatest environmental consciousness, while its 3P program has been highlighted frequently in business journal articles and environmental publications focusing on the relationship between business and the environment (Ferguson, 1989; Kirkpatrick, 1990; Mitchell, 1989; *New York Times,* 1988). Indeed, through 3P and subsequent programs, 3M has argued that it has reduced hundreds of thousands of tons of air pollutants, water pollutants, and sludge, and saved hundreds of millions of dollars from reduced manufacturing costs or operating costs for pollution control or for "retained sales of products that might otherwise have been taken off the market as environmentally unacceptable" (U.S. Congress, 1990). In this way, 3M has sought to define itself as a pollution prevention success story, its claims especially noteworthy in light of recent arguments that pollution prevention is best accomplished by industry on a nonregulatory, voluntary basis. It is this intersection of the claims of voluntarism (by a company that prides itself on innovation) with 3M's actual performance on which this analysis is focused.

The "Business" of Innovation

The origins of 3M (formerly the Minnesota Mining and Manufacturing Company) provide an instructive view of the company's approach to its core issues of industrial innovation, pollution prevention, and voluntarism. The company was founded at the turn of the twentieth century by five Minnesotans who bought a plot of heavily forested land on the shores of Lake Superior, northeast of Duluth, in order to mine corundum, used by sandpaper manufacturers as a grinding-wheel abrasive. Once the mining commenced, however, company officials discovered that their corundum "wasn't corundum at all, but a low grade anorthosite, unfit for effective abrasive work," as a company biographer put it (Huck, 1955; Mitchell, 1989).

The company tried selling its own sandpaper, using corundum shipped in from the East, but failed to establish a strong market presence. As a consequence, 3M was forced to innovate by establishing new product lines with high value added. Its first major innovation success was a waterproof sandpaper called "wetordry" whose primary market turned out to be the paint industry. The company was especially focused on the English market, given that a major legislative battle had erupted during the 1920s over whether to ban white lead in paint due to its role as an occupational hazard in industries such as automobile manufacture. Support for a ban had intensified with the release of a 1924 report by the undersecretary of state for Britain's Office of Home Affairs. The report revealed that between 1910 and 1923 there had been 1500 paint-related cases of serious occupational lead poisoning, which included 300 deaths. In the midst of this battle, 3M's "wetordry" sandpaper was introduced into the English market as a product capable of reducing dust emissions and thus eliminating the need to ban lead ingredients in paint. 3M's approach allied the company politically and financially with lead paint companies such as the Brimsdown Lead Company and the Associated Lead Manufacturers trade association which had been in the forefront of the effort to oppose the lead paint ban (Comfort, 1962).

While company biographers and company promotional materials have suggested that the introduction of wetordry sandpaper in England could be seen as an effort to reduce hazards by "easing the health problem of sanding dust,"(Comfort, 1962), it simultaneously undercut a prevention-oriented government action and thus allowed lead to be used in paint for another several decades. The development of wetordry, however, ultimately became most directly associated with 3M's capacity to innovate and its related decision to place a strong emphasis on its research and development activities. This approach was initially derived from the company's response to production problems experienced by its varied industrial customers. During the 1930s, 3M's research emphasis expanded to include development of consumer products along with large-scale advertising to differentiate and promote its products as well as to highlight the company's approach to research and product innovation. By 1937, when 3M decided to allocate additional resources to product development and engineering, the company slogan, "more research, greater growth," (Huck, 1955) had become its dominant operational philosophy. This emphasis on research and innovation became a 3M trademark, inspiring favorable commentary about the company's ability and willingness to meet customer demands for new products (particularly its industrial and commercial customers) and to provide an environment for experimentation in product development.

Through the 1940s, '50s, and '60s, 3M's ability to innovate and diversify into new product lines grew primarily from its base in coating and bonding technology and the core role of its chemical engineers in the area of research and development. New ventures were established in such areas as magnetic sound-recording tape and videotape, thermo-fax copying processes and dry-silver microfilm, fabric protectors and cleaning pads, and new electro-mechanical and medical and dental products. 3M's "business of innovation" (*R&D Magazine,* 1990) also evolved in terms of quantitative goals—the more tries at product innovation, company officials decided, the more likely a commercial success would result. As a consequence, the company structured itself to help maximize the number of "tries" as well as "hits," while enabling it to also tolerate "failure." As 3M grew in size—by the 1950s it was already listed among the elite ranks of the Fortune 500— it maintained a significant degree of decentralization to sustain an internal culture of innovation. New divisions were formed based on the success of new products, as more than 50 divisions were eventually established by the early 1990s along specific product lines. When any division became too big or unwieldy in relation to the need for further R&D and innovation, it was encouraged to split into new units. In recent years, that trigger has been defined as $200 million in sales as a threshold level for subdivision. Decentralization thus became at once an organizational strategy designed to establish a more intimate work environment and a setting more conducive to innovation.

It was at the divisional level that 3M established the organizational objective most directly associated with its culture of innovation—the goal of achieving twenty-five percent of sales from products that had not existed five years earlier. To accomplish this goal, 3M devised the concept of the "new venture team," groups created within a division to undertake the necessary research and development for a new product idea. New venture teams consisted of full-time staff recruited from the technical, manufacturing, marketing, and sales areas within a division. The team's responsibilities included designing a product as well as developing the ways to produce and market it. Team members thus established "ownership" over the product's lifecycle and in turn benefited from its growth as long as conventional corporate measures and standards of performance were met (Dumaine, 1990).

Through the venture team concept and related approaches, 3M's operational philosophy came to focus on institutionalizing procedures to prevent prematurely killing off a potential project. Tom Peters, in his book *In Search of Excellence,* described 3M's "eleventh commandment," as: "thou shalt not kill a new product idea" (Peters and Waterman, 1982). For example, any staff member unable to find a home for a potential project idea in one of the existing divisions is still allowed to devote as much as 15% of his or her own staff time to pursuing development of the product idea in order to prove it workable (and ultimately marketable). As a further incentive, 3M established the Genesis grant, an internal system of project development awards (currently ranging between $27,000 and $80,000) first initiated in 1984. The Genesis program was designed to "encourage growth by promoting technical innovation," and was aimed at kickstarting new projects that did not fit within existing division boundaries. By 1993, nearly 100 Genesis grants were provided annually (3M Genesis; Botten 1993).

Two additional operational approaches that encouraged innovation at 3M were internal technology sharing and its identification with and ability to work closely with customers. Although the company encouraged decentralization for product development, its industrial processes have remained reasonably similar, maintaining a base in chemical engineering and coating and bonding technology. Technology sharing within and between divisions has also become a profitable means for the company to retool old industrial processes or to adapt new ones to its various manufacturing divisions. Such sharing has been promoted through in-house technology conferences as well as by sharing employees across divisions.

At the same time, the concept of "staying close to the customers" has been critical to the ability of the company to develop new products and expand into new markets. Customers, particularly industrial customers, have long provided the inspiration for 3M's approach to product development by their ability to define very specific needs, a definition that can then become the basis for the establishment of the venture team. However, even when a product is developed in advance of such a definition of need, the company still attempts to find an appropriate customer to try to identify a need for the product rather than rely on developing products only after markets have been identified. In this way, the product itself tends to drive company decisionmaking, with markets developing from, rather than framing, such decisions.

The well known, perhaps apocryphal story of how Scotch Tape became a 3M product underlines this concept of a product-driven (rather than exclusively market-driven) company. As Peter Drucker tells the story, a 3M engineer, unable to find an industrial customer for a new tape he had developed was at first discouraged because the company seemed prepared to abandon the product. After bringing samples home with him one night, the engineer, to his surprise, discovered that his teenage daughters had used the tape samples to hold their curls in place overnight. Suddenly, a new customer for the product had been identified. With the need verified, the engineer was able to convince the company that it could now introduce and market "Scotch Tape," perhaps 3M's best known product today (Drucker, 1985). In this context, company salespeople, crucial participants in both the venture teams and the overall operations approach, have long been seen as central to the process of identifying needs and developing new products.

3M's emphasis on innovation has influenced the kinds of products developed, the company's organizational structure, and some of the environmental problems that have resulted from its activities, including its approach to product development. Its "business of innovation" has also allowed it to establish new market niches, as well as maintain high growth rates for the company as a whole. As it grew in size and product base, 3M also expanded its role as a multinational manufacturing corporation. In 1992, it ranked thirty-fourth on the Fortune 500 list, with approximately $13.8 billion in sales while employing 87,000 men and women in 57 nations. Overseas markets accounted for 50 percent of total worldwide sales. As part of this expansion, it had also become the world's largest producer of coated products (3M, 1992b).

As a leading "blue chip" company, 3M became known as one of the world's premier new-product industry innovators, developing and manufacturing more than 60,000 products for business, industry, government, and consumers around the globe. It began to average as many as one hundred new products each year. By 1990, more than 30 percent of 3M's sales derived from products introduced during the previous five years, thus exceeding its core operational philosophy of new product development. By the early 1990s, 3M had secured its place as a dynamic, innovative, technology and chemical engineering-driven Fortune 500 company, with, parenthetically, a strong environmental reputation. At the same time, the evolution of 3M revealed a less publicly visible, contentious history of toxics generation and regulatory conflict. Ultimately, a conundrum had emerged in relation to the company's reputation: innovation toward what end (and with what environmental outcomes), new products for what purpose?

3M's Environmental Issues

Despite its wide variety of products including tapes, coated abrasives, specialty chemicals, information, imaging, and electronic technologies, and medical products, 3M has come to depend on a set of core technologies and processes, many of which relate to the company's historical ties to coating and bonding technology and its more recent developments in non-woven materials, ceramics, and magnetics. An in-house survey revealed that only about 75 basic technologies are used at 3M. These technologies are in turn modified through a range of process changes and product manipulations to produce the more than 60,000 company products that reach the market (Bacon, 1991; Katauskas, 1990).

3M's technology processes essentially involve adding "sticky stuff" to a film base, as one 3M manager put it (Adams, 1991). VOC-based solvents have long been used as the base medium for placing coating on film. At the end point of the process, solvents are emitted into the ambient environment producing 3M's heavy volume of toxic air emissions. In recent years, a handful of new technologies have been explored as possible replacements for some of the more toxic solvents as a base medium for coating and bonding functions. Such replacement possibilities have included hot-melt (applying coating directly on film), water-based, and radiation-cured applications. Nevertheless, the use of chemical-based solvents still dominates nearly all 3M production systems and product innovations.

The widespread use of solvents and other toxic chemicals in 3M operations caused the company to become, during the 1970s and 1980s, a major target for permitting and related regulatory activities at both the state and federal levels. These activities included specific regulations on a medium-by-medium basis: air emissions, water discharges (including sludge and wastewater), RCRA wastes, and so forth. Although 3M was already known for its emissions of air pollutants and waste discharges and had been identified as a responsible party at a number of Superfund sites, it was only when Toxics Release Inventory numbers first became available that the extent of 3M hazardous waste generation and particularly toxic air releases became more evident.

The release of TRI data, first made public in 1989 (using 1987 figures), was a powerful event for 3M, clearly marking the company as one of the largest polluters in the country. 3M was situated among the top ten companies in total toxic releases and transfers and among the top two or three in terms of toxic air releases within the United States (see Table 12.1). Several 3M plants were also among the top ten polluters (by individual facility) in terms of air emissions, water discharges, and total toxic releases

Table 12.1 **3M Toxic Release Inventory Figures**

1989[a]	
Releases	
Nonpoint Air	969,519
Point Air	73,757,008
Water	15,503,726
Land	16,220
Underground Injection	0
Total Releases	90,246,473
Transfers	
POTW	772,820
Off-site	19,868,256
Total Transfers	20,641,076
Total Releases and Transfers	110,887,549
1990[b]	
Releases	
Nonpoint Air	2,284,795
Point Air	62,355,303
Water	3,976,617
Land	29,233
Underground Injection	20
Total Releases	68,645,968
Transfers	
POTW	815,060
Off-site	6,044,826
Total Transfers	6,859,886
Total Releases and Transfers	75,505,854

[a]Ranked 6th for total releases and transfers.
[b]Ranked 8th for total releases and transfers.

and transfers.[1] When 3M (reluctantly) joined EPA's 33/50 Industrial Toxics Project in 1991, it found itself to be the largest single generator (both in terms of total toxic releases and air emissions) of the 17 chemicals targeted by 33/50 for reduction (U.S. EPA, 1993). Due in part to its heavy use of solvents (the TRI identified the company as the second largest emitter of solvents in the country), 3M also became the single largest source of teratogenic chemical releases, primarily methyl ethyl ketone and toluene. Specific 3M plants in turn represented a significant source of pollutant releases in the communities where they were located (many in nonattainment areas under the Clean Air Act). This factor was most pronounced in areas where 3M facilities had emerged as the single largest source for toxic air releases or discharges at both county or state levels, most notably with its facilities in Minnesota, Illinois, Texas, Indiana, and California (U.S. EPA, 1991).

Aside from its becoming identified as a major source of toxic releases, 3M also came to be associated with a number of occupational and product-based hazards. In 1992, for example, the Minnesota Department of Health released a preliminary study initiated on the basis of worker complaints that identified an elevated cancer rate among 3M maintenance craftsworkers at the company's major facility in the St. Paul area. While the report failed to investigate more directly 3M production activities potentially responsible for the high cancer rates, it recommended further review to begin to identify causative factors (Minnesota Department of Health, 1992; Shipp, 1993).

Thus, as with other large users of toxic and hazardous materials, 3M became a visible regulatory target, subject to wide ranging enforcement actions, including fines for operational problems (e.g., leaking radioactive matter from air guns), permit violations, safety violations, and reporting violations (e.g., its failure to comply with TSCA prenotification requirements which resulted in the largest single fine—$1.3 million—in TSCA history) (*Chemicals in Progress*, 1992). These enforcement actions, as well as the publicly available reports such as TRI which began to document 3M's environmental impacts, became a significant concern for a company that long prided itself on its reputation as both an innovator and as a successfully managed company with a high public profile. For 3M, environmental issues touched on the very nature of that reputation.

The Rise of 3P

Prior to the development of its 3P ("Pollution Prevention Pays") program in 1975, 3M had largely ignored and at times resisted addressing its own environmental impacts, including those subject to regulatory review. Bert Cross, 3M's chairman during the 1960s, became a leading industry critic of environmental regulations in the late 1960s and early 1970s. In that capacity, Cross was appointed by President Richard Nixon to be the first chair of the National Industrial Pollution Control Council, a quasi-governmental, industry advocacy group responding to environmental laws and regulations affecting large producers. NIPCC, consisting of the heads of the 52 largest U.S. corporations and whose meetings and minutes were secret, became a leading industry opponent of toxics legislation, lobbying heavily to modify Clean Air Act rules and against the early versions of what eventually became the Toxic Substances Control Act (Vietor, 1979). 3M executives, in this and other industry-based groups, argued that environmental controls increased the cost of capital as part of overall production costs and thus created an inflationary burden on companies during a period when inflation had become a major impediment to plant or product expansion (Brunner, 1981).

Even where the company sought to address an issue with potential environmental implications, as with its "Commute-A-Van" program established during the early 1970s, it tended to justify such programs for reasons other than environmental purposes. The van program was initiated to facilitate access to the company's main center at the eastern edge of St. Paul as well as in response to increasing public unwillingness to fund further highway improvements to accommodate the company's growth. Thus, from the outset, the project was defined in the context of transportation (and public relations) needs for the company, and not in relation to its potential environmental benefits (reduced air emissions and energy use) (Owens and Sever, 1974).

By 1975, however, 3M decided to reconsider its approach toward environmental regulation. This occurred as a consequence of its inability to reduce compliance and pollution control costs in the midst of economic recession. In one particularly noteworthy episode, the company obtained a government contract to develop a rapid fire-extinguishing agent for petroleum fires, only to discover that the product initially developed would not meet EPA permit requirements under the Clean Water Act. Company researchers subsequently identified substitutes for two chemicals used in the product, allowing it to meet the permit requirements, and, as it turned out, lower overall production costs (Brunner, 1981).

The fire extinguisher episode influenced the discussions taking place within the company about the costs of environmental compliance in a high inflation/major recession climate during which powerful public support continued to be generated for environmental protection. The question of public relations also emerged as a major issue confronting 3M, which was then in the midst of a major scandal related to the indictment (and subsequent conviction) of top 3M officials who had made illegal contributions to Richard Nixon's 1972 reelection campaign (Smith, 1980).

Out of these discussions 3M's Pollution Prevention Pays, or 3P, program was organized to slow down the rapid increase in compliance costs and reverse negative public relations. With 3P, 3M proclaimed an end to its earlier environmental image of noncompliance and/or resistance to environmental laws and regulations, while also suggesting that its own powerful emphasis on research and product innovation could be translated into new environmental approaches.

As a first step in reorienting its environmental approach, the 3M Board of Directors in 1975 formally adopted a six-part "corporate environmental policy." At the core of the new policy was the concept of avoidance, defined both in terms of the avoidance or prevention of pollution generated by or emanating from 3M facilities as well as the reduction of costs associated with regulated wastes, emissions, or discharges. A well-managed business was one that "avoids conflict," argued Joseph Ling, the key company official responsible for the development of the 3P concept. Thus a corporate manager's goal, in this context, was to keep 3M "away from environmental conflict—away from confrontation with state or federal pollution control agencies, away from product criticism and community challenges over environmental concerns" (Brunner, 1981).

To accomplish those objectives, the 3M "corporate environmental policy" (Bringer and Benforado, 1989) would strive to:

- Solve one's own environmental pollution and conservation problems

- Prevent pollution at the source wherever and whenever possible

- Develop products that will have a minimum effect on the environment

- Conserve natural resources through the use of reclamation and other appropriate methods

- Assure that 3M facilities and products meet and sustain the regulations of all federal, state, and local environmental agencies

- Assist, wherever possible, governmental agencies and other official organizations engaged in environmental activities

While 3M's environmental policy statement covered environmental concerns both internal to the company and in relation to government regulation, it realized early on that by adopting what would be considered a proactive, voluntary approach, it could, in the long run, realize a number of significant gains: minimizing government intervention, creating greater efficiencies of production, reducing actual as well as potential compliance costs, and achieving a positive environmental image (crucial for a company like 3M with its own high profile product lines) in a period when companies were being substantially criticized for their environmental problems. At the same time, the program was also structured to emphasize the third "P," that pollution prevention *pays*. According to then chairman and chief executive officer Lewis Lehr, 3P had to derive "some monetary benefit to the 3M Company. This could conceivably be accomplished through reduced or deferred pollution-control or manufacturing costs, increased sales of an existing or new product, or other reduction in capital or expenses" (Brunner, 1981).

To implement its six-part environmental policy, a number of organizational and management reforms were implemented. 3M located the 3P program inside its Environmental Engineering and Pollution Control (EE&PC) division, which had previously been established to handle environmental compliance issues. In addition the company established a 3P Coordinating Committee consisting of management personnel from EE&PC on the corporate side as well as from the engineering, laboratory, and manufacturing organizations. An EE&PC supervisor was selected to carry out the 3P Coordinating Committee plans and programs, which included establishing criteria for 3P recognition, making recommendations for awards based on those criteria, and publicizing such awards. Unlike the Genesis program, however, 3P awards have not been monetary. An award for a new innovative technology for environmental purposes, for example, results in "a handsome walnut plaque [given] at a special function," while an award for application of an existing technology results in a certificate presented at that same function (Bringer and Benforado, 1992). In contrast, Genesis grants (which have almost invariably not been designated for environmental projects) can involve, aside from significant funding, far greater prestige for recipients (Botten, 1993).

3P also generated a significant corporate public relations operation, which primarily centered on updated accounting of both dollars saved and pollutant releases reduced. A 3P submittal form was developed to quantify, in the first year of any new "prevention"-oriented project, the tons or gallons of pollutants reduced. These would be noted on the basis of four specific categories:

- *Product Reformulation*—developing nonpolluting or less-polluting products or processes by using different raw materials or feedstocks

- *Process Modification*—changing manufacturing processes to control the formation of byproducts

- *Equipment Redesign*—modifying equipment to perform more efficiently under specific operating conditions or to make use of available resources

- *Resource Recovery*—reclaiming or recycling byproducts for sale or for use in other 3M products or processes

This accounting, in turn, was structured in terms of specific wastestreams subject to regulation (e.g., RCRA wastes, CWA-related wastewater and sludge discharges, CAA air pollutant releases). 3P thus emerged in its early years as a broadly defined organizational philosophy regarding environmental compliance and cost avoidance, a mechanism to give recognition to company activities defined as meeting the objectives of that philosophy, and a promotional effort to publicize both the philosophy and the accomplishments identified with the program.

Nearly all of the initial activities recognized by the company through 3P (and thus highlighted as examples of the commitment to pollution prevention) were the kinds of efficiency or housekeeping measures most commonly characterized as "low hanging fruit" opportunities for waste minimization. In a 1979 article published in the *EPA Journal*, for example, EE&PC vice president Joseph Ling identified three examples of the 3P approach which represented such opportunities: a process change that increased a conversion ratio for producing a bulk adhesive and thus reduced foul smelling exhausts that had generated substantial community complaints; recycling cooling water that enabled the company to scale down a planned wastewater treatment facility; and the redesign of a resin spray booth for more effective recycling of the overspray which had required special incineration disposal as wet scrap (Ling, 1980).

Through the late 1970s and 1980s, 3M became a visible proponent of efficiency and avoidance-related waste minimization programs it defined as "pollution prevention." At the same time, it sought to influence environmental policy in favor of both market incentive programs and decreased regulation, including reporting requirements under right-to-know legislation, permitting provisions at both the state and federal level, and/or pollutant-specific or clean up and liability provisions that directly affected 3M operations. In relation to legislation and regulations, 3M's EE&PC division became directly involved, as part of the 3P approach, in lobbying at the state and federal level *against* a wide range of pollution prevention and waste-related initiatives. 3M officials argued that bringing about reduction, or, rather, avoidance objectives, was best accomplished without regulatory oversight and through the company's own programs established to reduce environmental impacts.

This idea of reducing government regulation as a strategy for accelerating industries' active involvement in pollution reduction is illustrated by 3M's embrace of market incentive programs. It argued strongly that market incentives minimized government interventions at the operational level, while increasing company and facility flexibility in meeting (or redefining) the spirit of environmental compliance. One such example, for 3M officials, was its experience at a tape-manufacturing facility in Pennsylvania. The facility was able to earn credits by developing new techniques to reduce certain solvent emissions, which it then used to postpone either retrofitting or installing new control technologies on other production activities at the facility whose emissions had not been in compliance with Clean Air Act provisions (Brunner, 1981). Another example involved a 3M plant in Ventura County, California that decided to apply some of its "banked" pollution credits to establish a Clean Air Fund for the county, designed in part to offset the negative publicity from TRI reports which had identified the plant as the county's largest emitter of TRI chemicals (primarily of methyl ethyl ketone and toluene) (Miller, 1991).

Through the 1980s, 3M became adept at highlighting its program at various government and business forums, in press stories, and in publications presenting the 3M approach. Its pitched battles with regulators contrasted with its effective promotion of 3P objectives, much of which was defined in relation to its reductions of regulated pollutants quantified through its submittal forms. This little-publicized tension between the company's voluntary programs and its hostility to regulatory activity became more of a concern when TRI figures became available, that underlined 3M's heavy chemical use and substantial volume of toxic releases.

In 1989, the same year that TRI figures were first released, 3M announced a revision and expansion of the 3P program, called 3P+. New policies (such as placing more emphasis on prevention at the product-design stage), new sets of objectives, and new organizational structures were added to the original 3P program. 3P+ also included a commitment to incorporate environmental objectives directly into the corporation's "business plan" (thus suggesting added importance in top management's decisionmaking procedures).

3P+ committed 3M to a series of specific pollutant reduction targets and corporate standards, such as air, water, and land release reductions and reduced waste generation. Air pollution emission reduction credits earned through market incentive programs would also be returned to government for air quality improvement. Additional goals (several of which simply involved compliance with already established regulatory mandates or rules), highlighted by the company in its 3P+ promotional literature, included the phase out of all ozone-depleting chemicals and PCBs, implementation and completion of asbestos removal objectives, and the upgrading of underground tanks and piping.

3P+ organizational changes included an expanded auditing system, new evaluation procedures, management plans, and research opportunities (primarily for "avoidance" opportunities) at the divisional level, and longer-range environmental research and development planning, with funds to be divided between corporate labs (where much of the long-term environmental research has occurred), and division labs (where much of the product research occurs) (Bollbs, 1993). Influencing these new organizational initiatives in the R&D area, however, has been the company emphasis on the "D" in R&D, resulting from a decline in performance by certain of its divisions in the recessionary period of 1989–1992 (when 3P+ was also first instituted). This has produced a stronger company focus on market issues that tend to be divorced from environmental inputs (Cianci, 1993; Landry, 1993).

From the outset of 3P, 3M sought to present the quantitative and qualitative results of its environmental program as a major pollution prevention success. The 3P submittal form, developed in the first years of the program to continually update dollars saved and pollutant releases reduced, has been the major evaluative tool, highlighted in both public and private forums. In the Senate and House Reports of the 1990 Pollution Prevention Act, for example, 3M figures on sludge, wastewater, air emission, and solid waste reductions as well as cost savings were used to specifically identify the benefits of pollution prevention (U.S. Congress, 1990). According to a subsequent report, 3M officials stated that more than 3,000 specific 3P projects (e.g., those identified in various submittal forms) had "prevented over 575,000 tons of pollution" between 1975 and 1991, including 134,000 tons of air emissions, 16,900 tons of water pollutants, 426,000 tons of sludge and solid waste, and 1.65 billion gallons of wastewater (Bringer and Benforado, 1992). The 3,007 3P projects instituted during that period were also said to have represented cost savings for the company of $537 million, an average of $17,850 saved per project.[2]

Beyond the numbers, 3M officials have also argued that the company's environmental approach has encouraged significant qualitative changes both in the relationship between industry and the environment and in the relationship between government, industry, and the environment. These relationships, 3M officials suggest, have been changed because 3P has proven that voluntary source reduction both eliminates pollution and saves money and that such improvements represent benefits for both business and the environment.

In relation to government, 3M officials have argued that its 3P program has influenced the shape of environmental policy. Congressional committees and U.S. Environmental Protection Agency staff have been a constant target of presentations and meetings with 3M officials and lobbyists on the centrality of voluntary pollution prevention initiatives. 3M officials have eagerly sought validation of their approach, at one point undertaking (in 1992) a major lobbying effort to influence (and revise) an EPA pollution prevention award that had failed to name the company.[3]

Within the company, the development of the 3P+ program expanded the level of staff-based environmental expertise available at various entry points in 3M's complex R&D and product development processes. Particularly during the era when 3P+ was first initiated, the program was designed to establish within the company a more heightened emphasis on the "green trend" then visible in the larger society in the period shortly prior to Earth Day 1990. However, that environmental expertise came into play only when formally invited to participate at the division or venture team level—often when questions about the toxicity of a particular chemical, environmental impacts from a particular process operation, or regulatory issues associated with each aspect of the product's development needed to be answered. Although 3P+ included language about bringing environmental considerations into the design stage, the venture team concept and product development framework have not incorporated green product design as an R&D objective. As 3M's director of corporate research argued: "Green markets are not a 3M strategy; we're interested in how to make our products so that they pollute less, and thus cost less in terms of additional treatment or other regulatory costs" (Bollbs, 1993). Thus, at the venture team or division level, environmental information has largely remained external to the R&D process, except insofar as environmental issues come to be identified and require information on how best to be addressed. At the company-wide level, however, 3M environmental staff, primarily housed in the Environmental Engineering and Pollution Control Division, have sought to initiate research in response to division-related concerns, such as solvent emission reductions and possible product substitutions, adhesives issues, and questions of recycling and reuse of products and materials. Yet it is at the division level where design stage decisions first take place and where environmental questions vary substantially in how they are (or even if they are) addressed.

Thus, the overall thrust of the 3P/3P+ program, as it evolved during its first twenty years, reinforced 3M's embrace of environmental "voluntarism" for its internal operations (and its simultaneous opposition to environmental regulations and legislation), and extended its strategy of "avoidance" in defining and identifying the company's environmental goals. During these years, the environment became central to 3M, but on a track distinct from its "business of innovation" and in opposition to any external influences in defining what in fact constituted 3P's stated goal of pollution prevention.

Environment and Product Design: Two Examples

With the development of 3P, two threshold questions emerge: (1) how has the company integrated the 3P environmental framework into new product development—the centerpiece of 3M's corporate philosophy, and (2) how has the company's promotion of 3P as a voluntary program of environmental objectives influenced its approach to environmental regulation. As an avoidance strategy, 3M's approach to pollution prevention has primarily focused on the numerous legal and cost factors related to the kinds of materials, processes, and technologies utilized in the design and production of its continuous flow of products. As a company that maintains a powerful commitment to innovation and new product development, 3M has had strong opportunity to "design in" environmental concerns, including pollution prevention, throughout an entire product line in a relatively short period of time. Such a process could conceivably represent a model "design for the environment" approach so widely discussed today. Yet pollution prevention has remained an external rather than derivative function of the design stage of product development, particularly at the division level where nearly all design issues are worked out. With divisions (which have their own research labs) functioning autonomously, the pollution prevention message (that is, how best to cope with regulation and how best to avoid certain costs or constraints on production) only enters into a product cycle once the design decisions have been made. The development of two recent products (one designed after the 3P program was launched in 1975; the second introduced after the more ambitious 3P+ effort was initiated in 1989) effectively illustrate this distinction between design and avoidance.

Post-It Notes

A key product that potentially rivals the importance of Scotch Tape for 3M's growth and identity is Post-It Note Pads, one of the five top-selling office supply products in the U.S. Arthur Frye, a 3M scientist, according to the company's well-publicized story of the origins of Post-Its, first came up with the idea of a removable sticky-backed product (originally intended as a book marker) while singing in a church choir. He subsequently pursued the idea through 3M's policy of "bootlegging," where researchers can spend 15% of their work time exploring their own research ideas independent of the venture team structure. Frye was also able to utilize a new adhesive technology developed through the corporate research labs and available to other divisions for possible application. Once Frye's product was officially approved for new business development and test marketing, the company's significant abilities to define and secure a new market for a particular product came into play (Mitsch, 1990).

While the design of Post-Its, similar to a number of other key 3M products utilizing bonding and coating technology, was both simple in conception and in its subsequent production, it ultimately presented a complex range of environmental impacts that were present throughout the product lifecycle. Once the concept (that is, producing removable note paper based on a less permanent adhesive) and related market need was established, the manufacture of Post-Its also became relatively straightforward; that is, production lines of huge rolls of papers were coated with an adhesive, then modified to produce different paper forms and sizes. To begin manufacturing Post-Its, 3M decided to expand a relatively small facility in Cynthiana, Kentucky which was equipped with an existing coater. The expansion of the plant included the addition of several boilers, more than a dozen storage tanks, 5 mix kettles, 3 coating lines, and a spray booth. As sales (and the production) of Post-Its rapidly increased, the toxic air emissions and off-site transfers of toxic pollutants from the Kentucky site also significantly increased. In 1991, for example, toxic air emissions from the Cynthiana plant included 4,530 pounds of methyl ethyl ketone, 34,950 pounds of toluene, 8,140 pounds of methyl isobutyl ketone, and 10,900 pounds of cyclohexane.[4]

It was only at the point when expansion of the production facilities was already well underway—that is, at a point when the product had already been well developed and the specific chemical solvents required for the adhesive selected—that 3M environmental staff from the EE&PC group became involved in monitoring the product's environmental impacts.

These impacts included the significant VOC emissions and (subsequently) the concerns related to the recyclability of the product. Yet the nature of EE&PC involvement in general has been, according to one of the staff involved, to "familiarize the facility people with the rules they have to follow, involving all the different kinds of compliance issues related to wastes, emissions, occupational health and safety guidelines, etc.," but not product design questions (Schutt, 1993). When the EE&PC staff were brought in around 1984 to help monitor the manufacturing of Post-Its, they didn't raise any direct concerns about air toxics releases since the regulatory process (primarily the NESHAPs process through the Clean Air Act) had yet to set standards or establish regulations requiring compliance with respect to the specific VOCs being emitted at Cynthiana. Regulatory avoidance was thus not a factor. Nor was the EE&PC staff focused on how or even whether to limit the kinds and volumes of chemicals then being used in the production of the product. "We never explored alternative formulations or different processes," the EE&PC staff person recalled. "All of our involvement was after production had begun" (Schutt, 1993).

By the late 1980s, environmental concerns associated with the manufacture of Post-It Notes began to be raised. These included toxics release issues, made visible by TRI numbers, as well as recycling concerns (heightened by the increased interest in solid waste issues at that time). With its introduction as a major new item discarded primarily into the commercial waste stream, Post-It Notes presented a significant obstacle for paper recycling programs, due to the comingling of Post-It discards with other waste paper. Recyclers who only accepted white ledger paper (e.g., from office paper collections) refused to accept any collection source which included Post-It Notes, while a number of recycling firms involved in mixed waste paper collection for recycling also refused to accept papers which included Post-Its (primarily due to a refusal by recyclers to accept papers with yellow colorants) (3M Commercial Office Supply Division 1992).

Wary of the criticisms about the adverse environmental consequences of Post-It production and use that could potentially impact its carefully nurtured environmental reputation, 3M sought to counter these concerns. It did so, first, by seeking to lower toxic emission levels through the use of an in-plant incinerator in Cynthiana, and, second, by attempting to make Post-It Notes more "recyclable" by using recycled paper fiber which included limited amounts (15%) of post-consumer waste by total weight. These two approaches in fact reflected 3M's perspective on pollution prevention which incorporated both treatment (e.g., incineration) and recycling.[5] Neither of the approaches, however, directly addressed more fundamental product design considerations (solvent use, adhesive, and colorant impacts on recycling).

The Post-It experience specifically pointed to the dichotomy between preproduction design and postproduction avoidance at 3M. EE&PC environmental engineer Dave Schutt (the EE&PC staff liaison with the Post-It production facility in Kentucky) summarized the Post-It experience as underlining the limits of the avoidance approach. "EE&PC staff," Schutt argued, "get involved too late, by trying to address something that's already been done. As a result, we don't have as big an impact as we'd like. We tend to get involved after the authorization from the company has been made to build a factory and plans have already been drawn about what it's going to look like and how the product will be manufactured" (Schutt, 1993). Though Schutt remains concerned that the environmental staff has not been as successful in communicating with senior 3M management about the range of environmental issues at stake in a 3M product cycle, he does suggest that the lines of communication have improved in recent years, with environmental issues within the company becoming more prominent in the wake of Earth Day 1990, the launching of 3P+, and the emergence of new public relations concerns associated with the release of TRI information (Schutt, 1993; Bollbs, 1993).

Scotchcolor Single-Use Camera

Though both 3P and 3P+ specifically identified design issues as an appropriate arena for pollution prevention initiatives (whether in terms of product reformation, process modification, or equipment redesign), innovation at 3M still focuses primarily on creating new markets or maintaining existing ones. The evolution of 3M's Scotchcolor brand single-use camera during the late 1980s and early 1990s (subsequent to the initiation of 3P+) underscored the importance of these market-related development considerations.

Like other "disposable" consumer products, the single-use camera has been a focus of strong environmental criticism since its introduction by Fuji in 1987, criticism found even within 3M itself. In the February 1993 issue of *Today*, the 3M internal newsletter, two readers commented on the tension between 3M's "good environmental track record" including the "goal of reducing waste" and 3M's recent decision to manufacture and market its own single-use camera product. John Gregerson, the photo color systems division staff person most responsible for the development of this product, responded in the same 3M publication by arguing that the product was initiated to retain the company's "industry position" in the film products business, even as division staff remained concerned about the need to be "environmentally responsible." In a subsequent interview Gregerson explained that 3M had initially been hesitant to develop the product because staff felt consumers wouldn't be interested in purchasing that type of single-use product. But by 1990, single use camera sales had increased substantially and 3M had become concerned that certain camera manufacturers saw the rise of this product as an opportunity to expand into the film business itself, since film was included in the single-use camera product. While 3M had not developed its own camera product, it did maintain a leading position in the film business, a position that could be eroded by increased sales of single use cameras equipped with film (Gregersen, 1993).

3M staff in the photo color systems divisions thus decided to create a new group to explore the possibility of 3M developing a single use camera in order to protect its film business. As a first step, the group established focus groups to explore issues of design, production, and marketing considerations. This included an investigation into a number of environmental-related issues (e.g., whether to eliminate an outer package for the camera; whether to require the finisher to send back the camera for potential reuse as its own product; and whether to encourage finishers to send back the outer package for recycling purposes). With the exception of the possibility of establishing a limited reuse program for the product, the 3M team rejected incorporating most of the environmental approaches for market considerations on the basis of the focus group response (for example, focus group participants expressed preferences for double-layer packaging, and "health concerns" associated with reuse—including, incredibly, the possibility of their contracting AIDS from the prior user). As a consequence, the production of a Scotchcolor brand single-use camera with the additional packaging was launched in 1992 (despite the likely negative environmental feedback) in order to compete with other single-use cameras already on the market. To counter the negative environmental associations with its product, 3M sought to market its product as "recyclable," by encouraging finishers to send back to 3M the outer paperboard package for recycling purposes. Despite this effort, 3M photo division staff remained skeptical of the viability of recycling any part of the product, both in terms of a lack of incentive for finishers (since it represented an additional cost for 3M and thus a significant cost break would not be provided to the finishers as a way to encourage a returns policy) and in relation to the production issues involved in the ability to recycle specific product parts, such as the paperboard used for the packaging (Gregersen, 1993). Ultimately, 3M's single-use camera remained the classic throwaway, another symbol of product as waste.

As the two case studies suggest, 3M's efforts at "daily environmental management" or creating "sustainable products" (to use the language in the 3P+ literature), has remained constrained by market- and "development"-driven factors which most directly influence the company's product cycle within the company and which can also significantly contradict or erode the company's environmental goals. New product innovation to establish new markets—not environmental criteria—drives production decisions. The actual design choices in each of the cases substantially contrasts with the concepts of prevention and environmental management that are located throughout the literature on the 3P program. Although 3P and 3P+ included language about bringing environmental considerations into the design stage, the environmental impacts of Post-It Notes and the single-use camera ultimately surfaced as peripheral issues that became significant primarily as external constraints, not product considerations. Environment and product design were separate, distinctive routes in a decisionmaking matrix. As one division manager put it, the corporate (EE&PC) pollutant reduction objectives can be characterized as a "thou shall not" philosophy, which contrasts with the division objective of creating new products (the "thou shall" imperative) (Gregerson, 1993; Schutt, 1993). Underlining these two separate decisionmaking paradigms, the imperative for divisions to develop new products (i.e., the production goal of achieving 25% of company sales through products that are less than five years old) remains the basic rationale in deciding if a product ought to be developed and what, if any, environmental consideration comes into play.

One possible approach to the imperative of bringing new products to market, even those with substantial environmental costs, is for 3M to incorporate green product design as an R&D objective. Yet 3M remains disinterested in green product concepts as an actual design criteria, preferring instead to keep environmental considerations separate from the research and development processes at the division level—the place where all new product designs originate. The introduction of Post-It Notes and the 3M single use camera bear out those distinctions.

Regulatory Issues

The company's interpretation of an environmental management approach is also reflected in its hostility toward regulatory mandates, perceived as environmental constraints on production decisionmaking. As a company dedicated to manufacturing an ever-increasing variety of chemically based products, 3M must constantly deal with federal and state regulators. Indeed, the original line responsibility of the Environmental Engineering and Pollution Control Department (before it took on 3P implementation) was to oversee company compliance with federal and state regulations. And while the 3P/3P+ philosophy of regulatory avoidance has been more visibly identified as efforts to reduce regulatory compliance costs, such a definition has also included efforts to oppose specific regulatory interventions at both the federal and state levels.

3M has had a relatively consistent history of opposition to certain key environmental legislative and regulatory measures. At the federal level, it became most involved during the 1980s and 1990s in lobbying against pollution prevention and right-to-know legislation and regulatory activities. The company was specifically concerned with the question of definitions of pollution prevention. It argued forcefully against any approach that excluded recycling options (beyond closed loop in-process recycling) as integral to pollution prevention, given the company's reliance on (off-site and on-site) recycling and (both on-site and off-site) incineration, which are technically end-of-pipe strategies. This position placed 3M as the single most vigorous industry opponent of the 1990 Pollution Prevention Act (which defined pollution prevention as source reduction) at a point when most industry groups, including the Chemical Manufacturers Association, had decided to support the Act as a limited (and largely voluntarist) measure (Schaeffer, 1993; Bringer, 1992).

At the same time, 3M officials strongly opposed any extension of regulatory activity on the basis of pollution prevention objectives, particularly in the areas of permitting and enforcement. In this respect, EPA's Source Reduction and Regulatory Review initiative, which was launched in 1992 and sought to establish the basis for a cross-media approach to permitting and enforcement, was opposed by 3M lobbyists as a potentially unwelcome intrusion into company activities. Former 3M CEO Allen Jacobsen summarized these objections when he referred to the establishing of "certain barriers to pollution prevention and our ability to compete globally that a growing body of environmental regulation presents" (Jacobsen, 1991).

In Minnesota, 3M has played a significant role in opposing a range of environmental laws and regulations, associated with its role as the state's biggest polluter. The three top facilities reporting toxic releases in Minnesota are 3M plants. These three manufacturing sites alone accounted for over half of all toxic releases reported in the state in 1988—43.7 million pounds out of 81.2 million pounds (Minnesota Department of Public

Safety, May 1991). In addition, one of these facilities, Chemolite—the hazardous waste incinerator for all of the company's domestically produced waste—was found by the Minnesota Pollution Control Agency (MPCA) to have repeatedly violated Clean Air Act standards and to be negligent in reporting violations to the Agency. In 1989, 3M was fined $1.5 million for these violations—the largest fine ever levied in the state for pollution. Though 3M signed a negotiated stipulation agreement with the MPCA and paid the fines, the company nevertheless refused to admit liability "for any of the alleged violations," arguing that it did so "solely to avoid time-consuming and costly litigation" (Minnesota, 1989).

3M's environmental role in Minnesota has primarily focused on influencing state efforts to monitor and regulate industrial sources of pollution as well as to assigning responsibility in paying for the costs of clean-up associated with those sources. In the early 1980s, for example, it was the single most important lobbyist contesting the state legislature's effort to pass a Superfund law, which included a "joint-and-several liability" provision to help pay for cleanup costs. 3M felt particularly vulnerable since it had already been identified as a source of waste discharges at a state Superfund site which included other potential responsible parties no longer in operation. Lewis Lehr, the chairman of the 3M Company at the time (and the CEO also responsible for initiating 3P), lobbied then Governor Rudy Perpich to veto this legislation. Calling it "bad for the business climate in Minnesota," Lehr threatened to relocate a proposed major 3M expansion outside of Minnesota if the law was signed (*St. Paul Pioneer Press*, May 11, 1983). Despite the threat, Perpich signed the law, and the company (ultimately citing other factors) did locate its new facility in Austin, Texas, transferring hundreds of 3M corporate and R&D staff from its 3M Center in St. Paul. Two years later, in 1985, 3M, along with the Minnesota Chamber of Commerce, successfully lobbied the state legislature to repeal the "joint-and-several liability" provision and replace it with a weaker "victim's compensation fund" for persons harmed by exposure to hazardous waste (Jensen, 1991).

Like the Superfund episode, 3M also actively opposed state pollution prevention legislation that broadly paralleled federal legislation in this area. In 1990, the Minnesota state legislature, following the lead of several other states including Massachusetts, Oregon, and New Jersey, debated passage of a state Pollution Prevention Act. The Minnesota legislation required industries to develop and make public a pollution prevention plan, with the granting of pollution permits linked to the implementation of the plan. 3M sought from the outset to reduce the authority of this Act, arguing that industry's participation in pollution prevention had to be voluntary, that pollution prevention plans should not become public documents subject to review, and that permitting also not be linked to implementation. 3M launched a highly visible and successful lobbying effort that eliminated provisions requiring plans to be made public and decoupled any link of implementation to permitting (Minnesota, 1990).

The most protracted environmental conflicts between 3M and state regulators in recent years have been related to the attempts by the Minnesota Pollution Control Agency (MPCA) to develop air toxics rules (including those mandated by the Clean Air Act Amendments). Air toxics conflicts involving 3M and MPCA date back to the early 1980s when some of the state's rules were first being formulated. As these conflicts intensified over the next decade, 3M primarily sought to limit MPCA jurisdiction in order to preserve maximum operational flexibility while specifically opposing any efforts to force changes in 3M operations through regulatory or public pressures. For example, it consistently opposed including product line information in its TRI reporting, thus preventing any evaluation of the specific product source for particular emissions or discharges in facilities where more than one product line can be found (e.g., 3M's large Minnesota facilities in St. Paul and Hutchinson). Even when 3M was obliged to provide MPCA with air concentration limits for certain substances used in those facilities, it still blanked out all numbers on the different chemicals identified when the document was released for public consumption. In other states, 3M has also used "confidentiality" provisions (e.g., with its Cynthiana, Kentucky plant), which inhibit any effective identification of specific releases traced to specific processes or product lines (Hagedorn, 1993; Kentucky, 1993).

3M's rationale for the uncoupling of regulatory permitting and prevention is the need to provide companies with sufficient flexibility in production decisions. One such decision parameter long considered crucial by 3M officials involves the choice of production technologies, particularly best available control technology (BACT) as stipulated within Clean Air Act provisions. In addition, flexibility and voluntarism are also seen as linked, given that companies with approaches like 3P are *ipso facto* defined as the most likely candidates for voluntary prevention initiatives.

One example of this flexibility/voluntarism argument was 3M's decision to install pollution control equipment at its Hutchinson, Minnesota plant, an action which emerged as one of the company's most successful 3P-related publicity coups promoting the value of a voluntarist approach. In a front page story in the business section of the February 3, 1991 edition of the *New York Times* entitled "Hutchinson No Longer Holds Its Nose" (Holusha, 1991), reporter John Holusha commended 3M's effort to reduce VOC air emissions at its Hutchinson plant by voluntarily installing $26 million worth of carbon absorption recycling technology to recycle and burn off solvents from the production of Scotch sealing tape and videotape. The article, however, did not pursue either the context for the company decision, or an analysis of how the reduction numbers were derived. According to Jerry Liefert, the permit engineer at the Minnesota Pollution Control Agency responsible for all 3M facilities, 3M was in fact intending to expand both its magnetic media facility and its customer products facility at Hutchinson (which would increase actual emissions at these sites). Before expansion could take place, however, federal rules specific to magnetic media facilities required that 3M reduce emissions by at least 90% of the "allowable" VOC level in order to increase its operating capacity. While voluntary at the time of its introduction, 3M had in fact installed the carbon absorption technology to meet the soon-to-be implemented requirements (Liefert, 1991). Even after the reductions achieved by its end-of-pipe technologies, the Hutchinson site, with toxic air emissions of 12.64 million pounds a year, retained its status as the single greatest source of air toxics in the state of Minnesota and the fourth largest nationally (U.S. EPA, 1993; Liefert, 1991).

In view of the plant's daily emissions of over 35,000 pounds of air toxics, it is difficult to see how the application of pollution control technology at Hutchinson could be characterized as pollution prevention. "In my experience with the company, the term '3P' is likely to refer to pollution control equipment rather than process changes," an MPCA air toxics regulator stated in characterizing the 3M approach (Sensi, 1993). In this case, the representation of carbon absorption technology as pollution prevention rather than as a control technology directly reflected 3M's defining "prevention" more narrowly than nearly all other sources, including those used by U.S. EPA and the MPCA. The Hutchinson episode in fact provided another direct example of how 3M's environmental approach has served as a proxy for its definition of prevention as avoidance.

Conclusion

Since its origins nearly one hundred years ago, 3M has continued to be driven by its ability to innovate and quickly bring new products to market. As part of that corporate signature, it has defined its success in part by its ability to reduce or eliminate bureaucracy—both internally and externally (Mitchell, 1989). This ability also allows the company to be extremely flexible and rapid in its product cycle: the time required between design and bringing a new product to market is continually reduced. Such speed and flexibility, the company argues, provides it with a comparative advantage in a global marketplace which is continuously shifting its demand for products.

In many ways, the environmental question at 3M is seen as a form of imposed bureaucratic laws and regulation, similar in intent to any other bureaucratic constraint at 3M—that is, something to avoid, something to get out from under. The pollution prevention program emerged in part as a means to minimize the degree to which the company needed to respond to one crucial factor associated with such environmental bureaucracy: end-of-pipe pollution control regulation. If there are reduced pollutants, Joseph Ling had argued in advocating 3P, there will be less to regulate. As a result, 3M's own environmental bureaucracy became itself primarily focused on the question of how to avoid or reduce regulation as a way to establish advantage in comparison to other more regulated companies. Yet, despite its much heralded programs and its efforts at avoidance, 3M has remained a highly regulated producer and a major polluter, a function in part of the kinds of products produced and processes used as well as of the company's design and innovation orientation in which environmental factors remain external, or after the fact.

At the same time, the 3M approach to regulation and environmental review has been consistent with its central focus on voluntarism. For 3M, voluntarism in relation to environmental activity maintains flexibility and prevents interference with product development considerations. But while 3M has developed a comprehensive environmental management program to implement a scenario of pollutant reductions, cost savings, and regulatory avoidance for the company, its continuing environmental impacts appear at first glance to be out of sync with its policy goals and management plans. This tension exists not only in terms of the absolute levels of pollution still generated, but also in terms of 3M hostility to various forms of environmental regulation and public accountability. But such a tension between a company's well-publicized and much admired environmental policy and the realities of product development might not in fact be contradictory. Instead, the issues associated with the case of 3M throw into relief the very question of pollution prevention voluntarism itself. The key question about what drives environmental change at the production and design level suggests in part that industry's contribution to pollution prevention might directly require new and expanded rather than reduced forms of public input in order to keep such initiatives focused on the opportunities for prevention throughout a production cycle. If 3M is to be judged as a model, it represents both the limits of voluntarism and the unanswered questions regarding the appropriate relationship between public policy and industry activity.

References

Adams, 1991. Personal communication with Georjean Adams, August 6, 1991.

Bacon, 1991. Personal communication with Dale Bacon, September 11, 1991.

Benfardo, 1990. Personal communication with Dave Benfardo, May 9, 1990.

Berger, 1989. "Into 'Pollution Prevention' Before EPA," Jon A. Berger, *Waste Age,* November 1989, pp. 147–150.

Bollbs, 1993. Personal communication with Theodore Bollbs, 1992.

Botten, 1993. Personal communication with Bee Botten, 1993.

Bringer, 1988. "Pollution Prevention Program Saves Environment and Money," Robert P. Bringer, *Adhesives Age,* September 1989.

Bringer, 1992. Letter from Robert P. Bringer to Susan B. Hazen, director, Environmental Assistance Division, U.S. Environmental Protection Agency, October 15, 1992.

Bringer and Benforado, 1989. "Pollution Prevention as Corporate Policy: A Look at the 3M Experience," Robert P. Bringer and David M. Benforado, *The Environmental Professional,* Vol. 11, pp. 117–126.

Bringer and Benforado, 1992. "3P Plus: Total Quality Environmental Management," Robert P. Bringer and David M. Benforado, presentation at the 85th Annual Meeting of the Air and Waste Management Association, Kansas City, Missouri, June 21–26, 1992.

Brunner, 1981. *Corporations and the Environment: How Should Decisions be Made?,* David L. Brunner, Will Miller, and Nan Stockholm, (Los Altos: Committee on Corporate Responsibility—Stanford University, 1981).

Chemicals in Progress, 1992. *Chemicals in Progress,* U.S. Environmental Protection Agency, Vol. 13, No. 2, September 1992, p. 35.

Cinci, 1993. Personal communication with Jeffrey Cinci, 1993.

Comfort, 1962. *William L. McKnight, Industrialist,* Mildred Houghton Comfort, (Minneapolis: T.S. Denison & Co., 1962).

Corporate Report Minnesota, 1986. "Waste Laws Fixed, Landfills Nixed," *Corporate Report Minnesota,* January 1996.

Crosby, 1993. Personal communication with Brenda Lee Crosby, March 3, 1993.

Dawson, 1984. "Perpich is 'Ready to Respond' to 3M Complaints," Jim Dawson, *Minneapolis Star and Tribune*, February 24, 1984.

Doerr, 1991. Personal communication with Lisa Doerr, 1991.

Drucker, 1985. *Innovation and Entrepreneurship: Practice and Principles* (New York: Harper & Row, 1985).

Dumaine, 1990. "Ability to Innovate," Brian Dumaine, *Fortune*, January 29, 1990.

Ferguson, 1989. "Good to Be Green," Anne Ferguson, *Management Today*, February, 1989, pp. 46–60.

Franklin, 1988. "Air Cleaners at Plants Recalled," Ben Franklin, *The New York Times*, Tuesday, February 9, 1988.

Gelbach, 1993. "Toxic Shock: Minnesota's Tough New Hazardous-Waste Law has Business Down in the Dumps...," Doris Gelbach, *Corporate Report Minnesota*, September 1983.

Gibson, 1985. "Minnesota Mining Says It Told EPA of Spray's Hazards," Richard Gibson, *The Wall Street Journal*, March 13, 1985.

Gregerson, 1993. Personal communication with John Gregerson, March 30, 1993.

Guerrette, 1986. "Environmental Integrity and Corporate Responsibility," Richard Guerrette, *Journal of Business Ethics* 5 (1986) 409–415.

Hagedorn, 1993. Personal communication with Steve Hagedorn, 1993.

Hartman, 1993. Personal communication with Carolyn Hartman, 1993.

Hazardous Waste Consultant, 1993. "3M Company," *The Hazardous Waste Consultant*, September–October 1993.

Holusha, 1991. "Hutchinson No Longer Holds Its Nose," John Holusha, *New York Times*, February 3, 1991.

Horwitz, 1985. "Scotchguard Fatalities Disclosed by 3M: Firm Warns of Hazards If Spray Misused," Sari Horwitz, *Washington Post*, March 15, 1985.

Huck, 1955. *Brand of the Titan: The 3M Story*, Virginia Huck, (New York: Appleton-Century-Crofts, 1955), p. 16.

Inskip, 1983. "Perpich's Rift with Head of 3M," Leonard Inskip, *Minneapolis Star Tribune*, July 20, 1983.

Jacobsen, Allen, 1991. Letter to William Reilly, administrator, U.S. Environmental Protection Agency, March 29, 1991.

Jensen, 1991. Personal communication with Diane Jensen, 1991.

Katauskas, 1990. "Follow-Through: 3M's Formula for Success," Ted Katauskas, *Research and Development*, November 1990.

Kelly, 1991. "3M Run Scared? Forget About It," Kevin Kelly, *Business Week*, September 16, 1991, pp. 59–60.

Kentucky, 1993. Kentucky Emissions Inventory System "1993 Database," Kentucky Division for Air Quality, 1993.

Kirkpatrick, 1990. "Environmentalism: The New Crusade," *Fortune*, February 12, 1990.

Kurschner, 1991. "3M's Pollution Record: Cloudy and Clear," Dale Kurschner, *City Business*, Vol. 9, No. 26, December 9, 1991.

Kurschner, 1992. "3M Co. Launches Far-reaching Program to Reduce Costs," Dale Kurschner, *City Business*, January 27, 1992.

Labatt, Sonia. "A Framework for Assessing Discretionary Corporate Performance Towards the Environment," *Environmental Management*, Vol. 15, No. 2, pp. 163–178.

Leifert, 1991. "3M Company's Pollution Prevention Plus Program at Hutchinson, Mn," memo from Jerry Leifert, Minnesota Pollution Control Agency, June 1991.

Ling, 1980. "Industry: Making Cleanup Pay," Joseph Ling, *Environment*, (1980) Vol. 22, No. 3, pp. 42–43.

Management Today, 1989. "Good to be Green," *Management Today*, February 1989, pp. 47–51.

Marcus, 1984. "The Recycling of Chemical Waste," Steven Marcus, *The New York Times*, January 8, 1984.

Meersman, 1993. Personal communication with Tom Meersman, 1993.

Miller, 1991. "430 Tons of Toxic Air Emission Reported," Joanne Miller, *The Los Angeles Times*, December 1, 1991, Ventura County Edition, B-1.

Minnesota, 1989. 1988 Toxic Chemical Release Inventory. State of Minnesota. A Preliminary Summary of Toxic Chemical Report Forms for Calendar Year 1988. November 1989.

Minnesota, 1990. State of Minnesota Pollution Prevention Act of 1990.

Minnesota, September 1990. 1989 Toxic Chemical Release Inventory. State of Minnesota. A Preliminary Summary of Toxic Chemical Report Forms for Calendar Year 1989. September 1990.

Minnesota, December 1990. A Study on Expansion of the Toxic Chemical Reporting Requirements: Report to the Legislature. Minnesota Emergency Response Commission, December 1990.

Minnesota, 1991. 1989 Toxic Chemical Release Inventory: Summary Report. State of Minnesota. May 1991.

Minnesota Department of Health, 1992. A Report to 3M Company and Employees on the Cancer Occurrence Among Maintenance Craftsmen Currently or Formerly Employed at 3M Center, MCSS Epidemiology Report 92:1, Minnesota Department of Health, June 29, 1992.

Mitchell, 1989. "Masters of Innovation: How 3M Keeps Its New Products Coming," Russell Mitchell, *Business Week*, April, 10, 1989.

Mitsch, 1990. "Three Roads to Innovation," Ronald A. Mitsch, *Journal of Business Strategy*, Sept./Oct. 1990, p. 18.

Nerlean, 1991. Personal communication with Cathy Nerlean, 1991.

New York Times, 1983. "Minnesota Mining to Clean Up Waste Dump," *The New York Times*, July 21, 1983, p. A13.

New York Times, 1988. "9 Get Corporate Conscience Awards," *The New York Times*, March 1, 1988.

Owens and Sever, 1974. *The 3M Commute-a-Van Program: Status Report*, Robert D. Owens and Helen L. Sever (Saint Paul: Minnesota Mining and Manufacturing Company, 1975).

Moylan, 1985. "State's Radioactive Waste Getting Harder to Get Rid Of," Martin Moylan, *CityBusiness/Twin Cities*, 1985.

Pratt, 1993. Personal communication with Greg Pratt, 1993.

Parkinson, Gerald. "Reducing Wastes Can be Cost Effective," *Chemical Engineering*, July 1990.

Peters and Waterman, 1982. *In Search of Excellence: Lessons from America's Best-Run Companies*, (New York: Harper & Row, 1982), p. 227.

R&D Magazine, 1990. "Follow-Through: 3M's Formula for Success," *R&D Magazine*, November 1990.

Renner, 1991. Personal communication with Rich Renner, 1991.

Schaeffer, 1993. Personal communication with Eric Schaeffer, 1993.

Schutt, 1993. Personal communication with David Schutt, April 11, 1993.

Sensi, 1993. Personal communication with Carol Sensi, 1993.

Shapiro, Stacey. "Firms Detail Environmental Policies," *Business Insurance*, December 3, 1990.

Shipp, 1993. Personal communication with Dale Shipp, 1993.

Short and Kahn, 1983. "Perpich Signs 'Clean Environment' Bill," Allen Short and Aaron Kahn, *St. Paul Pioneer Press*, May 11, 1983.

Sigford, 1993. Personal communication with Kris Sigford, March 3, 1993.

Smith, 1980. "The Lures and Limits of Innovation," Lee Smith, *Fortune*, October 20, 1980, pp. 84–94.

3M (no date a). "Genesis: Growth Through Technical Innovation."

3M (no date b). "Invitation to Innovation," *Pollution Prevention Pays. Managing for a Better Environment*.

3M (no date c). "Technology for a Better Environment," *Pollution Prevention Pays. Managing for a Better Environment*.

3M (no date d). "The Community and 3M: Safety, Health, Environment," *Managing for a Better Environment*.

3M (no date e). "Toward a Cleaner Environment: An Environmental Commitment," *Pollution Prevention Pays.*

3M, 1990. 1990 Annual Report. *Lab to Market Leadership: Winning Worldwide,* 1990.

3M, 1991a. Quality Environmental Management Program. The President's Environmental and Conservation Challenge Awards Environmental Quality Management Category, 1991.

3M, 1991b. "Special Report: The Environment," A progress report for 3M employees on 3M's environmental programs. *Today* magazine, July 1991.

3M, 1992a. "Commonly Asked Questions About Post-It Notes and Recyclability," Commercial Office Supply Division, 3M, 1992.

3M, 1992b. Form 10K, Securities and Exchange Commission, for the year ending December 31, 1992.

U.S. Congress, 1990. "Waste Reduction Act" Report 101-55, 101st Congress, 2nd Session, House of Representatives, June 25, 1990.

U.S. EPA, 1991. State Fact Sheets, 1991 Toxics Release Inventory, U.S. Environmental Protection Agency, Office of Pollution Prevention and Toxics (TS-799), (Washington D.C.: Government Printing Office, 1993).

U.S. EPA, 1993. 1991 Toxic Release Inventory Public Data Release, U.S. Environmental Protection Agency, EPA 745-R-93-003 (Washington, D.C.: General Printing Office, May 1993).

Vietor, 1979. "NIPCC: The Advisory Council Approach," Richard H.K. Vietor, *Journal of Contemporary Business,* Vol. 8, No. 1 (First Quarter 1979), 57–70.

Vlerebome, 1984. "3M Will Bring Zest for Technology to Austin," Peggy Vlerebome, *Austin American Statesman,* February 26, 1984.

Wall Street Journal, 1988. "Minnesota Mining's Sale of Some Ionizers Is Suspended by NRC," *Wall Street Journal,* January 26, 1988, p. 40.

Wall Street Journal, 1990. "NRC Proposes Fine of $160,000 for 3M," *Wall Street Journal,* June 13, 1990, p. 16.

Weisner, 1993. Personal communication with Carol Weisner, 1993.

Willis, 1983. "3M Chief Blasts Business Costs, Superfund Bill." Judith Willis, *St. Paul Pioneer Press,* May 11, 1983.

Notes

1. As a major multinational corporation, 3M activities outside the United States (which accounted for more than 50% of total sales for the

company) have not been subject to reporting procedures equivalent to the TRI and thus its company-wide totals for toxic releases and transfers (as well as potential shifts in production accounting for increases and/or decreases in those amounts at a facility, state, or national level) are not available.

2. It might be noted that the 3M form and other industry efforts to "quantify" prevention or waste minimization goals, often fail to identify human health or environment or community-related criteria as potentially quantifiable outcomes.

3. Personal communication on a background basis with a U.S. EPA staff member involved in the selection process (1993).

4. TRI figures 1991. It's worth noting as well that the substantial increase in the use and release of various air toxics also had significant occupational implications which have not been directly identified or addressed.

5. On the "recyclability" issue of Post-It notes, see "Commonly Asked Questions and Answers About Post-It Notes and Recyclability," 3M Commercial Office Supply Division, (3M: St. Paul, Minnesota, 1992). In this handout aimed at recyclers, 3M made the argument that a mixed waste paper recycling program was "more inclusive" than a white ledger or computer printout paper recycling program, because it "diverts more waste from the landfills" which is "the ultimate goal of recycling." That position (necessary in promoting Post-It notes as a recyclable product) contrasted with the analysis that defined recyclability as "the number of times a material can be recycled before being discarded," a definition that assigned greater weight to white ledger paper recycling programs. Similarly, in terms of the on-site incinerator at the Cynthiana plant, reduction of emissions to meet regulated standards also contrasted with a reduction approach that reduced the use of a substance or material prior to treatment or recycling, the definition used in the 1990 Pollution Prevention Act as applied to TRI (which was vigorously opposed by 3M)

Conclusion: Barriers and Opportunities for Pollution Prevention

Robert Gottlieb

In 1992, OPPT research director Harry Freeman and four other colleagues from EPA published an extensive review of the state of pollution prevention activities, describing the wide reach of programs and policies instituted during the previous half decade.[1] These were the "new policies, technologies and processes that prevent or minimize pollution," as then President George Bush put it,[2] which constituted what Freeman and colleagues called "the new regulatory agenda." Their approach (a big tent concept of prevention which incorporated much of the EPA agenda) sought to be as inclusive as possible. It included such programs as EPA's 33/50 and Green Lights programs as well as broad-based industry efforts like the Chemical Manufacturers Association's Responsible Care. But these programs, by their eclectic and, at times, contradictory nature, also pointed to the *ad hoc* nature of pollution prevention activities, whether in terms of environmental policymaking, industry's organizational culture and decisionmaking about products and processes, or the broader question of industrial structure. By the early 1990s, as the Freeman group's survey suggested, pollution prevention, despite its presumed new status as the linchpin for policy and industry activity, provided little guidance for the formation and implementation of policy and industry decisionmaking.

At EPA, pollution prevention remained marginal to the centers of authority and decisionmaking within the agency—the media-specific program offices which continued to spend the lion's share of the Agency's budget and maintained the key levers of power in permitting, standard setting, and enforcement. Pollution prevention programs, such as the 2% set aside for funding established by Bush's EPA head William Reilly, largely existed outside the structure of Agency power. It situated pollution prevention as external to Agency decisionmaking and often reflective of its voluntarist (as opposed to regulatory) frame of reference inside EPA itself. Even when Agency officials, such as Clinton's EPA head Carol Browner, proclaimed that pollution prevention would become the dominant reference point in toxics policy, such declarations failed to easily translate into actual restructuring of the logic and outcomes of EPA's media-specific, program office approach.

In Congress, despite the passage of the 1990 Pollution Prevention Act, the focus of debate and possible new legislation also continued to be pollutant- or media-specific (for example, in discussions regarding the rewrite of the Clean Water Act, Superfund, or the Resource Conservation and Recovery Act). This remained the case even as the rhetoric of pollution prevention and legislative provisions with specific reduction objectives were incorporated into the debates or the language of the legislation. Similarly, the lower priority status associated with efforts to reauthorize TSCA also suggested that the separation of environmental policymaking from industry decisionmaking would likely remain intact.

In this context, pollution prevention as a form of industrial or economic policy remained a taboo subject for policymakers. In situating pollution prevention policy, a clear distinction emerged between the more acceptable opportunities for pollutant- and media-specific initiatives (often framed as encouraging voluntary changes) and those policies designed to address facility-wide or industry-wide issues (which, at best, had only limited legislative or regulatory reference).

The policy debates of the early 1990s also continued to be influenced by the agendas of key industry groups such as the Chemical Manufacturers Association and companies such as 3M or Monsanto. These were aimed at reducing public input into Agency decisionmaking processes, in part by elevating "science" in comparing risks to guide the setting of policy, yet denigrating current risk analysis as uncertain, with a propensity to overestimate actual risks. At the same time, industry groups aggressively promoted voluntary pollution prevention against more direct forms of policy intervention, while maintaining, within the regulatory discourse, a focus on regulated wastes (particularly RCRA wastes) rather than a focus on hazards generated throughout a production cycle. Finally, industry groups sought favorable market incentives (as opposed to policy directives and/or "environmental" taxes, such as the proposed 1993 carbon tax) to allow for greater flexibility and control over production decisions.

The uncertain state of pollution prevention policy paralleled the uneven application by industry of prevention approaches to production choices. Structural barriers, some based on long-term industry trends, not only impeded the progress of pollution prevention but limited its scope because of upstream influences. Efforts to incorporate pollution prevention as a matter of organizational behavior at a plant- or industry-wide level have also been bounded by the conditions imposed on such activities by the industry groups or companies themselves. Whether undertaking research into toxicology or risk analysis, reviewing product or process issues, making decisions about new technologies, or seeking to regain public confidence by reducing environmental impacts through production-related changes, companies and industries have often established a narrow (and at times inconsistent or contradictory) reference for what they have defined as pollution prevention. Thus, in terms of either policy inputs or industry outcomes, pollution prevention has remained a much sought-after paradigm shift that still lacks coherence or consistency, whether in terms of its definition, its organizational or institutional applications, or its day-to-day implementation.

Our analysis has sought to both identify structural and organizational barriers for pollution prevention and to explore the arenas where both policy and industry decisionmaking intersect. Changes in these areas, we argue, need to reflect new kinds of relationships between community and industry and within the workplace at each stage of a production cycle. These exchanges must also be reflected in the relationship between the "public" (as articulated through public policy) and the "private" (as expressed in relation to private sector behavior). To accomplish such changes, the development of pollution prevention requires the restructuring of both specific environmental policymaking (capable of intervening at the level of industry "sectors," as EPA officials have begun to define the focus for pollution prevention) as well as a fundamental integration of environmental and economic policy that would differ considerably from the current emphasis on deregulation or the longstanding assumptions about the division between industry (i.e., jobs) and the environment.

How this paradigm shift can be accomplished remains the threshhold question for pollution prevention, although the seeds of change can be identified. In terms of a community/industry relationship, tentative first efforts have taken place with respect to allowing community representatives to participate in corporate environmental audits or in establishing community advisory committees to monitor plant activities that are independent of the company. For example, at a Rhone–Poulenc petrochemical plant in Manchester, Texas, the company agreed to pay for an independent environmental audit that would be supervised by both local residents and a statewide environmental organization, Texans United. Similarly, a community inspector program to monitor a Chevron refinery in Northern California (based on a safety expert team that reported to community residents but was paid for by the companies involved) was proposed and initially approved by the local city planning commission only to be overruled by the city council after a successful lobbying campaign by Chevron.[3] On a more ambitious scale, community groups addressing pollution impacts from high-tech industries like semiconductors have advocated that the government-funded SEMATECH industry consortium supporting high-tech R&D ventures should explore community input concerning design for environment-type production initiatives.[4] More broadly, the enormous interest stimulated by the information made available through the Toxics Release Inventory established under EPCRA and expanded by the Pollution Prevention Act has elevated community right-to-know as a potential policy tool and possible source of influence with respect to industry decisionmaking. (It should be noted, however, that right-to-know information remains bounded by the quality and accessibility of the information and the ability of specific constituencies to act on such information).

Perhaps most significantly, community activism in the toxics area has begun to force both policymakers and industry officials to examine the community/industry relationship beyond the question of facility siting (and more effective risk communication) and to address the issue of stakeholders within a given industry setting. Such a stakeholder process, as suggested by one innovative effort initiated by the Environmental Defense Fund focused on the printing industry in the Great Lakes region,[5] could involve the range of industries associated with a given production cycle, the communities affected at each stage of the production, the workforce within those industries, the various government agencies and public officials involved, and various environmental or public interest groups concerned with broader environmental or ecosystem impacts.

Rethinking pollution prevention as a workplace strategy with respect to industry decisionmaking is another potential transforming approach. In its crucial 1986 study, *Serious Reduction of Hazardous Waste*, OTA briefly explored the question of greater worker involvement at a facility level in identifying opportunities for waste reduction.[6] A summary document by the OECD published in 1992 also raised the issue of worker participation in pollution prevention. The OECD authors argued that "only through greater involvement by the workforce can pollution prevention become a reality."[7] Both documents described opportunities for prevention (notably in the areas of wasteful or inefficient processes or operational procedures) as well as by initiating and/or expanding opportunities for broader-based workforce input into how products and processes are designed. 3M's efforts in this direction are notable in suggesting how expanding opportunities for product innovation among certain segments of the workforce provides a measure of success in company performance. Its approach, however, remains limited both in who gets to participate in such activities and how such activities are defined in relation to environmental and/or prevention goals. Although EPA, in fact, has argued that management strategies for greater workplace involvement such as TQM (or TQEM—Total Quality Environmental Management—the new buzzword among certain industry groups and government regulators)[8] are supportive of pollution prevention initiatives, neither the Agency nor industry trade associations nor specific companies have yet to incorporate worker participation as an actual prevention tool, whether in terms of voluntarist programs or regulatory approaches. The absence of workplace participation strategies in pollution prevention is also reflected in the divorce between occupational and environmental policies; a separation that must be overcome, as we have argued, in order for pollution prevention to succeed as a holistic approach.

The new forms of decisionmaking necessary for the success of pollution prevention can ultimately be situated as a question of public and private responsibilities in the environmental arena. If the absence of pollution is defined as both a public good and a public right, then prevention or reduction strategies can be seen as a system value for each of the stakeholders involved in a given industry setting. Whether in terms of industry decisionmaking, regulatory or other governmental activities, or community or worker input, pollution prevention needs to become (in terms of this definition of system value) a core basis for how production is organized and how products and processes are designed and ultimately function. The incorporation of this ethic of responsibility is not simply a stated goal for behavior, as implied in such approaches as the CERES principles, but a defining principle of production, whether imposed through regulation (or encouraged by incentive or disincentive approaches) and/or integrated directly into the decisionmaking processes of industry.

It is in this context of a conceptual change in how production is organized that pollution prevention can be understood as a form of industrial policy. As the discussion of the efforts to stimulate an electric vehicle industry (including the creation of public support mechanisms) has pointed out (efforts also related in part to narrow, more traditional media-specific environmental goals), pollution prevention in this instance would represent both a more holistic approach to industrial planning and a core design strategy, based on such tools as life cycle analysis or environmental design. Similarly, in the rapidly emerging area of military facility conversion (perhaps the most striking and comprehensive example of industrial policy that will be unfolding in the years to come), the extent of the existing pollution problems at such facilities presents both an argument for the necessity for pollution prevention as a planning strategy and some of the difficulties imposed on it by the current realities of the pollution already generated and by the specific causes of such pollution.

Pollution prevention, then, can be seen as a clearly articulated strategy for policy and decisionmaking as well as a goal of production requiring the rethinking of production values and a more effective integration of economic and environmental objectives. For planners, scientists, engineers, government regulators, community residents, industry workers and management, and environmentalists alike, pollution prevention not only challenges assumptions about existing roles and the knowledge base associated with those roles, but it also, crucially, provides a starting point in the development of new forms of environmental governance and decisionmaking essential to the health and environment of the planet.

Notes

1. "Industrial Pollution Prevention: A Critical Review," Harry Freeman, Teresa Harten, Johnny Springer, Paul Randall, Mary Ann Curran, and Kenneth Stone, *Journal of the Air & Waste Management Association,* Vol. 42, No. 5, May 1992, pp. 618–656.

2. In his same October 1990 remarks, Bush characterized the 1990s as "the decade of pollution prevention." Cited in Freeman *et al.*, pp. 617, 619. See also *Pollution Prevention Strategy,* U.S. Environmental Protection Agency, January 1991.

3. The Rhone-Poulenc and Chevron (Richmond, California) examples are described in "Making Our Local Industries Clean and Safe through Neighbor–Labor Audits," Sanford Lewis, The Good Neighbor Project, Waverly, MA, May 1994.

4. See *The Legacy of High-Tech Development: The Toxic Lifecycle of Computer Manufacturing,* Ted Smith and P. Woodward, (San Jose: Silicon Valley Toxics Coalition, 1992); "How Fabulous Fablessness: The Environmental Planning Implications of Economic Restructuring in the Santa Clara Semiconductor Industry," Janice Mazurek, Master's Thesis, UCLA Graduate School of Architecture & Urban Planning, June 1994.

5. Great Printing Project, Environmental Defense Fund, 1994; Interview with Manik Roy, 1993.

6. U.S. Congress, Office of Technology Assessment, *Serious Reduction of Hazardous Waste: For Pollution Prevention and Industrial Efficiency,* OTA-ITE-

317, (Washington D.C.: U.S. Government Printing Office, September 1986).

7. See also *Economic Aspects of International Chemicals Control,* Organization for Economic Cooperation and Development, (Paris: OECD, 1983).

8. See, for example, *Total Quality Environmental Management: The Primer,* (Washington D.C.: Global Environmental Management Initiative, 1992).

Glossary of Acronyms

ACGIH	American Conference of Government Industrial Hygienists
ANSI	American National Standards Institute
BADCT	Best available demonstrated control technology
BAT	Best available technology
BCME	Bischloromethylether
BOD	Biological Oxygen Demand
CBI	Confidential business information
CERCLA	Comprehensive Environmental Response, Compensation, and Liability Act (1980)
CFCs	Chlorofluorocarbons
CMA	Chemical Manufacturers Association
COE	U.S. Army Corps of Engineers
CPSA	Consumer Product Safety Act (1972)
CPSC	Consumer Product Safety Commission
CWA	Clean Water Act (1972) [Also Federal Water Pollution Control Act Amendments of 1972]
EPCRA	Emergency Planning Community Right-to-Know Act (Title III of the 1986 Superfund Amendment)
FWPCA	Federal Water Pollution Control Act (1948)
HAP	Hazardous Air Pollutant

HSWA   Hazardous and Solid Waste Amendments (to RCRA) (1984)

IMIS   Integrated Management Information System

LAER   Lowest achievable emissions rate

MACT   Maximum available control technology

METH   Methylene chloride

MSDS   Material Safety Data Sheets

NAAQS   National Ambient Air Quality Standards

NEPA   National Environmental Policy Act (1970)

NESHAP National Emission Standards for Hazardous Air Pollutants (Section 112 of the CAA)

NIOSH   National Institute for Occupational Safety and Health

NOAA   National Oceanic and Atmospheric Administration

NOES   National Occupational Exposure Survey (1984)

NOHS   National Occupational Hazard Survey (1974)

NPDES   National Pollutant Discharge Elimination System

OPPT   Office of Pollution Prevention and Toxics (formerly Office of Toxic Substances)

PCBs   Polychlorinated biphenyls

PMNs   Premanufacture notices

POTW   Publicly owned treatment works

PPA   Pollution Prevention Act (1990)

PRP   Potential responsible party

PSD   Prevention of significant deterioration

RACT   Reasonably available control technology

RCRA   Resource Conservation and Recovery Act (1976)

RRA   Resource Recovery Act (1970)

SDWA   Safe Drinking Water Act (1974)

SIC   Standard Industrial Classification

SIP   State implementation plan

SRRP   Source Reduction Review Project (EPA—1992)

THM   Trihalomethane

TLVs   Threshold Limit Values

TRI   Toxics Release Inventory

TSD   Treatment, Storage, Disposal

TSCA   Toxic Substances Control Act (1976)

Index

436

Index

Conventional pollutants, 19
Copper/brass radiators, 335, 351–353
Copper Development Association
(CDA), 351
Copper mining, 136
Corporate environmentalism, 3, 80, 188–
194, 198
Cost-benefit analyses, 48–49. *See also*
Economic costs of pollution
control/prevention
Council on Environmental Quality
(CEQ), 45, 59, 81
Crisis in the Workplace (Ashford), 95
Crisis management focus of pollution
policies, 11, 17–18
air pollution, 27–28
chemical regulation, 60–61
consumer product hazards, 110, 111
environmental audits, 180–181
environmental citizenship, 194
waste sites, 43
water pollution, 34
Criteria pollutants, 28
Cross-medium/pollution prevention
action, 84
Custom fillers in aerosols industry, 365–
366, 370–371
Cutting Chemical Wastes, 183, 265

Decisionmaking, industrial, 3, 67
environmental audits, 180–183
environmental citizenship, 194–197
green marketing/labeling, 188–194
life cycle analysis, 183–187, 280–284,
288, 313–318
organization/management issues, 176–
177
production outcomes, 197–199
tetraethyl lead, 170–176
3M, 404–409
toxicology and risk assessment,
177–180
worker involvement in pollution
prevention, 424–425
Definition debates over toxic policies,
124

linking terms to policy, 149–152
NRC/OTA/EPA reports, 125–128
prevention, pollution, 153–157
reducing or eliminating hazardous
substances/waste, 128–131
right-to-know proposals, 131–139
risk assessment, 139–143
state/local efforts, 143–148
Deodorants, aerosol, 361–362
Diapers, 190
Dibromochloropropane (DBCP), 96, 97,
178
Dimethylaminopropionitrile (DMAPN),
97
Dioxin, 61, 69
Diseases associated with chemical expo-
sure, 96–97. *See also* Health issues/
standards
Disinfection byproducts, 38–40
Disjointed incrementalism, 17
Dow Chemical
clean technology, 264
METH, 375
Pollution Prevention Act, 74
recycling, 148
solvents, chlorine-free, 380
tetraethyl lead, 177
TSCA, 60
voluntary approach by industry to
accomplishing prevention goals, 80
Drinking water contamination, 38
Drucker, Peter, 393
Dry basis and mass of waste generation,
238
Dumps, open, 11, 40–44
Du Pont, 170–178, 212, 263–264, 363
Du Pont, Coleman, 175
Du Pont, Irenee, 172

Earth Day, 26
Economic costs of pollution
control/prevention, 2
aerosols industry, 372
anti-regulatory backlash, 48–49
automobile recycling, 317–318
chemical industry, 246–248, 266–269

Program-dominated internal structure,
EPA's, 59
Propellants in aerosols industry, 115–116,
362, 369, 379
Propylene polymerization, 257
Public access to information. See Right-
to-know proposals
Public health. See Health issues/standards
Public Interest Research Groups
(PIRGs), 128
Publicly owned treatment works
(POTWs), 36, 37
Public transit development, 32

Quayle, Dan, 81, 142

Radiator repair industry, 332–333
background on, 334–335
control system, pollution, 344–348
eliminating risk, 353–354
exposure and risks, 338–342
OSHA, 342–344
process involved in, 335–338
substitutions, 348–353
Radionuclides, 39
Radium, 110
Randolph, Jennings, 96
Raw material usage in chemical indus-
try, 238–240
Reaction chemistry in reactor technolo-
gies, 257
Reaction injection molding (RIM), 297
Reactor technologies, 255–260
Reagan, Ronald, 38, 42, 44, 48, 69, 115
Reasonably available control technology
(RACT), 29
Recycling waste, 74, 77, 127
automobiles, 292, 317–318
batteries, 307–311
camera, single-use, 408–409
plastics, 298
Post-It Notes, 406–407
state policies, 48
Red blood cell destruction, 339
Redington, Dennis, 266
Reducing Hazardous Waste Generation—An

Evaluation and Call for Action (NRC),
125
*Reducing Risk: Setting Priorities and
Strategies for Environmental Protection*
(EPA), 139, 141
Regulations. *See also* Control system,
pollution; Media-specific legislation;
Policy-making process; Single-
medium basis for regulations;
Technology-based standards
aerosols industry, 377–381
alternative modes of, 21, 22, 33, 67
ambiguities of pollution prevention
policy, 73–85
anti-regulatory backlash, 43, 48–49,
115
classical forms of, 20–21, 30, 49–50
command-and-control format, 15
definition of, 20–21
front-end, 63–64. *See also* Prevention,
pollution
generic classes of policy tools, 21–22
multimedia basis for, 14
program-based, 47
Regulatory Analysis and Review Group
(RARG), 48
Reilly, William, 79, 80, 139, 421
Renal damage, 339
Reporting requirements, 21, 74–75, 130.
See also Toxics Release Inventory
(TRI)
Reproductive capacity, 97, 340
Research and CAA Amendments, 71
Resource Conservation and Recovery
Act (RCRA)
chemical industry, 211, 237–238
EPA, 127
exemptions, 136
federal role increased through, 12
hazardous substances/waste, 13, 41–42,
68–69
land disposal, 43–44
Reagan administration, 48
Resource Recovery Act (RRA) of
1970, 40
Respiratory protection, 102, 347